D0871800

Reasoned Faith

NORMAN KRETZMANN

REASONED FAITH

❦

Essays in Philosophical Theology
in Honor of
Norman Kretzmann

E D I T E D   B Y

ELEONORE STUMP

Cornell University Press

Ithaca and London

First published 1993 by Cornell University Press.

International Standard Book Number 0-8014-2571-9 (cloth)
International Standard Book Number 0-8014-9796-5 (paper)
Library of Congress Catalog Card Number 92-33439
Printed in the United States of America
Librarians: Library of Congress cataloging information
appears on the last page of the book.

⊗ The paper in this book meets the minimum requirements of the American National Standard for Information Sciences—Permanence of Paper for Printed Library Materials, ANSI Z39.48-1984.

FOR NORMAN

δαιμόνων δέ που χάρις βιαίως
σέλμα σεμνὸν ἡμένων.

Aeschylus
Agamemnon 182–83

Contents

Contents

Reasoned Faith

ELEONORE STUMP

Introduction

Perhaps because of our increasing appreciation of non-Western cultures, where religious passion is frequently a dominant force, or perhaps because of our increasing apprehension concerning inadequacies in our own secular culture, there has been a reviving interest in religion of all sorts in this country. Among philosophers, too, there has been a great revival of interest in the philosophy of religion and a consequent outpouring of work on the subject. Two things have characterized this new work.

The first characteristic is a broad extension of subjects seen as appropriate for philosophical scrutiny. Not so long ago work in philosophy of religion was largely confined to discussions of the meaningfulness of religious language and examinations of arguments for the existence of God. In the work currently being done, however, philosophers have gotten their courage up and ventured into such areas as providence, creation, conservation, and God's responsibility for sin, areas where analytic precision is more difficult to attain but where the scope of the investigation is less constrained.

The second feature of the new work in philosophy of religion is a willingness to bridge boundaries with related disciplines, most notably with theology but also with biblical studies. Since the three major monotheistic religions are each rooted in a sacred book, the data of religion include information about and doctrines gleaned from sacred books. In leaving biblical studies entirely to historical scholars of the texts, contemporary philosophers were cutting themselves off from a fruitful source of data about individual religions and the contributions those data make to issues relevant to philosophers. The

1

burgeoning interest in broader, richer questions has required philosophers to master some of the literature and scholarly tools of the
neighboring disciplines, which, no doubt, accounts for the fact that
the interdisciplinary forays have been largely confined to an explora-
tion of Christianity. (Venturing no further afield than Judaism and
Islam, whose histories are intertwined with the history of Christianity, requires yet an additional set of scholarly skills, which puts
such work outside the ambitions of even those philosophers of religion who would otherwise welcome the opportunity for explora-
tion.) Even with its restricted ambit, however, this interdisciplinary
focus is providing some of the most interesting, as well as conten-
tious, new work in the field. Both the interest and the contention are
especially notable in recent work by philosophers of religion on the
philosophical presuppositions of biblical studies.[1]

   That philosophers of religion are willing to take on richer topics
and to branch out into other disciplines is a sign of a change not just
in philosophy of religion but in philosophy as a whole. Philosophers
in various branches of the discipline are finding it incumbent on
them to explore topics that once might have been considered "un-
philosophical" and to enmesh themselves with some competence in
the details of their corresponding disciplines. So, for example, philosophers of science now routinely know a great deal about a particular science; they often consider themselves philosophers of physics
or philosophers of biology rather than just philosophers of science.
The work of these more interdisciplinary philosophers of science appears not just in philosophy publications but also in the journals of
the sciences they investigate. Similarly, philosophers of mind are
now commonly well versed in developments in neurobiology or cognitive psychology or computer science, and they serve on the edi-
torial boards of such publications as the *Journal of Cognitive Neuro-
science*. New developments in philosophy of religion reflect this
broader movement within philosophy. Philosophers of religion have
begun to feel the necessity of some academic competence in religion,
some grasp of theological doctrines of individual religions, some
awareness of the history of religious thought, and some familiarity
with texts held to be divinely revealed. For philosophy of religion,
this development has had a liberating effect, because it has become
respectable to investigate and discuss a whole array of interesting

---

[1] See, for example, *Hermes and Athena: Biblical Studies and Philosophical Theology*, ed.
Eleonore Stump and Thomas Flint (Notre Dame, Ind.: University of Notre Dame
Press, 1993).

subjects that philosophers would not have attended to in the preceding period.

This volume contributes to that welcome trend in philosophy of religion. It contains fourteen essays, none previously published, which manifest the new developments in the field, bringing philosophical techniques and skill to bear on particular religious doctrines or on texts held by Judaism and Christianity to be divinely revealed. The title of the collection, *Reasoned Faith*, reflects the theme uniting all the essays, faith examined by reason.

The Judeo-Christian tradition presents a comprehensive worldview that it wants and expects people to take on faith. It holds that there is an omnipotent, omniscient, perfectly good deity who freely chose to create the world and to people it with creatures who can themselves make free choices. As creator of the world, God somehow transcends it. He is, for example, outside space and not material; many but not all adherents to Judaism and Christianity have also supposed that he is outside time. Because as creator God is transcendent, it is not clear that our language can describe him adequately or that attributes can be predicated of God and creatures univocally. Some have gone so far as to maintain that God is transcendent in such a radical way that we cannot say anything positive about him at all. Orthodox Judeo-Christian tradition has also held, however, that God interacts with his creatures and lovingly provides for them. This claim is maintained in the face of an explicit recognition of all the suffering in the world. In fact, Christianity maintains that out of love for his creatures God himself voluntarily suffered in order to bring about atonement between himself and human beings, and those who avail themselves of this atonement can have hope of eternal life with God. The somber side of this good news is the claim that those who do not find their way to heaven in this fashion face everlasting life in hell. These religious doctrines are derived by faith from biblical texts, on the grounds that the texts embody a revelation of God to human beings. And not only is this worldview, derived in faith from sources taken to be revealed, to be accepted on faith, but faith is itself somehow meritorious or pleasing to God, who has arranged things in such a way that understanding of him and life with him can be reached only through faith.

What role is there for reason here? Many of the adherents of the Judeo-Christian tradition have thought that there was an important role for reason within the tradition. In the patristic and medieval periods, when the outlines of this worldview were first hammered out and many details filled in, the requirement for faith was not considered to be inconsistent with the full-fledged application of reason to religion. Augustine, for example, supposed that although we must accept this worldview on faith, having accepted it on faith, we investigate it by reason in order to further our comprehension of it, to develop and deepen our grasp of religious truths. Anselm codified Augustine's attitude in the watchword "faith seeking understanding". There is, clearly, also plenty of room for the investigations of skeptical, as well as believing, reason, since this picture of the world obviously raises many questions. In fact, the same questions might occur to both skeptic and believer. Augustinian believers will occupy themselves with these questions so that reason might enrich their understanding of faith; skeptics will see in such questions the start of reasons for rejecting the religion.

Perhaps the most obvious of such questions has to do with the requirement of faith itself. Why should it be the case that we need to accept religious doctrines on faith, and why should it be that faith is meritorious, required by God, or pleasing to God? At least since the Enlightenment, Western thought has commonly supposed that we have epistemic duties, including the use of reason and the careful weighing of evidence. In this century some philosophers have held that any failure to base one's beliefs on appropriate propositional evidence is a violation of epistemic duty or constitutes irrationality. If this view is right, then faith would be a defect, not a virtue. Furthermore, it is hard to see why faith should be thought meritorious in any way since it does not seem to be within our power to bring it about that we hold a particular set of beliefs.

Philosophers of religion have only recently begun to address the problematic claim that these religious doctrines are derived from divine revelation preserved in biblical texts. What attitude toward such texts does this claim require? How are they to be read, and how are they to be reconciled with other sources of knowledge arrived at by reason, such as science?

The account of God raises questions, too. There are general questions stemming from the claims about God's transcendence. Is God so far separated from creatures that we can't know anything about him except what he is not, or is it after all possible to say something positive about him? And if it is, how is the language fashioned for communication about created things to be applied to their creator? A traditional list of particular divine attributes also stimulates questions. Why should we suppose that God has these attributes rather than some others, and is it clear that all the attributes on the list are compossible?

Finally, questions are provoked by the account of God's interactions with human beings. The most important of these interactions for Christianity is expressed in the doctrine of the atonement, but what exactly the atonement consists in and how human beings are to avail themselves of it are not simple questions. Perhaps the most difficult and perennial question in this context, however, has to do with the existence of evil in the world—and in the next world too, given the doctrine of hell. How could a good God allow human beings to suffer as they do in this world, or even himself inflict suffering on them, as the doctrine of hell seems to say he does in the next world?

In this volume various skeptical and believing philosophers bring reason to bear on these questions, using reason to defend or deepen understanding of religious doctrine or else employing reason in the enterprise of elucidating defects and weaknesses in the Judeo-Christian account. The four sorts of questions which I have suggested are raised by the Judeo-Christian worldview correspond generally to the four parts of the volume.

The first part, "The Role of Reason in Faith", consists of three essays challenging, in different ways, the familiar contemporary assumption that if faith is to be justified, rational, or otherwise epistemically acceptable, it must be based on sufficient evidence. Robert Adams's "Truth and Subjectivity" is an interpretation and critical examination of Kierkegaard's assertion that truth is subjectivity. In taking this position, Kierkegaard does not confuse truth with the subjective attitude of the believer. In fact, Kierkegaard seems to have held a correspondence theory of truth. His famous and controversial statement arises from a question about human beings: How can human beings correspond to or be in conformity with an infinite God? Kierkegaard's answer is that we do so not by theoretical speculation but by passion. Adams presents and explains this view, shows how it becomes more complicated when it is applied specifically to Christianity, and then evaluates it within the context of contemporary work on religious epistemology.

Scott MacDonald, in "Christian Faith", sets out the common view that faith has both a cognitive and a conative component, and he explores the puzzles that arise from this marriage of intellect and will in faith. He first focuses on the puzzling claims that constitute "doxastic voluntarism", the view that the cognitive component of faith must itself be voluntary. Such doxastic voluntarists as Thomas Aquinas and John Hick suppose that this account of the cognitive component of faith is required in order to support certain claims traditionally made about faith, most notably that it is meritorious. MacDonald argues against Aquinas and Hick that the traditional claims can be explained without resorting to the theory that the beliefs held on faith are under voluntary control. Having rejected the views of doxastic voluntarism, he goes on to consider whether it is nonetheless necessary to suppose that faith requires some degree of cognitive uncertainty. Here he argues, against Robert Adams and Kierkegaard, among others, that cognitive uncertainty is not required for faith.

Concluding the first part, Robert Audi, in "The Dimensions of Faith and the Demands of Reason", discusses the connections between faith and reason by examining the notions of a person of faith and the standards of rationality appropriate to faith. He sets his discussion within the wider context of recent discussions in epistemology on reliabilism, coherentism, and foundationalism, and he argues that current work in the intersection of philosophical theology and these new discussions in epistemology has not been sufficient to reconcile faith and reason. On Audi's view, besides doxastic faith, there is another, non-doxastic kind of faith important in religious life, and he argues that the appropriate standard of rationality for non-doxastic faith is less stringent than the standard for doxastic faith. One sort of non-doxastic faith is essentially a state of the will, a matter of religious resolve or settled determination to live one's life in a religiously appropriate way. Audi goes on to explore the sort of considerations which would make such non-doxastic or volitional faith rational.

The next part, "Reason and Revelation", brings the philosophical use of reason to bear on texts traditionally taken by Jews and Christians as revealed and generally accepted by them as the basis for religious doctrine. Both the essays in this part look at the biblical book of Genesis in some detail. In "Genesis and Evolution" Peter van Inwagen contrasts fundamentalist worldviews, based on a literalist reading of Genesis, with the worldview van Inwagen calls 'saganism', that is, the sort of worldview associated with Carl Sagan. Van Inwagen argues for the inadequacy of both these worldviews. He argues against the "saganist" thesis that natural selection among random variations is the sole mechanism for evolution. The position he defends concerning evolution and Genesis is intermediate between the fundamentalist and the "saganist". In the process of explaining and defending his own position he raises some important considerations about philosophically justifiable approaches to texts held to be revealed.

Harry Frankfurt's essay "On God's Creation" also consists in a philosophically detailed interpretation of Genesis. Frankfurt's interest, however, is not so much in the question whether the biblical account is compatible with science as in the details of the account of creation given in the biblical text. He examines what the text says about the nature of the creative process and God's activity in that process. He argues that the account of creation given in Genesis raises two puzzles, because it suggests that God's concern with human beings is at least to some extent motivated by self-interest and that God is in some ways dependent on the conduct of human beings. Both these essays make an interesting contribution to the new work on biblical texts by philosophers of religion.

In the third part, "Reason and the Nature of the God of Faith", the results of bringing reason to bear on religious ascriptions of certain attributes to God are considered. In "Aquinas on Theological Predication: A Look Backward and a Look Forward", William Alston examines the Thomistic view that language used to predicate attributes of God must be neither equivocal nor univocal but rather analogical. Aquinas's reasons for taking this position about language applied to God are based on his adherence to the doctrine of divine simplicity, the view that all God's attributes are united in the radical unity that is God's nature. Alston examines Aquinas's views and argues that they are unacceptable. Although he agrees with Aquinas that even our best efforts to talk about God are inadequate, he presents an alternative explanation of why this is the case and an alternative suggestion for interpreting religious language.

In "The God above the Gods: Can the High Gods Survive?" George Mavrodes examines the contentions of certain theologians that we can say nothing positive or affirmative about God at all, that God is transcendent in a radical way. He considers claims by Paul Tillich that the true God is above the "God of theism", and he argues that Tillich's God is not a proper object of religious concern, that there being such a God is irrelevant to religion. Mavrodes also discusses Hick's idea of the Real, one transcendent reality underlying all the different deities worshipped by the adherents of diverse world religions. Mavrodes argues that as Hick construes the Real, the Real is in danger of collapsing into the individual deities of particular religions. Mavrodes concludes that radically transcendent gods of the sort advocated by Tillich and Hick either are not religiously interesting or are after all identical to the customary gods worshippers give allegiance to.

The other articles in this part examine individual divine attributes. Richard Swinburne's essay "God and Time" is a study of the doctrine that God is eternal, in the sense of everlasting. Swinburne argues that this view of God's eternality has several advantages over the view that takes God to be eternal in the sense of being outside time. Swinburne discusses the nature of time, deriving conclusions also about the nature of causation, including the conclusion that both backward causation and simultaneous causation are impossible. These views of time lead him to reject the doctrine that God is outside time. Swinburne interprets the doctrine of God's timelessness as committed to the view that God exists at a single instant, and he argues that his examination of the nature of time has ruled out such a possibility. Finally, he examines reasons for being dissatisfied with an account of God's being in time, and he tries to show that such worries are misplaced, because any constraints that existence in time place on God are, on Swinburne's view, only a consequence of a voluntary choice on God's part.

William Rowe's "The Problem of Divine Perfection and Freedom" is concerned with what Rowe thinks is a significant tension between the two divine attributes of perfection and freedom. Rowe claims that a perfect God would not be free to do any evil action and that such a God also would do whatever morally right actions he does out of necessity rather than freely. Even with respect to morally permissible actions, those that are not morally obligatory or morally wrong, Rowe claims that a perfect God would not in every case be free. To argue for this claim, Rowe considers whether God is free to select among the good worlds open to him to create. Arguing against Robert Adams, who has written in defense of the claim that it would not be wrong for God to create less than the best possible world, Rowe presents reasons for supposing that a perfect God could not create less than the best possible world. If there is no best possible world, Rowe argues, then it is inconsistent to suppose that the divine creator is perfectly good. If, however, there is one best possible world, then God is not free with regard to his choice to select it to create. Rowe concludes that the best we can say is that God's perfection places severe constraints on his freedom.

Thomas Morris, in "Perfection and Creation", considers Rowe's claims and related claims by other contemporary philosophers of religion. Morris examines the assumptions about the nature of goodness which he sees as crucial in Rowe's explication of the apparent tension between omnipotence and divine freedom, and he argues that some of these assumptions are not true or not applicable to God. On his view, Rowe's argument requires the assumption that the goodness of an agent can be additively increased by good actions. He examines two alternative theses about the relation between an agent's goodness and an agent's good actions: that the goodness of an agent's actions is productive of the agent's goodness or that the goodness of an agent's actions is simply expressive of the agent's goodness. Morris argues that the first of these suppositions cannot apply to God and that the second is true of God but not in the way necessary to give rise to Rowe's problem. He concludes with suggestions for ways in which the claims that creation is perfect and that God cannot create the best of all possible worlds might be reconciled.

The focus of the final part, "Reason and Faith on the Relation between God and Creatures", is on redemption and evil. William Mann's "Hope" is a philosophical examination of the theological virtue that is usually understood as the hope of salvation. Mann thinks that this virtue is in danger of collapsing either into faith—in which case hope consists in a belief that the one hoping will be saved—or else into love—in which case the one hoping desires salvation for himself and others. If we try to solve this difficulty by supposing that hope consists just in a desire for one's own salvation, then hope seems lamentably self-regarding and not a virtue at all. Mann considers the views of Augustine, Aquinas, and Luther on the nature of hope. Rejecting Luther's view, he argues in favor of Aquinas's understanding of hope as primarily a matter of hoping for one's own salvation, and he raises considerations designed to show that even so construed hope is nonetheless a virtue.

In "Abelard on Atonement: 'Nothing Unintelligible, Arbitrary, Illogical, or Immoral about it'" Philip Quinn looks not at human attitudes toward salvation but at the process of redemption itself. Condemned by the church in his day, Abelard's account of the atonement has never been popular, partly because it has been accused of exemplarism, that is, of holding that Christ's atoning work on the Cross constitutes an example for human beings and nothing more. Quinn argues that Abelard is not an exemplarist and that, in fact, his theory of the atonement comports better with our moral intuitions than that of such other philosophical theologians as Anselm or Aquinas. But Quinn thinks that Abelard's theory of the atonement is not without problems, so he presents suggestions for altering or developing Abelard's account so as to yield a theory that merits the praise in the title of his essay.

The last two essays in this part focus on the problem of evil. Marilyn Adams's essay "The Problem of Hell: A Problem of Evil for Christians" deals with the particular problem of evil raised by the

traditional Christian doctrine that allots human persons either a successful place in the scheme of salvation or a slot in hell. Adams
considers the claim that the doctrine of hell is incompatible with the
doctrine of God as omniscient, omnipotent, and perfectly good. She
examines various strategies for resolving the alleged incompatibility,
including rejecting the doctrine of hell itself and reconceptualizing
divine goodness in a way entailed by accepting the doctrine. Adams's
own solution consists in a development and extension of her solution to the more general problem of evil and the adoption of a universalist attitude toward salvation. She argues against several recent
attempts, most notably one by William Lane Craig, to reconcile the
existence of hell with the existence of a perfectly good God.

My essay "Aquinas on the Sufferings of Job" deals with the more
general problem of evil; it attempts to lay bare the foundations on
which our examination of the problem typically rests. To do so, I
consider the interpretation of the sufferings of Job given by Thomas
Aquinas. Aquinas, like other medievals before him, adopts the sort
of attitude toward human suffering which makes divine providence
seem most perplexing when it is apparent that *good* people are *not*
suffering. I show that Aquinas's attitude is a consequence of his
view of human happiness and his account of the human place in the
larger scheme of things. There are several natural objections to
Aquinas's account of suffering, including a morally indignant one
which finds his views repugnantly grim and inhuman. Aquinas's
account, I maintain, is intended to escape such objections and allo-
cates a significant place to joy in human life. What is most important
to see, I argue, is the degree to which our attitude toward the problem of evil is a function of our other metaphysical and ethical commitments.

It is notable that many of the essays in this volume, and not just
those by contributors whose areas of specialization include medieval
philosophy, discuss medieval thinkers to some degree or other.
Skilled and sophisticated philosophical reflection on religious issues
can be found throughout the history of philosophy, but there is an
especially rich vein of it in the medieval period, which for centuries
channeled its best minds into philosophical theology. Furthermore,
medieval philosophy is characterized throughout by the same devotion to care and precision in reasoning that marks contemporary analytic philosophy. So the recent growing pollination of contemporary philosophy of religion by medieval philosophical theology is
proving to be fertile.

Norman Kretzmann has been one of the most influential people in making medieval philosophy part of contemporary philosophical discussions, with a concomitant impact on philosophy of religion. And his own work in philosophy of religion, informed by his interest in and expertise at medieval philosophy, has made a difference to various issues currently under discussion in the field, including debates over the compossibility of certain divine attributes, questions concerning God's actions in creation, and arguments over the role of reason in faith. Like Augustine and Anselm, Kretzmann has refused to recognize any incompatibility or even any competition between faith and reason, and in recent years his work has been increasingly characterized by an insistence on the place of reason in the examination and defense of religious doctrines. His trust in the ability of reason to be successfully yoked with faith can be signally seen in his willingness to investigate and defend by reason even one of the most crabbed, counterintuitive claims of faith, the doctrine of divine simplicity.

This volume on reasoned faith was originally conceived as a festschrift for him, as a way for those who owe him a debt of friendship or filial piety to honor him on his sixty-fifth birthday. This group, it should be said, includes John Ackerman, director of Cornell University Press, whose generous aid and advice from the inception of the volume till now have been invaluable. While the book was in progress, we were stricken to discover that Kretzmann has incurable multiple myeloma. He himself has taken the news with a serenity and cheerful patience that most of the rest of us would not be able to imitate in his circumstances. The combination of philosophical reason and Christian faith in his reaction to this terminal illness is the crown of his commitment to reasoned faith. The contributors to this volume, his friends and former students, present this volume of articles to him, with admiration and affection, in recognition of his contribution to the field.

PART I

❦

THE ROLE OF REASON
IN FAITH

Robert Merrihew Adams

❦

Truth and Subjectivity

The words "Truth is subjectivity" are among the most famous that Kierkegaard wrote,[1] and among the most controversial. They are also among the most misunderstood. They have been derided as confusing truth with a subjective attitude of the believer,[2] and hence as implying a relativism[3] or non-cognitivism about religious beliefs, which Kierkegaard would doubtless have rejected if it were made fully explicit. It can be shown, however, that the statement, which forms part of a chapter title in *Concluding Unscientific Postscript*, is not meant, in the *Postscript*, to be inconsistent with an ascription of objective truth to religious beliefs. Far from confusing objective with subjective issues, the *Postscript* places some emphasis on distinguishing them.

Understanding is not helped by the fact that the idea of "truth is subjectivity" is often presented to students by way of brief excerpts from the *Postscript*, making it impossible to recognize the dialectical structure of the *Postscript*, in which two different religious points of view are developed. The thesis that "truth is subjectivity" is devel-

---

[1] Søren Kierkegaard, *Concluding Unscientific Postscript*, trans. David F. Swenson and Walter Lowrie (Princeton: Princeton University Press, 1941), p. 169. Parenthetical page references in the present essay are to this work.

[2] So, for example, Walter Kaufman, *Critique of Religion and Philosophy* (New York: Harper & Brothers, 1958), pp. 77–78.

[3] The charge of relativism is not supported, but noted, in C. Stephen Evans, *Kierkegaard's "Fragments" and "Postscript": The Religious Philosophy of Johannes Climacus* (Atlantic Highlands, N.J.: Humanities Press, 1983), p. 115. "Truth and Subjectivity", chapter 7 of Evans's book, is one of the best treatments of the subject known to me.

oped primarily in the exposition of "Religiousness A" and is accepted only subject to a major qualification in "Religiousness B", which is identified with Christianity and is clearly the focus of Kierkegaard's ultimate interest in the book.

There may still be grounds for criticizing the *Postscript* for excessive subjectivism. Whether the project really intended under the heading "Truth Is Subjectivity" can be carried through without infringing on a due recognition of objective rights and wrongs in religion and ethics is a serious question. I do not pretend to cover all aspects of that question here. But I believe that Kierkegaard's treatment of the theme contains insights into often neglected aspects of the relation between truth and subjectivity in religion and ethics, and I want to explore some of those insights.

In offering a reading of the *Postscript* on an important topic, I am keenly aware of the limitations of my Kierkegaard scholarship, including my ignorance of the Danish language. I also wander at times from the text into reflections that the text suggests to me. In the end, I suspect, Kierkegaard would not particularly like this essay. I am more fascinated than he probably was by the remarkable pieces of logical structure that crop up in his works, and I value reasonableness in ethics and religion in a way that Kierkegaard did not.

My main focus is on eliciting from the text possible views of ways in which the cognitive value of religious states of mind could depend on what the *Postscript* calls "subjectivity". In this I am using the *Postscript* as the book itself invites us to do. It denies that historical facts about an author's state of mind can be of any importance (or of any ethical or religious importance, at any rate) for the reader. All that an author can really give us, according to the *Postscript*, is a *possibility*, or a set of possibilities, that we may consider adopting for ourselves. That was one reason for Kierkegaard's writing under pseudonyms. In respect for his intentions, and as a reminder of the limits of my historical claims, I ascribe the *Postscript*'s contents to its fictitious author, Johannes Climacus.

1. Objective and Subjective Problems about Truth

The "truth is subjectivity" chapter of the *Postscript* begins with a disjunction: "Whether truth is defined more empirically, as the conformity of thought and being, or more idealistically, as the conformity of being with thought, it is, in either case, important carefully to note what is meant by being" (p. 169). This seems to presuppose that truth consists in some sort of conformity between thought and reality. That is, it seems to presuppose a *correspondence* conception of truth—while leaving open a variety of questions about the character of the correspondence, including the questions mentioned about the priority as between thought and being, and what is meant by being or reality. Appearances could be doubted here; one might wonder whether the apparatus of correspondence is introduced only as part of the *Postscript*'s satire on academic, particularly Hegelian, philosophy. But I think the idea of "truth is subjectivity" can be understood best within the framework of a correspondence conception of truth.

A distinction between an "objective problem" and a "subjective problem" of truth regarding Christianity is important for the structure of the *Postscript*, dominating the titles of the official main divisions of the work. Book 1 is titled "The Objective Problem concerning the Truth of Christianity", and book 2 is titled "The Subjective Problem: The Relation of the Subject to the Truth of Christianity: The Problem of Becoming a Christian". The problems are "objective" and "subjective" in the sense that one is *about* the *object* of thought (in this case, Christianity, or its historical and theological claims) and the other is *about* the *subject*, the thinker: "The objective problem consists of an inquiry into the truth of Christianity. The subjective problem concerns the relationship of the individual to Christianity. To put it quite simply: How may I, Johannes Climacus, participate in the happiness promised by Christianity?" (p. 20).

It would be a mistake to suppose that only the objective problem is concerned with a correspondence between thought and reality. Consider this point in relation to Christianity, since Christianity is the announced topic of the *Postscript*. Two things are required if Johannes Climacus is to have a *true* belief in Christianity. (1) Christianity must be true; that is, to put it crudely (and the *Postscript* is not overly subtle on this point), the facts about God and Jesus must be in conformity with the affirmations of Christianity. Whether this conformity does in fact obtain is the main "objective problem" of the *Postscript*.[4] (2) Climacus must really be a Christian, must really be-

---

[4] That is, it is the most important objective problem for the sense of the work as I understand it; and I shall refer to it as "the objective problem". Unfortunately, Climacus muddies the water by focusing at times on a different objective problem: What are, historically, the affirmations of Christianity, or of the New Testament? (See, e.g., the first sentence of p. 25.)

lieve in Christianity. Whether he is and does is the *Postscript*'s "subjective problem" as it applies to him. This too can be seen as a question of correspondence or conformity. The question is whether Climacus, in his thinking, is in conformity with the affirmations of
Christianity, and hence with the relevant facts about God and Jesus
(if the correct answer to the objective problem is affirmative).

The *Postscript* is much more concerned with the subjective problem than with the objective, as is suggested by the very unequal
length of the two "books" (33 pages for book 1 and 486 pages for
book 2, in the English translation). In fact the introduction to the
work flatly states that "our treatment of the problem does not raise
the question of the truth of Christianity. It merely deals with the
question of the individual's relationship to Christianity. . . . [I]t
deals with the concern of the infinitely interested individual for his
own relationship to such a doctrine" (pp. 18–19.). But the *Postscript*
clearly does assume that the objective problem about the truth of
Christianity has an answer. And, as we shall see, it sometimes supposes, at least for the sake of argument, an affirmative answer to
that or some related objective problem.

There is reason to interpret Climacus as setting the importance of
the objective problem (or of a correct answer to it) very high–almost
as high as that of the subjective problem. He writes, "Precisely as
important as the truth, and if one of the two is to be emphasized,
still more important, is the manner in which the truth is to be accepted" (p. 221), "the truth" and "the manner in which [it] is to be
accepted" corresponding here to the objective and subjective problems.[5] Moreover, the emphasis in both the *Postscript* (pp. 182, 378–
85) and the *Philosophical Fragments* on the *risk* involved in the "objective uncertainty" of faith seems to attribute great importance to the
answer to the objective problem. For the risk clearly can be identified with the danger that one's answer to the objective problem will
in fact be false. Indeed one is tempted to infer that the "infinitely
interested" subject idealized in the *Postscript* must care infinitely
about the truth of his religion, and hence about the correctness of
his answer to the objective problem. Some of the things that Climacus says in developing the idea that "truth is subjectivity" have
suggested to many that he does not care much, if at all, about answers to the objective problem; but I try to show that this interpretation is not forced on us.

---

[5] This text is cited, in support of the same interpretive point, by Evans, *Kierkegaard's
"Fragments" and "Postscript"*, p. 128.

2. Subjectivity

"Subjectivity" in "truth is subjectivity" obviously means something more than the mere reference to the subject or self who is thinking, a meaning that seems adequate to explain the sense of "subjective" in "subjective problem". But it still does signify thinking that bears a particular relation to the self of the thinker. Climacus raises, for example, the question of what it would be to think subjectively about "the problem of *what it means to die*" (p. 147).

> And if initially my human nature is merely an abstract something, it is at any rate the task which life sets me to become subjective; and in the same degree that I become subjective, the uncertainty of death comes more and more to interpenetrate my subjectivity dialectically. It thus becomes more and more important for me to think it in connection with every factor and phase of my life; for since the uncertainty is there in every moment, it can be overcome only by overcoming it in every moment. (P. 149).

Here subjectivity appears, at least in part, as an *integrative* tendency in thinking. It is part of an effort to unify one's life. The subjective thinker does not keep important questions in different pockets of the mind. If I have become subjective, I will "think" what I know about death, for example, "in connection with every factor and phase of my life". To the extent that this is what subjective thinking is, it is surely an intellectual virtue.

The effort to unify one's life and to maintain its unity through time is particularly important to Kierkegaard. In his writings it regularly characterizes "ethical" and "religious" as opposed to "aesthetic" ways of life and is to be achieved by a sort of "choice", by making and constantly reaffirming a decision. In the *Postscript* this theme is connected with an idea of "existence."

> The difficulty facing an existing individual is how to give his existence the continuity without which everything simply vanishes. . . . The goal of movement for an existing individual is to arrive at a decision and to renew it. The eternal is the factor of continuity; but an abstract eternity is extraneous to the movement of life, and a concrete eternity within the existing individual is the maximum degree of his passion. (P. 277)

Climacus does not regard *every* question as central in this way for the integration of one's life and selfhood, and hence as an appropriate topic for subjective thinking. He distinguishes between "essential" and "accidental" knowledge: "All essential knowledge relates to existence, or only such knowledge as has an essential relationship to existence is essential knowledge. . . . Only ethical and ethico-religious knowledge has an essential relationship to the existence of the knower" (pp. 176–77). Mathematical and chemical knowledge, for example, would not be essential knowledge. It would be silly to try to relate the Pythagorean theorem or the periodic table of elements to "every factor and phase" of one's life. So Climacus is not arguing for subjective thinking in mathematics or chemistry. This is not to say that mathematical or chemical knowledge or beliefs lie outside the scope of an integrative ideal of thought, or that they may appropriately be isolated from ethical and religious views in a hermetically sealed pocket in the mind. One's scientific knowledge is a "factor" or "phase" of one's life, and one's ethical and religious thinking should therefore be connected with it. For Climacus, however, it is only the ethical and religious thinking that provides the framework for integration of the self by being connected with every aspect of one's life, including the scientific. Self-integration does not require any interesting connection between knowing chemistry and having the ability to recite the names of the kings of Denmark.

The integration of a human life or "existence", according to the *Postscript*, depends on decision and passion. Subjective thinking therefore cannot be isolated from volition and emotion. It will be influenced by one's *caring*, from a distinctly personal point of view, about the questions considered. For my study this is perhaps the most important aspect of what is meant by "subjectivity" in "truth is subjectivity." It is one that Climacus most vividly emphasizes. He holds that subjectivity is both inwardness (a focus on one's own selfhood) and *passion*, declaring, in one of the most characteristic sentences of the *Postscript*, that "Christianity is spirit, spirit is inwardness, inwardness is subjectivity, subjectivity is essentially passion, and in its maximum an infinite, personal, passionate interest in one's eternal happiness" (p. 33).

At this point an integrative ideal of subjectivity is in tension with another sort of intellectual virtue—namely, with ideals of objectivity in thinking. Climacus illustrates the tension with a vivid simile:

> In sawing wood it is important not to press down too hard on the saw; the lighter the pressure exerted by the sawyer, the better the saw operates. If a man were to press down with all his strength, he would no longer be able to saw at all. In the same way it is necessary for the philosopher to make himself objectively light; but everyone who is in

passion infinitely interested in his eternal happiness makes himself subjectively as heavy as possible. (P. 55)

One might formulate an ideal of objectivity by saying that one's judgments and beliefs ought not to be influenced by what one cares about from a personal point of view, or perhaps that they ought not to be influenced by any desire except that of believing what is (objectively) true. The influence of any more personal desire can be seen as pressure on "the saw", interfering with one's responsiveness to evidence and thus distorting one's judgment. We must recognize this tension, I think, though I am inclined to maintain more hope than I see in Climacus for an integration of ideals of subjectivity and objectivity.

3. "Truth Is Subjectivity"

Having surveyed the essential background for an interpretation of the thesis that "truth is subjectivity", I begin my interpretation with the point that the *scope* of the thesis is limited. It is an answer *only* to the *subjective* problem. This is manifest in one of the most careful statements in Climacus's development of the thesis, a statement italicized in the text: "*When the question of the truth is raised subjectively, reflection is directed subjectively to the nature of the individual's relationship; if only the mode of this relationship is in the truth, the individual is in the truth even if he should happen to be thus related to what is not true*" (p. 178). Not only does this present a recognizable version of the "subjective problem" already introduced. It is also explicitly contrasted with a version of the "objective problem" or rather with a way of treating the objective problem as decisive: "*When the question of truth is raised in an objective manner, reflection is directed objectively to the truth, as an object to which the knower is related. Reflection is not focussed upon the relationship, however, but upon the question of whether it is the truth to which the knower is related. If only the object to which he is related is the truth, the subject is accounted to be in the truth*" (p. 178).

Part of what is meant by saying that truth is subjectivity is that an individual's being "in the truth" depends on the answer to the subjective rather than the objective problem. It also signifies a particular answer to the subjective problem; but that answer is not indicated in the statements just quoted, and there are two more points to be noticed about them before we get to it. (1) The subjective approach admits the possibility of objective error, for it allows that one might be related rightly, as regards subjectivity, "to what is not true". Thus even the subjective approach presupposes that there is (objectively, no doubt) an answer to the objective problem.

(2) The scope of the thesis that truth is subjectivity is limited also to *essential* truth. It does not apply to mathematics and chemistry but only to ethical and religious truth. "The reader will observe", says a footnote to this passage, "that the question here is about essential truth, or about the truth which is essentially related to existence, and that it is precisely for the sake of clarifying *it* as inwardness that this contrast is drawn" (p. 178; emphasis mine).

The meaning of the thesis is further illumined by two examples Climacus gives. The first and more general is "the knowledge of God": "Objectively, reflection is directed to the problem of whether this object is the true God; subjectively, reflection is directed to the question whether the individual is related to a something *in such a manner* that his relationship is in truth a God-relationship" (p. 178). If being in the truth is approached subjectively and in relation to God, in other words, the question is what must be true of the individual if the individual is to be truly related to God. I think this may be taken without strain, in its context in the *Postscript*, as a question about correspondence or conformity of the individual with God. And this seems to presuppose that there is, objectively, a God to be conformed to.

It may be objected at this point that the subjective approach will collapse into the objective approach, on the ground that what is required for your relationship to be a God-relationship is that you intend to be related to an object that you conceive as having (enough of) the attributes that God actually has. Thus the crucial question will be, after all, whether "this object", as you conceive of it, "is the true God". This objection assumes, of course, that the conformity with God required for a true God-relationship is conceptual, a conformity of one's ideas with the divine nature. But that is just what Climacus seems to deny.

This emerges in his more particular and more vivid example, in which we hear literary echoes of the gospel parable of the Pharisee and the tax collector (Luke 18:9–14):

> If one who lives in the midst of Christendom goes up to the house of God, the house of the true God, with the true conception of God in his knowledge, and prays, but prays in a false spirit; and one who lives in an idolatrous community prays with the entire passion of the infinite, although his eyes rest upon the image of an idol: where is there most

truth? The one prays in truth to God though he worships an idol; the other prays falsely to the true God, and hence worships in fact an idol. (P. 180)

It is implied that each of these characters has something right; note that the question raised about them is which has *most* truth.[6]

The child of Christendom has "the true conception of God in his knowledge". It could hardly be more explicit that there is a true answer to the objective problem about God, and presumably it is objectively true. Moreover, Climacus seems to think he knows the answer to the objective problem—or at least that part of the answer that consists in the true conception of God. It is the conception that prevails in Christendom.

The other person has an erroneous conception of the divine. All that is said is that "his eyes rest upon the image of an idol", and that "he worships an idol". But surely praying with eyes on an idol does not constitute worshiping an idol unless one accepts some *conception* of the idol as being, embodying, housing, or correctly representing a deity. The child of idolatry therefore has a false conception of deity but is sufficiently conformed to God to be praying "in truth to God", because he "prays with the entire passion of the infinite". And infinite passion, we have already been told (p. 33), is the maximum degree of subjectivity.

Clearly Climacus is saying that there is *more truth* in being wrong with regard to the objective question but right with regard to the subjective question than in the reverse. I take this as implying that *one's conformity or correspondence with religious reality depends more decisively on one's subjectivity, as manifested in passion, than on one's ideas about God.*

Here I face a major choice in my interpretation of the text. C. Stephen Evans, one of its best interpreters, declares that the question who has most truth, in our parable, "is about which kind of *life* can best be described as true; *it has no bearing on the question of propo-*

---

[6] As noted by Evans, *Kierkegaard's "Fragments" and "Postscript"*, p. 128. It is also worth noting that the characters in this parable are not introduced as a Christian and an idolater, but as *living in* a Christian and an idolatrous *community*, respectively. This reflects Climacus's view that the one is not a true Christian and the other is much more than an idolater. It also carries a (very Kierkegaardian) suggestion that the characters' stances on the objective problem are determined socially, by their communities, rather than individually by their struggles in thinking. This is a distraction in the present context, however. For clearly you could be theologically eccentric, holding a conception of God quite different from your community's, and still be objectively right but passionless, or objectively wrong but passionate, about God.

sitional truth."[7] This is a possible reading. It may be supported by the undeniable emphasis of the book on issues of salvation, as exemplified by the fact that Climacus is prepared to state the subjective problem as "How may I, Johannes Climacus, participate in the happiness promised by Christianity?" (p. 20). A "true life" would be one that conforms to God's demands or purposes in such a way as to be headed toward participation in such happiness. On this reading the thesis that "truth is subjectivity" amounts to the relatively uncontroversial point that one's life can be more, or less, acceptable religiously than one's theology—supplemented by the more distinctively Kierkegaardian idea that the religious acceptability of one's life depends mainly on its subjectivity or passion.

I find this version of "truth is subjectivity" disappointingly tame. I also think it misleading to use "truth" as a category for the evaluation of *lives* without any particular reference to *cognitive* adequacy, and am reluctant to see the argument of the *Postscript* as depending essentially on such a usage. Moreover there are indications in the text that Climacus does think that the cognitive adequacy, or at any rate the intentional content, of one's religious thoughts is affected by the truth that depends on subjectivity. Some of these indications will emerge in my discussion. One we have already seen. Prayer and worship are religious conscious acts whose intentionality is seen as affected by passion or its absence when Climacus says that one person "prays in truth to God though he worships an idol" while another "prays falsely to the true God, and hence worships in fact an idol." This interpretation, on which "truth is subjectivity" is at least in large part a thesis about the cognitive adequacy or meaning of religious thinking, is the one I wish to pursue here, without claiming to establish it as the only correct one.

For this interpretation one of the most important statements in the *Postscript* is that whereas "objectively the interest is focussed merely on the thought-content", for subjectivity "it is the passion of the infinite that is the decisive factor and not its content, for its content is precisely itself" (p. 181). In other words, the "content" of religious passion, and its intentional object, are wholly determined by its intensity rather than by ideas associated with it. And I think the point is not merely that passion-content is better than idea-content but rather that passion is somehow the only content available for an authentic passion for the infinite. How one might think this to be true is the subject of the next two sections of the present essay.

---

[7] Evans, *Kierkegaard's "Fragments" and "Postscript"*, p. 126.

4. Subjectivity and Intersubjectivity

Climacus declares that "to bring God to light objectively . . . is in all eternity impossible, because God is a subject, and therefore exists only for subjectivity in inwardness" (p. 178). It is easy to hear the verbal echoes reverberating between "subjectivity" and "God is a subject." It is much harder to see a rational connection between the claims that "God is a subject" and that subjectivity is required for thinking of God. But Climacus does present views that might provide grounds for a belief that subjectivity is required, quite generally, for intersubjectivity—that passion is required for belief in other minds.

The idea that passion is important in some way for awareness of other people's subjectivity is not implausible. It seems likely that our beliefs and judgments about other people's states of mind rely heavily on empathy. It would be difficult to form such beliefs and judgments if we were so passionless as to care about nothing ourselves.

Climacus has a more distinctive problem about belief in other minds, however. Purely objective, speculative thought, for him, is "abstract," and its object is the possible as such: "All knowledge about reality is possibility. . . . [T]rue knowledge consists in translating the real into the possible" (p. 280). And "when I think about something that another has done, and so conceive a reality, I lift this given reality out of the real and set it into the possible; for a conceived reality is a possibility" (p. 285).

This gives rise to the question how one can think the reality of anything over and above its possibility. One's own reality one knows, for one experiences it, and the experience doubtless contains something more than the thought of its possibility: "The ethical, as being the internal, cannot be observed by an outsider. It can be realized only by the individual subject, who alone can know what it is that moves within him. This ethical reality is the only reality which does not become a mere possibility through being known . . . ; for it is the individual's own reality" (p. 284). But how can this subject know, or believe, or even think the reality of another being?

In the case of another person's reality he could have no knowledge about it until he transformed it from a reality into a possibility.

With respect to every reality external to myself, I can get hold of it only through thinking it. In order to get hold of it really, I should have to be able to make myself into the other, the acting individual, and make the foreign reality my own reality, which is impossible. For if I make the foreign reality my own, this does not mean that I become the other through knowing his reality, but it means that I acquire a new reality, which belongs to me as opposed to him. (Pp. 284–85)

From these epistemological considerations Climacus develops an ethical point, that "there is no immediate relationship, ethically, between subject and subject. When I understand another person, his reality is for me a possibility, and in its aspect of possibility this conceived reality is related to me precisely as the thought of something I have not done is related to the doing of it" (p. 285). Ethically, Climacus claims, it is not important whether a conceived reality is in fact the reality of another person's inner life. What is important is that it is a possibility that I must choose whether to realize in my own life. "To be concerned ethically about another's reality is also a misunderstanding, since the only question of reality that is ethically pertinent, is the question of one's own reality" (p. 287). Obviously one might take issue with this ethical judgment.

My present concern, however, is with a more semantical point. What would it mean to believe that a certain conception expresses not just a possibility but the reality of another person's inner life (whether or not it is ethically good to hold such beliefs)? What would be the content of the belief? To say that "a conceived reality is a possibility", after all, is to make the point that there is no more content in a proposition thought of as true than in the same proposition thought of as possible. The point is not new. Kant expressed it in his famous remark that a hundred real dollars contain not a penny more than a hundred possible dollars.[8]

Climacus offers no *general* solution to this problem, since he does not in general approve of an interest in other realities than one's own. He thinks differently about belief in *God's* reality, however. The concerns of religion, or at least of Christianity, are different from those of ethics. "The believer differs from the ethicist in being infinitely interested in the reality of another (in the fact, for example, that God has existed in time)."[9] Indeed this can provide a virtual definition of faith: "To ask with infinite interest about a reality which is not one's own, is faith" (p. 288). We can gather from this a suggestion about what it might be to believe in the reality of God or to believe something about the reality of God. If Climacus equates faith

---

[8] Immanuel Kant, *Critique of Pure Reason*, A 599/B 627.

[9] God (the eternal) existing in time is for Climacus a formula for the Incarnation.

with "ask[ing] with infinite interest about a reality which is not one's own", perhaps he thinks that the difference between thinking of a God-concept as expressing a mere possibility and thinking of it as actually characterizing a reality is to be found in a passionate interest that is required in the latter case.

Something of the same sort may be true about our belief in the reality of other *human* minds, if we are less abstemious in that than Climacus advises. It seems to be virtually universally true that if we think of another being as really having a mind or consciousness like our own, we will *care* about what happens to that being in a way that we would not if we regarded its mindedness or consciousness as a mere logical possibility. This is as true when our caring is hostile as when it is friendly. And it is tempting to call this point to our aid if we are perplexed in trying to understand the difference between thinking of another being as possible and as real. We may be reminded here of Wittgenstein's aphorism, "My attitude toward him is an attitude toward a soul. I am not of the *opinion* that he has a soul."[10] Wittgenstein's ideas in this area are doubtless quite different from those of the *Postscript*, but this is common to them: they try to deal with a problem about what it would be to believe in the reality of another mind by appealing to an *attitude* that one might have toward a being as having a mind or soul—an attitude not specified in Wittgenstein's aphorism but identified by Climacus with a passionate interest.

Of course belief in the reality of a merely human mind would presumably not be marked by an *infinite* passionate interest. An infinite passion would signify belief in the reality of a divine mind. In other ways, however, this line of argument does not seem likely to establish a unique relation of subjectivity to religious truth. If subjectivity is required for thinking of God as real because "God is a subject", then it would seem to be required also for thinking of other persons as real, since they are subjects too.

5. Divinity and Passion

I do not think the thesis that religious truth is subjectivity is adequately explained by the relevance of passion to the difference be-

[10] Ludwig Wittgenstein, *Philosophical Investigations*, edited by G. E. M. Anscombe and R. Rhees, and translated by G. E. M. Anscombe, 2d ed. (Oxford: Basil Blackwell, 1958), p. 178ᵉ.

tween thinking of something as a possibility and believing in it as a reality (even apart from any qualms we may have about the reductivism with which the notion of reality would be treated in such an explanation). The statement that the "content" or intentionality of the passion of the infinite "is precisely itself" suggests that purely intellectual concepts are viewed as inadequate to express even the possibility of an infinite Good. This is connected with Climacus's objection to any "immediate" or "direct" relationship with God. "The immediate relationship with God is paganism," he declares, "and only after the breach has taken place can there be any question of a true God-relationship" (p. 218).

Immediacy, in this context, is at least partly a matter of cognitive content. "All paganism consists in this, that God is related to man directly, as the obviously extraordinary to the astonished observer" (p. 219). Climacus imagines, and mocks, a very conventional person who would suppose that God could be met immediately and would notice God only if God were the obviously extraordinary, "if God, for example, had taken on the figure of a very rare and tremendously large green bird, with a red beak, sitting in a tree on the mound, and perhaps even whistling in an unheard of manner" (p. 219).

We should not let this example mislead us into supposing that the immediacy rejected here is only sensory. Climacus associates the speculative or intellectual with the aesthetic (pp. 283, 288), and an idea that can in principle be given, at one viewing, to speculative thought is for him just as much a part of immediacy as the giant green bird with its red bill. We also should not suppose that immediacy is meant here in the usual epistemological sense. Climacus is certainly *not* saying that religious beliefs cannot be "basic" but must be supported by other beliefs that serve as evidence or grounds for them.

It may, however, be part of his meaning that God cannot be directly experienced. This seems to be implied when Climacus says that, in contrast with the purported direct relationship of paganism, "the spiritual relationship to God in the truth, i.e. in inwardness, is conditioned by a prior irruption of inwardness, which corresponds to the divine elusiveness that God has absolutely nothing obvious about Him, that God is so far from being obvious that He is invisible. It cannot immediately occur to anyone that He exists, although His invisibility is again His omnipresence" (p. 219). This statement can glide smoothly enough past eyes versed in the literature of theism; of course God is invisible. But we do well to hesitate at this point. What about the mystics? Is all direct experience of God to be denied even to them?

In Kierkegaard's *Either/Or*, Judge William, the fictitious author of the second volume, presents a somewhat respectful but still very negative critique of mysticism from his "ethical" point of view. That text contains enough disclaimers regarding the limitations of its point of view to alert us to the likelihood that Kierkegaard himself, and Johannes Climacus as a "religious" writer, would not wholly agree with Judge William's criticisms. But I think Climacus would endorse the Judge's main idea, as it climaxes the following bit of argument: "Therefore, if a mystic were asked what the meaning of life is, he perhaps would answer: The meaning of life is to learn to know God and to fall in love with him. But this is not an answer to the question, for here the meaning of life is understood as an instant, not as succession."[11] The answer attributed to the mystic here, "to learn to know God and to fall in love with him", could perhaps be interpreted in a sense that would win Climacus's approval. Judge William, however, interprets the knowing and the falling in love as instantaneous, as things that are complete in a moment of time. And Climacus will agree with him that the meaning of life requires "succession"; that is, it must be found in something that takes time. That is a main theme in the *Postscript*'s discussions of "existence". For Climacus, as I have noted, an existing individual's goal "is to arrive at a decision and to renew it" (p. 277)—a formulation with which Judge William would heartily agree.

This may help us understand the "prior irruption of inwardness" that is supposed to distinguish a "spiritual relationship to God in the truth" from pagan immediacy (p. 219). I take it that what Climacus means is that no momentary experience is sufficient of itself to put a person truly in relationship with God. A genuine God-relationship can be constituted only by a *history*, which takes time. Something "prior" must have happened before any experience that is to have religious significance; and something had better happen after it, as Climacus would doubtless be willing to add. This history is to be an "inner history",[12] involving an "irruption", a bursting in, of "inwardness", as Climacus puts it (p. 219). And of course he has already

---

[11] Søren Kierkegaard, *Either/Or*, part 2, translated by Howard V. Hong and Edna H. Hong (Princeton: Princeton University Press, 1987), p. 249 (SV II, 224—reference to the standard Danish edition is given in the margins of the new Princeton translations).

[12] On "inner history," see Kierkegaard's *Either/Or*, part 2, p. 134 (SV II, 121–22).

told us that "inwardness is subjectivity, [and] subjectivity is essentially passion" (p. 33). His view, I think, is that what is required to constitute a true God-relationship is an inner history marked by persistent passionate (indeed infinitely passionate) striving.

Many mystics would agree that the authenticity of experiences of God is not independent of the persisting religious character of the lives in which they are embedded and that something that might be called religious passion is important to a religious life. Perhaps this agreement would not satisfy Climacus; perhaps he would insist that there is some error in what even these mystics claim about their experiences. I shall not pursue that possible disagreement, except to say that I would be inclined to defend the mystics in it. Here I am more interested in Climacus's positive thesis, that an inner history of religious passion is necessary if God is to be truly the object of one's religious consciousness.

There is something to be said for this thesis. Theistic beliefs are not necessarily *religious* beliefs. Belief in a first cause, "which all call God", can be just a piece of metaphysics. Even belief in a divine command theory could be just a piece of metaethics. And belief in a supernatural agent of eschatological fulfillment, if the eschatology really offers nothing more than "pie in the sky", is not necessarily more religious than the daily horoscope. It's not that I am against metaphysics, metaethics, or eschatology; on the contrary, I am for all of them. But if these beliefs are not connected with any impulse to *worship* God, I am inclined to say that religiously, they have missed the point.

Religiously there is at least something essential missing from one's conception of God if one does not understand that God is the Supreme Good. And that does not mean something just a little bit better than anything else. It means something transcendently wonderful. How does one understand that? One recognizes, of course, that it means that God is *much* better than anything else, actual or possible. Even so I think it is plausible to suppose that it is only in *love* for such a Good that one gets a real glimmering of what one is talking about—that without any impulse to worship the supreme Good, one does not really get the point. In other words, *caring* about God is important to a religious understanding of the concept of God.

This poses a problem for anyone who aspires to pure objectivity in thinking about God. Wallace Matson begins his book about *The Existence of God* by saying that he will try to discuss the subject "dispassionately and judiciously, as if we were arguing about the existence of the Himalayan Snowman, or the antineutrino."[13] He goes on to acknowledge that hardly anyone writes or reads a book on this subject without caring much more about it than about the Himalayan Snowman. But we may think that this leaves a more fundamental difference unacknowledged. It's not just that we in fact care more about God than about the Yeti. Our concept of the Yeti does not depend on our caring about it; whereas one's conception of God commonly is, and arguably should be, shaped by the way in which one cares about God.

Suppose that God does in fact exist, and thus that the answer to the "objective problem", in the *Postscript*'s sense, about the truth of theism is affirmative. Suppose also that one does not "get the point" of theism, or adequately grasp the concept of God, unless one has enough religious passion about it to have an impulse to worship God. Then it would seem to follow, as a legitimate answer to the "subjective problem" about the truth of theistic belief, that such passion is required if one's religious consciousness is to conform to the divine object and thus really attain to religious truth. Correct ideas about God would doubtless constitute a measure of truth (whether or not Climacus would admit it). Without passion, however, they may fall short of the truth in the most important respect.

I agree with Matson that it is commonly possible and desirable, though difficult, to discuss objectively a topic that engages one's passions.[14] But where religion is concerned (and also in ethics), it may be that only thinking that is shaped in some way by a sort of passion can be adequate to its subject matter. Religious (and ethical) truth may be wood that we cannot cut if we take all pressure off the saw (cf. *Postscript*, p. 55). This is not to say, of course, that believing whatever we want to believe is the way to truth in these subjects. It is only to say that some influence of passion on our thinking, and especially on our conceptions, may be needed here if our thought is to conform to its object.

Here I have wandered, intentionally, some distance from the text of the *Postscript*, pursuing what seems to me most reasonable in the idea that (ethical and religious) truth is subjectivity. I am purposely ignoring some related theses of the *Postscript*, about which I have serious doubts. Climacus seems to hold that the subjectivity re-

---

[13] Wallace I. Matson, *The Existence of God* (Ithaca: Cornell University Press, 1965), p. xi.

[14] Matson, *The Existence of God*, p. xii.

quired for religious truth is an *infinite* passion. But what is an infinite passion? And are we humans, in our finitude, any more capable of it than of adequate *ideas* of an infinite deity? About these questions, and about Climacus's view that an adequate religious subjectivity necessarily involves believing something uncertain or even highly improbable, I shall have nothing to say here; they are not my present topic.[15]

6. Idolatry Revisited

Let us return to the child of idolatry who "prays with the entire passion of the infinite, although his eyes rest upon the image of an idol" (p. 180). Can Climacus really mean, without qualification, that he "prays in truth to God", given that his ideas of God are erroneous according to Climacus? Remembering that Climacus's question about the case was whether there is *more* truth there than in the case of a person who has the right ideas about God without the right sort of passion, we may be tempted to read an implicit qualification into the claim. *In a way* the prayer that rises with such passion from the temple of idolatry is directed to the true God (by its passion); but in another way, less important to Climacus, it is directed to a false God (by its ideas).

I suspect, however, that Climacus should be read as asserting something more extreme. In line with his claim that the "content" of the passion of the infinite "is precisely itself" (p. 181), he may mean that it is *only* the quality of the passion that determines to what deity a prayer is directed—that defective ideas cannot deflect a prayer of infinite passion from the true God or even add an idol as a secondary object, nor can sound ideas present the true God as object in a passionless prayer. I would not wish to defend such a view for myself, but it may be worth inquiring how it might be developed within the conceptual framework of the *Postscript*.

It virtually forces on us a question that is often raised as a challenge to the statement "Truth is subjectivity." Is it implied that fanatical devotion to any end whatever is true religion? That would clearly be an unacceptable consequence. It is also a consequence that Climacus clearly means not to accept.

---

[15] I have discussed these questions in "Kierkegaard's Arguments against Objective Reasoning in Religion", *The Monist* 60 (1976): 228–43; reprinted in Robert Merrihew Adams, *The Virtue of Faith and Other Essays in Philosophical Theology* (New York: Oxford University Press, 1987), esp. pp. 33–40.

His discussion of this problem, or of one very like it, is in terms of madness, but what he says can easily be applied to fanaticism too. He observes that "the objective way . . . thinks to escape a danger which threatens the subjective way, and this danger is at its maximum: madness. In a merely subjective determination of the truth, madness and truth become in the last analysis indistinguishable, since they may both have inwardness" (pp. 173–74). The text goes on to argue that the objective way is not so safe as it thinks, since "the absence of inwardness is also madness" (p. 174). The point that presently concerns me, however, is addressed in a footnote:

> Even this [that madness and truth are indistinguishable] is not really true, however, for madness never has the specific inwardness of the infinite. Its fixed idea is precisely some sort of objectivity, and the contradiction of madness consists in embracing this with passion. The critical point in such madness is thus again not the subjective, but the little finitude which has become a fixed idea, which is something that can never happen to the infinite. (P. 174)

"Madness never has the specific inwardness of the infinite." Neither presumably does Nazism or any other fanaticism. But why not? What is the specific inwardness of the infinite? Climacus appears to be claiming that it is contradictory, and hence impossible, to embrace with infinite passion a sort of thing variously described as an "objectivity" or a "little finitude"; but how are we to understand that?

Here we may seek help from the elaborate theory of the nature of religion (or at least of a type of religion, "Religiousness A") presented in the *Postscript* under the heading of "Existential Pathos". "The 'initial' expression for existential pathos" is identified there with "the absolute direction (respect) toward the absolute *telos*" (p. 347). This "absolute direction toward the absolute *telos*" is virtually the *Postscript*'s definition of religiousness in general, echoed in the twentieth century by Paul Tillich's definition of religion as "ultimate concern".

The absolute direction is understood as an inner transformation of the individual's existence (pp. 347–52). And its definition and manifestation are primarily negative. "The first genuine expression for the relationship to the absolute *telos* is a total renunciation" (p. 362). This means a renunciation of every finite end, and of everything that can be presented to us outwardly as an object—hence of every "objectivity" or "little finitude". This is explicitly applied to the finite and outward aspect of religious phenomena and practices as much as to obviously secular finitudes and objectivities. Not that the religious individual altogether ceases to have finite and outward ends; in order to do that one would have to cease altogether to live a human life. What is required is that one *detach* oneself from the finite ends (p. 367), "making the relationship to the absolute *telos* absolute, and the relationship to the relative ends relative" (p. 365). In this sort of religious devotion "all finite satisfactions are volitionally relegated to the status of what may have to be renounced in favor of an eternal happiness" (p. 350).

It is a complication, unwelcome in relation to my present interest, that the absolute *telos* is typically identified in the *Postscript*, as in the passage last quoted, with "an eternal happiness", rather than with God. But Climacus does hold the two in the closest relationship, declaring that

> the significance of worship is, that God is absolutely all for the worshiper; and the worshiper is again one who makes the absolute distinction.
>
> One who distinguishes absolutely has a relationship to the absolute *telos*, and *ipso facto* also a relationship to God. (P. 369)

Given this closeness, we may venture to use things that Climacus says about the concept of an eternal happiness as clues to his view of the conception of God that goes with true religion.

His concept of an eternal happiness is shaped by the need to make "the absolute distinction" between it and all the finite ends that are to be renounced and relativized. This results in a very abstract conception of an eternal happiness.

> [The] highest end is not a particular something, for then it would be relative to some other particular and be finite. . . . But to will absolutely is to will the infinite, and to will an eternal happiness is to will absolutely. . . . And this is the reason it is so abstract, and aesthetically the most poverty-stricken of all conceptions, because it is an absolute *telos* for an individual who proposes to strive absolutely. . . . And therefore the resolved individual does not even wish to know anything more about this *telos* than that it exists. (P. 353)

But then is any content left to the notion of an eternal happiness? Has this absolute striving any intentionality? Here Climacus applies the principle that the content of the passion of the infinite is precisely itself. For "there is nothing to be said of an eternal happiness except that it is the good which is attained by venturing everything absolutely" (p. 382). May we also suppose that, for the theory of existential pathos at any rate, the content of the concept of God is similarly stripped down to its relation to the absolute direction or absolute striving?

If so, we get a neat answer to our questions about idolatry and fanaticism. One who has "the specific inwardness of the infinite" will be one who "makes the absolute distinction" and thus is constantly renouncing all the finite and outward ends with which she nevertheless lives. Such a person cannot be a fanatic, for fanaticism essentially involves investing a religious or quasi-religious devotion in some finite and outward end. And a qualification not obviously[16] contained in "the entire passion of the infinite" must be imposed on any prayer from the temple of idolatry (or anywhere else) that is to be "in truth to God". Your eyes may "rest upon the image of an idol" or on a page of philosophical theology, but you must make the absolute distinction between God and those representations if your prayer is to have the true God as its object.

7. "Religiousness A"

The religion thus proposed to us may be viewed as consisting principally in the rigorous rejection of all fanaticisms, idolatries, and inordinate affections for finite things, undertaken as a form of passionate striving for a very abstract end of infinite value. Perhaps this could provide an adequate answer to the charge that the *Postscript* condones fanaticism. But it may give rise to moral uneasiness on another score, since it seems to offer no positive guidance for ethical or religious living. Given that *all* finite ends are relativized and in principle renounced, how will we distinguish the good among them from the bad? What will lead us to prefer kindness, for example, to cruelty?

This is not, I think, an arbitrary question to put to Climacus. He does not quite raise such a question about the finite *moral good*, but he does discuss a related problem about finite innocent pleasures.

---

[16] Climacus might claim that it is already contained, though not obviously, in his original description of the case. For he argues that "it is a contradiction to will something finite absolutely, since the finite must have an end, so that there comes a time when it can no longer be willed" (p. 353). Since contradictions, as commonly understood, are impossible, he might argue that it is *impossible* to direct "the entire passion of the infinite" to anything finite. But I will not try to evaluate this argument here.

How, he asks at agonizing length, can one be religiously justified in taking an outing in the Deer Park (a favorite pleasure of Kierkegaard's own)? How can one put the idea of God together with such a finitude as an outing in the Deer Park? And yet an absolute direction to the absolute *telos* requires that everything one does be brought into relation with the idea of God. This, Climacus is prepared to say, is "the ultimate difficulty of human existence, which consists precisely in putting differences together (like the idea of God with an outing in the Deer Park)" (p. 449; cf. pp. 426–27). It is a particularly excruciating difficulty for the religious person; "he desires to do all, to express this religious absoluteness, but he cannot make the finite commensurate therefor" (p. 433). He must of course continue to perform finite actions; without doing so, one cannot live at all. The problem is that no such action measures up to the religious passion or its object.

This is one of the more strikingly original ideas of the *Postscript*: that not only the images and ideas but also the actions that we are able to realize in their full particularity or concreteness are inadequate "to express . . . religious absoluteness". If there is to be something in our lives that conforms to the divine in such a way as to satisfy the subjective side of the problem of religious truth, Climacus suggests, it must be something more inward and abstract. Most philosophers looking for something more abstract would fasten on an idea. Climacus focuses instead on a passion, the passion for the infinite, which he seems to think corresponds to the divine reality more adequately than any idea does. The thought that some other function of our minds might apprehend God better than ideas resonates with important themes of modern theology. For example, Schleiermacher and others can be read as claiming that sort of superiority for *feeling*. If Climacus claims it for *passion*, that would help explain why, in his view, the "content" of the passion of the infinite "is precisely itself".

But if a religious passion is that in us which can most adequately express the divine, it cannot itself find an adequate expression in concrete action. This is the source of a suffering that Climacus characterizes as "the 'essential' expression for existential pathos" (p. 386).

> But herein lies the profound suffering of true religiosity, the deepest thinkable, namely, to stand related to God in an absolutely decisive manner, and to be unable to find any decisive expression for this (for a happy love between human beings expresses itself in the union of the

lovers). This inability is rooted in the necessary relativity of the most decisive external expression. (P. 440)

The religiousness that has its essential center in this suffering is what the *Postscript* calls "Religiousness A". It seems to be a form of religious life in which ultimacy has triumphed totally over concreteness—to put the matter in terms borrowed from an illuminating passage of Tillich, which I assume to have been influenced by the *Postscript*:

> The phrase 'being ultimately concerned' points to a tension in human experience. On the one hand, it is impossible to be concerned about something which cannot be encountered concretely, be it in the realm of reality or in the realm of imagination. . . . On the other hand, ultimate concern must transcend every preliminary finite and concrete concern. . . . But in transcending the finite the religious concern loses the concreteness of a being-to-being relationship. It tends to become not only absolute but also abstract, provoking reactions from the concrete element. This is the inescapable inner tension in the idea of God.[17]

Now perhaps the concrete pole has not vanished from Religiousness A so completely as I have been suggesting. In particular, it may be doubted whether what is said about an eternal happiness, that it is something about which there is nothing to be said except about the mode of striving to be related to it, is really to be applied in all strictness to God, in Religiousness A. Climacus speaks freely of God as *Creator*, for example, in passages that do not clearly step outside the bounds of Religiousness A (*Postscript*, pp. 220, 296). It seems to be assumed in the theory of existential pathos (e.g., p. 369) that God has a role as agent and cause, and not only as object of religious passion. And we have seen that the parable of the children of Christendom and idolatry, which is presented within the bounds of Religiousness A, presupposes that there are objectively right and wrong ideas of God.

The more rigorously abstract interpretation of Religiousness A remains interesting, however, for its boldness. It offers a purely formal conception of true religion, as determined solely by the form of religious motivation, of religious passion or striving. It may remind us of Kant's attempt to give a purely formal account of true morality, as determined solely by the form of reason's governance of action.

[17] Paul Tillich, *Systematic Theology* (Chicago: University of Chicago Press, 1951), 1:211.

And in both cases there are problems about filling in the form so as to give definite guidance for concrete action.

8. "Religiousness B"

Perhaps Religiousness A, even in the less austere of the forms suggested in this essay, is too abstract to be anybody's real religion. In the *Postscript*, at any rate, it serves as a stage in the exposition of Christianity, which is presented as the sole instance of a type called "Religiousness B". And the statement "Truth is subjectivity" is initially, and in its most unqualified form, an expression of Religiousness A. Climacus indicates this by presenting Socrates as an exemplar of subjectivity as truth. Socrates has "the passion of the infinite", holding fast to his (Socratic) ignorance "with the entire passion of his inwardness" (p. 180). "In the principle that subjectivity, inwardness, is the truth, there is comprehended the Socratic wisdom. . . . for this reason Socrates was in the truth by virtue of his ignorance, in the highest sense in which this was possible within paganism" (p. 183).

Socrates is the hero of *pre*-Christian religiousness, in both the *Philosophical Fragments* and the *Postscript*. The theological problem, stated at the beginning of the *Fragments*, to which both works constitute an elaborate response, is whether and how a religious advance beyond Socrates is possible. This problem is restated at this point in the *Postscript* (pp. 183–85). Having called attention to the difficulty of making such an advance and the danger that one will think one is making it but really "come out behind Socrates", Climacus asks and answers a question: "Subjectivity, inwardness, has been posited as the truth; can any expression for the truth be found which has a still higher degree of inwardness? Aye, there is such an expression, provided the principle that subjectivity or inwardness is the truth begins by positing the opposite principle: that subjectivity is untruth" (p. 185). This indicates that in the religiousness ("B") that goes beyond Socrates, the truth will still be inwardness, subjectivity,[18] but that this thesis requires some qualification or supplementation that was not needed in Religiousness A.

Climacus immediately stresses that he is not, like "speculative philosophy", making a move "in the direction of the principle that

---

[18] This is confirmed when Climacus says that Christianity "fits perfectly" with the thesis that "subjectivity is the truth" (p. 206).

objectivity is the truth" but aims rather at "making the inwardness far more intensive", because more paradoxical. He proceeds (in agreement with the first chapter of the *Fragments*) to identify the "untruth" in which the individual begins as *sin*—indeed, original sin (p. 186). This may tempt us to make an easy reconciliation of his claims that "subjectivity is the truth" and "subjectivity is untruth." We would do this by taking 'subjectivity' in different senses in the two claims, as meaning infinite passion in the first claim, and one's attitude on religious issues, whatever it may be, in the second claim. Then we could interpret "subjectivity is untruth" as meaning that one's attitude in relation to religion is sinful precisely because it is *not* infinitely passionate, whereas "subjectivity is truth" means that one would be in the truth, religiously, if one did have infinite passion.

This interpretation is unattractive, inasmuch as it has Kierkegaard palming off on us a mere equivocation as if it were a paradox. There is also a powerful argument against it. Climacus conceives of Christianity as exclusive in the sense that it "extends sin-consciousness to the whole race, and at the same time does not know the whole race [but only true Christians] as saved" (p. 518; see pp. 210–15, 515–19). And since he identifies salvation with coming to be in the truth,[19] this implies that non-Christians are not in the truth. Despite his "passion of the infinite" (p. 180), therefore, Socrates, as a non-Christian, cannot be in the truth, according to Christianity (or Religiousness B) as Climacus conceives of it.

The indicated conclusion, I think, is that subjectivity, infinite passion, is *necessary*[20] but *not sufficient* for being in the truth, or in conformity with God, according to Religiousness B. This fits very well with what Climacus says about the relation between Religiousness A and B.

Religiousness A is the dialectic of inward transformation; it is the relation to an eternal happiness which is not conditioned by anything but is the dialectic inward appropriation of the relationship, and so is conditioned only by the inwardness of the appropriation and its dialectic. (P. 494)

---

[19] See Søren Kierkegaard, *Philosophical Fragments*, trans. by Howard V. Hong and Edna H. Hong, published in one volume with the Hongs' translation of Kierkegaard's *Johannes Climacus* (Princeton: Princeton University Press, 1985), pp. 18–19 (SV IV, 188).

[20] For the necessity, see p. 512: "He who does not possess this highest subjective passion is not a Christian."

In other words, this is the religiousness for which "there is nothing to be said of an eternal happiness except that it is the good which is attained by venturing everything absolutely" (p. 382).

> Religiousness B . . . does on the contrary posit conditions, of such a sort that they are not merely deeper dialectical apprehensions of inwardness, but are a definite something which defines more closely the eternal happiness. (P. 494).

It seems fair to infer that it is not as true of Religiousness B as of Religiousness A that "it is the passion of the infinite that is the decisive factor and not its content, for its content is precisely itself" (p. 181).

It is clear enough what Climacus thinks is the "definite something which defines more closely", not only the eternal happiness, but also the God-relationship for an individual in Religiousness B. It is "a something outside the individual", a historical fact—namely, "the determination of God in time as the individual man" (p. 498). It appears thus that the answer to the subjective problem of being in the truth, within Christianity as conceived by Climacus, requires *both* having the right inwardness, an infinite passion, *and* being related to the right object, the historic Incarnation. Concreteness also is not so totally obliterated by ultimacy in Religiousness B as in Religiousness A. The history of Jesus provides concrete content for Christianity; and we may speculate that Climacus, like Kierkegaard, would expect it to give concrete guidance for living the Christian life. This may afford some hope of solving the problem (noted at the beginning of section 7) of a religious basis for distinguishing the good from the bad among finite ends.

Climacus would think it much too easygoing, however, to rest content with the formula that (the right) subjectivity is necessary but not sufficient for truth in Religiousness B. He describes Religiousness B as "paradoxical"; and the "tension", as Tillich called it, between concreteness and ultimacy is central to the paradox. "The paradox consists in the fact that this apparently aesthetic relationship (the individual being related to something outside himself) is nevertheless the right relationship" (*Postscript*, p. 498). The stricture that an immediate relationship to God is paganism remains in full force in Religiousness B: "A direct God-relationship is aesthetic and is not really a God-relationship, any more than a direct relationship to the absolute is an absolute relationship, because the discrimination of the absolute has not been accomplished" (p. 497n). How is this failure of the God-relationship through inappropriate directness to be avoided in Religiousness B? How is an Incarnation different from meeting God as a huge green bird with a red beak? And is Religiousness B as well equipped as Religiousness A to escape the dangers of fanaticism?

Climacus seeks a solution to these problems in the paradoxical character of Religiousness B. The paradox is found in the fact that "the determination of God in time as the individual man" is believed, but "it is not possible to think this." And "if the paradox is not held fast in this sense, Religiousness A is higher, and Christianity as a whole is reduced to aesthetic terms" (p. 498). I take this to mean that the absolute distinction must be made, and the absolute *telos* respected by relativizing the finite, *within* the object of Christian faith. Only so will idolatry and fanaticism be avoided. One way in which Climacus thinks the Christian must do this is indicated in the *Fragments* (especially chapter 4). The believer must not suppose that anything that is or could be known historically, even by the closest contemporary of the supposed incarnate God, could establish the truth of an Incarnation of God, because of the incommensurability between the finitude of everything historically observable and the infinitude of the deity that is believed thus to enter human history.[21] A different sort of basis is needed for faith in an Incarnation.

This, in Climacus's view, is a paradoxical stance: seriously, indeed passionately, to believe in a revelation of the infinite and eternal God in something finite and historical, and at the same time to make the absolute distinction between finite and infinite. If not strictly a paradox, it is at least a very difficult tension to live with. Yet I believe that it is religiously wiser to accept this tension than to settle, as in the more extreme form of Religiousness A, for a totally one-sided triumph of ultimacy over concreteness. I do not think, as Climacus seems to, that this tension is peculiar to Christianity,[22] but rather, as Tillich holds, that it is an inescapable part of any approach to God that is worthy of serious religious attention.

[21] This point could be related to the Chalcedonian doctrine of the distinctness of the divine and human natures in Christ, but Climacus does not comment on that.

[22] Indeed I do not mean to give a general endorsement of Climacus's conception of Christianity.

SCOTT MACDONALD

Christian Faith

Without faith it is impossible to please him. For whoever would
draw near to God must believe that he exists and that he rewards
those who seek him.

Hebrews 11:6 RSV

Faith by itself, if it has no works, is dead. . . . You believe that God
is one; you do well. Even the demons believe—and shudder.

James 2:17,19 RSV

Many philosophers and theologians who have thought about the
nature of faith have agreed with the author of Hebrews, on the one
hand, that Christian faith essentially involves belief that certain
propositions are true, and with the author of the epistle of James, on
the other, that it involves more than mere belief. The passage from
James suggests that what distinguishes full-fledged Christian faith
from demonic belief is works, but this suggestion has typically been
construed as claiming not that works are somehow constitutive of
faith but that they are a natural and typical external manifestation of
an internal emotional or volitional state that *is* constitutive of faith.
This internal state might be thought to be a sort of volitional commitment, an attitude of trust in or love for God that is the analogue
in the one who has faith of the fear and hatred of God that causes
the demons to shudder.[1] It is a common view, then, that Christian
faith essentially involves both a cognitive and a non-cognitive or volitional element.

---

[1] The apparent allusion, in the passage from James, to the great commandment:
"Hear, O Israel: The Lord our God is one Lord; and you shall love the Lord your God
with all your heart, and with all your soul, and with all your might" (Deut. 6:4–5),
suggests that those whose faith is dead fulfill the first part of the commandment (in
believing that God is one) while lacking the wholehearted love for God required for
fulfilling the second.

Of course some philosophers and theologians have given pride of place in their accounts of faith to one of these two elements, but they have typically acknowledged the necessity of the other. Aquinas, for example, who holds that faith is primarily a kind of intellectual assent to the truth of certain propositions, nevertheless maintains that full-fledged, salvific faith is intellectual assent informed by an appetitive act of charity, that is, by love for God. Similarly, those, such as Martin Luther, who argue that faith is primarily a kind of trust have generally acknowledged that trust in God logically presupposes at least some beliefs, such as that God exists and that God's nature and purposes are benevolent.

I think it is fair to say that the view that faith is essentially a compound state composed of both a cognitive and a non-cognitive element, of both belief and trust or love, for example, constitutes the mainline view of the nature of Christian faith. Among those who occupy the mainline, however, there has been considerable disagreement over the precise nature of the cognitive and non-cognitive components of faith and their relations to one another. In this essay I present a particular version of the mainline view and defend it against mainline rivals. Of course there are important accounts of Christian faith that lie outside the main line. Due to the influence of non-cognitivist developments in ethics and Wittgensteinian views in the philosophy of language, for example, it has become fashionable to argue that faith can be conceived of in purely non-cognitive terms.[2] But I propose to leave accounts of this sort aside. I will have my hands full addressing the important issues internal to the mainline tradition, and I think exploring those issues in detail helps clarify what's important about the mainline view in general.

I should say at the outset that I am interested here only in an account of *Christian* faith, that is, the sort of faith that has been at the heart of the Christian tradition, the having of which might be said to *make* one a Christian. I do not consider what significant features (if any) Christian faith has in common with other sorts of religious faith or with phenomena that are sometimes taken to be instances or manifestations of a kind of non-religious faith. I suspect that much of what is definitive of Christian faith will be essential to the sort of faith endorsed by theistic religions generally, and that there will be significant differences between this sort of faith and the

---

[2] For a survey of views of this sort, see Louis P. Pojman, *Religious Belief and the Will* (London and New York: Routledge and Kegan Paul, 1986), chap. 12. Pojman defends his own view in chap. 16. See also Terence Penelhum, *God and Skepticism: A Study in Skepticism and Fideism* (Dordrecht: Reidel, 1983), chap. 7.

sort found in non-theistic religions, but I will not be concerned with these issues here. Henceforth, when I use the term 'faith' I mean by it 'Christian faith'.

I should also say that I will be using the term 'belief' and its cognates in their narrowly cognitive senses. It is important to be explicit about this slightly artificial restriction since, in discussions of faith, 'belief' is often used to refer to both the cognitive and non-cognitive sides of faith, sometimes indiscriminately, as when 'belief' is simply taken to be interchangeable with 'faith', and sometimes by design, as in the common distinction between *belief that* and *belief in*. I will use 'belief' exclusively to mean 'belief that', that is, as denoting the propositional kind of belief that constitutes the cognitive side of faith.

1. The Nature of Faith

I hold that Christian faith is a compound state the primary constituents of which are a cognitive state, namely, belief that certain propositions are true, and a particular sort of volitional response to the things and states of affairs represented in those propositions. I am not interested here in determining what propositions are essential to Christianity, what things are to be included in Christianity's cognitive core. I assume, however, that *some* propositions are essential and that they represent, among other things, the existence of a personal God who is active in seeking the good of his creatures in certain determinate ways. Hence, on my view, faith necessarily entails belief that these propositions are true.

The volitional component of Christian faith is a response to these truths which consists in a kind of love for the person of God. Many accounts of faith, especially within the Protestant tradition, have taken trust to be the primary non-cognitive component in faith, but I think that love not only includes what these accounts have taken to be important about trust but is also more basic than trust to Christian faith. Love for God encompasses or grounds many distinguishable emotional and volitional attitudes, including reverence toward God for the sort of being he is, gratitude to him for his attitudes and actions toward us, desire for intimate communion with God, and desire for and commitment to the actualization of God's purposes and goals.[3] On my view, then, Christian faith consists in volitional

---

[3] This specification of both the cognitive content and the volitional nature of Chris-

commitment to the person of God and to his aims on the basis of the belief that Christianity is true.

The two primary components of faith are bound together by necessary connections running in both directions. On the one hand, volitional states in general require antecedent acts of cognition or apprehension that present the will with its object. So the volitional state that I claim is partially constitutive of faith is necessarily connected with the cognitive component of faith insofar as belief apprehends the object to which the will responds. The sort of love for God I have identified as necessary for faith, in particular, presupposes belief that God exists and has a certain kind of nature and certain purposes. On the other hand, an apprehension of some thing or state of affairs as good or bad entails an appetitive reaction to that thing or state. Insofar as one believes an object or state of affairs to be good, for example, one will be appetitively drawn toward it.[4] Hence, insofar as a person believes the propositions essential to Christianity and judges the persons, things, and states of affairs represented in those propositions to be good, that person will be appetitively drawn toward them. Given that those propositions represent the existence of a personal God who loves human beings and actively seeks their good, the appropriate appetitive or volitional response to God will be a sort of volitional commitment broadly characterizable as love for the person of God. The necessary connections linking cognitive apprehensions with volitional responses, then, make it reasonable to hold that the cognitive state by which one believes the propositions essential to Christianity and the volitional state whereby one responds in love to the things and states of affairs represented in those propositions constitute a single compound state, which is faith.[5]

My account of the nature of the volitional component in faith and its relation to faith's cognitive component entails that, properly

---

tian faith is, of course, rough and incomplete. For an interesting discussion of the nature of loving personal relationships which helps fill out this sketch, see Norman Kretzmann, "A Particular Problem of Creation: Why Would God Create This World?" in *Being and Goodness: The Concept of the Good in Metaphysics and Philosophical Theology*, ed. Scott MacDonald (Ithaca: Cornell University Press, 1991), pp. 220–49.

[4] This is not to say that cognitive apprehension of some good is sufficient to move us to act so as to obtain or realize it; we may, for example, perceive some other, incompatible good to be better, judge that though it is good in some respect, it is bad in other respects that outweigh its good, or suffer weakness of the will (if weakness of the will is possible).

[5] For a more detailed account of these relations between cognitive and appetitive acts and states, see my "Ultimate Ends in Practical Reasoning: Aquinas's Aristotelian Moral Psychology and Anscombe's Fallacy", *The Philosophical Review* 100 (1991):31–66.

speaking, the object of the cognitive component is not individual atomic propositions such as that God exists or that God is triune but a set of propositions (or a complex conjunctive proposition). This is because the volitional commitment essential to faith—love for God and commitment to his purposes—presupposes fairly rich cognitive content. One cannot respond in the appropriate way to God on the basis of assent to the bare proposition that God exists. One must, in addition, conceive of God as having a certain nature and as having acted in certain ways and with certain purposes. As the passage from Hebrews puts it, one must believe that God exists *and* that he rewards those who seek him. One can be said to have faith with respect to individual propositions, then, only in a derivative sense, namely, insofar as one believes a larger set of propositions that includes them.

This account of faith seems to me straightforward and intuitively appealing, but many proponents of mainline views have found it inadequate, rejecting it not because they hold that what I claim to be necessary to faith is not necessary but because they think there are features essential to faith that my account leaves out. They think, in other words, that my account is too simple. I'm going to divide these arguments into two groups: in section 2 I discuss those claiming that there is more to the volitional component of faith than I have allowed; in section 3 I take up those claiming that there is more to the cognitive component. My general strategy will be to show that these arguments fail either because some feature they allege to be essential to Christian faith is not in fact necessary to it or because, if that feature is necessary, my simpler account can in fact accommodate it.

2. The Volitional Component of Faith

Most mainline accounts have agreed with my view that the volitional component of faith consists (at least in part) in a sort of loving or trusting response to God. But many have thought that faith requires the will to be operative not only in *responding* to the persons and states of affairs presented by the propositions essential to Christianity but also in *bringing about* belief in those propositions. On this view, the cognitive component of faith must itself be voluntary; that is, the person who believes the propositions essential to Christianity to be true must hold those beliefs freely or voluntarily if she is to have faith. We can think of this view, then, as holding that faith presupposes a sort of doxastic voluntarism. We are free with respect to believing or not believing the propositions essential to Christianity, and it is essential to faith that one believes them freely.

There have been at least two influential sorts of argument for including doxastic voluntarism of this sort in the account of faith. The first argues for the necessity of doxastic voluntarism on the basis of considerations having to do with the merit of faith. The second appeals to considerations having to do with faith's role in making possible a personal relationship between human beings and God. My strategy against both of these arguments will be to show that they fail to demonstrate that we *must* conceive of faith as involving voluntary belief. Hence, I intend to leave open the question of whether any of our beliefs are in fact subject to the sort of direct voluntary control the doxastic voluntarist has in mind. There may be independent arguments showing that doxastic voluntarism is untenable, and, of course, if there are, then an acceptable account of faith cannot presuppose it. All I need to do to defend my account of faith, however, is show that, even if some form of doxastic voluntarism is true, it is not necessary for faith.

2.1. Faith and Merit

The argument from merit derives from the view that faith is a virtue or a state without which we cannot merit the reward of eternal life. If faith is meritorious or praiseworthy, and if faith essentially involves belief that certain propositions are true, then it might seem that faith requires some sort of meritorious or praiseworthy believing. Merit and praise, however, presuppose responsibility, and responsibility presupposes voluntariness. Hence, for believing to be meritorious or praiseworthy it must be voluntary, and so faith requires voluntary belief.

Aquinas seems to have appealed to considerations of just this sort in arguing for the merit of faith. "Every human act that is subject to free choice of the will can be meritorious if it is related to God. But believing (*credere*) itself is an act of the intellect assenting to the divine truth on the basis of a command of the will moved by God through grace, and so it is subject to free choice of the will in its being ordered toward God. That is why the act of faith can be meritorious."[6] This passage identifies two necessary (and jointly suffi-

---

[6] Thomas Aquinas, *Summa theologiae* IIaIIae,2,9 (hereafter *ST*). All translations from

cient) conditions of an act's being meritorious: it must be subject to free choice of the will (*liberum arbitrium*) and appropriately directed toward God, the highest good. Aquinas endorses these conditions because he holds that merit implies both responsibility (which requires free choice of the will) and moral rightness (which requires an intention appropriately directing the act toward God).[7] In this passage he claims that faith can be meritorious only because the believing that constitutes it can satisfy both of these conditions.

Aquinas goes on to identify the act of will appropriately directing one's belief toward God as an act of charity, and so he claims that charity is the principle of merit in human acts.[8] In order to satisfy his second condition for meritoriousness an act must be done for the right reasons, that is, it must be done for the sake of the good. On Aquinas's view, God is the universal and perfect good, the ultimate end for the sake of which all human actions ought to be done.[9] Hence, he holds that if an act is to be meritorious, it must be directed by the agent in the appropriate way toward God and that an act's being directed in this way consists in its being done out of charity, that is, out of love for God.[10] He holds, then, that one's belief that Christianity is true will be a meritorious act of faith only when it is freely brought about by an act of will out of love for God.

Aquinas's account faces an obvious dilemma. If acts of faith are meritorious only when the cognitive component in faith is brought about by an act of will out of love for God, then one's love for God must be prior to any of one's meritorious acts of faith. Now, consider the act of faith by which one first has faith, one's act of conversion faith. Either conversion faith is brought about by an act of will out of love for God or it's not. If it is, then it's meritorious, but we're committed to the absurd view that the new convert loves God prior to believing that God exists. If it's not, then on Aquinas's account, conversion faith cannot be meritorious, which seems clearly wrong. Aquinas seems to recognize that his account faces this dilemma and grasps its second horn.[11]

Aquinas are my own. I have used the Leonine edition (Rome: Vatican Polyglot Press, 1882–).

[7] See *ST* IaIIae, 6 and 21; 114,1,ad 1; and Thomas Aquinas, *De veritate* 14,3 (hereafter *DV*).

[8] *ST* IIaIIae, 2, 9, ad 1; IaIIae, 114, 4.

[9] *ST* IaIIae, 3–5.

[10] See *ST* IaIIae, 65, 2; IIaIIae, 2, 9, ad 1; 2, 10, ad 2; 4, 5.

[11] See *ST* IIaIIae, 4, 7, ad 5 and *DV* 14, 2, ad 10.

I do not assess the details of Aquinas's account here.[12] For my purposes it is sufficient to see that the argument from merit fails to show that faith requires this kind of doxastic voluntarism. I am willing to grant that faith is meritorious and that merit requires responsibility, and hence voluntariness; but it does not follow from this that faith, which involves belief, must involve voluntary believing. Given an account of faith that includes both belief and a volitional state consequent on that belief, it is possible, and I think more plausible, to divorce merit and responsibility entirely from the *belief* and tie it instead to the volitional *response*. Faith seems meritorious because those who have it love God, whereas those who, like the demons, believe and yet shudder, lack merit because they hate and fear God. The loving and the hating of God are acts of will consequent on the cognitive states by which the Christian faithful and the demons apprehend the truth of Christianity.

My account, then, can locate the voluntariness required for meritorious faith in one's volitional response to God on the basis of one's perception that Christianity is true. In fact, we typically suppose that our considered volitional responses to and attitudes toward the people, actions, and states of affairs we perceive around us are paradigm cases of states of ourselves for which we must claim moral responsibility. When, on the basis of our belief that there is a good God who cares for us and is active in seeking our well-being, we respond to God in love and commit ourselves to his purposes, our response will typically be voluntary and an appropriate locus of merit.[13] An account of faith, then, needn't require that the cognitive component of faith be subject to our will in order to secure a place for merit. If I am right, faith can be meritorious even if doxastic voluntarism is false and none of our beliefs is subject to voluntary control.[14]

---

[12] See my "Demons, Doxastic Voluntarism, and Aquinas's Account of Faith", forthcoming.

[13] Of course if our volitional response to the truth of Christianity is to be a locus of merit, it must be voluntary in the sense necessary for responsibility. For this reason we should not think of it as a sort of brute emotional reaction, since these sorts of reactions are typically not the sorts of things for which we are responsible. Emotions of this sort are surely typical of the experiences of those who have faith, but the sort of love for God I claim to be essential to faith is nearer to the sort of love we consciously and deliberately undertake in a marriage vow or in a decision to have (or adopt) and nurture children.

[14] It follows from what I have said here that, on my view, all faith is meritorious since meritorious volitional commitment to God is essential to faith. Hence, so-called

Now, nothing in my argument shows that an adequate account of faith must *exclude* the possibility of voluntary believing; my account of faith is clearly compatible with the truth of doxastic voluntarism. It's a mistake, however, to build doxastic voluntarism into an account of faith unless it is clearly required, and the argument from merit fails to show the need.

2.2. Faith and Personal Relationships

Some have argued, however, that there are reasons other than those having to do with grounding merit for thinking that the cognitive assent of faith must be subject to voluntary control. John Hick, for example, has argued that it is essential to faith that it grounds the possibility of human beings' entering into a personal relationship with God and that it is a necessary condition of our participating in this relationship as full-fledged persons that we be cognitively free with respect to the truth of Christianity. "If God were to reveal himself to us in the coercive way in which the physical world is disclosed to us, he would thereby annihilate us as free and responsible persons."[15] On this view, the cognitive assent of faith must be uncoerced if it is to be possible for human beings to enter into relationship with God and embark on the process of soul-making, in which faith plays an integral role.

This point about faith's role in making possible a personal relationship between human beings and God is important and right, but the assumption that *cognitive* freedom of the sort Hick describes is necessary for that relationship seems mistaken. What is clearly required for a full-fledged personal relationship is freedom with respect to the appetitive or volitional attitude one takes toward the

---

dead and demonic faith are not genuine kinds of faith distinct from meritorious Christian faith. The demons and those whose faith is dead may assent to the truth of Christianity but fail to respond to that truth with the volitional commitment essential to faith; when they do so, they do not manifest an unmeritorious kind of faith: they merely believe those propositions. Their *cognitive* state with respect to the propositions of Christianity may be the same as that of someone who has faith (subject to the qualifications I endorse in section 2.2), but, by virtue of lacking the necessary volitional commitment, they fail to have faith. Thus, I deny a distinction that is central to Aquinas's account, namely, the distinction between unformed and formed faith: Aquinas allows, whereas I deny, that there is unformed, unmeritorious faith. See *ST* IIaIIae, 4, 3–4.

[15] John Hick, *Faith and Knowledge* (Ithaca: Cornell University Press, 1966), p. 134. See also Richard Swinburne, *The Existence of God* (Oxford: Clarendon Press, 1979), pp. 211–12, and Eleonore Stump, "Aquinas on Faith and Goodness" in *Being and Goodness*, ed. MacDonald, pp. 179–207.

other person. As the case of the demons shows, cognitive freedom is not necessary for this sort of appetitive freedom. It seems that the demons are in a position to be quite certain of the truth of Christianity; that is, their epistemic relation to the propositions essential to Christianity is such that they cannot help believing that they are true.[16] They are nevertheless displeased that reality is such that it makes those propositions true, and they hate God and flee God's presence. The demons, then, are free to reject God despite the fact that they are not cognitively free with respect to the truth of Christianity. Similarly, resistance fighters who know perfectly well that their country is under the heel of a ruthless and oppressive foreign power and that their efforts are sure to win only brutal retribution can nevertheless set themselves firmly on a course of resistance and go to their deaths cursing the power that executes them.

Perhaps, however, the cognitive content of Christianity is special in a way that undermines the general argument I have just offered. Hick develops the argument in this way: "God, if he is known to exist, can only be known as the One who makes a total difference for us. For he is known as infinitely higher than us, in worth as well as in power, and as having so made us that our own final self-fulfillment and happiness are also the fulfillment of his purpose for us. I cannot know that such a Being exists and be at the same time indifferent to him."[17] Thus, if propositions of a certain sort are included among those one believes in believing that Christianity is true, it might seem impossible both to believe that Christianity is true and either to reject or to remain indifferent to God. If this is right, then it would appear that there can be no freedom in one's volitional response to the truth of Christianity. Moreover, given these conditions, it could not be the case that the demons believe that Christianity is true and yet hate and fear God, for in believing the propositions essential to Christianity they would believe propositions that make it impossible for them to respond to God in that way. Hence, one might conclude that faith must, after all, presuppose *cognitive* freedom with respect to (at least some of) the propositions essential to Christianity. If one were coerced with respect to believing that Christianity is true, and if one's response to God is

---

[16] Hick dismisses the case of demons on the supposition that they are merely mythological and not actual beings (*Faith and Knowledge*, p. 21). But the possibility and not the actuality of the case of the demons is what's relevant, and demonic assent seems possible.

[17] John Hick, *Christianity at the Centre* (New York: Herder and Herder, 1970), p. 56.

determined by the truth of Christianity, then there would be no room for free human participation in a personal relationship with God.

Now, this argument hinges on the claim that certain kinds of belief necessitate or determine a certain kind of volitional response, but there are two sorts of consideration that would count against that claim. First, it seems clear that if genuine weakness of the will is possible, that is, if it is possible at one and the same time to judge or perceive that some course of action is the best alternative open to one and nevertheless voluntarily choose or act in favor of another, incompatible, course of action, then one's volitional response will remain undetermined regardless of the content of one's beliefs. One might, for example, judge that one's highest fulfillment is to be found in fulfilling God's purposes and nevertheless voluntarily act contrary to those purposes through sheer weakness of the will.

Second, even if this sort of clear-eyed weakness of the will is impossible, certain common features of human psychology allow for less dramatic breaks in the chain linking volitional response to belief. It is, no doubt, a consequence of our cognitive limitations that, at any given time, the vast majority of what we believe we believe merely dispositionally. Moreover, a belief's causal efficacy vis-à-vis other mental states can vary in accordance with its being occurrent or dispositional. This is true for a belief's impact on both our cognitive and volitional states. For example, my believing (occurrently) that Nancy Reagan is Ronald Reagan's second wife, together with my believing (occurrently) that if Nancy Reagan is his second wife, then Ronald Reagan has been married before necessitates my believing (occurrently) that Ronald Reagan has been married before. But if, while believing the conditional (occurrently), I fail actually to call to mind that Nancy is Ronald's second wife—something I know perfectly well—then it is possible that I fail to believe (occurrently) that Ronald Reagan has been married before. Similarly, I might fail to admire my neighbor for her courage simply because, in my evaluation of her character, I have failed actually to consider certain facts about her that I know perfectly well.

Failing, on some particular occasion, actually to call to mind things that one nevertheless believes is a common sort of phenomenon, but the possibility of it is particularly apparent and important in the case of our formation of considered volitional attitudes and commitments of the sort that constitute the volitional component of faith. We often undertake these sorts of attitudes and commitments at a particular time on the basis of conscious, reflective deliberation.

In order for our beliefs to inform these deliberations, however, we must call them to mind and include them in our reasoning. It is evidence of this that when deliberating about particularly complex and important matters, we take special care to guard against failing to consider relevant facts that are in our possession. Regardless of their relevance to or potential significance for our practical reasoning, any of our dispositional beliefs that we fail actually to consider will remain insulated from the volitional attitudes and commitments we adopt on the basis of that reasoning.[18]

Creatures with psychologies like ours, then, are capable of a kind of cognitive negligence: we can neglect—that is, fail to consider occurrently—what we nevertheless believe. Of course it may be that some of these kinds of cases are ones in which a person is not responsible for failing actually to consider what she believes dispositionally, but the cases nearest to the particular sort of case we are interested in seem to be paradigms of culpable negligence. It is often because of the state of our wills, our passions, or our characters that we fail to consider all the facts that we can and should consider. Conversely, it is often to our credit that, in the same circumstances, we do actually consider what we should.

Belief and volitional response can come apart, then, due to cognitive negligence. Moreover, the truth of Christianity is characterized by the sort of cognitive complexity that opens the door to this kind of negligence. First, Christianity's cognitive content is fairly rich; it includes a number of propositions representing (among other things) God's existence and nature, his relation to the world, and certain of his attitudes, purposes, and actions. Given this intrinsic complexity, it is possible for one to believe the set of those propositions dispositionally while basing one's considered volitional response to the truth of Christianity on occurrent consideration of only a proper subset of them. One might, for example, form one's considered attitude toward God on the basis of considerations about

[18] Moreover, given the nature of considered volitional attitudes and commitments, there is the risk that beliefs that we fail at one time to include in deliberations of this sort will become *permanently* insulated from our effective volitional states. Settled attitudes and commitments and the long-range intentions that instantiate or accompany them tend to restrict the scope of our practical reasoning in certain ways: for example, by making it unnecessary for us (other things being equal) to undertake at some future time the kind of deliberation that led us initially to form those attitudes, commitments, and intentions. This effect of considered volitional states makes it less likely (other things being equal) that a belief that is inefficacious on one occasion (due to its having been left unconsidered on that occasion) will have another similar opportunity to exercise its causal powers.

his power, neglecting to consider his moral goodness or benevolence.

That the particular parts of Christianity's cognitive content most clearly relevant to our volitional attitude toward God are normative or evaluative propositions introduces further complexity into Christianity's cognitive content. These evaluative propositions predicate supervenient properties—goodness, well-being, fulfillment, and the like—of certain beings, purposes, states, and activities. These things possess these supervenient properties in virtue of possessing certain other properties that constitute the properties' supervenience base. The property of contributing to human fulfillment, for example—a property that Christianity takes to hold of certain actions, mental states, and ways of life—supervenes on certain other properties belonging to those actions, states, and lives, such as their being charitable, their being virtuous, their constituting conformity to God's will, and so on.[19] In the case of propositions that predicate supervenient properties, then, it is possible to believe occurrently that something possesses certain supervenience-base properties while failing to believe occurrently that it possesses the evaluative property supervenient on that base, believing only dispositionally that those properties constitute the supervenience base for the relevant supervenient property. It is possible, for example, to recognize that a particular action is charitable without at the same time recognizing (occurrently) that it is an action that contributes to human fulfillment, because one fails to call to mind something one nevertheless believes, namely, that the property of contributing to human fulfillment supervenes on the property of being charitable.

It is easy to imagine a scenario in which the demons fall victim to (or take advantage of) the negligence that can occur in the face of this sort of cognitive complexity. Because of their cognitive acumen and their access to facts substantiating the claims of Christianity, the demons believe the propositions essential to Christianity, including, let's suppose, the proposition that their highest fulfillment is to be found in following God's will. Following God's will, however, consists in activities such as performing acts of charity and service with respect to other creatures. Faced with the prospect of performing acts of this sort, the demons call to mind the fact that these acts are

---

[19] Of course, some of these base properties might in turn supervene on other properties. For example, that a particular action (or omission) conforms to God's will might supervene on its being an act of worship (or an instance of refraining from theft).

difficult and require a certain amount of self-sacrifice. On the basis of that (negligently) narrow consideration, the demons judge that it is better to avoid acts of this sort, and they respond with hatred to God, whom they think of (occurrently) as the powerful person who enjoins burdensome acts. Nevertheless the demons believe (dispositionally) that their fulfillment consists in conformity to the will of God.[20] The demons' belief that Christianity is true, then, needn't itself be voluntary if the demons are to have the freedom to reject a loving personal relationship with God.[21]

My reply to Hick's argument, which depends essentially on the possibility of the sort of cognitive negligence I have identified, will not work, however, against an argument of Aquinas's. Aquinas holds that one's volitional state is unqualifiedly necessitated by its object when (and only when) that object is perceived as the perfect and universal good and is cognitively immediate to us.[22] In the beatific vision—the supernatural state in which one sees God's essence directly and as it is in itself—one has direct intellectual awareness of perfect goodness itself. In that cognitive state one's volitional state is necessitated: one cannot help loving God, the perfect good. Given Aquinas's conception of the nature of beatific vision, it will not be possible for us, when we are in that state, to believe any of the propositions essential to Christianity merely dispositionally since their truth will be inescapably open and occurrent to us. In that state we will be incapable of the sort of cognitive negligence that would allow us to reject or remain indifferent to the perfectly good God who is our ultimate goal and fulfillment.[23]

It seems, then, that if we grant the possibility of direct cognitive access to the truth of Christianity of the sort that characterizes beatific vision of God (and deny the possibility of outright weakness of will), then we must grant that the volitional freedom necessary for a person's freely choosing to enter a relationship with God requires that that person not have the beatific vision. Leaving aside the special case of beatific vision, however, one's volitional response to the truth of Christianity remains voluntary even if the propositions es-

---

[20] It may be possible by continual or repeated negligence of this kind to lose the neglected dispositional beliefs altogether, thereby ceasing to believe what one once believed. If so, this would be an example of one of the many ways in which our beliefs are subject to *indirect* voluntary control.

[21] My argument here is inspired by Aquinas's moral psychology of wrongdoing (sin) in *ST* IaIIae, 75–77.

[22] *ST* IaIIae, 10, 1–2.

[23] *ST* Ia, 62, 8.

sential to Christianity include propositions about ultimate human well-being and God's perfect goodness and even if one is not cognitively free with respect to those propositions. Those who respond to God in love might do so voluntarily in virtue of the voluntariness of their occurrent consideration of the relevant propositions. Those who believe that Christianity is true might nevertheless reject God or remain indifferent to him in virtue of a voluntary failure to consider occurrently certain propositions that they believe dispositionally.

I conclude that neither the argument from merit nor the argument from personal relationships gives us good reason to suppose that the will must be operative in bringing about the belief essential to faith. The kind of volitional response to God that I have claimed to be an essential part of faith is sufficient to ground the merit of faith and explain faith's role in allowing human beings to participate in a loving personal relationship with God.

3. The Cognitive Component of Faith

The most significant differences between my account of faith and rival mainline accounts have to do with faith's cognitive component. My account places only two restrictions on the cognitive component of faith, namely, that it consists in belief that certain propositions are true and that its content is rich enough to ground the sort of volitional response necessary to faith. All mainline accounts I am familiar with impose additional restrictions, and so we need to see whether there are good reasons to add to this part of my account.

3.1. Faith and Authority

A long and influential tradition of reflection on the nature of faith has distinguished faith as a particular kind of *epistemic* propositional attitude distinct from other kinds of belief. The tradition is rooted in Augustine who distinguished faith from another sort of belief— what he called understanding (*intellectus*)—on the basis of its epistemic grounds. According to him, faith is belief based on authority whereas understanding is belief based on reason.[24]

[24] See, for example, Augustine, *De vera religione*, Corpus Christianorum, series Latina XXXII (Turnholt: Brepols, 1962) xxiv, 45. See my "Augustine" in *Blackwell's Companion to Epistemology*, ed. Jonathan Dancy and Ernest Sosa (Oxford: Basil Blackwell, forthcoming), and Norman Kretzmann, "Faith Seeks, Understanding Finds: Au-

Aquinas follows Augustine in this, maintaining that an act of faith with respect to some proposition is an act of assenting to that proposition on the grounds that it is testified to or spoken by God. "The faith we are talking about assents to something only because it is revealed by God. Thus [faith] depends on the divine truth itself as on the middle term [of a syllogism]."[25] God's truthfulness guarantees the truth of any proposition to which God testifies. Hence, the divine truth is the formal object of faith; that is, faith assents to propositions insofar as they are perceived as falling under the divine truth.

Aquinas's view that faith is intellectual assent on the basis of the divine authority is closely connected with his view that faith involves voluntary believing. He holds that one's intellectual assent to a proposition is subject to a command of the will only when that assent is not necessitated by one's evidence. Intellectual assent to some proposition is necessitated when one sees that the proposition cannot be false, that is, when one takes the evidence as guaranteeing the truth of the proposition. On Aquinas's view, evidence that guarantees the truth of a proposition is either its self-evidence (as in the case of propositions that are seen to be analytically or conceptually true) or demonstrative proof on the basis of self-evident propositions.[26] Since the evidence provided by testimony falls short of guaranteeing truth in either of these ways, assent to propositions on the basis of authority can be subject to free choice of the will. For these reasons Aquinas denies that one can have both faith and the strictest kind of knowledge (*intellectus* or *scientia*) with respect to the same proposition at the same time: if one holds a given proposition on faith, one must believe it on the basis of authority, a kind of evidence too weak to ground the strictest sort of knowledge; and if one knows it in the strictest sense, one must believe it on a kind of evidence different from authority.[27]

By imposing no restrictions on the epistemic status of the propositions the believer holds on faith, I am departing from this traditional conception of the cognitive component of faith. No doubt author-

---

gustine's Charter for Christian Philosophy" in *Christian Philosophy*, ed. Thomas P. Flint (Notre Dame: University of Notre Dame Press, 1990), pp. 1–36.

[25] *ST* IIaIIae, 1, 1; see also *ST* IIaIIae, 2, 1, ad 1; 4, 5, ad 2; 5, 3; 5, 3, ad 1, and *DV* 14, 2, ad 9. See also John Calvin: "Faith is the knowledge of the divine will in regard to us, as ascertained from his word. And the foundation of it is a previous persuasion of the truth of God" (*Institutes of the Christian Religion*, trans. H. Beveridge [Grand Rapids, Michigan: Eerdmans, 1975], book 3, chap. 2, sec. 6, p. 474).

[26] *ST* Ia, 82, 2, IaIIae, 17, 6, IIaIIae, 1, 4.

[27] *ST* IIaIIae, 1, 5.

ity—scriptural evidence and the testimony of Christian believers (both past and present)—plays an important role in grounding the beliefs constitutive of faith, but I can see no compelling reason to suppose that it is essential to those beliefs or the only sort of ground open to them.[28] Hence, I think we ought to allow that the belief essential to faith might be based on any sort of evidence whatever. Typically, though this is no part of the concept of faith, one who has faith will have a variety of kinds of evidence for the various propositions essential to Christianity. That variety might include demonstrative proof or inductive evidence for some propositions (for example, the proposition that God exists), abductive evidence for propositions constituting a general theistic account of reality, scriptural evidence or testimony, and firsthand religious experience. So it seems to me that faith does not require a particular kind of evidential grounding and that one can have faith with respect to certain propositions that one also knows or has conclusive proof for as well as with respect to those for which one has only weaker justification.[29]

If we had good reason to suppose that some sort of general epistemic weakness or uncertainty is necessary to the cognitive component of faith, then we might have good reason to restrict the kinds of evidence that can ground faith. As we've seen, both Aquinas and Hick think that the belief essential to faith must be voluntary or free and that it can be voluntary only if we take our evidence for the belief to fall short of guaranteeing truth or being epistemically coercive. I have argued that this reason is not compelling. We need to consider, however, whether there are reasons other than this for holding that faith necessarily involves uncertainty.

3.2. The Necessity of Epistemic Uncertainty for Trust

On one popular conception, faith essentially consists in belief on grounds that are epistemically deficient in some respect. The views of Augustine and Aquinas surveyed in section 3.1 constitute a weak

---

[28] In fact belief based on authority is itself epistemically derivative insofar as it presupposes beliefs about the veracity or reliability of the authority. Augustine recognizes this; see, for example, De vera religione, xxiv, 45.

[29] Moreover, it seems that one might have very strong evidence for accepting certain authoritative witnesses as legitimate, perhaps strong enough (on some accounts of knowledge) to make the beliefs accepted on the basis of that authority genuine instances of justified belief or knowledge. See my "Theodicy, Natural Theology" in Handbook of Metaphysics and Ontology, ed. H. Burkhardt and B. Smith (Munich: Philosophia Verlag, 1991), 2:891–93.

version of this conception. Augustine and Aquinas maintain only that the evidence grounding faith must be less than paradigmatically strong. They thought that, although beliefs held on faith cannot have evidence sufficient to give them impeccable epistemic standing, those beliefs can nevertheless be supported by very strong evidence—evidence sufficient to ensure the rationality of those who believe.[30]

Robert Adams has developed an argument similar to Hick's argument from personal relationships which concludes to a weak version of the thesis that faith necessarily involves cognitive uncertainty. Adams claims that the attitudes of trust, dependence, and cooperation essential to close personal relationships require a sort of uncertainty or cognitive distance between persons.

> Suppose we always *saw* what people were like, and particularly what they would do in any situation in which we might have to do with them. How would we relate to people if we had such knowledge of them? I think we would manipulate them. I do not mean that we would necessarily treat them in a selfish or immoral way, but I think we could not help having an attitude of control toward them. And I think the necessity we would be under, to have such an attitude, would be conceptual and not merely causal. . . . Our actual uncertainty about what other people will do makes it possible to *depend* on another person in a way that is much more personal. It enables the other person to be more truly other.[31]

Adams supposes that cognitive uncertainty about another person is necessary to account for the element of risk that is essential to the sort of dependence and trustful cooperation found in close personal relationships, because one can be said to take a risk only when one is uncertain of the outcome of one's venture. Adams suggests that willingness to take great risks in the face of uncertainty is the distinguishing mark of the trusting faith of the biblical heroes, whom we take to be paradigmatically faithful.

[30] In fact the medieval tradition that Augustine and Aquinas represent can correctly be said to deny that faith is compatible with *knowledge* only if one means by 'knowledge' what they meant by *intellectus* or *scientia*. Given that most modern epistemology has abandoned their very strict conception of justification, it is at best misleading to characterize their view in that way.

[31] Robert M. Adams, "The Virtue of Faith" in his *The Virtue of Faith and Other Essays in Philosophical Theology* (Oxford: Oxford University Press, 1987), pp. 20–21. Adams seems not to commit himself on the issue of whether the sort of cognitive uncertainty he has in mind entails cognitive *freedom*, so we needn't take him as endorsing Hick's thesis that voluntary believing is essential to faith.

Now, it seems to me that Adams is wrong about the role of uncertainty in close personal relationships. It is no doubt true that our close personal relationships involve some element of uncertainty about what the other person is like, but in exemplary cases—one's relationship with a spouse or a lifelong friend and companion, for example—our knowledge of the other person is as complete as such knowledge can be in this life, and whatever uncertainty remains in these relationships is entirely unrelated to our attitudes of love, trust, dependence, and cooperation toward the other person. My ability to love and trust my wife, to commit myself without reservation to her well-being and to the goals and purposes we have chosen as definitive of our common life seems in no way dependent on my being uncertain about what she is like or what she will do. In fact I know in great detail what she is like, and, much to her chagrin, I can predict with extraordinary accuracy what she will do in various kinds of situations. None of that makes it any more difficult for me to depend on her or to refrain from adopting an attitude of control with respect to her than it is in the case of my neighbors whom I know much less well.

The explanation of these facts seems to me to be that our considered volitional attitudes toward another person are not (conceptually) determined by what we know about that person. That is why it makes sense to attach moral responsibility to these sorts of attitudes. I can neglect my small children and treat them callously despite my awareness of their fragile psyches and great physical and emotional needs, and I have acted reprehensibly when I do so. Similarly, I can act out of love and genuine care for them even in situations in which I know perfectly well what they are like and how they will act. It is not my knowledge of but my attitude toward the other person that determines whether I will view her as someone or something to be controlled and manipulated.

Distinguishing two sorts of trust will help clarify this point. Both sorts involve the taking of risks, and so both require the person who trusts to be uncertain in some respect, since one can be said to take a risk only when one is uncertain of the outcome of one's venture. But they differ in respect of the source of the uncertainty. In the case of the first sort of risk-taking trust, the risk is rooted in uncertainty about the person in whom one trusts. When I lend my (irreplaceable) personal copy of Tischendorf's eighth edition to a student, my action manifests considerable trust precisely because of the risk I am taking. My evaluation of the risk will be directly affected by how well I know the student. To the extent that I am uncertain of her character and personal habits I will judge the risk to be greater, and my loan of the book will manifest a greater trust. But this sort of risk-taking trust seems to me not to be necessary to close personal relationships; in fact the risk, and hence the trust, in the case I've described is a function of a kind of uncertainty about the student that is incompatible with our relationship's being close. It would be a mistake to suppose that this sort of trust is essential to faith.

In the other sort of risk-taking trust, the risk is rooted not in uncertainty about the person in whom one trusts but in uncertainty about some other factor relevant to the venture. I might be willing, for example, to risk losing my house by offering it as collateral for a loan that a close friend desperately needs to keep her business afloat. I am willing to take a great risk for her sake because of the value I place on her and her achievement of goals important to her. Unlike the risk in lending a precious book to a student, the risk in this case is not rooted in my uncertainty about what my friend is like or what she will do. I may be quite certain of both what she will do with the money and that she will do everything in her power to repay the loan. My uncertainty in this case is about the eventual success of the business, something that is (let us suppose) beyond her or anyone else's direct control. Risk-taking trust of this sort, then, seems to be a function of a volitional commitment to the other person rather than any cognitive uncertainty about that person, and it is typical of close personal relationships. The risk-taking trust of the biblical heroes seems to be of this sort: in their willingness to sacrifice a great deal for God's sake they demonstrated their commitment to God and his purposes rather than some uncertainty about what God is like.[32] (In the next section I'll return to the notion of risk taking as a manifestation of volitional commitment.)

It is a mistake, then, to suppose that the sort of risk-taking trust essential to close personal relationships rests on any kind of uncertainty about the other person. Some element of uncertainty of the sort Adams describes may be a common and perhaps an inevitable feature of close human relationships, but it is not a necessary condition for them.

---

[32] Richard Swinburne's exposition of what he calls the Lutheran view of trust makes it a necessary condition of trust in God that one have some reason for believing that God will not do for us what we want and need. This seems to me to confuse the trust that is a part of faith, the riskiness of which is rooted in what one may have to sacrifice for God's sake, with the other sort of risk-taking trust, the riskiness of which is rooted in uncertainty about what the person one trusts is like or is going to do. See Richard Swinburne, *Faith and Reason* (Oxford: Clarendon Press, 1981), pp. 111–13.

3.3. The Necessity of Epistemic Deficiency or Sufficiency for Faith

A more radical version of the view that faith essentially involves epistemic uncertainty takes one's having faith to consist at least in part in one's having beliefs that are only weakly supported by evidence if they are supported at all. Tertullian and Kierkegaard may have held extreme versions of a view of this sort according to which faith requires us to believe *against* the evidence.[33]

Two common objections have been raised against faith understood in this way. First, if having faith essentially involves holding epistemically *unwarranted* beliefs, then one who has faith is necessarily irrational. Second, even if faith is not irrational simpliciter, the person who has faith seems to be irrational in holding the propositions believed on faith with the high degree of confidence that is characteristic of faith.[34] Rational persons, we might suppose, proportion the strength of their beliefs to the strength of the evidence.[35] But according to the popular conception, one who has faith has (at best) weak evidence for the propositions of faith and yet claims certitude for them.

These objections arise and seem to me powerful precisely because the views against which they are directed make it part of the *concept* of faith that the beliefs accepted in faith have a particular kind of epistemic deficiency. But unlike these accounts of faith, the account I have been developing places no restrictions on the epistemic status of the propositions held in faith. On my view (apart from the requirement that the person who has faith with respect to certain propositions *believe* those propositions) it is no part of the concept of faith that the believer stand in any specific epistemic relation to them. Thus, a person who has faith with respect to certain proposi-

---

[33] For a discussion of Tertullian's view, see Norman Kretzmann, "Faith Seeks, Understanding Finds" in *Christian Philosophy*, ed. Flint; and "Reason in Mystery" in *The Philosophy in Christianity*, ed. Godfrey Vesey (Cambridge: Cambridge University Press, 1989), pp. 15–39. For discussion of Kierkegaard, see Robert M. Adams, "Kierkegaard's Arguments against Objective Reasoning in Religion" and "The Leap of Faith", both in his *The Virtue of Faith*.

[34] Calvin, for example, claims, "We add [to the definition of faith as knowledge of God and Christ], that it is *sure and firm*, the better to express strength and constancy of persuasion. For faith is not contented with a dubious and fickle opinion. . . . The certainty which it requires must be full and decisive, as is usual in regard to matters ascertained and proved" (*Institutes*, book 3, chap. 2, sec. 15, p. 482).

[35] For classic statements of versions of this objection, see John Locke, *Essay concerning Human Understanding*, 4.19.1, and W. K. Clifford, "The Ethics of Belief" in *Lectures and Essays* (London: Macmillan, 1879). See also Anthony Kenny, *Faith and Reason* (New York: Columbia University Press, 1983), pp. 72–84.

tions might at the same time know or be justified in believing those propositions, and her beliefs might be subject to ordinary appraisals of epistemic rationality. Beliefs held in faith, then, are neither necessarily irrational nor necessarily epistemically inferior to other kinds of beliefs. Hence, the first of these objections does not arise for my account.

In one sense, my account avoids the second objection raised, too, since I allow the possibility that the person who has faith believes the propositions of faith on evidence strong enough to warrant a high degree of epistemic confidence. But since I don't think this way of handling the second objection is fully adequate, I give it detailed consideration in the next section. Before I do that, however, I want to consider a mistake analogous to that of building epistemic deficiency into the account of faith, namely, building epistemic sufficiency into the account.

In *Problems of Religious Knowledge* Terence Penelhum makes it a necessary condition of one's having faith that one considers oneself *to know* the truth of certain propositions.[36] Presumably this means that in order to have faith one must believe that the grounds on which one accepts the truth of Christianity provide support sufficient (according to some suitable criterion) to render justified one's belief that Christianity is true. There are two difficulties with this requirement. First, it entails that no one can have faith who does not have a considered view about what makes a given propositional attitude knowledge rather than something else, for one cannot *consider oneself* to know that P without at least a rudimentary view of what conditions must be met if someone is to be considered to know P. But it seems possible that a person who lacks the sophistication required to consider himself to know the truth of Christianity might nevertheless have faith, because a person can believe that Christianity is true without having any views at all about the epistemic status of that belief.

Second, Penelhum's requirement seems too strong in another respect. It seems possible for the person who has faith to think that the evidence on which his belief is based is insufficient to make that belief knowledge. Given that different people have different views about what the conditions for knowledge are, some of which may be

---

[36] Terence Penelhum, *Problems of Religious Knowledge* (London: Macmillan, 1971), pp. 123–32. Penelhum seems no longer to hold this view; see his more recent *God and Skepticism*, pp. 177–78. Calvin defines faith as knowledge (*notitia*) of God and Christ—see n. 34 above.

very strict indeed, it might even seem likely that there will be people who have faith and yet do not consider themselves to know that Christianity is true.[37] Penelhum's primary reason for including this restriction in his account of faith is that, as he claims, "there seems no . . . appropriate way [other than by using the word 'know'] of speaking of the mode of experience characteristic of the great formative figures of the Christian tradition."[38] I think, however, that faith does not require epistemic certitude, and in the next section I turn to the defense of this position.

In this section I have argued that there are no compelling reasons to make either epistemic deficiency or epistemic sufficiency part of the account of Christian faith. I think that, in addition to my negative arguments, there is a good reason for excluding from the account any epistemic restriction of this sort. By building epistemic deficiency or sufficiency into the cognitive component of faith we turn into *conceptual* truths judgments about the rationality of the person who has faith. If to have faith is (in part) to accept the truth of Christianity on evidence that is epistemically insufficient (or sufficient), then the person who has faith is necessarily irrational (or rational). That seems a mistake. Judgments of rationality with respect to some belief must be made on the basis of a determination of what evidence there actually is or what evidence a given person actually has for the belief in question. We ought not to legislate in advance whether all, only some, or none of those who have faith believe rationally. So by imposing no restrictions on the epistemic status of the cognitive component of faith, my account has the virtue of leaving open what ought to be left open, namely, the assessment of a person's rationality in believing the propositions essential to Christianity.

3.4. Faith and Certitude

I have claimed that one common objection to the rationality of faith, namely, that faith requires epistemic certitude in the face of less than certain evidence, does not arise for my account since I allow the possibility that the person who has faith believes the propositions of faith on evidence strong enough to warrant a high degree

---

[37] As we have seen, Aquinas would not have considered himself to know (at least in the strict sense) many of the propositions essential to Christianity.

[38] Penelhum, *Problems of Religious Knowledge*, p. 129. Penelhum goes on to quote Hick (*Faith and Knowledge*, p. 209) in support of this claim.

of epistemic confidence. But even if this is possible, those who have faith typically do not have evidence for their belief that Christianity is true strong enough to warrant anything akin to certitude, and so I need to provide an explanation of the phenomenon to which the objection appeals.[39] Having developed that explanation, I will be in a position to defend the claim I pressed against Penelhum that Christian faith does not require epistemic certitude.

My account of faith allows us to identify a misunderstanding in the view that faith requires epistemic certitude, a misunderstanding of the nature of the confidence characteristic of those who have faith. In accordance with the cognitive and volitional components of the act of faith identified in my account, we should distinguish between epistemic and volitional confidence or commitment. On the one hand, one's epistemic confidence with respect to some proposition is a function of one's perception of the strength of the evidence for that proposition. Thus, as one perceives the evidence for a proposition increasing, one's epistemic confidence with respect to that proposition increases, reaching a limit in epistemic certitude in the case in which one perceives the evidence as guaranteeing the truth of the proposition. On the other hand, one's volitional commitment with respect to some object or state of affairs is a function of one's practical commitment to pursuing or trying to realize or sustain that object or state of affairs. Thus, in general, the higher one values an end, the higher the degree of volitional commitment one will exhibit with respect to it; that is, the more one will prefer it to other ends and be willing to sacrifice for its sake.[40] Because I place a very high value on my children's well-being, for example, I am willing to devote a great deal of my time and energy to pursuing it, and I view other ends of mine as subordinate to that end, sacrificing other things I value when they conflict with the realization of that end and undertaking courses of action to which I would otherwise assign a negative value. The role I give to my children's well-being in my practical reasoning and action is a measure of my degree of volitional commitment to that end.

Given this distinction, my reply to the charge that the epistemic certitude necessary for faith entails that faith is typically irrational is that the certitude or confidence characteristic of faith is not *epistemic*.

---

[39] For an ingenious attempt to construct a reply to the second objection along lines suggested by Aquinas, see Eleonore Stump, "Aquinas on Faith and Goodness" in *Being and Goodness*, ed. MacDonald.

[40] I leave aside concerns about weakness of the will.

Christian faith carries with it a high degree of volitional commitment but, on my view, no particular degree of epistemic confidence beyond that required for assent or belief.[41] Hence, those who have faith can proportion their epistemic commitment to the strength of their evidence, thereby satisfying the canon of rationality to which the objection appeals. Of course this is not to say that those who have faith always or typically do proportion their epistemic confidence in this way; but if they are guilty of an irrational degree of epistemic confidence, it is not because their having faith entails it.

Now, it might be thought that even if epistemic and volitional commitment are distinct, the high degree of volitional commitment characteristic of Christianity must be based on a high degree of epistemic confidence if it is to be rational. Christianity demands *total* volitional commitment to its ends. It demands that those who have faith love God above all things and act in accordance with God's will in all ways. Hence, those who have faith are typically quite resolute with respect to what general ends to pursue and are willing to forfeit a great deal in pursuing them. If that sort of resoluteness about what one must do and how one must act is not itself epistemic certainty, it seems at least an expression of it. It seems analogous to the case of a physician whose resoluteness about the course of treatment required for a particular patient rests precisely on conclusive results from diagnostic procedures. The physician's practical resoluteness about what to do is caused in part by epistemic certainty about the patient's condition.

But volitional commitment or practical resoluteness needn't be based on epistemically certain beliefs; in fact it needn't be based on belief at all. If I judge that there is a one-in-three chance that the house in which my children are sleeping is on fire, I am absolutely certain about what I must do—I must try to get them out of the house, whatever the cost. In this case my practical resoluteness about what I must do to guard against merely possible imminent catastrophe does not even require *belief* on my part since I do not believe that the house is on fire but only that there is a reasonable chance that it is. A fortiori, acting with such resoluteness or with a high degree of volitional commitment needn't arise from corresponding epistemic certainty.

---

[41] Robert Adams has seen this: "The certitude of faith has much more to do with confidence, or freedom from fear, which is partly an emotional state, than it has to do with judgments of certainty or great probability in any evidential sense" ("The Virtue of Faith", p. 18).

One reason for the failure of any direct correlation between degrees of volitional commitment and degrees of epistemic confidence is that the practical exigencies of the world often demand of us action, and hence practical commitment of some sort, in circumstances in which we lack firm evidence about important features of the case at hand. Given the value of my children's lives, I must act immediately to get them out of the house even if I have only a reasonable suspicion that they are in danger. It would be morally outrageous of me to postpone action so as to have the time necessary to acquaint myself more thoroughly with the facts of the case.

Now, Christianity is immediately practically relevant in the lives of those who have faith; it demands total volitional commitment. Those who believe that there is a being that exemplifies perfect goodness and is a person who created human beings, who desires to secure for humans their own highest fulfillment, and who has prescribed for them certain ways of life to guide them toward that purpose can be wholly resolute about what to do. They can be certain of how they must respond to God and of what courses of action and ways of life they must embark on. Given that they believe these things to be true, it would be morally outrageous for them not to respond. But nothing about their practical resoluteness requires of them anything epistemically stronger than belief that Christianity is true. Those who have faith can pursue the ends identified by Christianity with total volitional commitment while being less than epistemically certain of the truth of Christianity.

Gary Gutting has claimed that although Christian faith does not require epistemic certitude, it does require what he calls decisive assent.[42] Assent to some proposition is decisive if it terminates the process of inquiry into the truth of that proposition. Decisive assent is to be contrasted with what he calls interim assent, which accepts some proposition but also includes a commitment to the epistemic need for continuing inquiry into the truth of that proposition.[43] Gutting argues that the total volitional commitment characteristic of Christianity is incompatible with the sort of continuing reflection on its truth that is characteristic of interim assent: "[T]he very meaning

---

[42] "It is true that acting with total commitment to a belief does not require absolute certainty about the belief. I can rightly give my life for a belief that I acknowledge as merely probable and that I admit I might give up on the basis of new evidence. . . . Decisive assent is not an assertion of certainty but only of the lack of a present need to continue the project of inquiry" (Gary Gutting, *Religious Belief and Religious Skepticism* [Notre Dame: University of Notre Dame Press, 1982], p. 107).

[43] Ibid., p. 105.

of decisive assent shows that it is necessary for total commitment.
Even though I can rightly, for example, sacrifice my life or my fortune for a belief about which I am not entirely certain, it is simply
foolish to give up everything for a belief that I think requires further
discussion and evaluation. The very fact that I act so decisively on a
belief requires that my assent be decisive."[44]

I think that Gutting has fallen into the same sort of confusion as
those who suppose that faith requires epistemic certitude. It's simply false that it must be foolish (either epistemically or morally) to
risk a great deal for a belief that one thinks requires further discussion and evaluation. I may well think that the proposition that the
house in which my children are sleeping is on fire needs further
evaluation in respect of its truth. Because I believe that there is some
chance that the proposition is true, because I judge that my evidence
for the truth of the proposition is sufficient to assign it a probability
of one-third, and because I have a great interest in whether or not it
is true, I should surely like to know whether or not the house is in
fact on fire. Of course the exigency of the situation does not allow
me to undertake the investigation I judge to be necessary or desirable from an epistemic standpoint; it requires me to act immediately
on what is for me the mere suspicion that the proposition may be
true. In this case I terminate the process of inquiry and act, but not
because of the epistemic status the proposition in question has for
me. I terminate the process of inquiry because the practical requirements of the situation demand it. Hence, I don't have to assent to
the proposition at all, in interim or decisive fashion, in order to be
able to act with total volitional commitment and impeccable rationality.

The same thing can be said of the total volitional commitment
characteristic of Christian faith. Given the pressing and immediate
practical relevance of the reality presented to us in the propositions
essential to Christianity, we can rationally respond to that reality
with total volitional commitment regardless of the relative epistemic
strength of our belief that those propositions are true. We can act
decisively and take ourselves to be morally compelled to act without
delay at the same time that we acknowledge that the epistemic status of our beliefs is weak. Gutting has mistakenly taken the decisive-
ness that characterizes these sorts of actions and volitional commitments to be grounded in an epistemic feature of our beliefs when it
is in fact often grounded in purely practical considerations.

[44] Ibid., pp. 107–8.

On my view, then, the certitude or confidence characteristic of Christian faith is volitional rather than epistemic. And since volitional and epistemic commitment can come apart, I hold it to be possible, and in fact quite typical, for Christians to manifest a high degree of volitional commitment while at the same time judging the probability of Christianity's being true to be well below 1.[45] Moreover, it seems clear that those who are in this mixed epistemic-volitional state need not be guilty of any epistemic or moral impropriety.[46]

4. Conclusion

Hence, the most prominent arguments for thinking that the simple account of Christian faith that I have presented is insufficient do not in fact give us good reasons to extend that account. We can make sense of Christian faith if we think of it simply as belief that Christianity is true plus an appropriate volitional response to that truth. My account, then, is not only simple but also adequate, and those are great virtues in any philosophical analysis.[47]

[45] The state I am claiming to be typical of Christian believers should not be confused with the state of one who acts "as if" Christianity were true. On my account, faith requires belief. My point, then, is that the evidence grounding that belief needn't be very strong in order for the believer to manifest quite appropriately the strong volitional commitment characteristic of Christian faith.

[46] I do not claim that total volitional commitment is *necessary* to faith but only that the nature of reality, as Christianity portrays it, appropriately demands this sort of response. Those who have faith, however, will no doubt manifest a wide range of degrees of volitional commitment.

[47] I am grateful to Richard Fumerton, Norman Kretzmann, Steve Maitzen, Christopher Shields, and Eleonore Stump for comments on previous versions of this essay.

ROBERT AUDI

❦

The Dimensions of Faith and
the Demands of Reason

It is often said that there are many faiths. It is less often said, but certainly true, that there are also many kinds of faith. This second point must be borne in mind when we ask in what ways or forms religious faith can be rational. The relation between religious faith and rationality is a perennial problem in the philosophy of religion, though the question is often posed in different terms, for instance as one that concerns faith and justification, or warrant for religious belief, or the possibility of knowledge of God. In this essay I approach the topic of faith and reason by exploring both some major forms of faith, particularly the notion of a person of faith, and the standards of rationality appropriate to faith.

1. The Epistemological Context

In the past two decades, the field of philosophy of religion has reflected the impact of recent developments in general epistemology, and the effort to exhibit religious faith as a rational attitude has taken a new (though by no means historically unprecedented) turn. Until the middle 1970s, the dominant tendency in assessing religious rationality, whether that of faith or that of theistic belief in general, was evidentialist. The task was chiefly to formulate and assess the arguments for God's existence or for selected religious propositions. Much discussion focused either on the traditional arguments for the existence of God, especially the cosmological, ontological, and teleological arguments, or on other theistic arguments from presumptively plausible premises about the world or our experience of it.

More recently, philosophers of religion have argued that theistic beliefs can be rational even if the believer neither has nor can formulate cogent arguments for them.[1] The impetus for this approach derived in good part from a recognition that if we have *any* knowledge or justified belief, it is in some way based on knowledge or justified belief that is non-inferential in the sense that it is not grounded in arguments or prior premises. This is of course a major foundationalist thesis; but until the 1970s, there was insufficient awareness that foundationalism could be held without strong assumptions felt to be irreconcilable with the fallibilist scientific climate of our time. Once epistemologists showed how foundationalism could be both moderate in its claims and significantly holistic in its treatment of justification,[2] the appeal to non-inferential justification in the case of religious beliefs seemed less problematic. This is not to say that the philosophers of religion who appealed to such justification endorsed foundationalism overall; indeed, some have criticized classical and modern versions without indicating that their own views were broadly, if qualifiedly, foundationalist.[3]

A further epistemological development influencing philosophers of religion is reliabilism. Reliabilism, broadly speaking, takes the justifiedness of beliefs to be determined by the truth-conduciveness (reliability) of the processes by which the beliefs are produced (or sustained). If a belief is reliably produced, as ordinary perceptual beliefs presumably are, it is justified; there is thus no need for it to arise by some inferential route that runs through justificatory premises. This conclusion is not only consistent with foundationalism but difficult to square with coherentism. If what justifies my belief that there is a

---

[1] See, e.g., C. F. Delaney, ed., *Rationality and Religious Belief* (Notre Dame: University of Notre Dame Press, 1979); Alvin Plantinga and Nicholas Wolterstorff, eds., *Faith and Rationality* (Notre Dame: University of Notre Dame Press, 1983); and Robert Audi and William J. Wainwright, eds., *Rationality and Religious Belief: New Essays in the Philosophy of Religion* (Ithaca and London: Cornell University Press, 1986).

[2] Here one might note papers by Mark Pastin (who acknowledges an earlier debt to Roderick Firth), "Modest Foundationalism and Self-Warrant", *American Philosophical Quarterly Monograph Series* 9 (1975): 141–149; William P. Alston, "Two Types of Foundationalism", *Journal of Philosophy* 73 (1976): 165–185; and Robert Audi, "Psychological Foundationalism", *The Monist* 62, no. 4 (1978): 592–610.

[3] Plantinga is a case in point here; in his early papers arguing for the proper basicality of certain theistic beliefs, he talks as if he were not committed to major foundationalist assumptions, and I believe some readers have mistaken him on this point. Even a recent writer who does not mistake him allows himself to use the heading, "Foundationalism Founders", for a section in which it is the attack on a strong classical foundationalism that is explicated. See Kelly James Clark, *Return to Reason* (Grand Rapids: William B. Eerdmans, 1990), esp. pp. 136–43.

window before me is reliable (roughly, truth-conducive) production of the belief by the perceptual processes in which it is grounded, then its coherence with my other beliefs is not what justifies it. Indeed, one could expect that in most cases, if other beliefs of mine that are not thus "foundationally" grounded—say a belief that someone denies that there is a window before me—fail to cohere with it, it is these other beliefs that are the better candidates for revision.[4]

Is this anti-evidentialist approach—which, conceived positively, might be called *experientialism*—just fideism all over again? It is certainly not fideism if that implies rejecting the importance of rationality as a major desirable characteristic of theistic beliefs. The anti-evidentialist is not downplaying reason but stressing its independence of argumentation and even of derivation from tacit prior premises. Indeed, if we distinguish between *narrow evidentialism*—the view that a belief is justified only if based on adequate evidence one has as premises (in the form of objects of one's beliefs)—and *broad evidentialism*—the view that a belief is justified only if based on adequate *grounds*, whether they are believed propositions or, say, perceptual experiences—then anti-evidentialists may be seen as widening traditional, narrow evidentialism rather than as rejecting evidentialism as such.[5] Justified beliefs need not be arrived at through reasoning, and the believer need not be prepared to give an argument for them from premises already believed; but justified beliefs will in fact be well grounded, and hence a good argument to support them *could* be constructed from premises formulating the grounds—assuming they can be properly articulated, which, apart from utterly ineffable mystical experiences, seems possible in principle. Even a quite thoroughgoing experientialism, then, is consistent

---

[4] Note that the reliabilist, like the moderate foundationalist, need not deny that *incoherence* with other beliefs can defeat the justification of a belief that is reliably produced; the point is that the *source* of justification is not coherence among beliefs but something that is not even doxastic and need not even supply the believer with potential premises from which to argue for the belief so acquired. Just what defeats what, however, is an enormously complex problem.

[5] In one of the influential early anti-evidentialist papers Alvin Plantinga stressed that there are grounds for justified non-inferential theistic belief. See "Is Belief in God Properly Basic?", *Nous* 15 (1981): 41–52. That the requirement that there be grounds for even non-inferential justified beliefs may be considered a kind of evidentialism is suggested by Norman Kretzmann, who notes how widely the term 'evidence' has been used in the history of philosophy. See his "Evidence against Anti-Evidentialism", presented at a conference of the Society of Christian Philosophers in October 1990, in Lincoln, Nebraska.

with broad evidentialism and hence is not properly considered a fideist position in the usual sense implying that it is irreverent or is in some other way inappropriate to take theistic beliefs as in need of any justifying grounds.

To be sure, the anti-evidentialist does reject the demand for second-order justification—justification for believing that one *is* justified—as a condition on rational theistic belief. But that is surely an unreasonable demand, even apart from its leading to an infinite regress. Again, foundationalism is instructive: if even a moderate version is sound, then we cannot expect people to have an argument— if that requires any more than having some kind of ground—for every justified belief they have. Even the most rational person will, at any given time, harbor "ultimate" premises: propositions that are objects of non-inferential beliefs, beliefs which, though not necessarily indefeasible or even deeply entrenched, are not based on other beliefs. Foundationalism allows, but does not require, that one have the makings of a discursive justification for one's justified non-inferential beliefs: a justification presentable in the form of a cogent argument whose premises are drawn from among the propositions one believes or is disposed to believe.[6] To require this justificatory preparedness would not only imply what seems a vicious regress; it is also unreasonable in the light of actual cases. It would be rather like saying that one does not really have something unless one can provide defenses that will prevent its destruction. Preoccupation with skeptical demolition must not be allowed to make us underrate our natural resources.

The experientialist approach as most prominently represented in its first decade has received much criticism, and discussion of the relevant issues continues.[7] There have, however, been new developments in the experientialist tradition, for instance by both Alvin Plantinga and William Alston.[8] I cannot discuss these extensive

[6] Much of our evidence base with respect to some proposition, or indeed a whole range of propositions, such as theistic ones, may be implicit in the suggested way: we may be disposed, e.g., to believe justifying propositions for the belief in question, upon simply reflecting on it or why one should believe it, yet do not *already* believe them prior to the question's coming up. I call this "Structural Justification" and explicate the notion in a paper of that title, in *The Journal of Philosophical Research* 16 (1991): 473–92.

[7] See, e.g., Philip L. Quinn's and Robert Audi's papers in Audi and Wainwright, *Rationality and Religious Belief*. For more recent discussion see Clark, *Return to Reason*, and Kretzmann, "Evidence against Anti-Evidentialism".

[8] Alvin Plantinga's "Positive Epistemic Status and Proper Function" (*Philosophical Perspectives* 2 [1988]) gives a good picture of the epistemological theory underlying his

works here. For my purposes the main point is that they agree with traditional evidentialists on the *target* of the effort to harmonize faith and reason: belief. There is no question that belief is of the first importance in the philosophy of religion, and that if religious belief (of a suitably rich kind) can be shown to be rational, then the problem of reconciling faith and reason is at least largely solved. In my view, however, showing this is, while sufficient, not necessary for a solution, or at least a partial solution. Let me explain.

There is a tendency for philosophers writing on the relation of faith and reason to think that while religious faith implies more than believing certain propositions, for instance because it requires an attitude of trust, it is fundamentally doxastic. That is (for monotheists), having religious faith is a matter of what, with suitable accompanying attitudes, one *believes* about God in relation to the world. I contend that there is another kind of faith which is, or certainly can be, of great religious importance. It might be illustrated by faith that God has a plan for the ultimate future of humanity, where this is conceived as a distinct kind of (positive) attitude not necessarily implying belief of its propositional object. I have elsewhere argued for the following two theses crucial to the faith-reason problem. First, even when such faith concerning divine action does not embody belief of the proposition in question, say that God has a plan for us—and hence is *non-doxastic*—it can play a central role in a person's religious life; it does this in part because of what the person believes, but it is not itself a kind of belief toward its propositional object. Second, the appropriate standard of rationality for non-doxastic faith is *less stringent* than the counterpart standard for believing the same proposition.[9] This essay will build on those theses, though

---

recent approach (which I take to be essentially consistent with his views in the papers cited earlier); and William P. Alston, in *Perceiving God* (Ithaca and London, Cornell University Press, 1991), develops his doxastic practice approach in detail.

[9] The case is developed in my "Faith, Belief, and Rationality", *Philosophical Perspectives* 5 (199): 213–39, and in my "Rationality and Religious Commitment", in *Faith, Reason, and Skepticism*, ed. Marcus Hester (Philadelphia: Temple University Press, 1992). Those papers also argue against the almost standard view that propositional faith entails (or is a kind of) belief. As William L. Rowe put it in reference to two significantly representative major views, "Both Aquinas and James take the objects of faith to be *statements*, statements mainly about the divine. Faith, then, is the acceptance of certain statements concerning God and his activities. Sometimes, however, . . . we think of faith as trust in certain persons or institutions. . . . But since trusting some person or institution generally involves accepting or believing certain statements about them, faith in someone or something presupposes beliefs that certain statements about them are true". *Philosophy of Religion* (Encino, Calif.: Dickenson, 1978), p. 171.

to a considerable degree its success will be independent of the details of the arguments given for them earlier. It may be thought that, historically, the issue of faith and reason has been so closely associated with faith construed as entailing (or indeed being a kind of) belief that, in countenancing non-doxastic faith as an element that is crucial for the controversy, I am to some degree redefining the issue. If so, the redefinition may still be reasonable provided, as I contend, non-doxastic faith, when adequately deep and pervasive in people, is sufficient to qualify them as religious.

2. Some Dimensions of Faith

I begin with four basic fiduciary notions and then develop one of them and explore the rationality conditions appropriate to it. The four I have in mind are *propositional faith*, faith *that* something is so; *attitudinal faith*, faith *in* some being (or other entity, such as an institution); *doctrinal faith*, a religious faith; and *global faith*, the kind whose possession makes one a *person of faith* and can qualify one as religious. Let us take these in turn.[10]

If I have faith that God loves humanity, I have a certain positive disposition toward the proposition that this is so. This disposition is something more than hope but does not imply belief (though some philosophers have spoken loosely of degrees of belief in such a way that if one so much as takes, or even presupposes, a proposition to have any significant chance of truth, then one thereby has some degree of belief of it). Propositional faith is, to be sure, incompatible with believing that God does *not* exist, but that is a different point. Because of the positive way in which it is more than hope, it is also incompatible with a pervasive or dominating doubt that God exists, although it can coexist with some degree of doubt or even with a tendency to have moments of predominant doubt.[11]

---

[10] For much valuable discussion of various kinds of faith see the special issue of *Faith and Philosophy* on the Nature of the Christian Faith, 7, no. 4 (1990). It is noteworthy that one author, Nicholas Wolterstorff, stresses not only the existence of different kinds of faith but also that "the question, 'What is the nature of Christian faith?' is . . . ill-formed. Both in the Scriptures and in the Christian tradition this single word 'faith' is used to pick out a number of somewhat different phenomena. Each of those has its own 'nature'." Wolterstorff, "The Assurance of Faith," p. 397. For a different view see Robert M. Adams, *The Virtue of Faith* (Oxford: Oxford University Press, 1989).

[11] This is not to say, as Richard Creel does, following Tillich's claim (which he quotes) that "faith is the continuous tension between itself and the doubt within itself", that a mature faith "grows out of [doubt] or over against it. Doubt is a *structural feature* of a healthy, mature religious faith, for we do not want to commit our-

If I believe *in* God, I presuppose certain propositions about God, of the kind one might put forward as expressing (tenets of) one's religious faith. Having faith in God may be compatible with not having formed the specific belief that, say, God exists (this is in any case an odd belief for an unself-conscious theist to hold), but it does imply a readiness to form, under appropriate circumstances, both that belief and beliefs of many propositions about God. If one's propositional and attitudinal faith are religious, then having such faith implies certain attitudes, such as reverence and trust. But those attitudes, while they do imply a measure of conceptual sophistication (at least enough for comprehension of their objects) and certain cognitive attitudes stronger than hope, need not imply belief that God exists.

When we come to the third case, *a* religious faith, we are in the abstract domain, at least for the main sense of this phrase. To have, or "be of" a faith in this sense is chiefly to hold certain tenets and attitudes; and these are specified in such a way that one could speak of a faith no longer held by anyone, or of a faith people ought to aspire to. *The* faith in question is, then, the appropriate set of propositions; *holding* it is a matter of having the appropriate attitudes toward them; and there are many *ways* to hold it.[12]

The fourth case is the richest. The basic notion seems to be that of being a person of faith—roughly, of having religious faith—as opposed both to lacking faith and to having a particular religious faith, which implies adherence to certain doctrines, usually institutionally embodied doctrines. People with their own views of God who do not fit any existing religion can be persons of faith, though they do not belong to any faith in particular. There is indeed a secular notion

---

selves to that which is less than the absolute." Creel, *Religion and Doubt* (Englewood Cliffs, N.J.: Prentice-Hall, 1977), pp. 58–59; cf. pp. 80–81. I am not suggesting that *all* faith implies doubt, or even that non-doxastic faith has it as a "structural feature". One might claim that *whenever* one takes (or is disposed to take) a proposition to have a probability lower than 1/2 one doubts it to some degree; but this seems too strong and misses some of the distinctive character of doubting, and in any case non-doxastic faith does not imply any disposition to attribute a probability or even a specific range of probabilities to its propositional object.

[12] What I am calling a faith is the sort of thing that Keith Yandell calls a religion: "*a conceptual system that provides an interpretation of the world and the place of human beings in it, that rests on that interpretation an account of how life should be lived . . . and that expresses this interpretation in a set of . . . practices.*" "The Nature of Faith: Religious, Monotheistic, and Christian", *Faith and Philosophy* 7, no. 4 (1990): 451–69. There is controversy over just what constitutes a religion, or a faith in the relevant sense; my concern is simply to note a use of 'faith' that covers the same broadly doctrinal range.

of a person of faith; I suspect it parallels the religious concept I want to describe, but I do not explore that possibility here.

The relations among these four cases are complex. On the assumption that faith *in* implies the existence of the entity in question, attitudinal faith is not implied by propositional faith, which has no such existential import. Faith that the devil will be foiled does not imply his existence; but if—without inverted commas—we can truly say someone has faith in the savior, then the savior exists. There is, to be sure, a retrospective notion, as where one has faith in a deceased uncle in regard to his providing for his young children; but there is still an existential presupposition, even if it is of the specific kind satisfiable by a person who no *longer* exists. On the other hand, it would seem that the converse implication holds, that attitudinal faith implies propositional faith concerning the object of the former: could one have faith in God but no faith that (say) God loves humanity? Perhaps, however, *all* the propositional attitudes integral to attitudinal faith might be attitudes of (psychological) *certainty* toward the relevant propositions; a person's faith in God, for example, might be surrounded by certainty that God will protect us, chasten us, and so on. But it appears that if one is certain that *p* (some proposition), then one does not have faith that *p*, at least as 'faith' is used in standard parlance. It is not altogether clear, then, that attitudinal faith implies propositional faith. It is clear, however, that, as usually conceived, a person of faith will *have* faith of at least one of the two relevant kinds: attitudinal or propositional. Even this weaker conception may be too strong for special cases to be explored in Section 3.

We are now in a position to note some of the epistemic relations among the four cases. To simplify matters, I speak only of rationality, but parallel points apply to justification.[13] Attitudinal faith is not rational unless one at least *has* a rational basis for propositional faith of a related kind; for example, one's faith *in* God would not be rational if one had no rational ground for, say, faith *that* God is good. Propositional faith may be thought to be similarly dependent on grounds for attitudinal faith at least of a narrow sort: if one has rational faith that God loves humanity, one at least has some rational ground for faith in God *so far as love of people is concerned*. Attitudinal faith, however, is generally conceived rather globally, as im-

---

[13] I distinguish between rationality and justification, but they are parallel in important ways. I have developed the distinction in "Rationality and Religious Commitment".

plying a range of positive attitudes. One does not have faith in a colleague merely because one has faith that he will reject a large bribe. It may thus be possible to have rational faith that something is so, without having grounds for attitudinal faith concerning a person connected with it, at least of any full-blooded kind. The rationality of *a* faith—a set of tenets the holding of which in a certain way makes one a person of that faith—would presumably be relative to grounds accessible at the time in question: roughly, to say that *a* faith is rational is to say that, at the time in question (normally the time of the attribution), there are grounds available such that someone holding the faith *on* those grounds would hold it rationally.

The conditions for the rationality of being a person of faith are the most complex. The rationality in question will depend on the specific kind of faith held and on the person's grounds for it. There will, moreover, be volitional as well as cognitive elements. Not all the relevant cases can be discussed here. My special concern is to explore to what extent such global faith can be volitional as opposed to intellectual, and to articulate, in outline, rationality conditions for global faith conceived as volitionally as is plausible. My focus on the most strongly volitional kind of faith is not meant to suggest (what is surely false) that it is typical of global faith to be minimally doxastic, but my interest is mainly in this range of cases.

3. Global Faith

Clearly, *one* way to be a person of faith is by virtue of having suitably strong attitudinal or doxastic faith that is a central element in one's character. I believe, however, that there is a different way to be a person of faith. It is not that one could be such without meeting *some* cognitive constraints; as noted before, one could not *dis*believe (believe it is false) that God exists.[14] One must also have framework beliefs, the kind necessary to understanding the religious concepts, including that of God; such beliefs are needed for an outlook rich enough to permit genuine religious faith. One must also have normative beliefs, for example that God is wholly good and should be revered. It is only existential beliefs about God that are not part of this conception of faith. The point is that what constitutes being a

---

[14] At least where the disbelief is not outweighed, e.g. by a pattern of opposing beliefs including such beliefs as one to the effect that the disbelief is a product of manipulation.

person of faith need not be mainly one's beliefs, not even beliefs of such propositions as standard biblical teachings about God's activity in relation to the world, not even those central in faith as commonly understood. Let me describe this alternative.

Imagine a person, say Alice, who has been brought up in a Christian tradition but is intellectually shaped by scientific and philosophical training of kinds typical in higher education in the Western world. Her day-to-day life, however, is marked by several kinds of Christian behavior and attitudes, though her beliefs are also constrained by what she takes to be a scientific skepticism toward much purported evidence, whether about church doctrines or for scientific claims. There may be several dimensions of her life in which her faith is manifested.

First, she tends to see things in nature *as* created by God (or at least she is strongly disposed to see them thus), not in a belief-entailing sense of 'seeing as', but in the sense that she tends to view natural phenomena under the aspect of God's creation and certainly with a lively sense of the possibility of divine creation. This is particularly so when she experiences a beautiful scene, but she is also disposed to view even certain ordinary objects as having the sort of character that should be expected if they are created or ordered by God. Perhaps she believes that natural objects such as hills, brooks, lakes, and groves are the sorts of things God would create; and if she contemplates a rare tree, like a large copper beech with shapes and shadows in its smooth bark that give the impression of a countenance, she may see it as the kind of thing that might bespeak divine creation. But she does not believe (or disbelieve) that natural objects in fact are created by God. Call this pattern of attitudes and dispositions a *fiduciary perspective*.

Second, she tends to be regularly motivated by, and when necessary to remind herself of, religious attitudes and principles: that we are to love our neighbors, that Christ's example of charity is to be imitated, and that the sun should not set upon one's wrath. These tendencies might be grouped under the heading of *practical commitment*: she has the sorts of behavioral patterns appropriate to a Christian faith, and they are grounded in attitudes partly constitutive of that faith among those paradigmatically committed to it. In directing her life, she is inspired by the power of religious Scriptures, by historical examples of religious devotion and sacrifice, and by the coherence and beauty of the theistic conception of the world that go with them.

Third, and closely connected with her practical commitment, she

remains open to evidences of God's governance. This is not to say
that she has, or even strongly tends to form, beliefs to the effect that
God is working around her; but she does tend to take certain things
that happen *as* some ground to believe God is present. She also has
some tendency to see certain occurrences as manifesting divine purpose, again in a perspectival sense implying a way of viewing these
things, not a subsumption of the phenomena under antecedently
believed propositions. This element in her faith is a kind of *evidential
receptivity*. She is disposed to follow certain evidences to theistic conclusions but has not done so. This may be because the evidences are
insufficient for the steepness of the path or because the path is
blocked by counterforces or because of an inertial skepticism or for
some other reason.

Fourth, Alice seeks and, both emotionally and attitudinally, appropriately responds to, religious reasons to support or interpret—
or even qualify—things she does or plans. Thus, in everyday human relations she asks what the Christian thing to do might be; and
if she thinks of a deed as what God would wish, this tends not only
to motivate her to do it—as implied by her practical commitment—
but also to feel approval or disapproval, joy or sadness, or other
attitudes or emotions, in ways characteristic of Christians. She feels
joy on discovering that a person who prayed hard for recovery from
a disease did so, disapproval at the thought of holding a grudge,
and so on. In short, Alice is appropriately *moved* by life. She tends,
for instance, to be inspired by reading Scripture, to feel something
like gratitude on viewing the beauty of nature; and, in giving others
loving support, to have a sense not just of moral rectitude but of
adherence to a deep commitment of her religious tradition. This dimension of her religious life (which could of course be further an-
alyzed) might be called its *attitudinal-emotional responsiveness*.

Fifth, she engages in religious practices, such as attending services
and discussions, that help to sustain and mature her understanding
of her religious commitments and the concepts they require her to
grasp. These patterns are a kind of *institutional engagement*. They are
admittedly possible outside institutionalized religion, but they imply
a sense of the sort of structure of meaning and tradition that constitutes an institution even apart from a community of participants
who realize it.

I suggest that, while not all these conditions are strictly necessary
for global faith (if indeed any of them is), when they are all realized
in a certain way, we may think of the person (such as Alice) as a
person of religious faith even if she has a kind of intellectual stance

from which doxastic faith, as implying belief that God exists, is absent.[15] While it is not consistent with her being a person of faith that she believe there is no God—since that would constitute too negative an intellectual commitment—she may be intellectually so affected by such things as the apparently negative force of the problem of evil and the power of naturalism as a worldview that she is forced to suspend judgment on the proposition that God exists, or, less voluntaristically speaking, she simply does not form the belief that it is true. She is open to it, but she does not hold it. She may hope, and may even have non-doxastic faith, that it is true, but she need not have the stronger attitude of doxastic faith that it is.[16] If one insists that attributing any probability higher than zero entails having a degree of belief, then in *that* sense she may also have a degree of belief that it is so; but such probability ascription is surely not sufficient for what is normally called believing, and it is indeed consistent with disbelieving.[17]

With all these points in mind, my aim can be put simply. I am above all contrasting faith as a state of the intellect with faith as something more global, and I am suggesting that it is possible for global faith to be fundamentally a state of the will: a kind of *volitional faith*, as I shall call it. It is not that one can have such faith *without* intellect; one must have concepts and framework beliefs, such as those required for understanding religion, even to be a candidate for possession of such faith. A person with volitional faith would also normally have some kind of (non-doxastic) propositional faith, say that God watches over humanity, though weaker attitudes such as hope toward the relevant propositions would minimally serve. But it seems *possible* that a person's faith be fundamentally volitional, as opposed to propositional, provided there are dispositions to acquire propositional faith, say where circumstances force one to adopt some cognitive attitude toward specific theistic propositions. One need not believe, but must be attracted to believing, some of these

[15] The suggestion here is that 'global faith' expresses a concept with multiple criteria and exhibits what William P. Alston calls "combination of conditions vagueness". He illustrates this idea with respect to a related term, viz., 'religion', in *Philosophy of Language* (Englewood Cliffs, N.J.: Prentice-Hall, 1964), pp. 87–91.

[16] James Muyskens has argued for the sufficiency of hope in *The Sufficiency of Hope* (Philadelphia: Temple University Press, 1979). I am not here endorsing the sufficiency of religious hope for being a religious person, but clearly hope is a propositional attitude consistent with the non-doxastic conception of faith I am developing.

[17] I have argued for this briefly in "Rationality and Religious Commitment"; and the view finds welcome support in a number of points made by Wolterstorff, "The Assurance of Faith".

propositions. A person of volitional faith would in fact tend to be deeply satisfied if there were a way to become convinced of such theistic propositions. The point, then, concerns what constitutes volitional faith, not what motivates it: the intellect, through framework and normative beliefs, guides the will and is part of what moves it toward a religious stance in life; but the global faith I am describing resides in the will.

Perhaps in the end it is not possible that faith can be entirely constituted by a state of the will. It is perhaps enough that we may think of volitional faith as, at its core, mainly a state of the will, mainly a kind of religious resolve, or at least a settled determination to conduct one's life, including one's cognitive life, in a certain way: keeping certain ideals in view, looking at both nature and human life as divinely ordered, relating to others in a certain spirit. This is not a matter of producing belief tendencies in oneself, though they may indeed arise from it; and it does not require any specific theological beliefs, as opposed to dispositions to form them or to seek evidence for them. It is instead a kind of embracing of a perspective, of a framework of concepts and principles which one takes as an appropriate context for living one's life. The intellect supplies the concepts and principles essential to the cognitive content of the faith; but having the global faith in question is fundamentally a matter of one's volitional stance, not of one's intellectual assent.

Assuming such a perspective, say a Christian perspective on the world and humanitiy in it, is not simply living *as though* God existed, something a pragmatist might do in order to produce faith or belief that is not initially there. It is not merely behavioral: a disposition of the will may underlie, but is not equivalent to, any pattern of conduct. Nor may the appropriate attitudes be self-induced as a result of, say, a Pascalian wager. The fiduciary aspect of faith must be preserved; hence, while one may be said to be living as though God existed (except for the suggestion of disbelief this seems to convey), the pattern must bespeak a loyalty to a cherished conception of the world. It must come from certain attitudes and values, including a commitment to a tradition (or something with the potential to become one); it may not be merely a response aimed at protecting one's future.[18]

---

[18] Here and elsewhere the conception of faith developed differs from the pragmatic one presented by Joshua L. Golding in his valuable essay "Toward a Pragmatic Conception of Religious Faith", *Faith and Philosophy* 7, no. 4 (1990): 486–503. Among the differences are these: his conception (in part perhaps because it is pragmatic) does not entail the reverential and other attitudes appropriate to being a person of faith in the sense I intend, nor the *centrality* of the fiduciary commitments I have described; he

If the volitional faith I am describing must not be construed too behaviorally, it must also be distinguished from the sort of fiduciary construct appropriate to non-cognitivism in the philosophy of religion.[19] What I am describing is a perspective that construes religious statements as truth-valued and countenances the possibility of evidence or grounds for rationally believing them. Alice may in fact believe that some people *have* sufficient evidence or adequate ground for theistic beliefs; but either she does not believe that she herself has it, or, if she does believe this, she has been unable to overcome her skepticism, perhaps because she does not feel she adequately sees the force of her evidence. She may, and probably does, hope for evidence, and she may even hope to achieve a doxastic faith: neither volitional nor doxastic faith precludes one's taking a positive attitude toward the other. My claim is only that the former, even without the latter, is sufficient (if minimally sufficient) for being a person of faith. Provided the faith is rich enough and sufficiently influential in one's life, it in turn is sufficient to make one a religious person. Granted, one would not usually be called a person of faith unless one were regarded as a religious person in a sense implying doxastic faith; but the former notion might have a minimal interpretation on which it implies being religious, in the overall sense of the term, only to some degree. Both notions admit of degrees.

4. Volitional Faith and Rational Religious Commitment

If it is true that one can be a religious person without either having doxastic faith or— like the non-cognitivist—without taking such

---

requires that a religious person have the quite specific goal of *having a good relationship with God* (p. 487), whereas I would neither require a goal this specific nor take faith as subordinate to it in the way implied by construing it as "an assumption that God exists for the purpose of pursuing a good relationship with God" (486); and his view implies a belief that "there is at least a chance (however small) that God exists" (pp. 491 and 502), whereas I hold that neither being a person of faith nor having (non-doxastic) propositional faith entails having this belief.

[19] It is also different from Paul Tillich's view that "scientific truth and the truth of faith do not belong to the same dimension of meaning" and that "from the subjective side one must say that faith is true if it adequately expresses an ultimate concern. From the objective side one must say that faith is true if its content is the really ultimate." *The Dynamics of Faith* (New York: Harper and Row, 1957), pp. 81 and 96. The view I am developing is like that of Tillich (and most theologians) in not construing theism as a scientific hypothesis, but it also does not require distinguishing objective and subjective perspectives in the way Tillich does, or positing different "dimensions of meaning" *if* that implies a non-cognitivist notion of religious language.

faith to be misguided on the ground that religious faith never has propositional objects, then the rationality of religious commitment may be viewed in a new light. For while religious people must hold whatever beliefs are required to have an adequate *concept* of God, they need not have the theistic beliefs whose justification is most problematic: those commonly supposed to be warranted by arguments for the existence of God or by religious experience, whether mystical or perceptual.[20] This is not to suggest that religious commitment constituted by volitional faith is, so far as rational grounds are concerned, easy to come by. For one thing, I have granted that it *negatively* depends on belief—for instance, on not disbelieving that God exists—and there are many philosophers who think that the amount and kind of evil in the world, or other considerations, or both, warrant that disbelief. There may also be a painful tension in remaining doxastically uncommitted. Non-doxastic faith is often in an arduous quest of its object; theistic belief has already embraced the object. The easy thing for a person like Alice would be either to give in to the incredulity or skepticism pulling her one way or to join those of settled theistic belief pulling her the other way. But there are (or may be) people who live with the tension. What, then, can be said about the rationality of volitional faith?

To begin with, even taking a proposition as a serious candidate for truth requires having some grounds for it if this cognitive attitude is to be rational. I believe, however, that, from a combination of experience and prima facie evidences given in the Hebraic-Christian tradition, it is quite possible for a person to have sufficient grounds to take seriously the proposition that God is, for instance, sovereign in the universe. This is particularly so if we emphasize the openness to evidence and the positive attitudes I have stressed; for neither entails attributing any particular probability, and both are consistent with believing that the objective probability is below 1/2. It is possible to have these grounds, of course, without being able to show that one does; my point concerns the possibility of having the grounds, not of mounting an epistemological case that they *are* grounds or, especially, conclusive grounds.

Another dimension of the problem, in addition to the question of conditions for the rationality of whatever propositional attitudes are involved in volitional faith, is the question of the rationality of the

---

[20] This is not to suggest that all such attempts to argue for the existence of God must fail. My point is that there may be a sufficient rational basis for religious commitment, conceived volitionally, even if those approaches should fail.

entire pattern of behavior associated with that faith and of the accompanying attitudes, both propositional and non-propositional. The question is not whether some set of religiously significant propositions can be objects of reasonable belief or even rational non-doxastic faith; it is whether a person of faith can, overall, be rational at least in the minimal case of the relevant non-doxastic attitudes: minimal in both the content of those attitudes and the degree of conviction with which they are held. Here, I believe, the rationality issue may come out quite differently depending on both the religious tradition and the agent in question.

Return to Alice, who considers herself Christian. Does she *do* anything irrational? This will depend on *why* she does what she does, as well as on what she does, in expressing her faith.[21] Perhaps her doing deeds of extreme self-sacrifice for a Christian ideal might be criticized as irrational, but one must bear in mind that there are plausible secular moral traditions that defend making certain sacrifices for one's ideals. In any case, nothing in her behavior need even appear irrational in this way; indeed, for much of what she does, there will be *both* good secular reasons and religiously cogent reasons, and as a well-integrated person Alice may be motivated by both kinds of reasons simultaneously. Consistently with being a person of faith, she may even have a policy of not doing controversial deeds for religious reasons unless she is *also* motivated by adequate secular reasons and would do the deeds for them alone;[22] and she can live up to this without taking either secular or religious reasons as more cogent than the other, though she may in some cases take one or the other kind as more cogent (an attitude consistent with each being fully sufficient to justify the action in question). To be sure, when it comes to viewing a beautiful scene as if it were God's work, she may have no secular reason for so viewing it, but this mainly internal,

[21] I have argued for this point in detail in "Rationalization and Rationality", *Synthese* 65, no. 2 (1985): pp. 159–84. Indeed, the reasons *for which* one does what one does are even more important for one's rationality than *what* one does.

[22] In "The Separation of Church and State and the Obligations of Citizenship", *Philosophy and Public Affairs* 18, no. 3 (1989): 259–96. I have argued that in advocating or promoting laws or public policies that would restrict human behavior, such a principle is reasonable; this posture does not seem inappropriate to even traditional religious doxastic commitments at least on the assumption that God has so created the world that for correct actions of the kind in question we can in general discover adequate secular reasons. Further discussion of the issue is contained in Paul Weithman, "Separation of Church and State: Some Questions for Professor Audi", and my "Religious Commitment and Secular Reason: A Reply to Professor Weithman", both in *Philosophy and Public Affairs* 20 (1991): 66–76.

non-doxastic stance (which is also not an action) scarcely seems in need of much reason to sustain its rationality. It is not as if she expended either efforts or resources needed elsewhere; and the private domain of the heart is one in which the standards of rationality are quite latitudinarian.

If, as seems reasonable, a good prima facie reason for doing something is that one finds it enjoyable or rewarding and continues to want to do it after experiencing it under varying conditions, then we can certainly view much of the overall pattern required for volitional faith as prima facie rational. Is there any reason to think that there must be overriding reasons to the contrary? Is Alice manipulating herself or developing bad habits of mind? I cannot see that this is at all typical of the kind of person of faith I am describing. Indeed, the very fact that, from a purely intellectual point of view, she would suspend judgment on the proposition that God exists indicates that her critical faculties are working powerfully: her natural inclination, after all, runs the other way. There may be a tension between her fiduciary disposition and a skeptical outlook on the world; but we surely need not criticize her rationality because she exhibits a limited response to skeptical considerations.

One might think that the suggested position is close to the Jamesian view that it is sometimes rational to cause oneself to hold a belief despite evidence to the contrary, as where one must, in order to save one's life, cause oneself to believe (against the objective evidence) that one is able to jump a precipice and so, through the confidence gained by that belief, increase one's chance of succeeding. A belief so produced, the objection might continue, is not justified. I agree: a justifiedly induced belief is not thereby justifiedly held. But I reject the suggestion that I have at best sketched a kind of faith that it might be rational to cause oneself to develop if one could justify nothing stronger. I have been arguing that volitional faith can be rational, both because of the grounds one may have for holding that stance in life—for having one's will so disposed—and because of the available grounds (which are often motivating factors as well in such a person) for much of the behavior this faith produces, including the behavior most likely to stand in need of justification. It might in fact be rational to cause oneself to have such faith, but the conditions under which that may hold are not my concern here.

Nothing said in this essay implies that it *is* rational for anyone in particular to be a person of faith or even that there are grounds in the light of which someone may rationally be one. This has not been my aim; my purpose has been simply to show that the conditions for the rationality of being a person of faith are less stringent where the constitutive faith in question is volitional than they are where it is doxastic. Even this may be questioned; but it is surely plausible to hold the related view that one needs less in the way of grounds for non-doxastic faith that p than for belief or doxastic faith that p. To take a secular example, I need less warrant for non-doxastic faith that a world war can be averted than for belief that this is so, and hence for doxastic faith that it is, where this faith embodies the belief that it is so. Similarly, it seems obvious that a person of volitional faith might be warranted in thinking that, if only because of uncertainty about the matter of what God wills for human beings, one needs adequate secular grounds for what one is motivated to do (at least partly) by one's faith. Such a person may then seek, and may often acquire, adequate non-religious grounds for religiously inspired conduct; and so far as the rationality of that conduct is crucial for the rationality of the person's faith, these cooperating secular grounds can support the rationality of the global volitional faith.

Is the point, then, that narrow evidentialism is correct after all, but the typical anti-theistic evidentialists, having overlooked volitional faith, have exaggerated the level of evidence needed for being a person of rational faith? This is not my point; but it is true that if evidentialism of any kind, broad or narrow, should be sound, volitional faith would require significantly less in the way of grounds than doxastic faith or theistic belief. My approach is also entirely consistent with the rejection of at least narrow evidentialism: if there can be rational theistic beliefs non-inferentially grounded in experience, there can surely be non-inferentially grounded non-doxastic faith rational on the basis of the same sources. It is not as if such faith had no *content* and hence there were no propositions to receive support from the relevant experiences. Even if hope is the only propositional component of someone's volitional faith, there would be suitable objects to receive the experiential support. My effort is not to undermine anti-evidentialism but to widen the debate over the relation between faith and reason and to show that the doxastic construal underestimates the resources for reconciliation.

5. Conclusion

Whenever one defends an unorthodox conception of some important ideal, there is a danger of misunderstanding; it may look as if one is suggesting that the unorthodox conception is really superior, or at least as if one did not endorse the ideal as most commonly understood. I reiterate, then, that I consider the two kinds of faith complementary; indeed, doxastic faith may be a natural aim of someone with only volitional faith. But if we do not countenance something like volitional faith as sufficient for a person's being religious (even if not maximally so), our conception of religion and its fulfillment in everyday life is more narrow. Moreover, volitional faith may be what remains when certain people undergo intellectual change; to say that if they lose confidence in certain propositions they cannot remain religious is to exaggerate the importance of the doxastic side of religious commitment. For people in this plight, volitional faith may be a position of retreat; but it is not a position of surrender. And if it does not represent an ideal for faith, it is nevertheless a position from which ideal faith can develop.

This brings me to a further point. If we imagine someone with doxastic faith, but only the minimum satisfaction of the conditions I have sketched as crucial for volitional faith, we have too intellectual a commitment: this may be having *a faith*—having a kind of *doctrinal faith*, as we might call it—but not full-bloodedly *having faith*. Hence, just as it may be appropriate for someone with only volitional faith to aspire to doxastic faith, it may be appropriate for people with doxastic faith to explore the extent to which their conduct—inner and outer—reflects that faith. Faith in the richest sense is not just acceptance of doctrine, nor is it even that cognitive state together with acting consistently with the doctrine.[23] Faith, in the richest sense, is a pervasive condition of the intellect, the will, and the heart.

Suppose it is true that the rationality conditions for volitional faith are less stringent than those for doxastic faith, and that these conditions can be readily met for mature, well-integrated theists. If one's faith is only volitional, what may one tell one's children? After all, religious education requires saying things on whose truth one may have suspended judgment. There is no simple rule for dealing with this problem. Much depends on just what one says to one's children and how. Surely parents are warranted in introducing their children to their religious tradition, at least in a non-dogmatic way (and where the tradition is not patently irrational or outrageously immoral). But no matter how much one avoids dogma, it is likely to be

---

[23] Compare Kant's distinction between acting from and merely in accordance with duty. The latter acts have no moral worth; similar reasons support saying that their counterparts in the religious case have no religious worth.

impossible to introduce a tradition such as that of, say, Christianity or Judaism, without implying that one believes many of the theistic propositions expressed therein. It would be of some help to such a person to speak of Bible stories in a way that implies they need not always be taken literally, but there is still the question of how to explain prayer. An adult may pray in hopes of being heard by God even without definite belief that this will occur; but young children are less subtle. On the other hand, it is not long before children can begin to appreciate the difference between disbelief and non-belief, and between skeptical incredulity and open-minded suspension of judgment on something not so far held. And it must be remembered that the prima facie desirability of nurturing that very openness can make abstaining from introducing a religious tradition at least equally problematic morally. For, without introducing religion in early childhood, there is scarcely more hope of bringing children up so that they are able to become religious than of bringing them up so that they are able to appreciate music without introducing it, and even having children participate in it, early in childhood.

Thus, even if there should be neither cogent arguments for God's existence nor experiential grounds adequate to warrant unqualifiedly believing that God exists, rational faith is possible. It is possible, moreover, for such faith to inform one's life sufficiently to qualify one as religious. Such religious commitment can express itself in many ways: moral, aesthetic, and social, as well as spiritual. Some kinds of volitional faith may be more rational then others, as some cognitive religious commitments are more rational than others. But neither the nature of faith nor the rationality of religious commitment should be conceived as entirely a matter of rational beliefs.[24]

---

[24] For helpful comments on earlier versions I thank Daniel Howard-Snyder, David Reiter and, especially, Eleonore Stump.

PART II

REASON AND REVELATION

PETER VAN INWAGEN

❦

Genesis and Evolution

I am neither a theologian nor a biblical scholar nor a scientist. Indeed I cannot even claim to know much about Old Testament studies or evolutionary biology. Nevertheless, I am going to discuss the book of Genesis and the evolution of life. I offer three excuses for presuming to pronounce on matters of which I am largely ignorant. First, war is too important to be left to the generals. Other people than those whose professional training most obviously qualifies them to speak on these topics have something invested in the conduct of debates about science and the Bible, and often these other people feel—*I* do at any rate—that it would do the professionals no harm to hear from *them* for a change. Secondly, the blunders of beginners can sometimes help the experts to see that they have failed adequately to communicate some aspect of their subject to the public and can suggest ways in which in this communication might be better done. Quite often there is some technical idea or thesis or argument that could be explained to the lay public in a much more useful way than it has been—and it *would* be, if only the specialists were aware of prevalent misconceptions. If nothing else, perhaps what I say can help the clerks to see what it is that needs to be better explained to the laity. Thirdly, if I can claim little knowledge of what the experts have said about the book of Genesis or the history of terrestrial life, I do claim, as a philosopher, to be something of an expert at tracing the relations between disparate things, and perhaps I can bring some of my expertise to bear in this paper.

I begin with two terminological points about my title. In that title, and in the remainder of this essay, I mean by *Genesis* the first three chapters of the book of Genesis: that is, the book of Genesis from "In the beginning . . . . " to the expulsion of Adam and Eve from the Garden. Secondly, the word 'evolution', at least as it occurs in phrases like 'the theory of evolution' has a strictly biological meaning. It is a vulgar error to suppose that the word 'evolution' designates a sort of "force" that has been in operation from the very beginning of the universe and which has been responsible for the formation and development of the stars and the planets and everything else, and which, as a special case of this general activity, is engaged in pushing living organisms toward ever higher levels of complexity. Despite this fact about the meaning of the word 'evolution', however, and despite the fact that I shall have a lot to say about evolution in this strict sense, I have used the word in my title as a sort of catchall for a very diverse set of scientific considerations—cosmological and geological as well as biological—relating to various questions about how the earth and the cosmos got into their present forms.

Now as to the issue of the relation between these scientific considerations and the book of Genesis, a very wide range of positions is possible. But two positions stand out as extremes and have got the most publicity. The popular or journalistic names for these extreme positions are 'fundamentalism' and 'secular humanism'. But each of these names has been objected to on various grounds, and, rather than become embroiled in terminological disputes, I shall invent my own names for them. More exactly, I shall describe, and invent names for, two positions that I believe correspond to *some* of the things said by people who are popularly called 'fundamentalists' and *some* of the things said by people who are popularly called 'secular humanists'. I shall call the one 'Genesiac literalism' (or literalism for short) and the other 'saganism'—after one of its most illustrious and talkative ornaments.

I begin with a statement of Genesiac literalism. (I say Genesiac rather than *biblical* literalism, because I believe that the early chapters of the book of Genesis are a very special part of the Bible, and I mean to talk about them only. Nothing I say should be regarded as having any implications whatever for questions about how to read, say, Job or the Gospels or Revelation.)

"The planet earth came into existence about six thousand years ago, when God created it in a series of six twenty-four-hour days. On the third, fifth, and sixth of these days, God created all the various species of living things, concluding with a single pair of human beings, the first man and the first woman. Any appearance to the contrary in the geological record is due to a worldwide flood that occurred about forty-five hundred years ago; the geological distortions caused by that vast deluge created phenomena that the clever and perverse have—like someone finding internal evidence of Baconian authorship in *Hamlet*—interpreted as showing that the earth is not thousands but thousands of *millions* of years old, its present geological features supposedly being due to the effects of various natural processes that have been at work over this immense stretch of time.

"We know the facts I have outlined concerning the beginning of the earth and life and man because God revealed them to Moses thousands of years later and Moses wrote them down in the book we call Genesis, a book that God has ensured is historically accurate in every respect because it is a part of His Holy Scripture. It is true that Scripture contains metaphor and hyperbole—as, for example, when it tells us that the soldiers of the kings of Canaan were as numerous as the grains of sand on the shore of the sea—but any reasonably intelligent and well-intentioned reader can tell when metaphor or hyperbole are intended by Scriptural writers, and the main historical statements of Genesis are clearly intended to be taken literally."

So says the literalist.

The saganist tells another story: "The cosmos, the totality of the distribution of matter and radiation in space-time, is 'all that is or was or ever will be.' Ten thousand million years ago or more, it was concentrated in a very tiny volume of space, which was, nevertheless, all the space there was. This tiny volume expanded very rapidly, and certain processes, which we are beginning to understand, led, after a few minutes, to the three-to-one ratio of hydrogen to helium nuclei that we observe today. A few hundred thousand years later, the density of the expanding universe had fallen to a point at which electrons could arrange themselves around the hydrogen and helium nuclei, and the space between the atoms thus formed was suddenly filled with free radiation, radiation which, vastly attenuated, is still detectable. Gravitational effects caused matter to be concentrated in stars and stars to be collected into galaxies. In the stars, new elements like carbon and oxygen were formed and were dispersed when these stars came to the ends of their lives and exploded. The scattered atoms of these elements eventually became parts of new stars and of solid planets circling them.

"On at least one planet, but presumably on many, natural processes led to the formation of a complex molecule capable of replicating itself with variations. Owing entirely to the operation of natural selection, the descendants of this molecule achieved a sufficient level of internal organization for us to feel comfortable about thinking of them as living organisms. The blind but, in appearance, creative processes of natural selection continued to operate, and produced the cell, the multicellular organism, sexual dimorphism, and, eventually, representatives of all the phyla we see today (and some that we don't). In due course, owing to the interplay of variation and selection over hundreds of millions of years, intelligence appeared. (The broad outlines of the latter part of this narrative, the part dealing with biological evolution, have been accepted by every serious scientist since about 1870. Opposition to it is due entirely to theological obscurantism.) A short time later, perhaps through a social analogue of natural selection, intelligence developed *science*, a powerful, self-correcting mechanism for understanding the cosmos. Various older and much less efficient competitors with science—notably religion—survive, but, having tried and failed to destroy their new and dangerous rival in its infancy, they are steadily losing ground to it and will soon go the way of the saber-toothed tiger. Perhaps the final nail in their coffin will be the discovery of intelligent life elsewhere in the universe, a shock they are too narrow-minded and parochial to survive.

"As to the book of Genesis [here the saganists in the sciences are aided by their colleagues in the other culture] it was not written by Moses or by any single author. It is easy to see that it contains two incompatible accounts of the creation of humanity. One account, which roughly coincides with the second chapter, the detailed story of the creation of the first man and woman, is thought to have been put into its present form in something like the ninth century B.C., hundreds of years after the death of Moses. The first chapter of Genesis (and a bit more), the "seven days" story, was written by priests about three hundred years later, probably during the Babylonian captivity of Judah. What both sets of authors were doing was editing and rewriting traditional material (ultimately derived from primordial Semitic creation-myths) to bring this material into line with their own theologies, and with an eye toward the polemical requirements of the contemporary religious and political situations."

Well, here are two extreme positions. Probably every position one could take on the relation between the book of Genesis and the scientific study of the origins of the universe, the earth, and humanity lies on the continuum between them. One possible position, for example, is *deism*, which accepts most of the saganists' story but rejects its contention that there is nothing besides the cosmos. Deism postulates an intelligent Creator who set the universe in motion and then sat back to watch the show. (Like the typical Hollywood producer, this Creator seems to have rather a taste for shows that involve sex and violence—especially violence. It is, however, doubtful whether he shares Hollywood's taste for happy endings.)

What I mean to do in the rest of this essay is, first, to set forth a position on the relation between Genesis and scientific accounts of the history of the universe that is radically different from literalism and saganism (and from deism). I shall then offer critiques of both literalism and saganism from the point of view afforded by this position. I pick these two positions to criticize because, first, they have been getting the lion's share of the publicity, and, secondly, as a consequence of the fact that they are extremes between which most if not all the other possible positions on this issue lie, what I would say about other positions may perhaps be gleaned from what I say about the extremes.

Now a word as to my own religious beliefs. I am a Christian. More exactly, I am an Episcopalian, and I fully accept the teaching of my denomination that "the Holy Scriptures of the Old and New Testaments are the revealed Word of God"; that they "contain all things necessary to salvation and are the rule and ultimate standard of faith"; that "God inspired their human authors and still speaks to us through the Bible".[1] But I am not constructing a position that I recommend only to Episcopalians. I recommend this position to any Christian—and to any Jew—who regards the book of Genesis as divinely inspired and who, nevertheless, rejects, as I do, Genesiac literalism. I will add that a Christian is not logically committed, by the very fact of being a Christian, to regarding the Bible as being divinely inspired throughout. There are only two glancing references to Scripture in the creeds—"on the third day he rose again, in accordance with the Scriptures" and "he [the Holy Spirit] spoke through the prophets". One would suppose, therefore, that, as regards the Bible, a Christian is absolutely obliged to believe only that the Hebrew prophets were divinely inspired, and that the Resurrection is in some sense "in accordance with" (*secundum*) the Hebrew Bible. But such scriptural minimalism has not been the mind of the Church. While one might want to qualify this statement in various

---

[1] *The Book of Common Prayer: According to the Use of the Episcopal Church* (New York: Seabury Press, 1979). The first statement (p. 526) is from the Form for the Ordination of a Priest; the second (p. 877) is from Resolution II of the Lambeth Conference of 1888; the third (p. 853) is from the Cathechism.

ways, in the light of such things as Martin Luther's remarks about
the Letter of James, it seems roughly correct to say that all Christians
whose witness on the matter has survived have regarded the Bible
as being divinely inspired throughout, and I have no intention of
separating myself from this cloud of witnesses. How, then, shall
those who agree with me and the literalists that Genesis is the inspired word of God and who also agree with me and the saganists
that life and the earth and the cosmos have histories that are measured in thousands of millions of years explain themselves? This
question is not, in its essentials, a new one. A lot of people seem to
think that all Christians were literalists before the geological discov-
eries of the early nineteenth century. Under the impact of these dis-
coveries and the Darwinian account of evolution that was built upon
them (the story goes) some Christians began desperately to scramble
about to try to devise some way of reconciling science and the Bible.

This is historically false. Let us consider the greatest of all Christian theologians, St. Augustine (whose death in the year 430 places
him at a comfortable remove from the impact of nineteenth-century
science). Augustine argued that the "six days" account of creation in
Genesis could hardly be literally correct, since (among other reasons
he gives) it asserts that day and night existed before the sun was
made. (Let me assure you parenthetically that if the author of Genesis 1 did not know much about geology, he certainly did know that
daylight was due to the sun.) Now if Genesis is not a literally correct
account of the Creation—Augustine reasoned—then it must belong
to one of the many non-literal modes of presentation recognized by
the science of rhetoric (which, as we should say today, was Augustine's area of professional competence). But I do not propose to
discuss Augustine's hermeneutical theories; I am more interested in
the account he gave of what he took to be the literal reality behind
the non-literal presentation.[2] Augustine held that God had created

---

[2] Augustine's views on Genesis are found in his *De genesi ad litteram* ("On Genesis
according to the Letter"). The standard English translation by J. H. Taylor (New York:
Newman, 1982) is titled *On the Literal Meaning of Genesis*. The "literal meaning" of the
English title refers not to what we would today call "the literal meaning of the text"
but to what I have called 'the literal reality behind the non-literal mode of presentation'. To read an inspired text *ad litteram*, for Augustine, is to read it with an eye
toward discovering what its human author intended to convey; one could also read
an inspired text *allegorically*, with an eye toward discovering types or foreshadowings
of persons or events of later sacred history (which, if they are objectively present in
the inspired text, were presumably unknown to its human author). In the discussion
of Augustine in the text of this essay, I use the word 'literal' in its customary present-day sense. In this discussion, I have drawn heavily on Ernan McMullin's intro-

the universe all at once, and that, at the moment of its creation, the universe was, by present standards, without form, and was empty of things of the kinds it now contains. But there was *latent* form and there were things in which that form was latent. He calls these things *seed-principles*, using a botanical trope, as we use a political trope when we speak of the laws of nature. The newly created universe subsequently, by its own inner necessity, evolved into its present highly differentiated state, this present state having been implicit in its original state much as a field of grain is implicit in a mixture of seed and water and earth. (Or, at any rate, many aspects of the present state of the world were in this strong sense implicit in the initial state. Others may have been due to miraculous actions by God subsequent to the beginning of things. But if miracles did play a part in the development of the world, these miracles were not local acts of creation ex nihilo; they rather consisted in the miraculous activation of potentialities that had existed from the beginning.) This is not to say that Augustine believed in anything like what *we* call "evolution." He did not believe that elephants were remotely descended from fish. The idea of the mutability of species would have been quite foreign to his Platonism. Rather, elephants arose from one seed-principle and mackerel from another. The "days" of Genesis, Augustine says, represent *aspects* of the development of the world; perhaps—he is rather tentative about this—what is represented is six successive stages of the angelic understanding of creation. Augustine's science may strike us as quaint, but it is evident that his account of the origin and development of the universe is no more consistent with Genesiac literalism than is an article covering the same ground in last month's *Scientific American*. Nor is Augustine an isolated example of a non-literalist in the ancient world: the Alexandrian theologians, Gregory of Nyssa, and St. Jerome (who produced the Latin translation of the Bible that was the Church's standard for fourteen hundred years) were non-literalists. Jerome once remarked that, in his opinion, the author of Genesis had described the Creation mythically—"after the manner of a popular poet."[3] Genesiac non-literalism is, therefore, both ancient and

---

duction to the collection *Evolution and Creation* (South Bend: University of Notre Dame Press, 1985). In this account of Augustine's views, I have glossed over several important matters—such as the relation of the timeless reality of God to the unfolding temporal processes of the created world—that are irrelevant to our purposes.

[3] Attributed, without citation, by C. S. Lewis, *Reflections on the Psalms* (London: Godfrey Bles, 1958), p. 92.

fully orthodox: it would be a bold literalist who called the Bishop of Hippo a wishy-washy theological liberal. Non-literalism was, of course, *rejected* by many important authorities in the Western Church. St. Thomas Aquinas, for example, was a literalist who explicitly stated that the Creation took place over a period of six successive twenty-four-hour days. What it is important to note about Aquinas, however, is that, in his discussion of Augustine's "opinion that all the days that are called seven are one day represented in a sevenfold aspect", Augustine is, in the words of Jaroslav Pelikan "criticized but not hereticized". Pelikan goes on to say, "It took the Reformation to change that."[4]

I agree, although perhaps my "agreeing" on a point of church history with one of our greatest church historians has its comic aspect. Literalism before the Reformation was no doubt the majority opinion. The theory that the Bible is literally and in every sentence and in every respect inerrant is, after all, the simplest and most natural theory of the "reliability" of the Bible that must in some sense be a consequence of the doctrinal statement that the Bible is the revealed word of God—just as geocentrism is the simplest and most natural theory of the causes of observed celestial motions. But *militant* literalism, the literalism that makes the denial of plenary verbal inerrancy a heresy to be destroyed before any other is a child of the Reformation. (And not of the Counter-Reformation. To say that Galileo was condemned for contradicting the Bible on astronomical matters is, at best, a vast oversimplification of an extremely complex episode.) It is not hard to see why this should be, for one of the most important offspring of the Reformation is biblical individualism, the doctrine that individual Christians are perfectly capable of reading the Bible for themselves with no help from anyone but the Holy Spirit—or at the very most with no human assistance but that of their pastors. Now no one but an extreme theological liberal would be happy with the prospect of widespread radically diverse interpretations of Scripture. This prospect is avoided (in theory) in the Roman church by the concept of a *magisterium*, or teaching authority, that God has granted to his One, Holy, Catholic, and Apostolic Church, an authority that of course extends to matters of biblical interpretation, the Bible being one of many important things the Church has in her care. A denomination that espouses biblical indi-

---

[4] Jaroslav Pelikan, "Darwin's Legacy: Emanation, Evolution, and Development," in *Darwin's Legacy: Nobel Conference XVIII*, ed. Charles L. Hamrum (San Francisco: Harper & Row, 1983), p. 81. No citation of the words attributed to Aquinas is given.

vidualism, however, must avoid by some other means the danger of ubiquitous conflicting interpretations of the Bible, and it will find a theory about the Bible that minimizes the opportunities for diverse interpretations of a given text—as biblical literalism of course does—to be very useful. *Militant* biblical literalism, then, is not simply a product of the doctrine that the Bible is the revealed Word of God; its other parent is biblical individualism, a johnny-come-lately in the history of the Christian Church. Having said this, I must add that I do not mean to imply that all the great Reformers were themselves literalists. John Calvin, I understand, questioned the historicity of the book of Job.[5] But this qualification strengthens rather than weakens the credentials of non-literalism.

To establish the credentials of non-literalism, however, is not to establish its possibility. How can the Bible be the revealed word of God if, to take one example among many, it says that birds and fish came into existence on the same day, when the plain truth is that there were fish for hundreds of millions of years before there were birds? Well, I don't *know* the answer to this question, but I will do what St. Augustine did: I will present an answer that I find plausible and which I am willing to recommend. To do this, I must discuss both the content of Genesis and its formation. These two matters are intimately related, but I shall begin by treating them separately.

First, as to content. Suppose that someone who had never heard of the Bible and had never so much as thought about the beginning of the world were one day to read the book of Genesis and were to take everything it contained in a pretty literal sense and were to believe every word of it. This person would thereby come to believe many true things and many false things. Among the false things there would be two that we have already mentioned: the proposition that the alternation of day and night existed before the sun, and the proposition that Aves and Pisces are coevals. We could make quite a list of such false propositions. Here are some of the true ones. That the world is finite in space and time—at least time past. That it has not always been as it is now but has changed from a primal chaos into its present form. That it owes its existence and its features to an immeasurably powerful being who made it to serve His purposes. That it was originally not evil and not neutral as between good and evil and not a mixture of good and evil but simply good. That human beings are part of this world and are formed from its elements—that they were not separately created and then placed

---

[5] Lewis, *Reflections on the Psalms*, p. 92. Again, no citation is given.

in it like figurines in a china cabinet. That the stars and the moon are inanimate objects and are without any religious significance—that, at least in relation to human beings, their main purpose is to mark the hours and the seasons. That it is not only kings but all men and women who are images of the divine. That human beings have been granted a special sort of authority over the rest of nature. That these divine images, the stewards of all nature, have, almost from their creation, disobeyed God, and have thereby marred the primal goodness of the world and have separated themselves from God and now wander as exiles in a realm of sin and death.

So our imaginary credulous reader of Genesis comes to believe some true things and some false things. The first (but not the last) point to note about the credulous reader's situation is that the true things are much more important than the false things. In fact, the true things are among the most important there are, and the false things are not very important at all. Someone who believes that the world began six thousand years ago is wrong; so is someone who believes that Columbus was the first European to reach North America. For the life of me, however, I can't see that it is much more important to get the age of the earth right than it is to get the identity of the first European voyager to reach North America right. I can expect a protest at this point from both the literalists and the saganists. Each will tell me that the question of the age of the earth is of very great importance. The literalist will say that it is important because a mistake about the age of the earth could lead one to reject the Word of God, and the saganist will say that it is important because a mistake about the age of the earth could lead one to reject science and reason. But these protests rest on a misunderstanding. I am talking about the *intrinsic* importance of a mistake in this area, not about its *extrinsic* importance. Clearly any false belief whatever, however trivial its subject matter, *could* have disastrous consequences in special circumstances. We could easily imagine circumstances in which a woman's mistaken belief that her husband had stopped to buy a newspaper on his way home from work led her to suspect that he was lying to her about his movements and eventually destroyed their marriage. And, of course, a false belief about the age of the earth could lead to a disastrous repudiation of the reliability of something that *is* reliable and whose reliability is important. It could, in fact, lead one to devote a large portion of one's life to defending the indefensible—as, no doubt, false beliefs about Columbus have done. What I am saying is that the matter of the age of the earth is of little importance in itself. This is far from an empty platitude. The last few hundred years have seen thinkers who over-estimate the intrinsic value of scientific knowledge as absurdly as Matthew Arnold and F. R. Leavis overestimated the intrinsic value of a well-honed literary sensibility. Here is a quotation from the No-bel Prize–winning physicist Steven Weinberg that illustrates the evaluation I am deprecating:

> The more the universe seems comprehensible, the more it also seems pointless.
>
> But if there is no solace in the fruits of our research, there is at least some consolation in the research itself. Men and women are not content to comfort themselves with tales of gods and giants, or to confine their thoughts to the daily affairs of life; they also build telescopes and satel-lites and accelerators, and sit at their desks for endless hours working out the meaning of the data they gather. The effort to understand the universe is one of the very few things that lifts human life a little above the level of farce, and gives it some of the grace of tragedy.[6]

Against this, I would set the following statements of the "great champion of the obvious," Dr. Johnson:

> [W]e are perpetually moralists, but we are geometricians only by chance . . . . our speculations upon matter are voluntary and at leisure.

> [Scientific knowledge] is of such rare emergence that one man may know another half his life without being able to estimate his skill in hydrostatics or astronomy; but his moral and prudential character im-mediately appears.

> [T]he innovators whom I oppose are turning off attention from life to nature. They seem to think that we are placed here to watch the growth of plants, or the motions of the stars.[7]

Well, I have set before you a choice of values. If you think that the evaluation of scientific knowledge that is implicit in my quotation from Weinberg is the right one and that Johnson's belongs to the rubbish of history and good riddance to it, you will not believe a word of anything I am going to say. But at least don't mistake my position: I am not saying that science is unimportant; I am only de-

---

[6] Steven Weinberg, *The First Three Minutes: A Modern View of the Origin of the Universe* (London: André Deutsch, 1977), p. 155.

[7] Quoted by Michael D. Aeschliman, *The Restitution of Man* (Grand Rapids: Wm. B. Eerdman's, 1983), pp. 25–26. The quotations are from Johnson's essay "Milton", in his *Lives of the English Poets*.

nying scientific knowledge the central place in the proper scheme of human values that Weinberg gives it. I also deny this central place to a knowledge and appreciation of history or music or literature, each of which is neither more nor less important than scientific knowledge.

My first step in reconciling the thesis that Genesis is the revealed Word of God with the findings of science is, therefore, to contend that what Genesis is right about is of great intrinsic importance and that what it is wrong about is of little intrinsic importance. This contention, however, raises the question why Genesis, if it is the Word of God, is wrong about *anything*. I said that I should discuss questions both of content and of formation. I have said something about content. To discuss the question I have now raised I introduce some points having to do with the formation of the Genesis narrative— the genesis of Genesis, as it were.

What is the purpose of the first chapters of Genesis? What is their purpose in relation to the Hebrew Bible as a whole? The Hebrew Bible is mainly the narrative of God's covenant relationship with His people Israel. The opening chapters of Genesis are intended to set the stage for the story of that covenant. They are intended to describe and explain the relations between God and humanity as they stood when God made a covenant with Abraham. Thus, Genesis begins with an account of the creation of the world and of human beings, an account that displays God as the maker and sovereign of the world and the ordainer of the place of humanity in the world, and which does that in a way that militates against various disastrous theological misconceptions current among Israel's neighbors and conquerors—as that divinity is divided among many beings whose wills are often in conflict; or that the lights in the sky are objects of worship; or that the image of divinity is present in a few human beings—kings—but not in ordinary people. But then why doesn't Genesis get it right? I say that Genesis does get it right—in essence. W. J. Bryan may have been a fool in many respects,[8] but he had a more accurate picture of the cosmos than Carl Sagan (who, if we may trust the Fourteenth Psalm, is also a fool). Bryan believed that the world had been created by God, and that by itself is enough to outweigh all the matters of detail in which Sagan is right and

[8] But not nearly so big a fool as the character who bears his name in the almost wholly fictional movie *Inherit the Wind*. The popular account of the Scopes trial is one of the two great legends of the saganist history of Darwinism, the other being the story (as it is usually told) of the confrontation between T. H. Huxley and Bishop Wilberforce in 1860. Of course, each of these legends, like Piltdown Man, was put together from pieces of real things.

Bryan wrong. But why doesn't Genesis get it right not only in essence but in detail? Why doesn't Genesis get it wholly right? After all, we expect a reliable source to get even relatively unimportant details right, insofar as it is able, and God knows all the details. The beginning, but not the end, of the answer to this question is that if Genesis did get it right in every detail, most people couldn't understand it. Never mind the fact that only a person with years of rigorous formal training in mathematics can fully understand the current theories about the first three minutes of the existence of the cosmos. Consider only the *age* of the cosmos: more than ten thousand million years. You and I can in a sense grasp numbers like 10^{10}: we know how to do arithmetic with them. But how could the age of the universe be conveyed to most people at most times? Suppose the Bible began, "Ten thousand million years ago, God created . . . ". Suppose you are a missionary trying to explain the Genesis narrative to a tribe of Amazonian Indians. How shall you explain these words to them? Shall you leave off teaching them about important things like the sovereignty of God till you have taught them about unimportant things like the decimal system? (Do not suppose that teaching them the decimal system will be the work of an afternoon, for there is no basis in their culture for using the kinds of numbers it gives access to.) And most cultures have been like our imaginary Amazonian culture in that respect. A scientifically accurate rewriting of Genesis, therefore, would turn it into something all but useless, for the result would be inaccessible to most people at most places and times. Only a few people like you and me—who are simply freaks from the historical and anthropological point of view—could penetrate even its surface. I wonder how many of us believe, at some level, that God—if there is a God—regards scientifically educated people as being somehow the human norm and therefore regards Amazonian Indians or elementary-school dropouts as being less worthy of his attention than we; I wonder whether many of us aren't disposed to think that if the Bible were divinely inspired it would be written with the preoccupations of the scientifically educated in mind? I will not bother to quote the very clear dominical and Pauline repudiations of the values that underlie this judgment. Everyone is of equal value to God and the Bible is addressed to everyone. A Bible that was made easy for kings to understand at the cost of making it hard for peasants to understand would be in violation of this principle—if only because there are a lot more peasants than kings. And, of course, there are a lot more people who could not understand a scientifically accurate rewriting of Genesis than there are people who could.

To this I can expect the skeptic to reply along the following lines: "That's beside the point. Of course the universe is so complex—no doubt any *possible* universe would *have* to be so complex—that only a few highly trained people in a few very special cultures could understand a *detailed* account of its origin and development. But the writer of Genesis could have described the early history of the cosmos very *abstractly*. He could have included all of the theses that you regard as 'important truths', and, nevertheless, everything he said about the development of the physical universe could have been true as far as it went. When God inspired the author of Genesis, why didn't He inspire him to write it that way?"

The answer to this question is threefold. One of the three parts I am not going to explore. I will simply mention it and leave it. I do this because I think it is very important, but that it could not be adequately discussed within the scope of this essay. It is this: not all the truths that are revealed in Genesis can be said; some (to employ a distinction of the early Wittgenstein) can only be shown. These truths, I believe, truths relating to sin and knowledge, can be shown only by telling a very concrete story. I believe that as a result of knowing the story of the fruit of the knowledge of good and evil, I know something important that I cannot articulate; something that could not have been conveyed in discursive prose and which perhaps did not have to be conveyed by a story about trees and a serpent but which certainly had to be conveyed parabolically—that is, by means of *some* story about the actions of concrete, picturable beings.

I pass with relief to the two more straightforward points I want to make. First, that an abstract version of Genesis would have little pedagogical value for most people at most times. Even if it contained all the correct lessons, the lessons would not be learned—or would be learned only by rote, as "lessons" in the schoolroom sense. Secondly, the idea of God's inspiring Moses (or whomever) to write an "abstract" Genesis purged of all harmless error seems either to presuppose a primitive "dictation" model of inspiration or else to imagine God as purging His revelation of harmless error at a very high cost to the recipients of that revelation. I will illustrate these points with a parable.

Imagine that a doctor visits our Amazonian Indians with the intention of teaching them some useful medicine—say, some elementary principles of first aid and hygiene and antisepsis, and such pharmacological lore and simple surgical procedures as they can be trusted with in the absence of continuing supervision. What would be the best way to teach such things? One might give one's pupils a précis of a medical encyclopedia, deleting whatever material was not applicable to their condition. But this précis, because it was presented in a form that was without model or precedent in their culture, might well be forgotten or ignored or even be sung as a chant to accompany the application of traditional tribal medical procedures. Another, and perhaps more effective technique, would be to revise and purify and extend the existing medical lore of one's pupils, making use of literary and mnemonic devices indigenous to their culture. In applying this technique, one might simply not bother to correct parts of the existing medical lore that were harmlessly wrong. If one's pupils believed that childbirth fever was caused by demons, why should one not teach them that the demons must make their way into the bodies of new mothers via the hands of midwives, and that this path could be blocked by a scrupulous ritual washing before the delivery? If this teaching would lead to the same behavior on the part of midwives as a much longer lesson that involved an introduction to the germ theory of disease, and if the extra time required by the longer lesson were time that could be devoted to a lesson about making effective splints—well, one would have to ascribe a very high value indeed to truth in the abstract to recommend the longer lesson.

This parable has, I hope, presented an analogical case for the pedagogical ineffectiveness of an "abstract" Genesis. It also shows, by analogy, some of the difficulties God would encounter in getting an abstract Genesis into our hands, even granted that it would be advisable to do so. He might, of course, have dictated it, Hebrew word by Hebrew word, to a shining-faced Moses or to some terrified priest in the time of the Captivity. I do not want to say that revelation never occurs in that mode: perhaps the Name of God and the Ten Commandments were delivered to Moses in that way. But it is certainly clear that little, if any, of the Bible has been simply dictated by God: God's usual procedure has been to use as His instrument of revelation the whole person of an inspired author and not simply the hand that held the pen. If God had simply dictated Genesis, then He might as easily have dictated a "pure" abstract version of Genesis as any other. If, however, He proceeded, as He seems usually to have done, by inspiring modifications of the kind of story that it was natural to the author—who must be the concrete product of a particular culture, even as you and I are—to tell, then it would have been a very difficult business to produce an abstract Genesis. Not that anything is too hard for God, but, if God chooses to work with human tools, He subjects Himself to limitations inherent in the nature of the tools.

The human author or authors of Genesis, whatever their historical period may have been, would have had no natural disposition to tell a story like our imaginary abstract Genesis, a story utterly at variance with every model provided by their own culture and every other culture I know of. People are not naturally inclined to divest a story they want to tell of the concrete details that give that story its character, and the ancient Hebrews had very concrete minds indeed—as did all their contemporaries. No doubt the continued influence of the Holy Spirit could *eventually* have produced an abstract Genesis. I have no idea how long this would have taken, but certainly longer than it took to produce the concrete, suggestive, effective Genesis that we have. And what would have been the value of this costly thing? Only this: that a few saganists in our own time would have had to find some other excuse to reject the Word of God than its disagreement with the fossil record. I do not see why God, who values any six holders of endowed chairs neither more nor less than He values any six agricultural laborers in ancient Palestine, should have thought the price worth paying.

This completes my outline of the position that I oppose both to Genesiac literalism and to saganism. I shall now, as I have promised, offer critiques of literalism and saganism from the point of view afforded by this position.

To the literalists, I have little to say. Anything I said to them would be based on a premise that no literalist could accept: that "creation science" is pretty much nonsense. It's not that it's not science at all, as the rather silly—and certainly politically motivated—Arkansas decision would have it. It's that—in my view, at least—it's very bad science, consisting of contrived, ad hoc arguments and selective appeal to evidence.[9]

As to the saganists, I can happily accept a good deal of the story they tell about how the world got into its present state. The universe of modern cosmology is a cozy, tightly knit affair, entirely unlike the rather frightening infinite and amorphous universe of nineteenth-century popular science, a universe that, in my view, was not based on the actual content of nineteenth-century science but which was

---

[9] This is well documented in many publications. Howard J. Van Till, Davis A. Young, and Clarence Menninga, *Science Held Hostage: What's Wrong with Creation Science* and *Evolutionism* (Downer's Grove, Ill.: InterVarsity Press, 1988) is as good as any.

rather an ideological construct put together for the express purpose of making theism seem implausible. The nineteenth-century cosmos was made infinite and amorphous so that anything might happen in it given sufficient time. It was made eternal to ensure sufficient time—and, of course, to avoid awkward questions about where it came from. But the lovely universe the late-twentieth-century cosmologists have given us is as tidy and peculiar and homely as the medieval *mundus* of crystalline spheres.

I cannot, of course, accept the saganists' statement that the cosmos is all that is or was or ever will be. (Nor can I accept the fatuous attempt of the deists to append a Creator and Voyeur to the saganists' cosmos.) From my point of view, the cosmos depends from moment to moment on the sovereign power of God who is infinitely greater than it, and it would vanish, all in a moment, like a candle flame in a high wind, if He were to stop supplying it with the power to continue to be. And I believe that the Lord and sustainer of the cosmos, the only helmsman of the wide and single stars, the faithful guarantor of the laws of nature, has become locally involved in His creation in a special way, and that, as a result, a man has risen from the dead and many other miracles have occurred.

So I differ from the saganists on two points at least: the cosmos does not exist on its own, and the power that sustains it sometimes manifests its sustaining presence in ways radically different from the norm (that is, there are miracles). Now if I differed from the saganists on only these two points (and on such closely related points as the imminent end of the Church), they and I could accept pretty much the same science. Whether the world depends on a power outside itself, and whether there are miracles are not questions to be decided by science. (I do not of course deny that if science can provide a convincing natural explanation for a hitherto mysterious event, then that is an important piece of evidence that must be taken into account by anyone who is trying to determine whether *that event* is a miracle. But this point has nothing to do with the question whether there are miracles.) Thus it would seem that on one point at least the saganists and I agree against the literalists: we accept the same science, or, at least, they and I are no more likely to disagree about science than are any two saganists.

As a matter of fact, however, this is very far from being true. If the saganists' science were entirely correct, this would not trouble me a bit. Nevertheless, I'm very skeptical about some of it. It's just not clear to me that it all *works*. There are three points about which I am doubtful. The first of them has to do with the beginning of the cosmos. When it began to emerge that the cosmos had a beginning in time, or, at least, that the cosmos did not have an infinite past in which it was pretty much the same as it is now, saganists began to try to come to terms with this awkward fact—producing in the process such philosophically motivated theories as the now discredited steady-state theory, the pretty much discredited "oscillating universe" theory, and the currently rather fashionable theory that the cosmos began as a quantum fluctuation. All these theories are addressed to the same sort of questions as the cosmological argument. I will not discuss them. I want instead to raise some questions in the general vicinity of the argument from design. (But I am not going to discuss those very general features of the cosmos and the laws it obeys that have led some to observe that it appears to have been "fine-tuned" to permit the existence of life—the features that led Fred Hoyle to say, one might almost say to *complain*, that it looked as if a superintellect had been monkeying with the laws of physics.) The two theses that are important components of the saganists' science and about which I am doubtful are their theses concerning macroevolution and human origins. (To these two theses a third might be added: that life arose as the result of a purely natural process. But it would be hard to have a profitable discussion of this question, because, owing to the fact that the origin of life is at present wholly mysterious, wise saganists will probably want to say only that life arose by *some* natural process, and, while I am not as sure of this as they are, I see no particular reason to dispute it. I will remark only that if all life on earth is, as someone facetiously suggested, descended from bacterium-like organisms negligently deposited by extraterrestrial picnickers on the recently cooled surface of the earth, this would account perfectly for the earliest fossil evidences of life.)

Let us turn to the topic of macroevolution, the evolutionary differentiation of very broad taxa, such as phyla. Macroevolution, according to saganism, is microevolution writ large. The same principles of random variation and natural selection that have caused a pair of fruit flies blown by chance to the Hawaiian Islands to have descendants that belong to many different species have brought it about that that first self-replicating molecule has as descendants arthropods and vertebrates and the members of every other phylum.

There is, I think, no reason to believe this, beyond the bare fact that phylogenesis has in fact occurred. This is not to say that there is no reason to believe that all living organisms have a common ancestry. No doubt the fact that penguins and spiders and algae share at least one apparently arbitrary characteristic—the code by which nucleic acid specifies the structures of proteins—is best explained by the same hypothesis that explains the common features of the Hawaiian fruit flies: common ancestry. The common-ancestry thesis cannot be regarded as a fact that is known simply on the basis of induction on many observations since (I believe) no two known species, living or extinct, are such that it is universally agreed by the experts that one is ancestral to the other; even cases in which, of two known species, one is believed by some experts to be ancestral to the other (e.g., *Homo sapiens* and *Homo erectus*) are rare.[10] But the indirect arguments are persuasive. It is not that there are no difficulties with the common-ancestry hypothesis, but, as Cardinal Newman said in another connection, a thousand difficulties do not add up to a single doubt, and it seems reasonable to believe that these difficulties will someday be resolved. So I am not saying that the common-ancestry thesis is supported by no evidence beyond the bare fact that phylogenesis has occurred. What seems to me to have only that much evidential support is that the interplay of random variation and natural selection—I shall hereafter refer to this interplay as simply 'natural selection'—is the sole mechanism responsible for the genesis of phyla and other broad taxa. Or, since we are not disputing the common-ancestry thesis, we may say: for the *differentiation* of phyla and other broad taxa—that is, for macroevolution.

One of the strongest reasons for being skeptical about the hypothesis that natural selection is the only mechanism driving macroevolution is the absence of intermediate forms. This absence is striking, even at the level of the biological class. Amphibians, for example, are supposed to have evolved from lobe-finned fish in a sequence that involved no radical difference between one generation and the next. A few fish of some species, or so the story goes, got into some environmental situation in which, owing to natural selection, their descendants in due course formed a new species; a population of fish belonging to *that* species suffered a similar fate, and, eventually, across a bridge of many, many species, the original population of fish produced descendants with pentadactyl limbs and all the other taxonomic characteristics of amphibians. The trouble with

---

[10] The logical structure of this thesis could easily be misunderstood. Compare the following similar statement: No living human being is known to be descended from any *known* human being who lived before the fall of Rome. Indeed, it is possible (although unlikely) that no person known to history who lived prior to 400 A.D. has any currently living descendants.

this scenario is that the fossil record reveals none of these intermediate species. Full-blown amphibia simply *appear* at a certain point in the fossil record with no visible not-quite-amphibian antecedents. And this is not an isolated example: there are few, if any, even remotely plausible fossil candidates for intermediates between reptiles and amphibians or between any class and the class out of which, by general agreement, it is supposed to have evolved. And yet the theory of evolution by natural selection seems to predict that, if the members of class *A* are descended from a population belonging to class *B*, then there must once have existed a vast number of "transitional" organisms, organisms intermediate between the two classes. The theory seems to make this prediction because the members of any two classes are radically different in anatomy and physiology and because the effects of natural selection on a population accumulate very gradually.

Darwin was deeply troubled by the fact that no trace had been discovered of forms intermediate between broad taxa. His solution to the problem was to ascribe the absence of known intermediates to the inherent imperfection of the fossil record and to the fact that "only a small portion of the surface of the earth has been geologically explored and no part with sufficient care."[11] In Darwin's day, fewer than 1 percent of the fossils that have today been discovered and catalogued were known. My impression is that today few if any paleontologists accept his solution. If my amateurish researches have not led me astray, the current judgment of most paleontologists is that if, for example, amphibians had evolved from some population of fish as gradually as Darwin believed they must have, then the fossils of some forms intermediate between fish and amphibians would almost certainly have been discovered. The obvious move to make in the face of this judgment, if one wants to save the hypothesis that natural selection is the sole mechanism behind macroevolution, is to say that the evolutionary differentiation of the amphibia proceeded not gradually but explosively and that the number of generations separating true fish and true amphibian was consequently very small. ('Gradual', 'explosive', and 'small' are, of course, relative terms. Any evolution by natural selection must be "gradual" by some standards, since any generation of the most rapidly evolving population must be practically indistinguishable from

---

[11] Charles Darwin, *The Origin of Species*, 6th ed. (1872; New York: Collier Books, 1962), p. 327.

its predecessor. The idea is that, contrary to what Darwin thought, the time required for a species to become distinct is small in comparison with the average "lifetime" of a species of that sort.) In that case, the intermediate organisms would not have been numerous or widespread. If they were few and were confined to a small geographical area, then the discovery of even one fossilized intermediate could be highly improbable. And, of course, the same story can be told about all macroevolutionary transitions. It goes like this: *all* taxa at whatever level tend to be stable—particularly as regards the gross anatomical properties evidence of which is preserved in fossils—for long periods and then, under special environmental conditions, to differentiate locally and all but instantaneously. Now by the timetable of the geological record, "instantaneously" could comfortably encompass many thousands of generations of evolving organisms. The trick is to suppose that differentiation occurs slowly enough to be explained by natural selection and fast enough to account for the absence of intermediate forms from the fossil record.[12] Well, maybe this will work. But the skeptic will wonder whether such a rate exists, even as an abstract possibility. Despite my very real awareness of my ignorance of these matters, I make bold to confess that I find it difficult to believe that some fish was separated from some amphibian by only—to pick a figure that must be right within a factor of two or three—ten thousand generations, each of which differed from its predecessor only to the extent allowed by the operation of natural selection. Most biologists, apparently, find this easy enough to believe. The ignorant skeptic like myself, the village atheist, will wonder whether their ability to believe this is rooted in their nuts-and-bolts anatomical, physiological, and biochemical expertise, or whether it is a product of their belief that things could easily have happened this way because this is how things did in fact happen.

And then there is a statistical problem. Even if there were few enough intermediates between fish and amphibian for it to be highly improbable that we should have found any of their fossils, it could nevertheless be highly probable that we should have found fossils of

[12] These words are my own attempt to give a brief statement of the "theory of punctuated equilibria" in such a way that this theory is clearly represented as a Darwinian theory. For a description of the theory of punctuated equilibria by its most eloquent exponent, see Stephen Jay Gould, "The Episodic Nature of Evolutionary Change", in his *The Panda's Thumb* (New York: Norton, 1980).

intermediates between *some* two classes.[13] The statistical principle I am appealing to is illustrated by the following fact: If I am a member of a randomly selected group of twenty-three people, the odds are just short of 17 to 1 against any of the others having the same birthday as I, but the odds are better than even that *some* two people in the group of twenty-three will have the same birthday.

One can also raise the question whether the missing intermediates are even logically possible, given that evolution proceeds by natural selection alone. Let us ask the question this way. If you took the genotype of a given lobe-finned fish, could you change it into the genotype of a given primitive amphibian by a sequence of gradual steps of the kind that evolution—even explosive evolution—by natural section requires? (Here we think of natural selection as operating at the genetic level; we think of selection pressure changing the relative frequencies of the genes that make up a population's gene pool.)

It might be argued that it is easy to see that this would be possible. Suppose that the fish and the amphibian genomes each contain one hundred thousand loci and that, in our two selected organisms, the same genes are present at ninety thousand of them and different ones at the other ten thousand. Then to change the genotype of the fish into the genotype of the amphibian in a sequence of one thousand steps, we simply make the necessary gene replacements ten at a time. The problem with this argument is that there is no guarantee that such a procedure would produce at each a step a genotype that corresponds to a viable organism. In fact, I find it hard to believe that it would. Let me try to make my difficulties with this notion clear by means of an analogy.

Suppose we own a very sophisticated automated factory. Properly programmed, our factory is capable of turning suitable raw materials into just about any sort of finished product. At present, a stream of steel ingots is flowing into the factory and a stream of meat grinders of identical design is flowing out. Another program, which we have in our files, would cause the factory to produce meat grinders of a more advanced design. (No single part of the "advanced" meat grinder, not even the smallest nut or bolt, would be exactly like any

[13] But what about *Archaeopterix*? Is it not an intermediate between reptiles and birds? This is possible. There are, nevertheless, powerful arguments for the conclusion that *Archaeopterix* was simply a bird. See Chap. 8 of Michael Denton, *Evolution: A Theory in Crisis* (Bethesda, Md.: Adler & Adler, 1986) for a discussion of *Archaeopterix* and the coelacanth and other candidate "intermediates".

part of the current, "primitive" meat grinder.) Now let us examine printouts of the two programs. Each program consists of one hundred thousand lines, each line being a complex string of characters. Ninety thousand lines are the same in the two programs, and the rest different. Could you change one program into the other by a sequence of one thousand ten-line-at-a-time changes? Obviously you could. But would all the "intermediate" programs produce some sort of meat grinder—or anything at all? It is hard to see how this could be. The new instruction that you insert at line 27 tells a bolt-making machine to produce bolts of a size slightly larger than the bolts it contributed to the original meat grinder. In order to accommodate that change, you have to change the size of 24 holes to be bored in 16 pieces of metal produced by four stamping machines and two milling machines; you have to change the instructions that determine the sizes of the nuts intended to fit those bolts; you have to reprogram the devices that pick up and manipulate the nuts and bolts; it will now take only 960 bolts instead of 1,000 to fill a standard bolt-bin, so the bins will have to be emptied every 88 seconds instead of every 92 seconds or they will overflow, and so the rate at which the bolt-collecting machine moves among the bins will have to be increased by an appropriate amount—and so on and so on. Unless all of these modifications in the factory's behavior can be embodied in nine other one-line changes in the program—changes which do not themselves necessitate yet further changes—*any* ten-line change in the program that includes the change we have introduced at line 27 will produce not meat grinders but a lot of jammed milling machines and conveyor belts.

It seems to me that the genotypes that underlie the physiology and anatomy of a given fish and a given amphibian are probably in this respect a lot like the programs that underlie our two styles of meat grinder. That is, I doubt whether there is any path in logical space from one to another that proceeds by changing a small number of genes at each step: every path you try will (I suspect) eventually run up against organs and systems that are no longer coordinated—perhaps even against proteins that don't fold properly. You can only look from one to the other and shake your head sadly and say, "You can't get there from here." At least not by the mode of transport envisaged. Not by a sequence of steps the size that selection pressure can effect in a given gene pool in one generation. That is *local* transport. It can take you from light peppered moths to dark ones, and—a much longer ride—from one species of fruit fly to another. These are in different parts of the same town. It's no good if you want to go from Europe to Australia—that is, from the fish to the amphibia. I should also point out that even if there *are* possible "small-step" paths from fish to amphibia, these paths might compose only an infinitesimal region within the space of all the possible paths that confront the ancestral population of fish, and thus the evolution by natural selection of amphibia from fish might be so vastly improbable as not to be worth considering.[14] And—to return to our previous theme—it might be that all or most of the possible paths are too long to be consistent with the absence of intermediate forms from the fossil record.

Nevertheless—or so I believe—the amphibia did evolve from some population of fish. If this is right, there are two possibilities. There is the possibility that an intelligent being has been guiding evolution by a series of actions that directly affect the genes of the evolving organisms. If we think in terms of our "meat-grinder" analogy, such a being would correspond to a computer programmer who turns one program into the other in a series of steps each of which involves a very large number of carefully coordinated changes. And there is the possibility that there is some yet undiscovered mechanism that does the same thing—perhaps not as efficiently as an intelligent being, but efficiently enough. The second possibility is the one that should be investigated, if only because the first cannot be *investigated*.

Remember the cautionary tale of Lord Kelvin. Assuming that the mechanisms underlying solar radiation must be explainable in terms of the physics he knew, the great physicist calculated—correctly, I understand, given his assumptions—that the sun could not have been shining for more than about twenty million years. When the paleontologists told him that there had been life on earth for much longer than that, he contemptuously replied, "There are two sciences, physics and stamp collecting," meaning that a paleontologist's *estimate* of a period of time must fall before a physicist's *calculation* of a period of time. But if he had had an open mind, he might have looked at the paleontological data and said something like, "It

---

[14] We should remember, however, that vastly improbable events are not necessarily surprising events: the conception and birth of a human being with any *particular* genetic makeup is a vastly improbable event. It might be that the number of possible biological classes that could evolve out of *some* population of fish is so huge that it is not surprising that one such class did evolve, despite the fact that the prior probability of *its* evolving was all but infinitesimal. I cannot myself believe that logical space contains a suitably enormous number of possible classes that could evolve from some population of fish, but one's intuitions in this area are probably not of much value.

may be only an estimate, but it's a damned good one. It begins to look as if solar radiation may be produced by some mechanism other than heating due to gravitational compression, though I can't imagine what it might be." And, of course, there *was* such a mechanism, one that Lord Kelvin couldn't imagine because it was conceptually inaccessible to a physicist at the turn of the twentieth century.

Many areas of science present us with examples of cases in which long-term effects are produced by different mechanisms from those that produce short-term effects. Michael Denton has pointed out that this is true in the case of meteorology and geology: the mechanisms that underlie changes in climate are not those that underlie changes in the weather; mountain building is explained by mechanisms other than those that account for short-term, superficial geological change.[15] Nevertheless, it may be, for all I have said, that natural selection *can* account for macroevolution. Against the cautionary tale of Lord Kelvin should be set the cautionary tale of Sir Isaac Newton. Newton thought he saw that planetary orbits must be unstable, and he speculated that they were subject to periodic divine correction. Laplace, however, was able to show that Newton's own mechanisms—the laws of motion and the law of universal gravitation—entail that planetary orbits are stable enough to account for our observations. The point of this tale would be unaffected if Newton had postulated not supernatural interference with planetary dynamics but an unknown natural mechanism that supplemented the mechanisms he had discovered. The totality of the implications of the theory of evolution by natural selection, like the totality of the implications of Newtonian mechanics, cannot be grasped by the mind in a single flash of insight. But I say this: our understanding of macroevolution is either in the position of our understanding of orbital mechanics before Laplace or else in the position of our understanding of solar radiation before the advent of nuclear physics. If the former—well, the theory of evolution by natural selection has had in Darwin its Newton, but it has not yet had its Laplace. I think that our tentative conclusion should be that the theory of evolution by natural selection alone is doubtful in a way that many scientific theories are not. We may be confident that we understand, at least in very broad outline, where the stars get the energy to shine and what the forces are that cause mountains to rise. It is premature to believe that we have even in broad outline a satisfactory theory of macroevolution. If we temporarily suspend our belief in the theory

---

[15] Denton, *Evolution*, pp. 87–88.

that macroevolution is microevolution writ large, I cannot see that we shall thereby come to any harm. The theory does not *do* anything for us that I know of, beyond just sitting there and providing an explanation for the diversity of life. In this respect it is like the theory that the diversity of life is the work of an intelligent designer. There are many beautiful and satisfying explanations of microevolutionary phenomena in terms of natural selection. (My favorite is the explanation of the showy plumage of male dabbling ducks.) But I know of no explanation of any macroevolutionary phenomenon—sexual dimorphism, say—in terms of natural selection.

Let us now turn to the evolution of humanity, or, more exactly, to the evolution of those cognitive capacities that make humanity so strikingly different from all other species: I mean the capacities that allow us to do fantastic things like theoretical physics or evolutionary biology or drawing in perspective or, for that matter, making a promise or deciding not to plant wheat if there's a dry winter—things absolutely without analogues in any other species.[16] The evolution of these capacities, unique in the history of life, is a phenomenon of microevolution, and, therefore, even if macroevolution involves other mechanisms than natural selection, it may be that our special cognitive capacities are entirely a product of natural selection. It must be understood that by "cognitive capacities", I mean capacities determined by the physiology of the brain: not capacities that are conferred on one by one's culture and education, but capacities that are written on one's chromosomes. I think that no one doubts that our paleolithic ancestors—our ancestors of, say, thirty thousand years ago—had more or less the same cognitive capacities as we. A paleolithic infant, transported to our era by a time machine and raised in our culture, would be as likely to grow into a normal and useful member of our culture as an infant brought here by airplane from Tibet. Moreover, an immigrant paleolithic baby would be as likely to become a brilliant high-energy physicist or evolutionary

---

[16] When I wrote the pages that follow in the text, I was aware that they were inspired by a wonderful lecture of Hilary Putnam's, "The Place of Facts in a World of Values"—in *The Nature of the Physical Universe: The 1976 Nobel Conference*, ed. Douglas Huff and Omer Prewett (New York: John Wiley & Sons, 1979)—that I had read several years before. When I recently reread that lecture, in connection with preparing the present essay for publication, I discovered that I had remembered it better than I knew, and that in some places I had come close to reproducing Putnam's exact words. I have let these passages stand, on the principle that imitation is the sincerest form of flattery. (But Professor Putnam should not be held responsible for the ways in which I have used the materials he has provided.)

biologist as an immigrant Tibetan baby. If this is true, then the cognitive capacities needed to master—and to excel at—any modern scientific discipline were already present, in more or less their present statistical distribution, among our paleolithic ancestors. (A race of mute, inglorious Miltons indeed!) And this means, according to the saganists, that these capacities evolved by the operation of natural selection among the ancestors of our paleolithic ancestors. And this, in its turn, implies that there was some character, or set of characters, such that (a) possession of those characters by some of its members conferred a reproductive advantage upon some population composed of our remote ancestors and (b) the presence of those characters within the present human population constitutes the biological basis of the human capacity for theoretical physics and evolutionary biology.

Have we any reason to think that there exists any set of characters having both these features? (Let us arbitrarily call a set of characters having both features *special*; I choose an arbitrary designation because an arbitrary designation is at least not tendentious.) If we have indeed evolved by natural selection from ancestors lacking the biological capacity to do physics and biology, then the answer to this question must be Yes; after all, we're here, and we are as we are. But if we set aside any conviction we may have that our cognitive capacities were produced by natural selection, can we discover any reason to believe that there exists—even as an abstract possibility—a "special" set of characters? It might be said that we know that a special set exists because we can point to it: our collective name for it is "intelligence". Now "intelligence" is a pretty vague concept, but not so vague that we can't see that this suggestion is wrong. I expect that no one would care to maintain that if (say) Albert Einstein and Thomas Mann had been switched in their cradles,[17] Mann would have made fundamental contributions to physics—or even that he would have become a physicist. It is very doubtful whether Mann possessed (in however latent a form) the quality that Einstein's biographers call "physical intuition", a quality that Einstein possessed in an extraordinary degree and which even a run-of-the-mill physicist must possess in some degree. And yet it would be simply silly to say that Einstein was more *intelligent* than his fellow Nobel Prize winner. Einstein did not discover the general theory of relativity because he was so very bright—though doubtless high intelligence was a necessary condition for his achievement—but, insofar as a

---

[17] Actually, Mann was born in 1875 and Einstein in 1879.

"cause" can be named at all, because of his superb faculty of physical intuition. Couldn't we easily imagine a population whose members were as *intelligent* as we—if they were dispersed among us, we should hear them commended for their "intelligence" with about the same frequency as we should hear the members of any randomly chosen group of our fellows commended—but who were as lacking in "physical intuition" as the average accountant or philosopher or pure mathematician? (I mean, of course, to imagine a population that is *biologically* incapable of displaying any appreciable degree of physical intuition. No doubt certain genes must be present in an individual who possesses that enviable quality; what I want to imagine is a population of human beings within which some of these genes are so rare that the chance of the requisite combination of genes occurring in any of its members is negligible.) Couldn't such a population develop quite an impressive civilization—as impressive, say, as classical Chinese civilization or the civilization of ancient Egypt? The point raised by this question would seem to apply a fortiori to the reproductive success of such a population in a "state of nature". Why should a population with the gene frequencies I have imagined fare any worse in the forests or on the savannas than a population in which the genes that, in the right combination, yield the capacity for physical intuition are relatively numerous?

The saganists' answer to this question will, I think, go more or less as follows. "You are making mysteries where none exist. You might as well make a mystery of my contention—and I do contend it—that the ability to play the cello is a product of natural selection. Isn't that mysterious, the mystery-monger asks, when there were no cellos, not even primitive cellos, on the primeval savannas? But the capacity to play the cello—that is the biological capacity to be taught to play the cello in the right cultural circumstances, a biological capacity that was presumably about as frequent among our paleolithic ancestors as it is among us—is an aggregate of a lot of generally useful capacities. Two obvious ones are manual dexterity and the ability to discriminate pitches. Each was advantageous to our primitive ancestors, since they needed to chip flints and to interpret subtle changes in the chorus of insect noises in the forest night. We should also not neglect the fact that most, if not all, genes have many different effects on the constitution of the whole organism. It may therefore be that some of the genes whose co-presence in Einstein was responsible for his remarkable physical intuition were selected for in the remote past because of advantageous effects functionally unrelated to physical intuition. In sum, while we perhaps don't understand physical intuition all that well, there is no reason to doubt that its presence in a given present-day individual is due to a combination of genes that were, individually if not collectively, advantageous to our primitive ancestors."

Well, if there is no reason to doubt this, is there any reason to believe it? If I wanted to pick someone to learn to chip flints or to interpret insect noises, I should certainly pick a cello player over someone who was all thumbs or someone who was tone-deaf. But if you know nothing about a certain person except that he or she is a first-rate theoretical physicist, what can you predict that that person will be good at—other than theoretical physics? You know that the physicist will be of high general intelligence, but you don't need to look for a physicist if you want intelligence. You know that the physicist will have a certain flair for thinking in terms of differential equations, though not necessarily a degree of mathematical ability that would excite the admiration of a mathematician. And that's about it. I don't suppose that you can predict that the physicist will have much in the way of spatial intuition (in the sense in which spatial intuition is required by an architectural draftsman). Nor is the physicist particularly likely to be a good mechanic or an accomplished inventor of mechanical devices or especially good at balancing a checkbook or counting cattle.

Quite possibly the first person to have the idea of the bow and arrow or to conceive the idea of making fire from the heat produced by friction would have to have had the qualities that would make a good physicist. Nevertheless, the intellectual conception of the great prehistoric inventions must have been a pretty rare occurrence; I can't see the great, but very rarely operative, advantages to a population of having in its gene pool the capacities for making such inventions as exerting much selection pressure on the population's gene pool. But let us concede that a population of modern human beings transported to some vastly ancient time (and divested of modern knowledge) would have had a distinct reproductive edge on otherwise similar populations that lacked the biological basis of physical intuition, owing to its capacity to invent the bow and arrow and fire-by-friction. This concession simply raises a further question: How did the gene frequencies that ground this capacity get established before—it must have been *before*—there was a relatively advanced technology to confer on them the opportunity to be advantageous? I find this question puzzling, but it may well have a plausible answer, and I don't want to let my case rest very heavily on the assumption that it has no plausible answer. I rest my case primarily on two further points.

First, *is* it all that clear that the idea of making fire by friction and the idea of understanding gravitation as a function of the curvature of space-time were arrived at by the exercise of the same cognitive capacity? "This causes heat; greater heat than this causes fire; therefore doing this longer and harder may produce enough heat to cause fire" is a splendid piece of abstract reasoning. But is there any reason to believe that a population a few of whose members are capable of such reasoning must also contain a few people who are, genetically speaking, Newtons and Einsteins? I can see no reason to be confident about the answer to this question, one way or the other.

Secondly, the "cello" analogy is deeply flawed. Cellos are human artifacts and are constructed to be playable by organisms that have such abilities as human beings happen to have. The structure of the science of physics is certainly not arbitrary in the way that the structure of a cello is. A race of intelligent beings descended from pigs rather than from primates might have invented stringed instruments radically different in structure from cellos and quite unplayable by human beings. And music itself is rather an arbitrary thing compared with science. If there are intelligent extraterrestrials who, like us, derive pleasure from listening to rhythmic sequences of sounds among which there are certain definite relations of pitch, it does not seem to be very reasonable to expect that we could make much of their sounds. To adapt an aphorism of Wittgenstein's, if a lion could sing, we shouldn't want to listen. But if extraterrestrials have invented physics, their physics will have to be a lot like ours. Extraterrestrial physics must resemble terrestrial physics because physical theories are about the real world, and the same real world confronts pig, primate, and extraterrestrial. And yet (to take one example of the sort of thing physicists look into) the structures of the various families of elementary particles, and the forces by which they interact, can hardly have had any sort of effect on the evolution of the cognitive capacities of our remote ancestors. There is no reason for the paleoanthropologist to learn about the decay modes of the Z^0 boson in order to learn about how the brains of our ancestors evolved toward the possession of a capacity which is (among other things) a capacity to theorize about the decay modes of the Z^0 boson. Our ability to do elementary-particle physics seems to me, therefore, to be as puzzling as our ability to play the cello would be if cellos were not artifacts but naturally occurring objects, objects whose occurrence in nature was wholly independent of the economy of *Homo habilis*. Suppose, for example, that cellos grew on trees and only in a part of the world never inhabited by our evolving ancestors. Wouldn't it be a striking coincidence that some of us could learn to play them so well? Isn't it a striking coincidence that we can theorize about elementary particles so well?

I once heard Noam Chomsky say that our ability to do physical science depends on a very specific set of cognitive capacities, and that, quite possibly, the reason that there are no real social sciences may be that we just happen to lack a certain equally specific set of cognitive capacities. He went on to speculate that we might one day discover among the stars a species as good at social science as we are at physical science and as bad at physical science as we are at social science. He did not raise the question why natural selection would bother to confer either of these highly specific sets of capacities on a species. (Presumably the answer would have to be that the right gene combinations for success in physical science were just part of the luck of our remote ancestors' draw and that, having arisen by chance, these gene combinations endured because they were in some way advantageous to our ancestors. But we have already been over this ground.) Einstein once remarked that the only thing that was unintelligible about the world was that it was intelligible. He was calling attention to the (or so it seemed to him) unreasonable simplicity of the laws of nature, and he supposed, I think, that the world was intelligible because it was simple. That does not seem to me to be quite right. The ultimate laws of nature may be simple, but that does not make them intelligible to highly intelligent people—Thomas Mann, say, or Virgil, or J. S. Mill, or Nietzsche— who lack the very specific set of cognitive capacities that enables physicists to pick their way through the flux of the phenomena to the deep simplicities. What is "unintelligible" if anything in this area is, is that some of us should possess those capacities.

Saganists, therefore, owing to their adherence to natural selection as the sole engine of evolution, believe in what I have dubbed a "special" set of characters—a set of characters that *both* conferred a reproductive advantage on some population of our remote ancestors and also underlies our ability to do science. I, for reasons that I have tried to explain, am a skeptic about this. It seems to me that there is no very convincing argument a priori for the existence of a special set of characters and that the only argument a posteriori for its existence is that our scientific abilities could not be a consequence of natural selection unless such a set existed. For my part, however, I am going to suspend judgment about whether our scientific abilities are a consequence of natural selection till I see some reason to believe that there exists a special set of characters. Belief in a special set of characters, indeed, seems to me to be, in its epistemic features, very strongly analogous to belief in a Creator. More exactly, it is analogous to the type of belief in a Creator that is held by its adherents to rest on rational argument and public evidence—as opposed to private religious experience and historical revelation. There are, in my view, no *compelling* arguments for the existence or for the nonexistence of a Creator, no arguments that would force anyone who understood their premises to assent to their conclusion or else be irrational or perverse. There are compelling arguments for *some* conclusions: that the world is more than six thousand years old, for example, or that astrology is nonsense, but there are no compelling arguments for any conclusion of philosophical interest, whether its subject matter be God or free will or universals or the nature of morality or anything else that philosophers have argued about. Nevertheless, there are some very *good* philosophical arguments: serious arguments that are worth the attention of serious thinkers and which lend a certain amount of support to their conclusions. Among these, there are certain arguments having to do with God. The cosmological argument and the design argument, for example, appear to me to be arguments that are as good as any philosophical argument that has ever been adduced in support of any conclusion whatever. And yet the conclusions of these arguments (they are not quite the same) can be rejected by a perfectly rational person who understands perfectly all the issues involved in evaluating them.

I very much doubt whether there is any argument for the existence of a special set of characters that is any better in this respect than the design argument or the cosmological argument. It may nevertheless be that certain people—paleoanthropologists, perhaps—know that a special set of characters exists. It may be that they know this because of their mastery of a vast range of data too complex to be summarized in anything so simple as a single argument. By the same token, however, it may be that there are certain people who know that a Creator exists and know this because of their mastery of a vast range of data too complex to be summarized in anything so simple as a single argument.

My own guess is that neither sort of knowledge exists. If there are people who *know* that there is a Creator, this must be due to factors other than (or, perhaps, in addition to) the inferences they have drawn from their observations of the natural world; and no one knows whether there is a special set of characters. Belief in a special set of characters is based on nothing more than a conviction that natural selection must be the ultimate basis of all evolutionary episodes (except those so minor that, if no explanation in terms of natural selection is apparent, they may plausibly be assigned to genetic drift). And that conviction, like the nineteenth-century conviction that the universe has always been much as it is at present, is one that is held mainly because of its supposed anti-theistic implications. (Actually, it has no anti-theistic implications, but it is widely believed that it does.) Atheists often preach on the emotional attractiveness of theism. It needs to be pointed out that atheism is also a very attractive thesis. Very few people are atheists against their will. Atheism is attractive for at least two reasons. First, it is an attractive idea to suppose that one may well be one of the higher links in the Great Chain of Being—perhaps even the highest. (This idea is attractive for several reasons, not the least of which is that most people cannot quite rid themselves of the very well justified conviction that a being who knew all their motives and inmost thoughts might not entirely approve of them.) Secondly, there are very few atheists who do not admire themselves for possessing that combination of mental acuity and intellectual honesty that is, by their own grudging admission, the hallmark of atheists everywhere. The theist, however, is in a position to be an agnostic about the existence of a special set of characters, just as someone who accepts the saganists' science is in a position to be an agnostic about the existence of a Creator. Each is in a position to say, "Well, I don't know. There may be such a thing. What are the arguments?"

Confident and logically acute theists are not going to be impressed by arguments for the non-existence of God. Because they are logically acute, they will see that, while some of these arguments may be worthy of serious attention, they are not compelling in the very strong sense I spelled out above. Because they are confident, they will not abandon a worldview of which that belief is an integral part for anything less than a compelling argument. Similarly, confident and logically acute saganists are not going to be impressed by arguments for the non-existence of a special set of characters. Because they are logically acute, they will see that, while some of these arguments may be worthy of serious attention, none of them is compelling. Because they are confident, they will not abandon a worldview of which that belief is an integral part for anything less than a compelling argument.

In the past, theism has made important contributions to science. It has, in fact, been very plausibly argued that modern science did not (as the saganists suggest) arise in the teeth of clerical opposition but is rather a *product* of Western Latin Christianity, as closely connected with it (causally and historically, not logically) as is Gothic architecture. Those who accept this thesis, however, sometimes say that the umbilical cord connecting science to Mother Church has long since been cut, and that science now proceeds quite independently of the religious or anti-religious convictions of its practitioners. I wonder if the case of evolutionary biology doesn't show that this is at least a partial falsehood. Suppose I am right in suggesting that there are grave difficulties with the idea that natural selection is the only mechanism behind macroevolution and the evolution of certain specifically human cognitive capacities. Suppose that the allegiance of saganists—and saganism is certainly widespread among evolutionary biologists—to these two evolutionary theses is due not to scientific considerations but to the atheism that is a central component of saganism. Consider, finally, the following two evaluations of the situation in evolutionary biology. The first quotation, rather a famous one, is from the *Encyclopédie française* (1965). Its author is the naturalist Paul Lemoine, professor at the Museum of Paris:

> The result of this exposé is that the theory of evolution is impossible. Basically, despite appearances, no one believes it any more, and one says—without attaching any other importance to it—"evolution" in order to signify "a series of events in time"; or "more evolved" or "less evolved," in the sense of "more perfected," "less perfected" because such is the language of convention, accepted and almost obligatory in the scientific world. Evolution is a sort of dogma which the priests do not believe in any more, but which they keep up for the sake of their flocks.
>
> It is necessary to have the courage to say this in order that the men of the next generation may direct their research in another way.[18]

Now taken as a sober sociological thesis about the beliefs of scientists, this must be regarded as Gallic overstatement. Many of the priests, perhaps a large majority, really do believe sincerely in their dogma. But there is an important truth behind the overstatement—or so it seems to me in my ignorance. The truth is that the theory of macroevolution by natural selection alone is doing no scientific work, and that adherence to it consists mainly in talking in a certain way. This quotation, by the way, gives the lie to the saganist thesis that the only resistance to the theory of evolution by natural selection is provided by theological obscurantists. As a matter of fact,

---

[18] Paul Lemoine, quoted by Etienne Gilson in *From Aristotle to Darwin and Back Again* [a translation by John Lyon of Gilson's 1971 *D'Aristote à Darwin et retour*] (South Bend: University of Notre Dame Press, 1984), pp. 88–89.

there has been, ever since Darwin, a respectable body of scientific opinion opposed to the Darwinian account of evolution. For some reason, such opposition has been more prominent on the continent of Europe than in the English-speaking countries.

My second quotation is from the Australian biochemist Michael Denton:

> The overriding supremacy of the myth [sc., that natural selection accounts for all evolutionary phenomena] has created a widespread illusion that the theory of evolution was all but proved one hundred years ago and that all subsequent biological research—paleontological, zoological and in the newer branches of genetics and molecular biology—has provided ever-increasing evidence for Darwinian ideas. Nothing could be further from the truth. The fact is that the evidence was so patchy one hundred years ago that even Darwin himself had increasing doubts as to the validity of his views, and the only aspect of his theory which has received any support over the past century is where it applies to microevolutionary phenomena. His general theory, that all life on earth had originated and evolved in the gradual successive accumulation of fortuitous mutations, is still, as it was in Darwin's day, a highly speculative hypothesis entirely without direct factual support and very far from that self-evident axiom some of its more aggressive advocates would have us believe.[19]

May we not speculate that atheism is impeding progress in evolutionary biology? If there are actually other mechanisms at work in evolution than natural selection, and if atheism is emotionally (though not, of course, logically) wedded to the idea that natural selection is the only mechanism of evolution, perhaps a leaven of theists among evolutionary biologists would make a genuine search for such a mechanism possible. Perhaps, in fact, a more general allegiance among its practitioners to the important truths contained in the book of Genesis could be of real service to science. If that is possible, however, it is not probable. Owing to the general perversity of human beings—a feature of our species whose explanation can be found in St. Paul's reading of the third chapter of Genesis—there is likely to continue to be only one kind of interaction between the book of Genesis and science: silly squabbles between Genesiac literalists and saganists.[20]

---

[19] Denton, *Evolution*, p. 77. Denton's book is indispensable reading for anyone interested in the scientific difficulties faced by the Darwinian theory of evolution. Since this essay was written, another indispensable book has appeared: Phillip E. Johnson, *Darwin on Trial* (Washington, D.C.: Regnery Gateway, 1991).

[20] Parts of this essay were delivered as the Kraemer Lecture at the University of Arkansas, Fayetteville, Arkansas, in March 1989.

HARRY G. FRANKFURT

❦

On God's Creation

> Leazar said in Bar Sira's name: About what is too great for thee
> inquire not; what is too hard for thee investigate not; about what is
> too wonderful for thee know not; of what is hidden from thee ask
> not; study what was permitted thee; thou hast no business with
> hidden things.
>
> *Midrash Rabbah*

1. I propose to ignore these instructions.[1] I shall consider certain
hidden things. In just what way did God create the world? What
was the state of affairs before He created it? What was the nature of
the creative process? What, exactly, did He do? And how may we
understand, in the light of what He did, His relationship to the
world and to mankind?

Of course these questions are too great, too hard, and too wonderful. It is true that we have no business with them. Still, there are
other things in life besides business.

2. No one has yet produced, so far as I am aware, an adequate
biography of God. We have no systematic developmental account of
the character and activities of the deity whose career is related in the
Old Testament. It is plain, however, that He is responsive to human
behavior, and that He often reacts to it with great intensity. Moreover, it often seems that He regards Himself as being in some way
dependent on the conduct of mankind. The things people do appear
at times to affect Him in ways that even suggest a certain vul-
nerability on His part.[2]

A rather striking manifestation of this dependency is God's recur-

---

[1] The epigraph is from *Midrash Rabbah*, ed. H. Freedman and M. Simon (London:
Soncino Press, 1939), vol. 1 (Gen. 1), p. 56.

[2] Thus God responds to the sin of Adam and Eve not simply with anger and with
curses but also with fear (cf. Genesis 3:22).

rent interest in executing covenants with human beings. Insofar as a covenant is a contract, it is an agreement entered into for mutual advantage. If it is to rest neither on ignorance nor coercion, it must offer benefits of comparable magnitude to everyone who is to be bound by it. Now it is not difficult to understand how humans might profit by entering into contractual arrangements with a being of enormous power and energy, who is in an incomparably effective position to promote and protect their interests. But what is in it for God? In what way might He expect to benefit from any human performance? How could it be in His interest to obligate Himself to man? What difference can it make to Him how people act? Why does He care about it at all?

One line of response to these problems is grounded in the familiar image of God as an absolute and imperious ruler, an exigent and all-powerful issuer of commands and decrees. On this account, the reason people are obliged to obey and to worship God is not that doing so is inherently desirable or that it is beneficial to anyone. They are required to submit to God's will only because He demands their submission; and He demands this just because, whether out of pride or out of jealousy or out of sheer willfulness, He wants it. Thus the considerations that define the relationship between man and God are, from a moral point of view, quite arbitrary: human beings must do what God commands, and He commands it simply because it is what He wants. The ultimate relevant fact is that it pleases Him to be worshipped and obeyed. There is nothing more to be said about the matter than that.

Another line of response invokes a far different, though equally familiar, image of God as a loving parent. On this account, God is not motivated in His relationship with mankind by any willful desire for glorification. He does not regard people primarily as His subjects, but as His children. It is because He wishes them well, rather than because He is concerned with Himself, that He is preoccupied with their behavior. What He fears is that they may act in ways that will be detrimental to their best interests. For this reason, He devotes Himself paternalistically to instructing them and to guiding their conduct. When He berates them or provides them with inducements to do this or that, He does so entirely for their benefit. Since people are not always capable of understanding what is good for them, they cannot be left to themselves. For their own sakes, accordingly, God requires them to accept His authority.

Neither of these two lines of response goes deep enough. In both cases, the problem of understanding the relationship between man

and the divine remains wholly isolated from the problem of understanding creation. But there must be a profound connection between
these problems. It could hardly fail to be the case that God's view of
human beings is in some way determined or conditioned by how
their relationship began. Thus, there is every reason to think that a
clarification of God's creation would illuminate the curious sym-
biosis between Him and his most notable creature. After all, before
God was Lord or Father of mankind, He was the Creator of the
world.

3. What was the state of affairs when the process of creation began? Here is what we are told:

> When God began to create heaven
> and earth, the earth was
> unformed and void, and darkness
> was over the surface of the deep;
> and the spirit of God hovered over
> the water. And God said, 'Let
> there be light.' And there was
> light. (Gen.1:1–3)[3]

This is manifestly not an account of a creation ex nihilo. Whatever
basis there may be for supposing that the world was created out of
nothing, these opening lines of Genesis appear to be flatly inconsistent with that supposition. They seem to make it quite explicitly
clear that before God performed His first creative act—that is, prior
to His creation of light—there was already something. Indeed, quite
a bit. The text mentions three things: the earth, the deep, and the
spirit of God.

It may appear to be somewhat uncertain whether we are to understand that the earth was actually in existence at the beginning of the
creative process. The assertion that the earth was "unformed and
void" might naturally be construed as describing the condition of
the earth at a certain time in its history; and in that case it would
imply that the earth, although it did not yet have a specifiable form
or character, did then exist. But the assertion could also plausibly be
taken to imply instead that, at the time in question, the earth did not
yet exist. Everything depends on what is meant by saying of the
earth that it was "unformed and void".

---

[3] The translation is based on the New JPS Translation, in *Tanakh: The Holy Scriptures*
(Philadelphia: Jewish Publication Society, 1988).

Suppose that we accept Rashi's suggestion concerning how to understand this key phrase.[4] Then we will probably have to conclude that the earth did already exist when God's creative activity began. The Hebrew words translated as "unformed" and "void" are, respectively, *tohu* and *bohu*. Rashi says that "the word *bohu* has the meaning of emptiness and void". As for the other element of the phrase, he explains that "the word *tohu* has the meaning of astonishment and amazement . . . ; for a person would be astonished and amazed at the void in the world."

Now if we take this seriously, it is difficult to construe the assertion that the earth was *tohu* and *bohu* as consistent with the supposition that the earth did not exist. After all, what would be so surprising about the non-existence of the earth before creation began? No one examining the state of affairs prior to the creation of light would be astonished or amazed to discover an empty space at the location destined in due course to be occupied by the earth. That would surely not be surprising at all. On the contrary: before creation gets under way, one would naturally *expect* to find emptinesses and voids.

Perhaps, then, "the void in the world" does not refer to a simple vacancy or to an absence of matter. Perhaps it refers to a deficiency of another sort, which permits the supposition that the earth did in some way already exist. Rashi says that the void in the world is astonishing and amazing. Now what is it to be astonished or amazed? It is a matter of being more or less *dumbfounded*; and this means being to some degree *speechless*. A person who is struck with astonishment, or with amazement, is not immediately capable of giving an orderly and informative account of what has struck him that way.

The experience disorganizes him, and therefore he cannot readily describe it. This may happen when the experience is so unexpected that the person is thrown off balance. Then, because he is startled, the person is for the moment unprepared to grasp the nature of the experience confidently even though it is not something that is inherently difficult to comprehend. However, this is not to the point here. For, as has already been suggested, the terms employed to characterize the earth at the beginning of creation do not mean that the condition of the earth at that time was unexpected.

[4] Abraham ben Isaiah and Benjamin Sharfman, *The Pentateuch and Rashi's Commentary (Genesis): A Linear Translation into English* (Brooklyn: S. S. & R. Publishing Company, 1949), p. 3.

What the terms *tohu* and *bohu* convey is that prior to creation the condition of the earth was *indeterminate*. Genuine indeterminacy would certainly be dumbfounding. It would inevitably leave one speechless, because indeterminacy is precisely a matter of being insusceptible to coherent description. So the reason a person could not grasp the pre-creation condition of the earth discursively is not that the earth does not then exist; nor is it that the nature of the earth before creation would be so surprising that anyone observing it would be irresistibly taken aback. Rather, the person would be dumbfounded by the fact that the earth does not possess a definite nature at all: it exists, but it lacks distinct and fully articulated properties. This is the sense in which the earth is said to be "unformed". It is in a similar sense that the earth is said to be "void". It is void in the sense of being blank, with no identifiable character.

Prior to creation the earth was inchoate and hence not describable in the categories of intelligible speech. That is why anyone encountering it at that time would have been, as Rashi intimates, amazed, astonished, and (necessarily) speechless. Now this way of understanding what the passage says about the earth is confirmed by what it goes on to say about the deep. Here the text is quite unequivocal: the deep does already exist. Moreover, we may legitimately suppose that the deep was as inchoate as the earth, even though the text does not explicitly assert that it was unformed and void. For water is naturally and paradigmatically fluid, and this fluidity evokes by itself the notion of something that lacks a stable and determinate character. It is essentially characteristic of water to have no fixed place and no inherent form. Water flows and spreads freely, without inner constraint; and it accepts as its own whatever shape surrounds it. By its very nature, then, the deep is "unformed and void".

4. Although it was unformed when creation began, the deep did have a surface. We are told that there were two things over this surface: darkness, and the spirit of God (*ruach elohim*). Now why does the text refer here to the *spirit* of God? What is the significance of the fact that it does not refer simply to God Himself? The *spirit of God* and *God* are surely not the same. There is a difference between the spirit of a thing and the thing itself. Roughly speaking, the former provides the latter with its distinctive mode of animation. Of course, not everything has a spirit. Something has a spirit only insofar as (again, roughly) it is integral to its nature to be energetically purposeful. Then its spirit is the general tendency or style that in-

forms its various purposes. It is what sustains and guides the direction of its energy.[5]

Suppose the energy of an active being is sharply focused, its purposefulness wholly determinate. In that case, its spirit is fully defined. But it may be that a purposeful being does not have an altogether certain or determinate purpose. Although it is capable of purposefulness and is tending toward purposeful activity, it may not yet have settled into guiding itself steadily by any specific purpose. In that case, its purpose is not entirely actualized or clearly defined. Its spirit is, to one degree or another, still unformed. And its own nature is correspondingly indistinct.

The difference between the spirit of God and God is the difference between a relatively unactualized and a more completely actualized mode of divine existence. This corresponds to the difference between the formless state of the world before creation and the fully determinate state of the world subsequent to the creative process. At the beginning of creation, God was as unformed as the world. The divine was present and active only as an indistinct spirit; its reality was not yet that of God Himself. The nature of this divine spirit was indefinite, and its activity was vague. In the still indeterminate condition of things that prevailed prior to creation, neither the world nor God was wholly developed. The specific character of the deity— i.e., the exact direction of its purposefulness and power—had not yet been articulated or realized. Like the unshaped and fluid world itself, the divine presence was inchoate.

Consider how the text represents the divine before the sequence of creative acts, and compare this with how it refers to the divine when that sequence of acts begins. With respect to the time prior to creation, we have: "*the spirit of God* hovered over the water." With respect to the initial performance in the creative sequence, however, we have: "And *God* said: 'Let there be light.'" The spirit of God is present in the world before the initial creative act. When it comes to the performance of that act, however, it is not by the spirit of God that the act is performed. The act is performed by God Himself. Each subsequent act in the process of creation is also reported as having been performed by God rather than by the divine spirit.

A fundamental difference between the spirit of God and God is that the former, since it has no definite nature, cannot be genuinely

---

[5] Thus, "the spirit of '76". The same notion is involved when we say such things as: "His spirit will live on in the institution to which he devoted so much of himself," and "Although I cannot be present, I am with you in spirit."

active. Thus there is nothing in the text to suggest that it ever accomplishes anything or even that it ever attempts anything. One activity (and only one) is attributed to it: "the spirit of God *hovered* over the water." Now, hovering is a peculiarly vague and unproductive sort of activity. While it requires energy and may involve some movement, it closely resembles being completely at rest. Indeed, hovering is specifically designed to avoid any passage from one location to another. Its purposefulness is in this respect indecisive and without ambition. The distinctive goal of hovering is precisely to have no direction and to bring about no significant change of place. It is devoted essentially to going nowhere. Its whole purpose is to simulate and to approach total inactivity.

As long as it is devoted to nothing more than an indecisive hovering over the shapeless waters of the deep, the energy of the divine agency is basically inactive. Divine agency is then nothing more than the potentiality of an incipient but as yet unrealized God. The text explicitly marks the transition from this state of affairs to one in which the divine is more fully actualized and determinate. It does so by abandoning the term "the spirit of God", and by shifting to the term "God".

5. This transition is simultaneous with the start of the creative activity that transforms an inchoate world into an ordered cosmos. But there is more to be said. The process by which the divine becomes actualized and determinate not only *begins at the same time* as the series of acts by which divine agency fashions the cosmos. The two sequences *coincide*. Thus, each *begins with the same event*—viz., the creation of light. This first creative act both transforms a dark world into a lighted one and transforms the spirit of God into God.

What is the nature of the act? It is, of course, an act of speech: "God said, 'Let there be light'." Moreover, this act of speech is evidently effective *without any intermediation*: "God said, 'Let there be light'; and there was light." Between the utterance and its outcome, nothing intervenes. The act is not like the utterances of magic; creation is not accomplished by the work of some arcane power, subordinate to God, which is summoned and deployed by the casting of a verbal spell. Accordingly, the creative act of speech is not a command. Nor is the act effective by causing a response in something other than itself. The effectiveness of the act is provided entirely by its own creative power. It does not require or depend on anything else. Some words are spoken and, in the very speaking of these words, both the world and the divine are thereby altered. The world is lighted, and the divine spirit becomes God.

How are we to understand the relationship between these initial alterations of the world and of the divine? Consider the fact that the Hebrew word translated as "spirit", in the phrase "the spirit of God", is *ruach*. In certain other translations of the passage at hand, this word is translated as "wind"; and in still others, it is translated as "breath".[6] Now each of these three words refers to something elusive and indeterminate. Spirits, winds, and breaths are difficult to pin down. For one thing, they lack recognizable shapes or boundaries; for another, it requires considerable scientific sophistication to identify the material of which each is composed. With respect to each, then, neither its form nor its matter is easy to grasp.

Before God began creating, the divine nature was indefinite. It was present in the world only as a breath, or a wind, or a spirit. This changed when the divine began to speak. Uttering words involves shaping the breath. Similarly, the formation of a thought entails ordering the mind or spirit. Both speaking and thinking are matters of articulation, which create form by imposing distinctions upon what is previously undifferentiated. Whether it is considered an act of speech or an act of thought, then, "Let there be light" is an ordering or an articulation by which something with a distinct identity is formed. As its identity becomes definite, the spirit of God—previously formless and indeterminate—becomes God.

We must ask why the creation of the world began with the creation of light. The primary relevant difference between darkness and light is that in the light it is possible to make clear distinctions. In the darkness, no (visual) distinctions can be made. Under ordinary circumstances, of course, turning on a light reveals distinctions that already existed but that were concealed by the darkness. But the creation of light effects a more radical change. It makes possible, for the first time, the introduction of stable distinctions into a world that is previously fluid and unshaped. That is to say, it provides for the possibility of making a cosmos—an ordered and determinate system of being—out of what has hitherto existed only inchoately.

Before He began to articulate the utterances by which He created the world, God's will was formless and undefined. He had no deter-

---

[6] Rashi says, in commenting on Genesis 1:2: "The throne of glory stands [suspended] in the air and hovers over the face of the waters by the breath of the mouth of the Holy One, Blessed be He, and at His command, like a dove—which hovers over the nest" (ben Isaiah and Scharfman, *The Pentateuch and Rashi's Commentary*, pp. 3–4). Similarly, Freedman and Simon, eds., *Midrash Rabbah*, p. 20: "R. Berekiah commenced in the name of R. Judah b. R. Simon: By the word of the Lord were the heavens made, and all the host of them by the breath of His mouth (Ps. 39:6): not by labor or toil but only by a word; thus, And God said: Let there be light."

minate intentions or desires; and He did nothing but hover inde-cisively. It was only in formulating the clear-cut volitions expressed in His successive creative acts of speech that His active nature be-came focused and specific. These acts of speech were not addressed to anyone or to anything. They were resolutions, or determinations of intention, by which the spirit of God was transformed into a pur-poseful and active being. Thus *God was created by creating.* He was defined by His creation, just as the nature of the world that He cre-ated was defined by Him.

This sounds a bit like Spinoza's doctrines that God and the world are somehow one and that the order of the world is identical with the mind of God. Of course, Spinoza regards the divine order as necessary and thus as self-explanatory, while the view I am here attributing to Genesis is that a world without order is possible and in fact preceded creation. The Genesis account, as I construe it, is not rationalistic. It does not even attempt to explain *why* the incho-ate became ordered; it offers no understanding of what made the spirit of God transform itself into God. Perhaps the spirit of God possesses an inherent tendency toward order; or perhaps it *is* this tendency. Perhaps the assumption that there exists a divine spirit in the world means, in other words, precisely this: that the universe tends to acquire and sustain determinate characteristics and a stable order.

6. The final creative act is, of course, the creation of man. Now what God does in creating a man differs quite markedly and sug-gestively from what He does in His earlier creative activities. At each of the eight steps in the sequence of creation, God declares that something is to happen or to be done. The first seven declarations are uniform in pattern: (i) "Let there be light," (ii) "Let there be an expanse in the midst of the water," (iii) "Let the water below the sky be gathered into one area," (iv) "Let the earth sprout vegetation," (v) "Let there be lights in the expanse of the sky," (vi) "Let the wa-ters bring forth swarms of living creatures, and birds," and (vii) "Let the earth bring forth every kind of living creature." The eighth dec-laration diverges strikingly from this pattern. God's final utterance is: (viii) "Let *us make* man." When He comes to the creation of man, God's resolution is for the first time not that something should hap-pen or should be done, but that *He should do it Himself*.

Man is unique, then, in not having been created by an act of speech. The statement "Let us make man" enunciates the intention to create man, but it does not itself accomplish the creation. The actual creation of man is reported separately, as follows: "And God created man in His image, in the image of God He created them, male and female He created them." That the creation of human beings was not accomplished by speech is confirmed by the second account of creation. At Genesis 2:7, there is no reference to any utterance. The text there refers instead to another sort of activity altogether. "The Lord God formed man from the dust of the earth, He blew into his nostrils the breath of life, and man became a living being." In forming man out of dust, God created him, so to speak, *by hand*.[7]

In the earlier stages of the creative process, the "Let . . . " utterances are creative by themselves. They require no further or separate activity of implementation. Thus, in the account of every earlier stage except one, the report of the utterance is followed immediately, and with no indication of any intervening events, by a report ("And it was so") that the relevant creation has been accomplished.[8] There is no suggestion of mediation between the act of speech and the realization of the intention it expresses. In order for the first seven features of the world to be created, it suffices that the divine spirit or will be resolved. God creates them simply through the formation of His own nature.

When it comes to creating man, however, that is not how God does it. He begins by making up His mind, or by becoming re-

[7] Rashi says: "For everything was created by [divine] decree but he was created by the hands [of God]. For it is said (Ps. 139:5), 'And thou hast laid thy hand upon me.'" ben Isaiah and Scharfman, *The Pentateuch and Rashi's Commentary*, p. 14.

[8] The one exception is the sixth utterance ("Let the waters bring forth swarms of living creatures, and birds that fly above the earth across the expanse of the sky"), which is not followed by "And it was so." Instead, it is followed immediately by this: "God created the great sea monsters, and all the living creatures of every kind that creep, which the waters brought forth in swarms, and all the winged birds of every kind." In this respect, the account of the sixth step may seem to resemble that of the eighth; for both appear to report that God does something in addition to speaking. But I think that the significance of this resemblance must be discounted. First of all, it makes no theological sense. Second, there is a more reasonable way to explain the resemblance than by assimilating the creation of sea creatures to the creation of human beings. The statement that God created the sea monsters and the rest may be understood as merely an elaborated report of what His sixth utterance accomplished rather than as the report of additional activity undertaken to implement the sixth utterance. That utterance is creative by itself, and the report that "God created the great sea monsters" does not mean that He performed a further implementing act. It simply reports what the sixth utterance created. This way of construing the sixth step clearly cannot be employed with respect to the eighth. For the eighth utterance ("Let us make . . . ") is unmistakably *prospective*. It cannot be understood except as proposing to perform a further act of creation.

solved, to create man. But this resolution of His will does not suffice. It is only preliminary to the activity by which the creation of man is actually accomplished. Unlike every other step in the sequence of creation, God's final creative act is manifestly not an act of self-definition. He does not create man by forming Himself but by shaping some dust—that is, by *doing something to something else*. The creation of man does not come about by a simple articulation of God's volition or thought or breath. It is a mediated process, in which forming the intention is one thing and implementing it effectively is another. God does not create man by a purely reflexive act, which is creative just by advancing the development of His own nature. The creation of man requires work.

This has a large and resonant import. It means that man, unlike all other creatures of God, is genuinely an artifact. Human existence and human nature are not created sheerly through the self-definition of the divine; God's formation of humans is not tantamount to His formation of Himself. Their coming into being is distinct from any modification of the divine will. The creation of man is unique in being emphatically not identical with the articulation of an intention. And since human existence was not begun by a determination of God's volitional nature, human history is therefore not unequivocally subject to the determinations of God's will.

This implies that, with respect to man, God's omnipotence is limited. Just as the creation of human beings required that God do some real work—it being evidently insufficient for Him merely to resolve that humans should exist—so God cannot exercise direct power over mankind by mere acts of the divine will.[9] In creating human beings, God created something separate—something whose being is distinct and radically other than His own. In other words, mankind does not exist just as an articulation of God's will. Therefore, human beings are not wholly dependent on divine volition or immediately subject to it.

Man is a product of God's handiwork. In producing people, God produced creatures whose nature is independent of the direct or unmediated control of His will. This explains, for example, why God, when He expels Adam and Eve from Eden, posts guards at the gates. He cannot achieve His intention that Adam and Eve stay out

---

[9] Of course God can exercise *indirect* power over human beings by volition alone, since the rest of nature does respond without mediation to His will. So God can endeavor to control man indirectly by directly affecting conditions (i.e., just by making up His mind) which are important to human interests.

of Eden simply by forming a volition that they do so. Insofar as the world is formed by the formation of His own will, God can shape it by shaping Himself—i.e., by articulating His own thoughts and volitions. But in dealing with man, whose being is distinct and separate from Himself, God can exercise control only through intermediaries.

But why did God create something distinct from Himself? By introducing into the world a being other than His own, whose behavior is determined by its own nature rather than by His will, He appears to abandon unequivocal control over His creation. Thus he seems deliberately to undermine His own omnipotence. Why would He do this? Perhaps He did it because in a world in which everything is determined simply by His will, there would really be nothing other than Himself; and His omnipotence would therefore be meaningless. God's control of the world would in that case be nothing more than self-control. It would be power over nothing but Himself!

There is a kind of paradox in the notion of omnipotence. A being enjoys absolute omnipotence only if its effective exercise of unlimited power requires nothing more than a determination of its will. If its intentions themselves do not suffice but must be implemented by further exertions, its power is to that extent qualified. The insufficiency of its volition implies some external resistance, which cannot be overcome without work. It follows that a being possesses unlimited omnipotence only if there is nothing other than itself over which to exercise its power. For (a) unequivocal omnipotence entails unmediated control, while (b) the being of anything that is subject to unmediated control belongs to whatever exercises that control.

Thus, a wholly omnipotent being would necessarily be alone. There would be nothing other than itself over which to exercise power. It could do nothing but form intentions and thereby alter its own nature. In a sense, then, it would be quite powerless. God needs a being other than Himself, then, in order to exercise His power at all meaningfully. But this means that for the meaningful exercise of His power, He needs a being over which His power is not absolute.

7. The fact that God and man are separate is the source of an ineradicable tension in the careers of each. The story of man's yearning to diminish the distance between himself and the divine has often been explored. Less familiar is the story of God's struggle to accommodate the reality of a being other than His own.

The texts make it clear that God has found this struggle frustrating and even demoralizing. Indeed, at the time of Noah it actually led Him to believe for a while that His creation of man had been a mistake:

> And the Lord regretted that He had made
> man on earth, and His heart was
> saddened. The Lord said, "I will blot out
> from the earth the men whom I created—
> men together with beasts, creeping
> things, and birds of the sky; for I regret
> that I made them." (Gen. 6:6–7)

Only by the heartening example of Noah was God persuaded to change His mind about this:

> Noah was a righteous man; he was
> blameless in his age; Noah walked with
> God. (Gen. 6:9)

Despite his distinctness as an independent being, and his capacity therefore to diverge from God's will, Noah was not distant from God. On the contrary, he "walked with God". It was in this cohesion with God that his righteousness and his blamelessness consisted. The example of Noah convinced God that, even though men are beyond the control of His unmediated will, it is not inevitable that there be a distance between His will and the will of man.

God yearns, just as man does, to overcome the distance between them. Since man is separate and can therefore act only by his own will, this cannot be accomplished unless man accedes voluntarily to the divine order. Accordingly, it is necessary for God to threaten, to persuade, and to bargain. This accounts for the importance of covenant.

But why does God care whether men act in harmony with His will? Why does He so badly want man to walk with Him? The answer is that He requires man to accept a divine order so as to complete His creation both of the world and of Himself. It is through the articulation of order that God's being is realized and defined. And it is only to the extent that the inchoate is transformed into a cosmos that He exists with a determinate and actualized nature. As long as there is anything outside that cosmos, neither the world nor God Himself is complete. They remain to some extent formless and unactualized.

If man's will is disharmonious with the will of God, there is a boundary beyond which divine order does not prevail. In that case, God is not omnipresent. Being is ultimately fragmented. As there is a limit to the extent of divine order, so the cosmos is incomplete and the actualization of the divine is unfinished. It is for this reason that the distance of man is a threat to God.

It is understandable why Genesis does not report that, after creating man, "God saw that this was good." Nor is it any wonder that God may sometimes be inclined to think that He made a mistake in creating man. But God has resolved not to destroy mankind. Instead He negotiates, He cajoles, He tries to make a deal. Endlessly, he seeks to induce man to accept at least some kind of coherence with the divine. This would not erase the separateness of God and man; human volition would be as independent as before. But it would at least entail that human life is ordered as God wishes it to be ordered. Hence it would entail that His order prevails universally, albeit not exclusively by His unmediated volitional control. God has no better hope for completion. God and humans can never be one and the same, as God is one and the same with the rest of His creation. He needs man to walk with Him. He depends on mankind's cooperation. Without it, divine order cannot be sustained throughout the world.

According to one Talmudic view, God reckons the creation of the world as having been finished only when the Tabernacle was erected. That is, there was a complete and fully ordered cosmos only when His law was decisively established as determining the affairs of Israel.[10] The point is not merely that the created world is *unsatisfactory* until human beings accept the divine law but that it is not *complete* until then.[11] Until there is a coherent harmony between man and God, there is no universal order; that is, the cosmos is unfinished. God cannot complete the process of His creation alone.[12]

---

[10] "At the erection of the Tabernacle, as it says, And he that presented his offering *the* first day (Num. 7:12) meaning, the first of the world's creation, for God said, 'It is as though on that day I created My world'" (*Midrash Rabbah*, p. 25).

[11] As the editors of the Midrashic text point out: "The world is not really created until man does God's will, here symbolized by the erection of the Temple, and thereby His original design to be at one with man is fulfilled" (ibid., n. 4).

[12] The ideas I have tried to develop in this essay derive from conversations with R. Sidney Morgenbesser.

Part III

❦

REASON AND THE NATURE
OF THE GOD OF FAITH

WILLIAM P. ALSTON

❦

Aquinas on Theological Predication:
A Look Backward and a Look Forward

i

The question of how to understand predicates in their application to God has preoccupied religious thinkers for as long as they have been reflectively aware of the following two facts. (1) The terms we use in speaking of God are taken from our talk of creatures, particularly human beings. That is, we first understand what it is for a human being to make something, to communicate a message, to condemn and to forgive, what it is for a human being to have powers, virtues, and attitudes. Then, on the basis of that understanding, we use such terms to say something of God. (2) God is so fundamentally and so enormously different from human beings and other creatures that it seems impossible for terms to be true of God and of creatures in just the same sense. Hence it would seem that if we are to have any chance of speaking truly about God, the terms we use will have to undergo some change of meaning from their original use in talk about creatures. And just what change is that, and what does it leave us with?

A great variety of positions has been taken on this matter over the course of some two thousand years, and the issues are very much with us today. In this chaotic scene one treatment stands out: that of St. Thomas Aquinas. Because of the exceptional power of his intellect and his sensitivity to many aspects of the problem, Thomas produced an account of unmatched subtlety, complexity, and depth. As I shall be arguing, he attempted to hold together more themes than can comfortably coexist in a single coherent account, and, even insofar as it is coherent, his view and the arguments for it are subject to criticism. Still, in our philosophical endeavors we stand on the shoulders of giants, and preeminent among those giants on this topic is St. Thomas. There can be no better way to advance our understanding of this issue than to work through his treatment and use what we learn therefrom in our attempts to move forward.

A word about sources. My discussion focuses on the explicit discussion of this problem in the two Summas, the *Summa contra gentiles (SCG)* and the *Summa theologiae˘ (ST)*. These sections represent Thomas's most extensive mature discussion of the topic. We must remember, however, that much of Thomas's treatment of fundamental philosophical issues comes up incidentally in the discussion of one or another theological issue, and a number of these discussions are relevant to the understanding of my central texts. These treatments have to do with the semantics of terms, the nature and origin of concepts, the general metaphysical background, and, most centrally relevant, the nature of analogically related meanings. Hence I draw on various bits of the Thomistic corpus in my interpretation of the discussion of theological predicates in the two Summas. But since this essay makes no pretensions to be a work of Aquinas scholarship, I will not be exploring those sources in the way I would if that were my aspiration. Instead, much of that work is behind the scene, and I rarely cite chapter and verse.

I am all too well aware of the enormous quantity of literature to which this tiny stretch of the Thomistic corpus has given rise. One who offers to add to this already swollen stream must justify such apparently gratuitous behavior. My apologia is in two parts. (1) No one, in the literature with which I am acquainted, has noted the particular stresses and strains in the Thomistic view with which I shall be dealing. (2) As for criticism of the view, after the internal tensions have been resolved, most of the literature is too respectful of the master to dare to criticize, or if this inhibition is lacking, the criticism is generally marred by (usually gross) misunderstandings of the target. There is still work to be done.

ii

In both Summas, before Thomas develops his view of the analogical meaning of predicates in application to God, he establishes certain basic points concerning theological predicates. Following the order in *ST* I, 13, Thomas first, in article 1, answers various objections to the possibility of using any term to say anything that is true of God.[1] Then in article 2 he contends that terms can be said of God *substantialiter*, to say something of *what God is*, rather than what He is not or how He is related to other things. In article 3 he argues that some terms can be used literally (*proprie*) of God[2], namely, those that do not include in their meaning the imperfect mode in which a perfection is realized in creatures, for example, such terms as 'being', 'good', and 'living'. Let's call these "pure perfection terms". By contrast, those terms that do include a creaturely mode in their meaning, for example, 'rock' and 'lion', can be said of God only metaphorically. Finally, in article 4 Aquinas rebuts the suggestion that because of the simplicity of God, the fact that there is no real distinction between different aspects of God, all words said of God are synonyms. The crucial move in response to that claim is to invoke the principle that words signify things through the concepts we form of those things. Since we cannot think of the divine nature in one fell conceptual swoop but only as divided up conceptually into different aspects, our talk about God will inevitably inherit that limitation. Thomas clearly recognizes that this implies a fundamental inadequacy in our talk of God. The upshot of these articles is that we can make significant and true predications of God, in which the terms are used literally and nonsynonymously, and which succeed, though inadequately, in specifying something of what God is. These results set up the problems of how "pure perfection" terms are to be understood when applied to God, just what they are telling us of what God is, and how this is related to what they tell us about creatures when applied to them.[3]

Aquinas's positive doctrine concerning the semantics of predicates in application to God is put in terms of the trichotomy: univocal, equivocal, analogical. The first thing to note about those terms is

---

[1] Aquinas, along with many other writers on this subject, does not make explicit the 'truly' qualification. He puts the objection just as "nullum nomen potest dici de Deo" (no word can be said of God). But the truth constraint is obviously in the background. If it doesn't matter whether what we say is true or not, and if we avoid category mistakes (if that qualification is needed), obviously any term can be predicated of God. The only chance for a serious problem, with respect to terms that are commonly predicated of God, such as 'forgives', 'preserves', 'is omniscient', is as to whether they can be *truly* predicated of God, whether we can use them to make explicit something that is true of Him.

[2] One reason for translating *proprie* as 'literally' is that the main contrast to *proprie* is 'metaphorically'.

[3] In the subsequent discussion I refer to various points Thomas makes in these articles.

that they have to do with the semantic relation of two or more uses of a term. It makes no sense to ask of a word apart from any contexts of its use, "Is it univocal?" or "Does it have a univocal meaning?" That would be like asking of a thing whether it is similar or whether it is twice. Similar to what? Twice what? And so with univocity, and so on.[4] A term is *univocal* in two or more uses when it bears the same sense (meaning) in those uses. A term is *equivocal* in two or more uses when it bears different senses in those uses. Analogy, in the semantic sense that is in question here, is a species of equivocity. A term is used analogically in two or more employments when it is used in different senses but those senses are related to each other in appropriate ways. Just what those appropriate ways are remains to be considered.

When working with this trichotomy, Aquinas always takes the first order of business to be to show that terms are not, and cannot be, used univocally of God and creature. All Aquinas's reasons for this, at least all those that make explicit the differences between God and creatures that prevent univocity[5], stem from one basic divine attribute—simplicity. Twentieth-century philosophers, in arguing against univocity, are more likely to cite divine immateriality or atemporality, and theologians are more likely to make unspecific appeals to "otherness" or to God's not counting as "a being". But we hear none of that from Aquinas. He certainly didn't take the immateriality of God to be a bar to univocity, though he clearly recognizes that certain terms need to be refined before they can be literally predicated of God, to remove elements of their meaning that render them predicable only of material substances.[6] For him it is simplicity that makes all the difference.

---

[4] It is a currently fashionable view that no word has a meaning, or indeed any semantic properties at all, apart from contexts of use. I certainly don't wish to subscribe to any such doctrine as that. We can specify the meaning(s) a word has in the language without "putting" it in a context of use in order to do so. (Of course, we can illustrate these points by citing contexts of use; and it is also true that for a word to have a meaning is for it to have a certain potentiality, which is realized by using it in various contexts.) Univocity, equivocity, and analogicality are distinguished from other semantic terms in having to do with the ways different uses of a term are semantically related.

[5] For an argument that is not explicit in this way, see *ST* I, 13, 5, sed contra. The second argument there is based on the thesis that "God is more distant from any creature than any two creatures are from each other". No attempt is made to specify what differences are in question.

[6] See, e.g., his suggestion that we remove the reference to bodily goings-on in emotion terms to render them applicable to God (*ST* I, 20, 1, ad 1).

Since it is so important for the argument against univocity, I had better say a word about simplicity. It is a matter of there being no distinction at all between any divine parts or aspects of any sort whatever. This means not only that God has no spatial or material parts but also that there is no distinction between different properties, states, or activities of God, no distinction between God, the individual, and His nature or essence, and no distinction between essence and existence. Whatever you say truly of God, it is the same "thing" that makes it true. There are many different things to truly say of God, but that diversity is not reflected in any diversity in what makes all these sayings true.[7]

This very fundamental difference between God and any creature is reflected in each of the specific reasons Aquinas gives for the impossibility of God-creature univocity. In *ST* I, 13, 5, the argument that occupies center stage in the Responsio runs as follows.

> The perfection words that we use in speaking of creatures all differ in meaning and each one signifies a perfection as something distinct from all others. Thus when we say that a man is wise, we signify his wisdom as something distinct from the other things about him—his essence, for example, his powers or his existence. But when we use this word about God we do not intend to signify something distinct from his essence, power or existence. When 'wise' is used of a man, it so to speak contains and delimits the aspect of man that it signifies, but this is not so when it is used of God; what it signifies in God is not confined by the meaning of our word but goes beyond it. Hence it is clear that the word 'wise' is not used in the same sense of God and man, and the same is true of all other words, so they cannot be used univocally of God and creatures.[8]

Why is it that when we apply a predicate to God "we do not intend to signify something distinct from his essence, power or existence"? Obviously, because we realize that God is simple, and hence we would not intend to say anything that could not be true of a simple

---

[7] *ST* I, 3. Thomas's rock-bottom characterization of God would seem to be that He is Being Itself, or Existence Itself, the complete richness of Being, the pure act of existing. This has to be understood in such a way that the pure act of existing can include, without any real internal distinctions, everything that it takes to make a being supremely perfect—including perfect knowledge, power, and so on—and the activity that springs from that supreme perfection.

[8] Translations from *ST* I, 13 are by Herbert McCabe, O.P., in volume 3 of the Blackfriars edition (London: Eyre & Spottiswoode, 1964).

being.[9] And because the wisdom of a simple being is not really distinct from his powers, his activities, or his knowledge, we would be saying something false if we spoke of God with that intention.

Again, the first argument of the sed contra is as follows.

> 'Wisdom', for example, means a quality when it is used of creatures, but not when it is applied to God. So then it must have a different meaning, for we have here a difference in the genus which is part of the definition.

'Wisdom' does not "mean a quality" when applied to God, just because a quality is ipso facto something distinct from the bearer of the quality. And God does not "have" qualities in that way, because no such distinction can be found in Him.

Let's turn to *SCG* I, 32, "That Nothing Is Predicated Univocally of God and Other Things". In section 2, Aquinas argues that "the forms of the things God has made do not measure up to a specific likeness of the divine power; for the things that God has made receive in a divided and particular way that which in Him is found in a simple and universal way".[10] And he takes this to show that no term can be applied univocally to creatures and God. We shall scrutinize this inference later.

In section 3 he goes on to argue that "even though the rest of things were to receive a form that is absolutely the same as it is in God, yet they do not receive it according to the same mode of being. For . . . there is nothing in God that is not the divine being itself, which is not the case with other things" (p. 144). And the same conclusion is drawn. Again, simplicity is the crucial assumption ("there is nothing in God that is not the divine being itself").[11]

---

[9] Thus Aquinas's theory of theological predication would seem to be applicable only to the religious discourse of those who do recognize the simplicity of God. Does this exclude most believers? Presumably Aquinas would appeal to some doctrine of "implicit knowledge" unsophisticated believers have of such matters as divine simplicity. Anachronistically, he could make use of Hilary Putnam's doctrine of the "division of linguistic labor", according to which some of the semantics of a term, even as used by the unsophisticated, is carried by what the experts in the society know about what the term applies to.

[10] Translations of *SCG* are from *On the Truth of the Catholic Faith*, trans. A. C. Pegis (Garden City, N.Y.: Doubleday & Co., Inc., 1955), Bk. I: God. This passage is on p. 143 of vol. I.

[11] The other arguments in chap. 32 depend on other features of the Thomistic metaphysics and account of predication, e.g., on the notion of "participation" in a form, which holds of creatures and not of God, and on a certain way in which God is prior

Aquinas then argues that "we are not merely equivocating when we use the same word, as some have said, for if this were so we could never argue from statements about creatures to statements about God" (*ST* 13, 5, R). And, of course, the claim that we can make valid arguments of this sort is crucial for Aquinas, since he holds that all our natural knowledge of God is based on such arguments. Indeed he holds that our natural conception of God is built up in this way, by thinking of God as what is related to creatures in certain ways, for example, as their ultimate cause. In *SCG* I, 33, we find this argument along with others.

> For in equivocals by chance [the use of the same word for two quite unrelated meanings] there is no order or reference of one to another. . . . But this is not the situation with names said of God and creatures, since we note in the community of such names the order of cause and effect. . . . (Sec. 2)

> Furthermore, where there is pure equivocation, there is no likeness in things themselves; there is only the unity of a name. But . . . there is a certain mode of likeness of things to God. [For God makes creatures as so many modes of likeness of His nature.] (Sec. 3)

All these arguments against pure equivocity stem from the basic idea that God is the cause of the existence of creatures, and in such a way that, as with all causality according to Aquinas, what is produced in the effect preexists, perhaps in a different mode, in the cause.

iii

If these terms are applied neither univocally nor purely equivocally, only one possibility remains. "We must say, therefore, that words are used of God and creatures in an analogical way, that is in accordance with a certain order [*proportionem*] between them" (*ST* I, 13, 5, R). Aquinas is speaking here only of "pure perfection" terms

---

to creatures—by virtue of the fact that everything is predicated of God "essentially". Most if not all of these arguments themselves rest on the simplicity assumption. For example in the last argument "things being predicated of God essentially" is explained as follows. "God is called being as being entity itself, and He is called good as being goodness itself". God does not just *share* in goodness; He *is* goodness. If this were a work of Aquinas scholarship I would go through all the arguments. But I take the ones cited in the text to be the most important ones.

(*hujusmodi nomina*); others, if appropriate in any way, are, as we have seen, said of God metaphorically. Let's keep firmly in mind the point that 'analogical' is being used here to designate a certain relation between two different senses of a term, a relation that is such as to make the senses linked to each other or relevant to each other in a way in which "purely equivocal" senses are not, as when 'pen' is used both for a writing implement and an enclosure for keeping pigs. We must be careful not to read Thomas on analogy in terms of the dominant current meaning of the term in which it has to do with some likeness or similarity between things. Analogically related uses of terms, or the things they are applied to in these uses, need not be markedly similar to each other. Similarity is only one of the relations that can tie together analogically related senses. *Analogia* is a Latin term of Greek derivation, and in the Greek it was originally used for mathematical proportions, or equality of ratios. In the course of its career it broadened out to encompass relations of any sort, and that is the dominant meaning in Thomas. Most basically, when two uses are related "analogically," they are related by virtue of some significant relation between what they signify or the things to which they are applied. So the crucial question we need to answer in order to understand Thomas's dictum that pure perfection terms are said analogically of God and creatures is: By virtue of what sort of relation are the two senses significantly connected to each other?

In order to attend properly to what is said about this in the two Summas we have to set aside a great weight of Thomistic tradition. In 1498, Cardinal Cajetan (Thomas de Vio) wrote his *De nominum analogia (The Analogy of Names)*,[12] and it quickly became established as the definitive systematization of the Thomistic doctrine of analogy. In this treatise Cajetan distinguished three basic types of analogy— inequality, attribution, and proportionality. The first need not concern us here. Analogy of attribution is found where the term is primarily applied to one subject (or applied to one subject in the primary sense), and the understanding of the other application is given by some relation that the subject of that application has to the former subject. This is often a causal relation. Aquinas's favorite example is 'healthy', as applied primarily to an animal, and then applied by analogy to urine as a sign of animal health, to medicine as a cause of animal health, to diet as conducive to animal health (here

---

[12] *The Analogy of Names and the Concept of Being*, trans. E. A. Bushinski and H. J. Koren (Pittsburgh, Pa.: Duquesne University Press, 1953). The passage on which Cajetan principally relies for his interpretation is found in the *Commentary on the Sentences*, Bk. I, Dist. 19, Q. 5, a. 2, ad 1.

we would be more likely to say 'healthful'), and so on. Analogy of attribution is omnipresent in language. Thus if we think of 'academic' as applied primarily to a certain range of activities (teaching, learning, etc.), we can say that 'academic salaries' are salaries paid for engaging in such activities, 'academic buildings' are buildings in which such activities go on, and so on.

Analogy of proportionality is found where there is a likeness of two relationships. (A proportion is a relation; proportionality is a similarity between two proportions.) Thus we may say that the way a computer is related to some material that appears on a monitor is similar to the way a human being is related to some recalled information, a similarity that undergirds analogically related senses of 'remember'. Again the relation of a human being to what she does is similar to the relation of an inanimate body to its reaction to the forces acting on it, in such a way as to give rise to analogically related senses of 'behave' or 'act'. It may be objected that in these cases, and other putative cases of analogy of proportionality, one could find or construct a term that could be used univocally to say what is in common in the two cases by virtue of which the relations are similar. Even if this were so, it would not show that the terms in question—'act', 'behave', 'remember'—are not used in accordance with an analogy of proportionality. But it would encourage us to suppose that this kind of analogical talk could be replaced by more fine-grained talk in which all the terms are used univocally. That is, we could replace unspecific references to similarity with a precise specification of the respects of similarity and dissimilarity. However, the Aristotelian-Thomistic tradition has been committed to the thesis that certain predications are essentially or irretrievably analogical, in that we are incapable of getting below the proportional similarity so as to specify features that are wholly in common. The favorite examples for this are the "transcendentals", terms that apply across the Aristotelian categories. Thus it is frequently said that 'being' is said analogically of substance, quality, quantity, relation, and so on. A substance and a quality each *is* in a way appropriate to its category, but there is no way of specifying a neutral sense of being, such that a term for that sense is univocally predicable of things in any category. Needless to say, this is all highly controversial. I find it illuminating to think of the "essential analogy" thesis as amounting to the claim that at certain points we can manage at best an "imperfect abstraction"; we cannot go all the way in forming a concept that applies equally to each item in the extension of the term; instead the best we can do is to form a cluster or family of related concepts. We can "see" or "show" their mutual "belongingness", but we can't spell it out in terms of strictly common properties. A currently prominent species of this genus of "imperfectly abstracted concepts" is the Wittgensteinian concept of family resemblance terms.[13]

Cajetan held that the analogy of proportionality is the only "true" analogy of names and gave it pride of place in his treatment. And until quite recently the Thomistic tradition has followed him in this. Thus it has been widely supposed that in holding that terms are said analogically of God and creatures, Aquinas was attributing an analogy of proportionality to these uses.[14] If one approaches the discussion in the two Summas against the background of this tradition, one will be quite surprised to learn that Thomas gives us no hint of a similarity of relations or any of the other distinguishing features of the analogy of proportionality. On the contrary, he seems for all the world to be saying that predications of a term to God and creatures are related according to an analogy of attribution.

> We can distinguish two kinds of analogical or 'proportional' uses of language. First there is the case of one word being used of two things because each of them has some order or relation to a third thing. Thus we use the word 'healthy' of both a diet and a complexion because each of these has some relation to health in a man, the former as a cause, the latter as a symptom of it. Secondly, there is the case of the same word used of two things because of some relation that one has to the other— as 'healthy' is used of the diet and the man because the diet is the cause of the health in the man.
>
> In this way some words are used neither univocally nor purely equivocally of God and creatures, but analogically, for we cannot speak of God at all except in the language we use of creatures, and so whatever is said both of God and creatures is said in virtue of the order that creatures have to God as to their source and cause in which all the perfections of things pre-exist transcendently. (*ST* I, 13, 5, R)

The exposition is quite parallel in *SCG* I, 34, 1–4. The only significant difference is that it is made more explicit that the analogy in theological predication is according to the second of the two types. "Now, the names said of God and things are not said analogically according to the first mode of analogy, since we should then have to

[13] See Ludwig Wittgenstein, *Philosophical Investigations*, trans. G. E. M. Anscombe (New York: Macmillan Co., 1953), pt. I, secs. 66–67.

[14] See, e.g., Jacques Maritain, *The Degrees of Knowledge*, trans. G. B. Phelan (New York: Charles Scribner's Sons, 1959), Appendix II; R. Garrigou-Lagrange, *God: His Existence and His Nature*, trans. Dom Bede Rose (St. Louis & London: B. Herder Book Co., 1946), vol. I, pp. 213–23; G. B. Phelan, *St. Thomas and Analogy* (Milwaukee: Marquette University Press, 1948), p. 35.

posit something prior to God, but according to the second mode" (*SCG* I, 34, 4).[15] Thus in both Summas Thomas clearly puts forward the analogy of attribution as the one by which divine-human predication is to be construed.

But how can this be? This would seem to come into stark conflict with a thesis at the heart of the Thomistic philosophical theology, namely, that there is a divine-human commonality with respect to "perfections". This is usually put by saying that the perfections of all things are in God.

> All the perfections of all things are in God. . . . This may be seen from two considerations. First, because whatever perfection exists in an effect must be found in the producing cause: either in the same formality . . . or in a more eminent degree. . . . Since therefore God is the first producing cause of things, the perfections of all things must pre-exist in God in a more eminent way. . . . Second . . . God is being itself, of itself subsistent. Consequently, He must contain within Himself the whole perfection of being. . . . Now all the perfections of all things pertain to the perfection of being: for things are perfect precisely so far as they have being after some fashion. It follows therefore that the perfection of no thing is wanting to God.[16] (*ST* I, 4, 2, R; see also *SCG* I, 29, "On the Likeness of Creatures to God")

And so it would seem to follow that any pure perfection, like goodness or knowledge, will be found both in God and creatures, though, as we shall note in more detail, in a different mode.

[15] It is not entirely clear that Aquinas's reason for rejecting the first mode is cogent. Presumably his thought is as follows. Where the analogy between asserting P of x and y is of the first sort, it holds because each of them is to be explained in terms of a relation in which they stand to a third item, z. But that would require that a predication of P to that third item is prior to the predication of P to God. And nothing is prior to God. But as we shall note later, Aquinas does acknowledge that "from the point of view of our use of the word we apply it first to creatures because we know them first", even though "from the point of view of what the word means it is used primarily of God and derivatively of creatures, for what the word means—the perfection it signifies—flows from God to the creature" (*ST* 13, 6, R. See also *SCG* I, 34, 5–6). But in order to have an analogical use according to the first mode, the "analogy of many to one", it need only be true that the one is prior to the many "from the point of view of our use of the word". It need not also be prior in causality. Indeed, in Aquinas's favorite example of this mode of analogy, what is prior to the two analogical uses, viz., health of the animal, is not prior in the order of causality but only in the order of the use of the word. However, whatever is to be said about this argument, it seems clear that, as Thomas is thinking of it, the sense of 'God is wise' is to be understood by the relation of God to human wisdom, rather than both of them being understood by their relation to some third subject to which 'wise' is applied.

[16] Translations from *ST* other than I, 13, are taken from *Basic Writings of Saint Thomas Aquinas*, ed. A. C. Pegis (New York: Random House, 1944). The translation is a revision by Pegis of the translation by Laurence Shapcote.

The reason this seems to conflict with the central passages on analogical meaning is that in Aquinas's paradigm case of the analogy of attribution the analogy does not involve any commonality, or even similarity, of property predicated by the term in each attribution. What makes urine, medicine, or diet *healthy* (or 'healthful') is certainly not the same as, or even similar to, what makes an animal body healthy. What it is for a body to be healthy is, let's say, that its vital functions are being carried out properly. But what makes the medicine healthful is that it tends to correct certain deviations from the former: what makes the urine healthy is that it is an indication of the former; and so on. It is by virtue of these relations to animal health, not by virtue of any similarity between what we are saying of the secondary analogates[17] and animal health, that the term is analogically applied to them all. But if this is our model for the analogical predication of goodness to God and creatures—an analogy based on the causal relation between the analogates—then in saying that God is good, we would simply be saying that God is the cause of goodness in creatures, just as in saying that this medicine is healthful we are saying that it is the cause of health in an animal body. We would be doing this rather than attributing an intrinsic property to God, one that is shared to some extent by, or imitated, or participated in by, the creature. And just this interpretation is roundly rejected in *ST* I, 13, 2.

> Firstly . . . God is just as much the cause of bodies as he is of goodness in things; so if 'God is good' means no more than that God is the cause of goodness in things, why not say 'God is a body' on the grounds that he is the cause of bodies? . . . Secondly, it would follow that everything we said of God would be true only in a secondary sense, as when we say a diet is 'healthy', meaning merely that it causes health in the one who takes it. . . . Thirdly, this is not what people want to say when they talk about God. When a man speaks of the 'living God' he does not simply want to say that God is the cause of our life. (*ST* I, 13, 2, R)

Thus Aquinas not only rejects the interpretation of 'God is good' that his explicit discussion of analogical meaning would seem to suggest. He seems in the passage just quoted to distance himself from the very example he used to explain the relevant mode of analogy.[18]

[17] An "analogate" is the subject of an analogical predication.

[18] All this provides aid and comfort to the Cajetan party. For according to Cajetan's general account of analogy, the analogy of proportionality is the only one that involves "intrinsic attribution" in all the analogates, that is, the only one that involves an important commonality in the properties attributed.

If there is a way out of this impasse, it will be based on the point that the health example is designed to illustrate some features of the theological analogy and not others. In particular, it is designed to illustrate the fact that attributions of, for example, goodness to God and creatures are related via a relation of the analogates, in this case a causal relation of a special sort (creator to creature). That fact is a defining feature of the analogy of attribution. But that there is no important commonality in what is attributed to each of the analogates is not a necessary or invariable feature of this mode of analogy. That is true of the health example, but since it is not essential to analogy of attribution, we are not constrained to extrapolate that as well to the divine-creature case. And in fact Aquinas gives us sufficient warning not to do so, though he could have been more explicit about this. At the end of the canonical statement of theological analogy quoted from *ST* I, 13, 5, he says that "whatever is said both of God and creatures is said in virtue of the order that creatures have to God as to their *source* and cause *in which all the perfections of things pre-exist transcendently*" (emphasis added). Consider also what, to my knowledge, is the closest Aquinas comes to telling us in so many words what the analogically related sense is in which a predicate like 'good' is applied to God. In *ST* I, 13, 2, after giving his reasons for rejecting the purely causal and the purely negative interpretations, he says: "'God is good' therefore does not mean the same as 'God is the cause of goodness' or 'God is not evil'; it means that *what we call 'goodness' in creatures pre-exists in God in a higher way*." To expand on this a bit, the meaning of 'God is good' is not derived from 'Sam is good' in terms of a purely causal relation, as in the health example, for that would not preserve the intention of attributing a commonality of property (form). On the other hand, the causal dependence of creatures on God is fundamental for the analogy; it is because of this that we can significantly speak of God in terms originally applied to creatures. *But the causality here is of such a sort as to involve transmission of form (perfection) from cause to effect.* Hence in deriving the sense of the predicate in application to God from its sense in application to creatures we are exploiting the causal dependence of the prior analogate on the posterior one (in the order of meaning derivation), but we are doing so in awareness of the fact that by virtue of this causal dependence there is, and must be, a commonality in intrinsic form, though possessed in more and less perfect ways. Hence though the analogy here is an analogy of attribution, like the case of health in animal and medicine, and also like it in being based on a causal relation, it is unlike it in that the crucial relation guarantees a commonality of intrinsic property between the analogates, and hence that commonality is part of what is being asserted in the derivative attribution.

This approach to the matter is put by Battista Mondin in terms of a distinction between an "extrinsic" and an "intrinsic" analogy of attribution.[19] Both the health case and the goodness of creature and God case exemplify the analogy of attribution, because in both cases the analogy is based on a relation between the analogates. But in the one case this relation founds a commonality in intrinsic property, and in the other case it does not. This runs counter to Cajetanist orthodoxy, according to which commonality of intrinsic property is found only in the analogy of proportionality.

Note that in specifying the divine sense of pure perfection terms in this way Aquinas makes no pretense of giving a positive account of what this higher way is in which the perfection exists in God. Thus his account is much less specific or contentful than it might conceivably be. He does lay down a number of negative specifications, all of which are involved in the doctrine of simplicity. The perfection is not possessed by God in any way that requires having a body, that requires His being distinct from the perfection possessed, that requires this perfection being distinct from others, and so on. But Aquinas gives every indication that he does not by any means aspire to give a concrete positive sense of what it is for a simple being to know something or will something or love someone or to be omniscient or omnipotent. He does, indeed, apply various general principles concerning these perfections to God, for example, that one wills only what one cognizes as good and that one knows other things by way of a "species" of the thing in the mind.[20] But all this too is stated in terms appropriate to nonsimple beings. There is no attempt to say what it is for a cognitive subject to "have" a species of the object known in such a way that the species and the knowing are not distinct from the knower. Again, Aquinas does say that for God the "species" through which He knows everything He knows is His own nature. But, again, no attempt is made to give us a concrete sense of how that is possible, and, more crucially, how it is possible that that "nature" through which S knows x

---

[19] See Battista Mondin, *The Principle of Analogy in Protestant and Catholic Theology* (The Hague: Martinus Nijhoff, 1968), chap. 2, secs. 8–11, and chap. 4. I have learned much from Mondin's treatment of the whole topic. An alternative non-Cajetanist approach is set forth powerfully and persuasively in Ralph M. McInerny, *The Logic of Analogy: An Interpretation of St. Thomas* (The Hague: Martinus Nijhoff, 1961).

[20] I will return to this point in another connection.

is not distinct from S itself, from S's existence, and S's other activities.[21]

Thus someone who is looking for as full-blooded a conception of God's knowledge, volition, love, or power as we have of human knowledge, and so on, will be disappointed with what he gets from Aquinas. But then that would have been a thoroughly misguided expectation. As we shall see in more detail in the next section, given the fact that all our forms of thought and speech are fitted to deal with complex beings, it should come as no surprise that we are unable to develop a robust conception of the nature, properties, and activities of an absolutely simple being in which no real distinctions are to be found.

One more gap needs to be filled before we have a fully rounded picture. In *SCG* I, 34, 1, Thomas explains analogical predication as being "according to an order or reference to something one". In *ST* I, 13, 6, R, he makes it explicit that in analogically related predications there is a primary analogate by reference to which (by virtue of relations of other analogates to which) the other analogically related predications have to be explained.

> Whenever a word is used analogically of many things, it is used of them because of some order or relation they have to some central thing. In order to explain an extended or analogical use of a word it is necessary to mention this central thing. Thus you cannot explain what you mean by a 'healthy' diet without mentioning the health of the man of which it is the cause; similarly you must understand 'healthy' as applied to a man before you can understand what is meant by a 'healthy complexion' which is the symptom of that health. The primary application of the word is to the central thing that has to be understood first.

Thomas goes on to say that "all words used metaphorically of God apply primarily to creatures. When used of God they signify merely a certain parallelism between God and the creature." But as for pure perfection terms, "from the point of view of what the word means it is used primarily of God and derivatively of creatures, for what the word means—the perfection it signifies—flows from God to the creature. But from the point of view of our use of the word we apply

---

[21] Perhaps Aquinas's realization of the lack of any positive account of what these perfections are like in God is reflected in his statement in the introduction to Q. 3 of *ST* I, the question on simplicity, that "because we cannot know what God is, but rather what He is not, we have no means for considering how God is, but rather how He is not."

it first to creatures because we know them first. That . . . is why it has a way of signifying that is appropriate to creatures."[22]

Thus Aquinas holds that there are two contrasting orders of priority for pure perfection terms, one appropriately called *causal* or *ontological* and the other appropriately called *semantic*. He says that the term is applied primarily to God in the first order and applied primarily to creatures in the second. I must confess that I can't see why Aquinas thinks that the first order is an order that has to do with words. There is no doubt but that, in his system, God's goodness, knowledge, or power is prior causally and ontologically to creaturely goodness, and so on, because the realization of the second is completely dependent on the first. But this would not seem to be a point about the predication of terms but about causal relations that hold independent of the structure of language. Be that as it may, I am concerned here, as Aquinas is primarily concerned in these discussions, with semantic order, with what meanings are derivative from what others, with what meanings have to be explained in terms of what others. And on that point he is quite clear that the application to creatures is semantically prior: "we apply it first to creatures because we know them first". And he carries that principle out in practice. In a passage quoted above we saw him explaining what is meant by 'God is good' in terms of the goodness of creatures ("what we call 'goodness' in creatures pre-exists in God in a higher way", *ST* I, 13, 2, R). But we never find him explaining what it is for a creature to have knowledge or the like in terms of what it is for God to have knowledge.

iv

So far, perhaps, so good. We have developed a coherent, interesting interpretation of the Thomistic position that pure perfection terms are predicated of God and creatures analogically, and we have brought out Thomas's reasons for this position. It holds that such terms are predicated of God in a sense not exactly the same as that in which they are predicated of creatures but in a sense that is related to the latter by virtue of the dependence of creatures on God for their existence and for what they are. By virtue of this relation

---

[22] Cf. *SCG* I, 34, 5–6, where it is pointed out that a parallel opposition in priorities holds for health. Health of the medicine or diet is causally prior to health in the animal, but as for the use of the word, we explain the former in terms of the latter.

the divine sense of the predicate 'wills that *P*', for example, is something like "does something of the same sort as what we call willing by creatures, except that it is in a higher mode". Understanding the divine sense in this way does not give us as much as we might like to have by way of a detailed conception of what it is for God to will that *P*, for example, but (a) it is more than nothing (it does give an intelligible sense to the term), and (b) it is the most we can expect to have, given the constraints, especially simplicity, within which we are working.

But before I close the book on all this, I must attend to another prominent feature of these stretches of the Summas that may seem to sort ill with the doctrine of analogy I have been expounding. This is the distinction between the "perfection" or property signified by a predicate term (*perfectio significata, res significata*) and the mode of signification (*modus significandi*).

> We have to consider two things . . . in the words we use to attribute perfections to God, first the perfections themselves that are signified— goodness, life and the like—and secondly the way in which they are signified. So far as the perfections signified are concerned the words are used literally of God, and in fact more appropriately than they are used of creatures, for these perfections belong primarily to God and only secondarily to others. But so far as the way of signifying these perfections is concerned the words are used inappropriately, for they have a way of signifying that is appropriate to creatures. (*ST* I, 13, 3, R. See also *SCG* I, 30, 3.)

This distinction renders the problem more complicated than it appears from the passages concerning univocal, equivocal, and analogical meaning. For in terms of this distinction we have to give semantic treatment to each of the two aspects that have been distinguished.

Aquinas gives us a hint as to what sort of thing is involved in the "mode of signification" by contrasting abstract and concrete terms.

> Since we come to know God from creatures and since this is how we come to refer to him, the expressions we use to name him signify in a way appropriate to the material creatures we ordinarily know. Amongst such creatures the complete subsistent thing is always a concrete union of form and matter; for the form itself is not a subsistent thing, but that by which something subsists. Because of this the words we use to signify complete subsistent things are concrete nouns which are appropriate to composite subjects. When, on the other hand, we want to speak of the form itself we use abstract nouns which do not signify something

as subsistent, but as that by which something is: 'whiteness', for example, signifies the form as that by which something is white. (*ST* I, 13, 1
ad 2. Cf. *SCG* I, 30, 3.)

Although Thomas was writing before the full flowering of the
movement known as "speculative grammar", it is tempting to interpret the above distinction in terms of that theory. The speculative
grammarians[23] distinguished two levels of the semantics of words,
one the more specific or lexical, by virtue of which the meaning of,
for example, 'cat' differs from that of 'dog', and a more general
meaning that is shared by all members of a given grammatical category. This latter is the *modus significandi*. Thus 'dog', 'cat', and all
other concrete nouns have the same modus significandi. The modus
significandi has both semantical and syntactical significance; it fits a
word for certain positions rather than others in sentences, and at the
same time it constitutes one aspect or level of the word's meaning.
The fact that 'dog' signifies a kind of *substance* is an integral part of
its meaning. Furthermore, the "modistae" took there to be ontological correlates of the various *modi significandi*, more specifically different aspects of a thing referred to (*modi essendi*).[24] Thus Aquinas:

> A noun signifies a thing as coming under some description, verbs and
> participles signify it as enduring in time, pronouns signify it as being
> pointed out or as in some relationship. (*ST* I, 13, 1, ad 3)

Let's return to the third quotation back, from Q. 13, 3, R. That
ended with the statement "But so far as the way of signifying these
perfections is concerned the words are used, inappropriately, for
they have a way of signifying that is appropriate to creatures". What
way is that? A part of the answer is given in the second quotation
back, from Q. 13, 1, ad 2. Our language, and thought, is designed
for application to material substances; that is the subject matter for
which we are cognitively fitted. "Amongst such creatures the complete subsistent thing is always a concrete union of form and matter. . . . Because of this the words we use to signify complete subsistent things are concrete nouns which are appropriate to
composite subjects. When, on the other hand, we want to speak of

---

[23] Because of their emphasis on modes of signification they were known as "modistae".

[24] For more on the modistae see Jan Pinborg, "Speculative Grammar", in *The Cambridge History of Later Medieval Philosophy*, ed. Norman Kretzmann, A. Kenny, Jan Pinborg, and Eleonore Stump (Cambridge: Cambridge University Press, 1982).

the form itself we use abstract nouns which do not signify something as subsistent." Thus we are in a bind. God is both subsistent and simple. The conceptual and linguistic resources at our disposal enable us to speak either of something subsistent and complex or of something simple and non-subsistent, but they give us no way to speak of something as both simple and subsistent. Hence when we speak of God, we are forced to misrepresent Him so far as the *modus significandi* aspect of our terms is concerned.

> Whatever our intellect signifies as subsisting, therefore, it signifies in concretion; but what it signifies as simple, it signifies, not as *that which is*, but as *that by which something is*. As a result, with reference to the mode of signification there is in every name that we use an imperfection, which does not befit God, even though the thing signified in some eminent way does befit God. (*SCG* I, 30, 3)

But is our situation really that desperate? Why can't we just construct terms to fit the bill? Why can't we just stipulate that we are going to use a certain term, 'gwise', to signify a being that is both subsistent and simple? Why is that beyond our powers?

To respond to this query we will have to go more deeply into this problem than Aquinas explicitly does in the passages we have been considering. Suppose we do say 'God is gwise', having tailor-made the term 'gwise' for application to a being that fits Thomas's specifications for God. There are still two aspects of our modes of signification that render what we say unsuitable for talk about God. First, our forms of speech and thought[25] require us to distinguish between subject and predicate in order to make any assertion whatever about anything.[26] But because God is absolutely simple, there is no distinction between God Himself and one of his properties or activities. Hence, by virtue of a deeply rooted feature of human thought and language we cannot think or speak of God without misrepresenting Him in this respect. Second, we are forced to distinguish between various properties, features, or aspects of God. We can't sum it all

---

[25] Let's not forget that language mirrors thought for Aquinas and inherits its fundamental features from the thought it expresses.

[26] Strictly speaking, this claim holds only of subject-predicate statements. In the twentieth century we see more clearly than our predecessors that not all statements are cast in this mould. However, the basic point I am concerned to make here is that our forms of statements impute complexity to what we are speaking of; and that point can be made for all statement forms.

up in one simple concept.[27] We have to first say that God is *wise*, then that He is *omnipotent*, then that He *exercises providence over His creatures*, and so on. For both these reasons it is endemic to the constitution of human thought that we cannot speak of God, whatever terms we use, without thereby violating our solemn assurance that God is absolutely simple: "as to the mode of signification, every name is defective" (*SCG* I, 30, 3). This idea that the aspect of the meaning of terms known as *modus significandi* is derivative from the way terms function in our forms of thought and speech is itself deeply rooted in the thought of the modistae. *Modi significandi*, though they have semantic and ontological significance, are in the first instance a matter of syntactical function; it is from the latter that they are discerned and distinguished. Hence any ineluctable features of the forms of our thought and talk will be reflected in what is possible for us with respect to the *modi significandi* of our terms.

Now let's look at the relation of this discussion to Thomas's doctrine of univocal and analogical meaning. What would the latter look like if formulated in terms of the *res significata–modus significandi* distinction? At least this much is clear: pure perfection terms as applied to creatures are unsuitable for application to God, so far as their *modi significandi* is concerned. But what about the more specific aspect of the meaning—the perfection signified? Although Aquinas isn't using the language of univocity-equivocity-analogicality when he deploys this distinction, he certainly gives the impression that all is clear sailing, univocity-wise, with the perfection signified. "So far as the perfections signified are concerned the words are used literally of God" (*ST* I, 13, 3, R). "And so with reference to the mode of signification no name is fittingly applied to God; this is done only with reference to that which the name has been imposed to signify. Such names, therefore, as Dionysius teaches, can be both affirmed and denied of God. They can be affirmed because of the meaning of the name; they can be denied because of the mode of signification" (*SCG* I, 30, 3). There is no hint in these passages that the *res significata* side of the matter forces a change in the meaning of pure perfection terms when applied to God. And, indeed, at least most of the

---

[27] "Since we know God from creatures we understand him through concepts appropriate to the perfections creatures receive from him. What pre-exists in God in a simple and unified way is divided amongst creatures as many and varied perfections. . . . Thus the words we use for the perfections we attribute to God, although they signify what is one, are not synonymous, for they signify it from many different points of view." (*ST* I, 13, 4, R)

ways in which we found Aquinas arguing earlier from simplicity to a denial of univocity would seem to yield a lack of univocity only with respect to the *modus significandi* side of the matter. Thus, for example, he pointed out that wisdom is not a quality of God (since not really distinct from God Himself) though it is a quality of creatures, and that each of the words signifies something distinct from each of the others when applied to creatures, but that they cannot appropriately do so when applied to God. These are two ways of pointing out the unsuitability for divine predication of the modes of signification words display when predicated of creatures.

But if the lack of univocity attaches only to the *modus significandi* side of the matter, there is no room for analogically related senses. For, as we have seen and as Aquinas insists, we can't change the creaturely mode of signification into one that is suitable for a divine application. We are stuck with the former, and the best we can do is to lament the fact that "as to the mode of signification, every name is defective". And as for the *res significata* side of the matter, on the present interpretation, that is just fine as it stands; there is no need to look for an analogically related divine sense of the term, so far as that aspect of the meaning is concerned. Hence it appears that the doctrine of an analogical meaning of theological terms has been frozen out; there is no place for it. Instead of analogically related creaturely and divine senses, what we have are creaturely senses all up and down the line, together with the recognition that one aspect of each such sense is ineluctably inappropriate for application to the divine.[28]

This would be a striking result indeed. On Aquinas's own showing there is no room for an analogy of meaning for creaturely and divine applications of terms. At one point in my decades-long reflection on this topic, I thought that this was the last word. But fortunately for Thomas and for Thomism, there is a hitherto (almost) suppressed side of the matter. On a number of occasions Aquinas testifies that there can be no strict sharing of form between God and creature.

---

[28] Note that I have not arrived at this conclusion by supposing that a term could have just lexical meaning (just signify a perfection) without also displaying a mode of signification and for that reason be perfectly univocal as between creaturely and divine attribution. Such univocity is clearly impossible, as Aquinas would no doubt agree, just because of the fact that the semantics of terms is intimately connected with their uses in larger syntactical complexes; a term would have no meaning at all if its meaning did not fit it for playing a distinctive role in assertions and the like.

> Any creature, in so far as it possesses any perfection, represents God
> and is like to him, for he . . . has pre-existing in himself the perfections
> of all his creatures. . . . But a creature is not like to God as it is like to
> another member of its species or genus, but resembles him as an effect
> may in some way resemble a transcendent cause although failing to
> reproduce perfectly the form of the cause. (*ST* I, 13, 2, R)[29]

Since the specific "lexical" meaning of a predicate consists in the fact
that it "signifies" the property (form) it does, then since no form can
be common to God and creature, we cannot use any predicate with
the same lexical meaning of God and creature if we are to have any
chance of saying something true in both cases. This is made quite
explicit in *SCG* I, 32, 2–3, a passage that I quoted in part when initially canvassing Aquinas's reasons for non-univocity. First we have
the "no form in common" point applied to yield the implication of a
lack of univocity.

> An effect that does not receive a form specifically the same as that
> through which the agent acts cannot receive according to a univocal
> predication the name arising from that form. . . . Now, the forms of the
> things God has made do not measure up to a specific likeness of the
> divine power: for the things that God has made receive in a divided and
> particular way that which in Him is found in a simple and universal
> way. It is evident, then, that nothing can be said univocally of God and
> other things. (Sec. 2)

In case one missed the point that this is a difference in lexical
meaning due to difference in form signified, that point is underlined
in the next section by distinguishing it from the additional point that
the mode of being of the form in creatures is different from that in
God (and hence, although Aquinas does not make this explicit,
terms will always differ in their mode of signification).

> If, furthermore, an effect should measure up to the species of its cause,
> it will not receive the univocal predication of the name unless it receives
> the same specific form according to the same mode of being. For the
> house that is in the art of the maker is not univocally the same house
> that is in matter, for the form of the house does not have the same
> being in the two locations. Now, even though the rest of things were to
> receive a form that is absolutely the same as it is in God, yet they do not
> receive it according to the same mode of being. For as is clear from
> what we have said, there is nothing in God that is not the divine being

---

[29] See also *ST* I, 4, 3; *SCG* I, 29.

itself, which is not the case with other things. Nothing, therefore, can be predicated of God and other things univocally. (Sec. 3)

This is a very revealing passage. Note that both difference of form and difference of mode of being of the form are derived from the same basic divine creature difference: the simplicity of God. There can be no exact reproduction of form just because creatures have in a divided way what is found in God in an absolutely simple way, without any real distinction between the perfections. And, again, the mode of being is inevitably different because anything God "has" is identical with His being. Thus we have what we might call a certain "leakage" from the ontological correlate of the mode of signification to the ontological correlate of perfection signified. The divine simplicity not only makes the forms of our speech inapt for talk about God (difference in mode of signifying) but also interferes with any identity of form between God and creature.

Thus the full story here is that in neither aspect of their meaning—the "lexical" or the "grammatical"—are creaturely terms fully suitable for application to God. And so there is a place for analogy after all, at least on the lexical side. Though no real improvement can be hoped for on the grammatical side, the lexical meaning can be altered from its creaturely form so as to fit better the divine subject. And yet it is not as if the lexical meaning can be shaped so as to signify the divine perfection in as complete or specific a fashion as that in which it signifies the creaturely approximation. The best we can do is what Aquinas suggests in his earlier explanation of the meaning of 'God is good'. We can attribute to God a more eminent analogue of the creaturely perfection but without saying specifically just what that is. We can adumbrate the analogous divine perfection only by relating it, by supereminence, to the creaturely version of which we do have a satisfactory grasp. Thus "every name is defective" in both aspects of its meaning, even though we can go some distance toward making the lexical meaning more appropriate.

V

Now that we are straight as to just what the Thomistic account is of the meaning of predicates in their theological application, I turn to criticism. Let's consider the common complaint that on the Thomistic interpretation theological statements lack what is required for their intended function. They (1) lack determinate truth conditions and (2) cannot figure in reasoning in the ways they are supposed to in Thomistic, and other, theology. These criticisms are related in a moderately complex fashion. If (1) is valid, that is going to play havoc with any attempt to perform inferences to or from theological statements. If it is indeterminate just what it takes to make a given (putative) statement true, then what follows from the statement, or what it follows from, will certainly be indeterminate, because what the statement "says" is indeterminate. But, of course, (2) can make trouble even if theological statements are as determinate as you please. For the determinate theological meaning might not be such as to underwrite the inferences that Aquinas and other theologians purport to perform. Hence we must consider both criticisms.

The *res significata–modus significandi* distinction further complicates matters. For each of the above disabilities might stem from differences between theological and non-theological meanings in one or other of these aspects, or both. I shall proceed by looking at the possible contributions of each aspect of theological meaning to the alleged difficulties, beginning with the mode of signification.

First off, it is clear that the inaptness of our *modi significandi* for theological application is not going to affect inferences insofar as they depend on the specific meanings of the terms employed, for the mode of signification is distinguished from that. Thus, to the extent that implications of divine knowledge or will or goodness depend on the specific content of those concepts, it will not matter that our grammatical forms are ill-suited to talk about God. Any trouble here will come from differences in the *res significata*.

Then why should defects in the mode of signification be thought to adversely affect truth or validity? It would have to be something like this. Our grammatical forms make a contribution to the truth conditions of our statements. Thus when I say that Jim forgave Sally, part of what it takes to make my statement true depends on the fact that 'forgave' picks out one attribute rather than another, and 'Jim' and 'Sally' are being used to refer to certain persons rather than others. But the truth conditions also reflect the grammar of the statement. What is being said is that the action designated by 'forgave Sally' was performed by Jim, and that relationship has to hold in order for the statement to be true. But that means that the statement can be true only if there is such a relation holding between Jim and this action of his, and that means, in turn, that a condition of truth is that there is a distinction between Jim and this action. And so it is for anything else we say or think in the complex discursive forms available to us. But then that means that none of the statements we make about God can be (wholly) true. For a necessary condition of the truth of each is that what we are asserting of God is related to Him in a certain way, and hence is distinguishable from Him.[30] And that condition contradicts divine simplicity. Precisely what makes all our terms for God defective in their *modi significandi* prevents anything we say of God from being true. And if truth goes, the game is up with theology, at least on the traditional construal as a discipline that gives us truth about God.

If Aquinas has any defense against this, it will be by supporting the denial that grammatical form contributes to truth conditions in the way just adumbrated. We might defend this denial by adverting to the way in which grammatically inapt or misleading sentences are successfully used to make true statements in any area of discourse. The work in this century by analytic philosophers on "systematically misleading expressions" and the distinction between "grammatical form" and "logical form" provides abundant resources for such an argument.[31] Let's assume that existence is not a predicate and that existentially quantified statements, rather than subject-predicate statements, give an adequate representation of what we are asserting when we make positive and negative existential claims. Nevertheless, we surely do often succeed in saying something true when we use 'exists' as a grammatical predicate, as when we say "Margaret Thatcher exists" or "The Great Pumpkin does not exist". If, as certainly seems to be the case, the statement "Margaret Thatcher exists" is completely, unqualifiedly, 100% true (and not just partly true or approximately true or close enough to being true for practical purposes), then it must be that the grammatical form does not enter into the truth conditions in the way suggested above. For otherwise part of what we would be asserting in saying "Margaret Thatcher exists" is that existence is related to her as one of her properties or attributes, and so, on the assumption we are making about existence, what we are saying would not be completely true.

---

[30] Making this point is less straightforward when we are asserting an attribute like goodness or wisdom. For there, on one interpretation, what we are saying to be related to the subject in a certain way is not a "part" or aspect of itself, but a separate, "abstract" entity. However, even here, I believe it can be successfully argued that when we assert that X is good, we are also committed to X's *goodness* being related to X in a certain way, and hence being distinguishable from X. I won't have time to go into all that in this paper.

[31] See, e.g., Bertrand Russell, *The Philosophy of Logical Atomism*, in R. C. Marsh, ed., *Logic and Knowledge* (London: George Allen & Unwin, 1956); Gilbert Ryle, "Systematically Misleading Expressions", in A. Flew, ed., *Logic and Language*, 1st series (Oxford: Basil Blackwell, 1952).

For another familiar example consider the many turns of phrase in which we use an existential form of statement without seriously committing ourselves to the existence of what we would be committing ourselves to if the grammatical form were taken to make a full contribution to the truth conditions. We say things like "There is a possibility that he will come", "There is a chance of rain", and "There is merit in your suggestion" without committing ourselves to the real existence of such entities as possibilities, chances, or merits.[32] Assuming there are no such things as chances and so on, if the grammatical form did contribute to the truth conditions in the way mentioned, then we would not ever be saying anything true when making statements like this. But obviously we do often make wholly true statements with these forms of speech.

These cases are unlike the theological case in that we have the resources for making our truth claims in an apt, rather than in an inapt, grammatical form. Instead of saying, "Margaret Thatcher exists", we can say, "There is such a person as Margaret Thatcher". Instead of saying, "There is a chance of rain", we can say, "There might be rain". On Thomas's view, however, we are unable to replace "God is wise" with a grammatically perspicuous formulation. But this difference leaves unaffected the point that it is possible to make statements that are wholly true even though the grammatical form is unsuitable for what is stated. At least so I claim. I cannot prove that the possibility of making a wholly true statement by saying "Margaret Thatcher exists" is not dependent on the possibility of making the same statement by saying "There is such a person as Margaret Thatcher." Nevertheless, it seems highly plausible to me that there is no such dependence. Suppose we had the subject-predicate form of statement but that existential quantification had not been developed. Would it then be impossible to make true positive or negative existential statements by the use of the subject-predicate form? I cannot see that it would. Indeed, perhaps we all learn the subject-predicate form before learning existential quantification. If so, would that make it impossible for a child at that stage to make true existential statements? I cannot see that it would.

But surely it is better to have an apt, perspicuous form of statement for what we want to say. This can hardly be denied. But if the

---

[32] I am not suggesting that it is impossible to commit oneself to the existence of such entities, or even that there may not be good reasons to do so. I am merely pointing out that in making statements of the sort just cited we are not making any such commitments.

inapt form does not interfere with complete truth, then what is inferior about it? Perhaps the most promising answer is that the inapt form is not the better choice just because it is, or can be, misleading. It can give rise to inappropriate, or even false, suggestions, inferences, or interpretations. The subject-predicate form does not adequately represent existential facts just because it is liable to suggest that existence is among the properties of an existing thing. And any form of statement fails to represent God adequately just because it is liable to suggest that there is complexity in the divine being, that God is distinct from His nature, properties, and actions. But being liable to spawn false suggestions is not the same thing as being false. I can have said something wholly true by saying, "There is a long way yet to go", even though I didn't express it in what is ontologically the most perspicuous fashion. In just the same way I can say something wholly true by saying, "God created the heavens and the earth" or "God spoke to Moses", even though my statement carries, by virtue of its form, false suggestions concerning the divine being.

If this is a satisfactory defense of Thomas-style theological statements against the charge of a failure to satisfy truth conditions, by reason of defects in the mode of signification, we can move on to the stickier double problem that arises with respect to the *res significata*: (a) a lack of determinateness in the theological meaning and (b) the mere fact that the theological meaning differs from the creaturely meaning. The problems significantly interact. I begin with the former.

I have already noted the rather low level of determinateness exhibited by theological statements on Thomas's interpretation. To say that God forgives Butler's sins is to say that the act of forgiveness (directed to Butler) "attaches" to God, but in a higher form. Thus apart from the inaptness of the subject-predicate form, about which nothing can be done, there is the fact that even the perfection signified is not fully specified; instead we simply indicate that it is a higher form of a creaturely perfection but without being able to say just what the higher form is. And insofar as it is indeterminate what we are attributing to God in saying this, to that extent it is not clear what the truth conditions of the attribution are. Hence it is not clear exactly what is being asserted of God.

How serious a problem is this? We can live with a certain degree of indeterminacy in our assertions. It conveys real information to tell someone that London is large city, even though there is no precise lower limit for the largeness of a city. But the difficulty here is that

Thomas, by his own showing, is not in a position to map, delimit, or demarcate the area or extent of indeterminacy. In the case of London we can give the population and make the statement much more specific, thereby making it clear that the largeness of London is on the order of magnitude of, say, New York City, rather than San Francisco. But that is just what we cannot do in the theological case. We can't replace the indeterminate assertion with anything more determinate, nor can we separate out a determinate part from a shadowy penumbra. At least, Thomas has given us no hint as to how this could be done, and it would seem to be indicated by his theory that there could be no such way. Thus we would seem to be at a loss in determining just what we are saying of God when we say that He is good or omniscient or that He created and sustains the world. This looks to be a crippling disability indeed.

The seriousness of the disability can be brought out by considering its consequences for inferences to and from statements about God. In this brief discussion, let's concentrate on the implications, both theoretical and practical, that can be drawn from statements about God.[33] I will begin with the former. Actually, it will prove most convenient to start the discussion with difficulties that arise from the mere fact that the theological meaning of a term *differs* from the creaturely meaning, whether the former is perfectly determinate or not. Indeterminacy will then be seen to play a crucial role when attempts are made to resolve these difficulties.

The most pressing worry about theoretical implications has to do with the application of general principles, arrived at from the study of creatures, to God. If 'knows' or 'wills' has a somewhat different meaning as applied to God and humans, then we cannot automatically transfer to divine knowing or willing principles we know (have reason to think) to hold for human knowing or willing. For it cannot be accepted without more ado that what is true of human knowing is also true of knowing in a different sense of 'know'. Thus when Aquinas takes it, on the basis of our understanding of human knowing and willing, that divine knowing takes place via a "species" of the object known, and that God necessarily wills what He understands to be the good, we will have to ask for some further reason to think that principles true of knowing or willing in one sense are also true of knowing and willing in another sense. He gives us no such reasons. (In terms of "theoretical implications" the

---

[33] Theoretical implications have been most emphasized in the critical literature, but the practical implications are at least equally important.

question is as to whether "God knows Moses" entails "God is aware of a species of Moses", etc.) Nor is Aquinas in a good position to do so. For, and this is where indeterminacy is crucial, he has disavowed any attempt to be specific about what knowing or willing come to in the divine case, except that they constitute a "higher mode" of the sort of thing we have in human knowing or willing. But if we can't spell out the ways in which this higher version is like and unlike the lower analogue, how can we even address the question of whether principles that hold of the lower form also hold of the higher form? This difficulty strikes at the heart of the Thomistic theology, for at many crucial points it depends on taking principles (assumed to be) true of human so-and-so's to be true of divine so-and-so's. The whole argument for the central thesis that the perfections of all things are in God hangs on the principle that whatever the cause bestows on the effect preexists in the cause,[34] a principle that is drawn from reflection on causal relations in the created order. Just to take one other example, the treatment of divine love depends on applying to God the scheme of passions drawn from the human case.[35] And so if the interpretation of theological predication renders such extrapolations invalid, Thomistic theology is in big trouble indeed.

Thomas would, presumably, reply that the ways in which divine perfections surpass their created counterparts are not such as to invalidate the applications of these principles to the divine case. But how, on his own principles, can he know this, or even be reasonably assured of it? By his own admission he is in no position to spell out the respects of similarity and dissimilarity between divine and human causal agency, willing, and so on. Therefore, how can he be assured that the dissimilarities are not such as to undermine the application of principles arrived at by a consideration of the creaturely analogues?

The difficulties with practical implications run parallel with the theoretical. Consider the inference from "God wills (commands) us to love one another" to "We ought to love one another". This seems quite in order until we ask whether the higher form of volitions (commands) has the same practical implications as the human form of volitions (commands)? And again, Aquinas is not in a good position to answer.

Because of these difficulties it would behoove us to reexamine

---

[34] *ST* I, 4, 2; *SCG* I, 29, 2.
[35] *ST* I, 20, 1

Thomas's argument for the lack of univocity of even pure perfection terms, with respect to their lexical meaning, in creaturely and divine applications. Let's recall that this argument depends on an inference from the statement "divine wisdom [for example] is not exactly the same as human wisdom" to the statement that "wise" cannot be univocally predicated of God and man.

> It must be said that nothing can be predicated univocally of the creature and God, for in all univocals the intelligible nature signified by the name (*ratio nominis*) is common to each of the things of which that name is univocally predicated. . . . Now however much it may imitate God, no creature can ever attain to this, that anything the same in its very intelligible essence should be common to it and to God. . . . [w]hatever is in God *is* His own proper act of existing. . . . Consequently, since the act of existing proper to one thing cannot be communicated to another, it is impossible that the creature should have anything in common with God quidditatively, even as it cannot possibly acquire the same act of existing as His. (*De veritate*, II, 11)[36]

> An effect that does not receive a form specifically the same as that through which the agent acts cannot receive according to a univocal predication the name arising from that form. (*SCG* I, 32, 2)

> It is impossible to predicate anything univocally of God and creatures. Every effect that falls short of what is typical of the power of its cause represents it inadequately, for it is not the same kind of thing as the cause. (*ST* I, 13, 5, R)

In all these cases Aquinas is arguing from "God and creature do not share exactly the same forms" to "No terms can be predicated univocally of God and creatures". But this argument clearly assumes that the meanings of the terms in question exactly mirror the objective facts of the matter. And because for Aquinas terms signify immediately our concepts, and through them what these are concepts of, this claim is based on the assumption that our concepts reflect precisely the ontological character of their objects. If divine volition has a quite different ontological status from human volition, then it follows without more ado that our concept of divine volition is correspondingly different from our concept of human volition, and hence that the meaning of 'wills' as applied to God is correspondingly different from the meaning of 'wills' as applied to human beings.

---

[36] This translation is from J. F. Anderson, *An Introduction to the Metaphysics of St. Thomas Aquinas* (Chicago: Henry Regnery Co., 1953).

But this may well be questioned. Why suppose that our concepts are that closely conformed to the nature of the things conceived? Why suppose that I cannot form a concept of, for example, *believing* that applies truly both to human and canine believing, even though there are many crucial differences between believings of these two sorts.[37] To do so I have to abstract from many of the salient features of each sort of belief, but on what grounds can it be denied that such abstraction is possible? Why suppose that our conceptual operations are so closely tied to the character of what is conceived that we cannot form concepts that prescind from some of those features? Indeed, Thomas himself recognizes that this is possible. In a famous passage on analogy from the *Commentary on the Sentences* XIX, 5, 2, ad 1, he distinguishes three modes of analogical predication: "(1) solely as regards the concept involved; (2) as regards the act of existing, but not the concept; (3) as regards both the concept and the act of existing". He explains the second of these categories as follows.

> The second mode of analogical predication is in effect when several things are put on an equal footing under one and the same common concept, although the nature that they share in common exists diversely in them. Thus all bodies [however diverse they may be in their actual existence] are on a par so far as the concept of corporeity is concerned. Thus the logician, who considers intentions only, says that the term body is predicated univocally of all bodies, and yet corporeity does not exist in corruptible and in incorruptible bodies in the same mode.[38]

Thus we can form a very general concept of corporeity that abstracts from the difference between corruptible and incorruptible bodies,[39] and hence can be predicated univocally of both. Why, then, should it be impossible to form a concept of willing, knowing, forgiving, or loving that abstracts from the differences in the ways in which these forms are realized in God and creatures, and hence can be predicated univocally of both?[40]

[37] Human beliefs, but not canine beliefs, are often linguistically encoded. An important part of what it is for a human being to believe that p is for that human being to be inclined to draw inferences from p. And so on.

[38] The translation is taken from Anderson. Note that this is a part of the text that Cajetan principally relies on in developing his interpretation of the Thomistic doctrine of analogy.

[39] According to Thomas's Aristotelian astronomy, the heavenly bodies, unlike terrestrial ones, are composed of incorruptible matter.

[40] The position adumbrated here is quite similar to the positions of both Scotus and Ockham on this point. See Duns Scotus, *Philosophical Writings*, trans. Allan Wolter

I do not claim to have shown the possibility of forming a concept that is restricted to what is common to divine and human knowing, willing, or whatever; and especially have I not shown the possibility of forming such a concept that has enough content to be interesting and important.[41] I don't know of any way of demonstrating this possibility short of exhibiting the actuality by actually constructing such a concept. I fancy that I have done this in other publications,[42] and I will not repeat the performance here. Suffice it to say that, so far as I can see, by using a functionalist approach to the construal of psychological concepts we can specify a very abstract structure that can plausibly be claimed to be equally found in God and in creatures with psyches, though the mode of realization of this abstract structure is, no doubt, enormously different. Just to give a hint of the general idea, if what it is for a human being to know something is, in part, for that being to have a tendency to direct its action in a certain way, this fundamental aspect of knowledge could equally apply to God, and a term constructed so as to embody this aspect, and only this aspect, could be univocally predicated of God and man. Of course, to show that a certain term with a certain meaning could be truly predicated both of God and creatures we would have to go into what we are warranted in supposing that God is like, for that obviously puts limits on what can be truly predicated of God.[43] I cannot go into all this within the limits of this essay. Here I restrict myself to arguing that Thomas has radically undersupported his claim that it follows from the thesis that "no creature can ever attain to this, that anything the same in its very intelligible essence should be common to it and to God" that no term can be predicated uni-

---

(Indianapolis: Hackett Publishing Co, 1987), pp. 20–25. (This is from the *Opus Oxoniense*, I, dist. III, q. i.) See also William of Ockham, *Philosophical Writings*, trans. Philotheus Boehner (Indianapolis: Hackett Publishing Co., 1990), pp. 102–13. (This is from the *Ordinatio*, D. II, Q. ix, P sqq., and from the *Reportatio*, III, Q. viii.)

[41] If the question is merely whether one can form *any* concept that applies equally to God and human beings, that is easily answered. Try *not identical with Richard Nixon* or *possible object of thought*.

[42] See my "Functionalism and Theological Language" and "Divine and Human Action" in *Divine Nature and Human Language* (Ithaca: Cornell University Press, 1989).

[43] This is one of the paradoxical aspects of this problem area. We have to employ talk about God in order to determine what terms with what meanings can be truly predicated of God, and we have to do the latter to determine the semantic status of talk about God. Thus we have to have a working grasp of the subject matter in order to arrive at a theoretical grasp of it. But it takes little reflection to realize that this is by no means peculiar to this topic. Any investigation of language, semantic or otherwise, requires us to use language meaningfully.

vocally of God and creature, and hence that if we are to say anything truly of God the term has to be used in a somewhat different, analogically related sense.

One might think that Thomas has resources for answering this criticism in his account of concept formation, according to which intellectual concepts are abstracted from material ("sensible forms" or "sensible species") presented by the senses.[44] Moreover, this process is such as to make a form of the object, indeed the essence of the object where that is what is conceived, present in the mind in an "intentional mode". Thus Thomas is committed to a very high assessment of human cognition in general and conceptualization in particular. The process is such as to guarantee an exact mental transcription of the form to be conceived. Indeed, "transcription" is too weak a term, for the form conceived is, so to say, "bodily" in the mind. That is, it is in the mind so far as its intrinsic content is concerned, for the mode of realization of, say, the essence of a goat, is far different in the goat and in a human mind! It might be thought that on this view there is no room for a discrepancy in content between a concept (and hence the meaning of a term that expresses that concept) and the real being of the form conceived. And in that case a difference in the forms of knowledge in God and creature would necessarily carry with it a difference in the concepts of divine and human knowledge, and, pari passu, a difference in the meaning of 'knows' as truly applied to God and to creature.

However, there must be something wrong with this argument, for we have already seen Thomas acknowledging that generic concepts are sometimes abstracted from differences in the forms they are used to grasp. And apart from that, we can see why the above argument has no tendency to show that our concepts of divine attributes and activities must reproduce with photographic accuracy every detail of those perfections. For the doctrine of the development of concepts by abstraction from sensible forms has no application to the development of our thought about God. God does not present Himself to the senses, and so there is no sensible species from which concepts of divine attributes and properties, much less the divine essence, are abstracted. On the contrary, by Thomas's own showing we form our concepts of the divine by derivation from concepts of sensorily perceivable creatures, concepts that are themselves formed in the way just mentioned. Thus the general account of concept for-

---

[44] See, e.g., *ST* I, 85. The account is actually much more complicated than this. But I am not able to go into it properly within the limits of this essay.

mation has no tendency to imply that our concepts of divine attributes and activities will embody the character of those attributes and activities in such a way that differences in attributes will necessarily carry with it a difference in concepts. And so the argument against univocity from a difference in the *res significata* still falls through.

The upshot of these remarks is that even if we go along with Thomas on divine simplicity, the best position to take on theological predication, keeping in mind the distinction between *res significata* and *modus significandi*, is that we may be able in some cases to use terms univocally of God and creature so far as the *res significata* is concerned, even though the mode of signification will misrepresent the divine being. This is not to say, of course, that all, or even most, or even more than a tiny fraction, of creaturely terms can be univocally applied to God. And it may be that no creaturely terms, as they stand, can be so applied. But even so, it may be possible to devise more abstract terms that capture something strictly in common between God and creature, as briefly adumbrated by my reference to a functionalist account of knowledge. That, of course, leaves vast stretches of discourse about the divine that are best construed in other terms—analogy, metaphor, and so on. But it would seem that when it comes to what Aquinas calls "pure perfection terms" he lacks any sound reason for denying that they can be univocally applied across the divine-creature gap.

If we jump ship on the simplicity doctrine, as I believe we should, then much of Thomas's reasons for the denial of any univocity disappears. What is left is only the "difference of specific form" argument I have just been engaged in discrediting. Moreover, we no longer have the worry about the inaptness of the form of our discourse. Since there are real distinctions in God between God and His attributes, properties, and activities, between essence and existence, and between different properties and activities, the fact that our forms of assertion presuppose such differences does not render them inappropriate. We can then attempt to determine what terms can reasonably be thought to be truly applied univocally to God and creatures. As I have already intimated, I think that these will be very abstract ones. For the rest we can explore the varieties of alternatives to univocal literal predication, including special technical terms that can be literally applied only to God, analogically related senses of terms, and various figures of speech. St. Thomas is a landmark figure in opening up this subject and helping us become aware of much of its complexity, but his doctrines need considerable modification if they are to survive critical scrutiny.

GEORGE I. MAVRODES

The Gods above the Gods:
Can the High Gods Survive?

"The Tao that can be told of is not the eternal Tao."[1]

This essay is not about Taoist thought. It is primarily about Christian theology and philosophy. I begin, however, with a quotation from the *Tao Te Ching* because it illustrates, from a quite different tradition, a "move" that has sometimes been made in Christian thought. Pending further examples, we might describe this move as follows. It consists of saying that the ordinary and primary object toward which the religion is oriented—the tao in this case, and God in Christian thought—is not the final and most profound reality. Behind it, or above it, or beneath it, there is something else, something more decisive and ultimate.

It is often claimed that the intentional objects of religious thought and attitudes are "transcendental" objects, entities that are supposed to be somehow beyond the pedestrian world of time and space, of ordinary human relations, and so on. If that is so, as seems plausible, then the sort of move proposed in the opening sentence of the *Tao Te Ching* might be called a "super-transcendentalizing" suggestion, the claim that the transcendent is itself radically transcended. I call this the "T-move".

The *Tao Te Ching*, then, begins with just such a move. Taken as it stands, the sentence quoted does not seem to cast any doubt on the

---

[1] Lao-tzu, *Tao Te Ching*, chap. 1. Translated by Wing-Tsit Chan under the title *The Way of Lao Tzu* (Indianapolis: Library of Liberal Arts, 1963), p. 97. This sentence has been translated in a variety of ways—e.g., "The tao that can be named is not the eternal tao."

existence or reality of a tao which can be told of. But it does say that
that tao, the one which can be told of, is not the eternal Tao. On the
most parsimonious reading of this sentence perhaps it does not assert that there is an eternal tao but only denies eternality of the "told
of" tao. More charitably, however, it certainly seems to suggest that
there is an eternal tao, and this reading is supported by the immediate context.[2] I take it then, that the intention here is to call attention
to, and to contrast, two taos. One of them can be told of and is not
eternal, and the other cannot be told of and is eternal.

A terminological peculiarity often accompanies the T-move. The
super-entity is here referred to by the same word, *Tao*, that is used
for the entity it transcends. The same strategy is employed by some
writers in the Christian tradition who use various expressions incor-
porating the word *God* to refer to the entity that is said to transcend
God.[3] Perhaps something of the sense that the repeated word bears
in its "lower-level" use, or some penumbra of connotation surround-
ing that use, is meant to be carried over to the application to the
super-object.

How do these taos differ? Two things are said of them here: one
of the taos is eternal and the other is not, and one of them can be
told of and the other cannot. It looks like the latter distinction is
used to generate the *reference* to the two taos, and then eternality is
ascribed to one of them and non-eternality to the other. But the
claim that there is a tao that cannot be told of generates a paradox,
at least superficially. For saying that this tao cannot be told of seems
itself to be a case of telling something of this tao. It seems to be a
description of the tao, an ascribing to it of a certain characteristic.
And the paradox is immediately compounded by going on to tell
something more about this tao, that it is eternal. This is, of course,
the stock paradox which, in Western philosophy and theology, af-
flicts claims to the effect that something is ineffable. Augustine, for
example, clearly recognized the paradoxical character of such claims,
describing them as "a contradiction in terms".[4]

---

[2] E.g., "The Nameless is the origin of Heaven and Earth; the Named is the mother
of all things," from the same chapter.

[3] A significant exception, to be noted in this essay, is in the recent work of John
Hick.

[4] St. Augustine, *On Christian Doctrine*, trans. by D. W. Robertson, Jr. (New York:
Liberal Arts Press, 1958), book I, sec. 6 (p. 11): "If what I said were ineffable, it would
not be said. And for this reason God should not be said to be ineffable, for when this
is said something is said. And a contradiction in terms is created, since if that is
ineffable which cannot be spoken, then that is not ineffable which can be called ineffable."

Perhaps, however, this paradox is only apparent and not genuine. Suppose, for example, that we take the expression "told of" to be a somewhat special or technical term, so that not every case of saying something about a subject, not every case of ascribing a characteristic to something, is to be counted as a case of something being "told of". That is, only certain kinds of description constitute "telling of". With that restriction the paradox may disappear, since saying of something that it cannot be told of, or that it is ineffable, or that it is eternal, may not itself be the crucial sort of description which is being ruled out.

Or consider an alternative translation, "The tao which can be named is not the eternal tao." A paradox is generated if we suppose that in order to refer to the super-transcendent tao we must have some name for it, or (perhaps more accurately) some referring expression—"the tao which cannot be named", perhaps, or "the eternal tao"—and thus it can be named after all. But this paradox may also disappear if we construe the naming that is to be ruled out to be a naming of a special sort. Of course, many of us now do not put much stock in names, and we do not recognize any interesting special sort of naming. We think of names as purely conventional, and so we suppose that I, for example, could have been named just about anything. It wouldn't make any difference. But in fact there is a long tradition in Western thought which says that some names are indeed purely conventional but that there are other names that are not conventional. And those other names are the *true* names of things. This tradition is now largely in the arcana of wizardry, etc., but it goes back at least to Plato[5] (or Homer?). If we were to interpret Lao-tzu in terms of those early Platonic notions, then we might say that conventional names are generally satisfactory for purposes of reference and predication and that there is no problem in the super-transcendent tao's having a conventional name (or any number of them, for that matter). And there is likewise no problem in our using a conventional name to identify and refer to this super-transcendent tao. But then what Lao-tzu intended to deny was that this tao could be named in that deeper sense in which (in Plato, for example) the gods know the true names of things but humans generally do not. Perhaps, that is, Lao-tzu meant that the true name of the eternal tao is absolutely beyond all human comprehension and use. Or he may have meant, more radically, that the eternal tao simply has no true name at all, in neither a human nor a divine

---

[5] Plato, *Cratylus*. There is an extensive and interesting fictional development of the idea of a true name in Ursula K. Le Guin's *Earthsea Trilogy*.

vocabulary. No doubt such a doctrine would be puzzling, and it might well be false, but when restricted in this way it does not seem to generate a paradox of self-referential incoherence. If, however, one insists on a completely unrestricted doctrine of ineffability, and so on, then indeed it will be hard to avoid the Augustinian "contradiction in terms".

Now, what I want to argue in this paper is that the "high gods" that are postulated in the T-move are in a peculiarly vulnerable position. They are threatened with one or another of two opposite fates. They may be kicked upstairs, into a realm that is religiously irrelevant (and therefore humanly irrelevant). There they may pursue their own interests, I suppose, assuming that they have interests, but they will have no bearing on human life. That will be left to the lower gods—perhaps to the tao that can be told of. On the other hand, the high gods may have a feature that is so religiously attractive that they will be "eaten", absorbed, by the lower gods by way of the claim that the lower god is, and always has been, simply identical with the postulated high god—e.g., the claim that the tao which can be told of is in fact the eternal tao.

I want to argue this point primarily with reference to the views of two twentieth-century philosophical theologians, Paul Tillich and John Hick, both of whom make the T-move, though in rather different ways. Tillich's God above God seems to me especially vulnerable to the first fate, because Tillich strips him of a feature essential to religious relevance. Hick's Real, however, is most in danger from the other side, because he is endowed with a feature that is so attractive religiously.

1. Paul Tillich and the God above God

More than two thousand years, along with deep theological and philosophical differences, separate the *Tao Te Ching* from twentieth-century theology within the Christian tradition. But the T-move has survived, or (more probably) it has independently arisen time and again. In the theological writing of this century it is associated prominently with the work of Paul Tillich. Tillich was deeply dissatisfied with God, but he was willing to cast in his lot with the God above God.[6] And the God with whom Tillich was dissatisfied, the God

[6] Paul Tillich, *The Courage to Be* (New Haven: Yale University Press, 1952), pp. 182–90. This book is based on Tillich's Terry Lectures at Yale University.

who is transcended in the T-move, is sometimes further specified as "the God of theism."[7] Thus he draws a contrast between the God of theism (who would be, I suppose, the God of many religious people) and the God above God.

Tillich evidently found the God of theism to be religiously unsatisfactory. For one thing, this God is not ultimate, apparently because he is not different enough from other things. "He is seen as a self which has a world, as an ego which is related to a thou, as a cause which is separated from its effect, as having a definite space and an endless time. He is a being, not being-itself."[8] And so this God is merely a part of reality, "subjected to the structure of the whole", and thus subjected to the "categories which constitute reality".

The God above God, however, presumably contrasts with the God of theism in these respects. The God above God is not a being: he (or it?) is being-itself. Absolute faith, Tillich says, consists of accepting an acceptance, but that acceptance is "without somebody or something that accepts. It is the power of being-itself that accepts and gives the courage to be." And he goes on to say that being-itself "cannot be described in the way the God of all forms of theism can be described. It cannot be described in mystical terms either. It transcends both mysticism and personal encounter."[9] Even theists, Tillich suggests, can become aware of the deep paradoxes concealed in their own thought and practice. They can realize, for example, that if they pray, then they are speaking "to somebody to whom you cannot speak," and they are asking "somebody of whom you cannot ask anything." And "each of these paradoxes drives the religious consciousness toward a God above the God of theism."[10]

Furthermore, it appears that in Tillich's thought the God of theism does not provide a solution to the pressing existential problem of how to face the anxiety generated by the threat of meaninglessness and non-being. For the God of theism, he suggests, "is not more real than any finite being," and that God "has disappeared in the abyss of meaninglessness with every other value and meaning."[11] But Tillich says, as we have already noted, that the God above God

[7] E.g., ibid., p. 186.

[8] Ibid., p. 184.

[9] Ibid., pp. 185, 186. It is curious that Tillich is apparently intent on rejecting any attempt to characterize the God above God in "substance" terms, even such general terms as "thing" and "being", but he himself readily uses action characterizations with reference to this God—He (or it) "accepts" and "gives the courage to be", etc.

[10] Ibid., p, 187.

[11] Ibid., pp. 186, 187.

does provide that existential solution, giving us the courage to be. *"The courage to be is rooted in the God who appears when God has disappeared in the anxiety of doubt."*[12]

I noted that Lao-tzu appears to begin in a way that accepts the existence and reality of both taos. What about Tillich and the gods? What seems clearest in this is that Tillich holds that the super-transcendent God, the God above God, does not exist. If he did exist, then he would be a being rather than being-itself, a thing among things, etc., and so he would be no better off than the God of theism. Therefore if atheism is defined either as the doctrine that God does not exist or as the denial of the doctrine that God does exist, then Tillich is an atheist *with respect to the God above God.*

Perhaps Tillich would object to the negative flavor of that characterization as an atheist (though not everyone counts "atheist" as a pejorative term). Tillich wants to take his stand within religion rather than outside of it, perhaps even within Christianity in some sense. He wants to talk about the God above God, and he finds—or at least claims to find—in that God the solution to the profound existential problem of doubt and despair. But if we ask an ontological question about the God to whom Tillich gives his allegiance, we seem to get, from Tillich himself, a negative answer.

Some philosophers might think of appealing to the notion of *reality* as an ontological category that is perhaps broader than that of *existence*, and which could be of use here. For example, John Hick, whom I discuss in the last part of this paper, also makes the T-move, and he refers to the super-transcendent entity as "the Real". So we might say that Tillich's God above God, though he does not exist, is nevertheless *real*. And that might provide enough ontological solidity, so to speak, to satisfy us. Tillich himself, however, seems to rule out this strategy also. For one of his major complaints against the God of theism is that he is "a part of the whole of reality" and that he is subjected to "the ontological elements and categories which constitute reality."[13] Presumably, then, the God above God should not be subjected to the categories that constitute reality. I suppose, therefore, that we should not consider him to be real.

The problem here—the religious problem—is that religious believers often (indeed, I would say, characteristically) distinguish between existence and/or reality, on the one hand, and illusion, imag-

---

[12] Ibid., p. 190. Italics in the original. This sentence concludes the book.
[13] Ibid., p. 184.

ination, unreality, mere possibility, and the like, on the other hand. And they want their gods to belong to the first branch of this distinction rather than to the second. Put in some Tillichian terms, they are inclined to think that nothing is worthy of ultimate concern if it does not have ontological solidity and standing. So if they become convinced that the erstwhile intentional objects of their worship and allegiance do not in fact exist, or that they are not real, then they are likely either to seek a new religion with better ontological credentials (or at least a stronger ontological promise) or else to give up the project of religion altogether. And so when Anselm says, in his paean of worship, "Therefore, O Lord my God, You exist so truly that You cannot even be thought not to exist,"[14] he is giving expression to a profound element in religious sensibility.

I suppose that Tillich would be quick to deny that the God above God was illusory, imaginary, or merely possible.[15] But such purely negative comfort, especially when coupled with the equally strong denial of the corresponding positive ontological claims, is probably insufficient to sustain a genuinely religious life. Unless the object of our worship and allegiance can be given some positive ontological standing, most of us will take the religious game to be up.

Well, that is a curious problem in Tillichian theology, and perhaps it ought to give Tillichians some concern. I leave it for the moment but will come back to it after thinking briefly about Tillich's views on the ontological status of the perhaps "lesser" God, the God of theism.

Christian theists, of course, have characteristically claimed that their God exists.[16] Anselm, as we have just seen, says indeed that

---

[14] Anselm, *Proslogion*, chap. 3. Translated by Jasper Hopkins under the title *A New, Interpretive Translation of St. Anselm's Monologion and Proslogion* (Minneapolis: Arthur J. Banning Press, 1986), p. 227.

[15] Indeed, I suppose he should say that the God above God is *not* possible at all.

[16] Eleonore Stump, an early reader of this essay, reminds me that there is a strong medieval Christian tradition that also construes God as being-itself but which should not be confused with the Tillichian view. As I understand it, these medievals, unlike Tillich, construe God as also existing, and therefore as a being, indeed as the most fundamental of all beings and the one who exists more truly than anything else. What seems to be involved here is something like a Platonic universal that is also self-instantiated. So God is being-itself and also the full and perfect instantiation of being-itself. That is why He exists incomparably more truly than anything else that exists. Tillich, on the other hand, might be thought of as holding that being-itself is a universal—a property or something analogous to a property—which is partially and imperfectly instantiated in existing things but which has no full and perfect instantiation. It is not self-instantiated, so it is not a being, and it is not fully instantiated in anything else.

God exists in some especially strong way, "so truly". And the existence claim has been a staple of Christian thought both before and after his time. In addition, many Christian philosophers and theologians have not only claimed that their God exists; they have undertaken to provide various epistemic supports for that claim. Some, for example, have advanced *arguments* for that purpose, arguments for the existence of God. Others have claimed that belief in the existence of God—the God of theism—is supported by religious *experience*. And so on. But what of Tillich?

I don't know whether Tillich ever said flatly that the God of theism does not exist. He does, however, speak approvingly of atheism, atheism with respect to the God of theism. He says, for example, that atheism "is justified as the reaction against theological theism and its disturbing implications."[17] Probably, therefore, we would not be going amiss if we said that Tillich is an atheist regarding the God of theism. And if so, then Tillich seems to be an atheist about both God and the God above God.

Whatever may be the rationale for Tillich's "uppercase" atheism, however, he doesn't seem to provide much of a ground for "lowercase" atheism. That is, the sorts of complaints which he makes against the God of theism don't seem to militate against the existence of that being. Suppose for the moment that it is true that the God of theism is (or would be, if he existed) a thing among things, a being rather than being-itself, an ego which is related to a thou, and so on. And suppose too that the God of theism does not provide the solution to the problem of existential despair in the face of non-being and meaninglessness. Would those facts, if they were facts, show that the God of theism does not exist? It wouldn't seem so. There are lots of existing entities that are things among things, beings rather than being-itself, egos related to thous, and so on. Take Mount Shuksan, for example, or even me. And there are many existent things which are not the answer to existential despair. Why then should we take these failings of the God of theism, if indeed they are failings, to preclude his existence?

These observations begin to bring us back to the curious problem I set aside a few pages back, the problem of the religious significance of denying the existence, and the reality, of the God above God. What is a Tillichian to do with the God of theism, if it turns out that the God of theism actually does exist? Perhaps the most attractive response to this problem, for a Tillichian anyway, would be to treat

---

[17] Tillich, *The Courage to Be*, p. 185.

this being as an interesting, and perhaps very important, part of reality but not as the final focus of religious life and faith. A Tillichian might accept the possibility that the God of theism exists—that is, she or he might accept the possibility that there exists a being which matches, in important respects, what theists have thought about God. But the Tillichian who admits that possibility will have to go on to deny that such a being could be *God*. He or she will deny, that is, that such a being is a suitable object of ultimate concern, a proper focus of worship, and so on. There would be something wrong, idolatrous perhaps, in orienting one's religious life toward that being.

But why would that orientation be wrong? Suppose, for example, that Anselm's God exists. That God would be a being than whom no greater could be conceived—not only the greatest actually existing being but the greatest *possible* being. He would be a being of unsurpassable goodness, love, power, wisdom, knowledge, and so on. That certainly looks like a strong candidate for a suitable object of worship and ultimate concern.

Might the Tillichian reply in turn that no existing entity could satisfy the Anselmian definition, because being-itself is greater than any possible being? That response would not seem to be successful. For one thing, being-itself (construed in the Tillichian way) is not a candidate in the Anselmian sweepstakes. Anselm's definition is intended to pick out the greatest conceivable *being*. But being-itself, according to Tillich, is not a being at all, whether great or mediocre. Consequently, being-itself is not a being greater than the God of theism (nor, for that matter, is being-itself a being greater than me). And so even if it were a fact that being-itself is greater than any possible being, it would still seem to be possible that some actually existing being—the God of theism—should satisfy the Anselmian definition.

No doubt the Tillichian, some Tillichians anyway, will think of responding that the properly religious attitudes and responses should be directed toward whatever is greatest and not toward any lesser candidate, regardless of whether what is greatest is the greatest possible *being*. Perhaps, indeed, this is a point which Anselm would accept. It seems to have an Anselmian flavor about it. And such Tillichians will go on to say that being-itself is indeed greater than any possible being. Fair enough; perhaps the argument of the preceding paragraph does lay too much stress on a particular wording. But this Tillichian reply will lead us, I think, to a deeper question. What reason is there for thinking that being-itself *is* in fact greater than any possible being? Suppose, that is, that we forget the word *being* for the moment, and simply say something like "Thou art that than which nothing greater can be conceived." Thus we would allow into the competition for greatness any actual existents, and any possible existents, and also anybody's favorite non-existent, such as being-itself. What reason is there to think that this, presumably more open, field of candidates will produce a different result in the end? Perhaps it is the God of theism, the God who "so truly" exists, who is greater than all other actual existents, and all other possible existents, and all those non-existents whose existence is not even possible.

I think that one would be hard put to find in the Tillichian approach any strong reason for ruling out that possibility, and for supposing that being-itself must be greater than any possible being.[18] Perhaps we can get a little better idea of the difficulties facing the Tillichian here by considering one of the ways in which Tillich thinks that the God of theism falls short, religiously, of the God above God. The God of theism, he suggests, cannot provide us with "the courage to be" in the face of the threat of non-being. Because such a God is a being, rather than being-itself, he "is not more real than any finite being", and so far as the courage to be is concerned he has "disappeared in the abyss of meaninglessness with every other value and meaning."[19]

But again suppose that we think of the God of theism construed in a more-or-less Anselmian way. That God, if he exists at all, exists *necessarily*. If he exists, then it is not even logically possible that he should fail to exist. As some of us now like to say, if he exists in some possible world, then he exists in every possible world. And so

[18] Indeed, it might be the case that *every* actual being is greater than being-itself. Maybe God, in creating the world, confers on every actual being a measure of the divine greatness which lifts that thing above the level of being itself.

An anonymous reader has called my attention to the following argument (taken from John Wyclif's *Tractatus de Universalibus*). The value of a thing is not less than the value that would be removed from the universe were that thing removed from the universe. If being-itself were removed, every individual being would also be removed. The totality of individual beings has a value greater than that of any individual being. Therefore, being-itself is greater in value than any individual being.

This is an ingenious argument, but it loses its force if being-itself is a self-instantiated universal—fully and perfectly instantiated in the God of theism whose essence, as some of the medieval philosophers held, is to be (see n. 16). In that case Wyclif's principle would entail that the value of God is not less than that of the sum of all beings (including Himself) and greater than that of any *other* individual being.

[19] Tillich, *The Courage to Be*, pp. 186, 187.

this God, the God of theism, constitutes an absolute barrier against the triumph of non-being. In the face of the God of theism there is no possibility at all that the threat of non-being should ever be realized. Any theist, therefore, who found himself or herself oppressed by that threat could take courage from the thought of an Anselmian God of theism.

Furthermore, if what oppresses the theist is the possibility of *his or her own* non-being, rather than that of non-being in general, the God of theism would seem to be existentially superior to the God above God. For the former, unlike the latter, is a being who *loves* his creation, who *cares* for his people, and so on. And so it would seem to be the God of theism, rather than the God above God, who could provide one with the courage to be, even in the valley of the shadow of death.

It seems quite possible, therefore, that even if we are willing to go along with Tillich in talking about being-itself, the power of being, the ground of being, and so on, we might still insist that none of these were suitable and proper objects of religious concern and adoration. For we might hold, and with some reason, that the God of theism is greater than being-itself, and that the power of being is nothing other than the power of that being who exists so truly that he cannot even be thought not to exist. The God above God would thus succumb to the first of the dangers I mentioned earlier. Pushed into a realm beyond existence, he loses touch with reality and thus with any human religious concern.

2. John Hick and the Real

John Hick is as much a super-transcendentalist as Paul Tillich, but he makes the T-move in a rather different way. Hick's motivation is largely ecumenical, a generous desire to "see the best" in all the great post-axial faiths that now dominate the world's religious geography, as well perhaps as in the pre-axial nature religions of which some scattered fragments remain, and in the "new religions", which some people scorn as cults. In all the post-axial religions, and perhaps in the others as well, Hick sees a soteriological process at work, something that is reorienting the lives of believers away from self-centeredness and toward reality-centeredness. We can actually see that happening in all the great religions, he suggests, in the saints, the bodhisattvas, the mahatmas, and so on. And other believers, though perhaps lagging far behind, are on essentially the same path. Hick, we might say, sees all these religions as enterprises that actually work—they are successful in bringing about a genuine spiritual transformation.

The great religions, however, really do constitute a plurality. They are not identical. In particular, these religions recognize an impressive diversity of "ultimates". Among these are the personal gods, the *personae*, of the theistic faiths and the impersonal absolutes, the *impersonae*, of the great non-theistic religions. So believers give their allegiance variously to Vishnu, Allah, Nirvana, the Father, Adonai, the Tao, Brahma, and others. Hick wants to take his own stand within one of these religious traditions, Christianity. But he wants also to survey this whole field of religious activity and faith with a sympathetic, ecumenical eye. What is such a person to say about this plethora of divine entities, personal and impersonal?

Hick rejects the suggestion that we should take all these names to be the many names of one and the same thing. Apparently he takes the "intentions", the connotations, of these names too seriously for that. For the various gods and absolutes are described in ways that make it impossible that any one thing should satisfy all the descriptions. As he says, "Surely these reported ultimates, personal and non-personal, are mutually exclusive."[20] The gods, therefore, as actually recognized and identified in the various religions are too different from one another to be plausibly thought of as really being identical.

The naturalistic theorist, Hick says, would simply "see all these systems of belief as factually false." But Hick has already argued that religious believers are fully reasonable in interpreting their experiences of the transcendent in a realistic way, and thus it is reasonable for them "to believe in the reality of that which is thus apparently experienced." With that conclusion in hand, he goes on to say, "One cannot dismiss the realm of religious experience and belief as illusory, even though its internal plurality and diversity must preclude any simple and straightforward account of it."[21]

Hick's own solution to this problem appeals to the distinction between noumena and phenomena, as developed by Immanuel Kant. The gods and absolutes of the particular religions, he suggests, are phenomenal entities (or at least something rather similar to phenomenal entities). They are experienced entities, constituted by some

[20] John Hick, *An Interpretation of Religion* (New Haven: Yale University Press, 1989), p. 234.
[21] Ibid., pp. 234, 235.

combination of an input from a more basic level of reality and a set of interpretive and constitutive categories. The categories, supplied by the religious traditions, differ from religion to religion, and that accounts for the diversity of gods. But there is a noumenal reality behind or beneath these phenomenal entities. And that noumenal reality Hick calls "the Real".[22] And so the thesis he proposes to explore, he says, is "that the great post-axial faiths constitute different ways of experiencing, conceiving and living in relation to an ultimate divine Reality which transcends all our varied versions of it."[23]

Earlier, I said that Tillich seems to be an atheist both with respect to God and with respect to the God above God. Hick, on the contrary, might more plausibly be thought of as a polytheist with respect to the gods and a monotheist with respect to the ultimate divine reality, the Real.

Now, Hick seems to use the expression "the Real" as a referring expression. To what does it refer? Well, it looks like a definite description. In the ideal case, I suppose, a definite description refers to the one and only thing that satisfies the description. If nothing satisfies the description, or if more than one thing satisfies it, then perhaps the situation is more cloudy. On the most hard-nosed interpretation, however, these would be cases in which the description has no referent at all; it simply fails to refer. But let us not worry about these more unfortunate possibilities now. Let us suppose that there is in fact exactly one thing (in some sense of "is" and "thing") which satisfies the description, "the Real". And let us suppose also that when Hick uses this expression he succeeds in referring to that thing.

Now, why should not the partisan of some particular religion, not so ecumenically minded as Hick, immediately take advantage of this success by claiming that the primary term in his own religious vocabulary also refers to this very same thing? Why, for example, should a Buddhist not claim that "Nirvana" refers to just the same thing as "the Real", and that therefore Nirvana is the Real? And someone else might say that Adonai is identical with the Real, and so on.

It seems pretty clear that Hick could not readily accept claims of this sort. For one thing, he holds that the *personae* and *impersonae* of the great religions are not identical with one another. Hence they could not all be identical with the Real. Indeed, if no two of them

[22] Ibid., pp. 236–49.
[23] Ibid., pp. 235, 236.

are identical with each other, then no more than one of them could possibly be identical with the Real. And the suggestion that just one such claim is true would not fit well with Hick's sort of ecumenism.

For another thing, Hick wants to make a sharp distinction of ontological level between the gods of the religions, on the one hand, and the Real, on the other hand. One possibility, he suggests, is that the various gods may be "projections of the religious imagination", which, while they "are not objectively existent personal individuals", nevertheless truly represent some aspect of the Real.[24] But presumably it is not possible that some projection of the religious imagination, some hallucination, could be identical with the Real. And so, on this interpretation of the gods, none of the claims we are considering could possibly be true.

The other possibility that Hick countenances is that the various gods (and also the *impersonae* of the non-theistic religions) are real—though they are not the Real. They are, in Kantian terms, *phenomena*. They are constituted "by informational input from external reality being interpreted by the mind in terms of its own categorical scheme and thus coming to consciousness as a meaningful phenomenal experience."[25] Hick explicitly says that his theory here is analogous to Kant's theory of sense perception, though Hick allows that the categories constitutive of religious experience may be culturally determined and culturally variable rather than universal features of human rationality. On this view, then, it would seem that the gods should be construed as real—real in the same sense as Kantian cantaloupes and oceans. But, just like Kantian physical objects, the gods are related to an underlying noumenal reality, and that underlying reality is what Hick calls "the Real". And since the Real is noumenal while the gods are phenomenal, no god could be identical with the Real.

In both of these possible cases, then, there is a pronounced ontological distinction between the gods and the Real. It would seem, therefore, that Hick could not accept the suggestion that Nirvana, say, or Adonai, is identical with the Real without giving up the governing principle of his view.

---

[24] Ibid., p. 273. Hick draws an analogy here with what some psychical researchers call "veridical hallucinations", apparitions of the dead in bodily form, speaking, and so on. These are hallucinations in the sense that no relevant body, sound waves, and so on are present to the experiencing subject, but they are veridical if, for example, they incorporate true information (psychically transmitted and received, presumably) about the circumstances of a recent death, etc.

[25] Ibid., p. 243.

But the enthusiast of Nirvana also has her case. After all, Hick either does or does not succeed in referring when he uses the expression "the Real". If he does not, then it would seem that the sentences in which that expression occurs will not express truths. And in that case perhaps we can just forget about this theory and go back to square one—go back, that is, to one or another of the particular religions, such as Buddhism. If, however, Hick does succeed in referring to the Real, then it must be possible to do so. And the enthusiast of Nirvana may then claim that this is just what she does. Perhaps there is some element in what Hick means by "the Real" that enables that expression to refer to the ultimate reality. If so, the Nirvanist claims that element as part of (or the whole of) her meaning for "Nirvana". And whatever referential intentions Hick has when he uses this expression, the Nirvanist claims those intentions as also being her own. And so she claims that if Hick succeeds, then she also succeeds. Nirvana, then, would be simply identical with the Real, and if the Real is noumenal rather than phenomenal, then Nirvana is that very same *noumenal* reality.

It might be suggested here that Nirvana, as construed by Buddhists, could not be identical with the Real, because Nirvana has properties that are logically incompatible with those of the Real.[26] That might possibly be so, but it is not at all obvious that it is so in fact. Any claim to that effect would have to be considered rather carefully.

Let us suppose, for the sake of the argument, that there is some property, P, such that it is logically impossible that something which has P is ultimately real. Consequently, it is not possible that an entity which has P also satisfies the description, "the Real". And suppose too that some Buddhists—or all Buddhists, for that matter—say that Nirvana has P. Would it follow from these suppositions that Nirvana is not identical with the Real? By no means. What would follow is that *if these Buddhists are correct in what they say or believe about Nirvana*, then Nirvana is not identical with the Real. But Buddhists are not bound to be infallible about Nirvana, just as Christians may sometimes be mistaken in what they think about God, and so on. Perhaps these Buddhists are simply mistaken in thinking that Nirvana has P. And in that case Nirvana may, after all, be identical with the Real.

Someone may continue the objection by observing that Nirvana is

---

[26] I owe also to Eleonore Stump the suggestion that I might consider this objection more fully.

a Buddhist concept, and so it is Buddhists who have the right to define it. The Buddhist definition, that is, should take precedence over mine. That may well be right—at any rate, I don't have any objection to it. But I don't really know whether there is an official Buddhist definition of Nirvana or, if there is one, what it is. In any case, the fact that Buddhists believe and say that Nirvana has P is not very strong evidence that P is an essential element in the concept of Nirvana. Maybe in saying such things they are not undertaking to define Nirvana but simply to make an assertion about it. After all, when we use referring expressions we are not usually defining them; often we are simply using them in the course of making non-definitional assertions about their referents.

That fact is what makes it possible for people to disagree about one and the same entity, and to express their disagreement in mutually incompatible propositions. People argue about what role George Bush played in the Iran-Contra affair. The various assertions made about Mr. Bush in this connection cannot all be true. But a crucial element in this impossibility is the fact that all of these assertions really are about the same person, George Bush. (If they were about different people, then they might all be true without much difficulty.) Consequently, the people who say conflicting things about Mr. Bush must all succeed in referring to him, even though some of them have mistaken beliefs about him and make false assertions about him. What these people say about Mr. Bush is not *definitive* of him, and mistakes in these assertions are not fatal to the reference of his name or other referring expressions. I would suppose that if the term 'Nirvana' refers at all (as Hick himself apparently supposes that it does), then it will be similarly resistant to the effects of falsity in the statements in which it occurs.

What I say here about Nirvana would apply also to the Real. Even if we suppose that Hick really does refer to something by using that expression, we need not be committed to thinking that therefore everything Hick says about the Real must be true. And not everything that Hick says about the Real need be taken as a definition of that term, nor must it be a crucial element in determining the reference of that expression. Hick too might be mistaken, mistaken about the properties of the Real. And so the alleged impossibility of Nirvana's being identical with the Real might be due to an error on that side rather than on the part of the Nirvanist.

Despite what I say here, it may be that Nirvana is not identical with the Real. I have argued only that the fact that incompatible claims are made by the enthusiasts of these things does not show that they are indeed disparate entities. We should need more than that.

Well, the Nirvanist might claim that Nirvana is identical with the Real. But, of course, it might be not only the Nirvanist who makes such a claim. Maybe a Muslim will say as much for Allah, the Jew for Adonai, and so on. Indeed, I suppose that this would not be an uncommon reaction. Probably it is part of the phenomenology of every religion that its more thoughtful adherents will suppose that the fundamental reality of their religion is the most fundamental reality there is—in other words, the Real.[27]

Now, Hick may well point out that these claims could not all be true, for the *personae* and *impersonae* cannot all be identical with one another. Or at least they cannot be identical unless almost all religious thinkers are wildly mistaken about their gods and ultimates. Allah, for example, could not be identical with Nirvana, since one of these is personal and the other is impersonal. And so they could not both be identical with the Real. Well, maybe that is true. But that fact, if it is a fact, does not count against the Nirvanist's claim. For the Nirvanist—at least the Nirvanist I imagine—does not claim that all the gods, etc., are identical with the Real. She claims only that Nirvana is identical with the Real. In a similar way, the Muslim may claim only that Allah is identical with the Real. And so also for the Christian, the Jew, and the others. But each one of these particular claims is perfectly compatible with the fact that they cannot all be true. In fact, all these enthusiasts may well make that latter fact part of their own theology.

What must be crucial here is Hick's conviction that all the religions must be on the same level, so to speak. So if the various gods cannot all be identical with the Real, then *none* of them can be identical with the Real.[28] But why must all the religions be thought to be on the same level?

Hick asks a closely related question at the end of his chapter on "The Pluralistic Hypothesis."

> But if the Real in itself is not and cannot be humanly experienced, why postulate such an unknown and unknowable *Ding an sich*? The

---

[27] "[Religion] says that the best things are the more eternal things, the overlapping things, the things in the universe that throw the last stone, so to speak, and say the final word." William James, "The Will to Believe," sec. 10, in his *The Will to Believe and Other Essays in Popular Philosophy* (New York: Longmans Green and Co., 1897), p. 25.

[28] And so, presumably, it would be impossible for there to be a religion which had the Real as its object of worship, ultimate concern, etc.?

answer is that the divine noumenon is a necessary postulate of the pluralistic religious life of humanity. For within each tradition we regard as
real the object of our worship or contemplation. If, as I have already
argued, it is also proper to regard as real the objects of worship or
contemplation within the other traditions, we are led to postulate the
Real *an sich* as the presupposition of the veridical character of this range
of forms of religious experience.[29]

And so the crucial argument would seem to be that which establishes that it is proper for us to regard as real not only the God of
our own religion but also the gods of all the other forms of religious
life. What is that argument?

Hick's own explicit argument seems to be the following: "Nor can
we reasonably claim that our own form of religious experience, together with that of the tradition of which we are a part, is veridical
whilst the others are not. . . . Persons living within other traditions,
then, are equally justified in trusting their own distinctive religious
experience and in forming their beliefs on the basis of it."[30] For Hick
had indeed argued earlier that the adherents of a great variety of
religious faiths (as well, indeed, as the rejectors of religion) were
justified in holding their particular positions.[31]

That earlier argument, supporting the rationality of a plurality of
faiths, seems to me to be correct in general. But that really doesn't
matter much for the point under consideration. For the fact that
many faiths are rational does not at all preclude our reasonably
claiming that our own faith, and the experiences associated with it,
are veridical while the others are not. To suppose that it does have
that effect is to confuse the idea of rationality with that of truth or
veridicality. But these ideas are distinct. In particular, the fact that a
certain belief is rational for a certain person does not show that his
belief is true. And the fact that a certain person is justified in taking
her experience (conceptualized in the categories supplied by her tradition, etc.) to be veridical does not show that her experience *is* veridical. Therefore, my accepting that it is rational for some other person to believe the things she believes, or that it is rational for her to
rely on her experience in forming her beliefs, does not at all commit
me to thinking that her beliefs are true, or that her experiences are
as likely to be veridical as some competing experiences to which I
am attracted.

[29] Hick, *An Interpretation of Religion*, p. 249.
[30] Ibid., p. 235.
[31] Ibid., pp. 210–30.

The reason for this is stated by Hick himself. "What is reasonable for a given person at a given time to believe depends in large part upon what we may call, in the cybernetic sense, his or her information or cognitive input." And he adds a little later that "the reference is to the rationality of the believing, not of what is believed. A proposition believed can be true or false: it is the believing of it that is rational or irrational."[32] That is, the rationality of believing is highly sensitive to the personal situation of the believer. The relevant situations include a variety of epistemic factors, and perhaps some non-epistemic factors as well.[33] And these situations vary from person to person. It certainly seems plausible to me to suppose that people who have lived their entire lives in cultures very different from my own, and whose religious views have been formed from childhood in traditions much different from mine, may be in substantially different epistemic circumstances from mine. I have, therefore, no great difficulty in supposing that it may be reasonable for them to hold the beliefs that they do hold. But that is not a reason for thinking that their beliefs are true or likely to be true.

Hick not only makes this point about the person-relativity of rationality, but he provides an example of it from his own perspective. For Hick holds that it was (or may well have been) rational for Jesus, living in first-century Palestine, to believe in demons, and to experience certain diseases (e.g., epilepsy) as cases of demon possession. And he also holds that we may be obliged to reject those same beliefs, because they do not cohere well with modern scientific beliefs.[34]

A more general argument for this same conclusion starts with the assumption that it is rational for a person to order his or her religious life within one or another of the great religions in accordance with his or her own religious experience.[35] It could hardly be rational for me to be, say, a Christian, worshipping God the Father, Son, and Holy Spirit, on the basis of my religious experience, unless it were also rational for me to take that experience to be veridical. In a similar way, a Hindu could not be rational in undertaking the worship of Vishnu on the basis of his religious experience, unless it were rational for him to take his experience to be veridical. The Buddhist could not be rational is contemplating Nirvana as the ultimate

---

[32] Ibid., pp. 211, 212.

[33] A classic and germinal discussion of the relevance of non-epistemic factors is William James's essay "The Will to Believe."

[34] Hick, *An Interpretation of Religion*, pp. 217–19.

[35] This is, of course, one of Hick's prominent theses.

principle unless she were rational in taking her relevant experiences to be veridical. And so on. But Hick himself holds that these gods and impersonal principles are often construed in such a way that it is not possible that all of them exist. "The gods of the monotheistic faiths", he says, "are thought of in each case as the one and only God, so that it is impossible for there to be more than one instantiation of the concept. . . . Surely these reported ultimates, personal and non-personal, are mutually exclusive."[36] If that is so, then I could not consistently take my own experience to be veridical without also rejecting the veridicality (though not the rationality) of at least some of the experiences that are constitutive of some other faiths.

The truth, then, appears to be that we cannot reasonably claim that our own form of religious experience is veridical unless we also claim that some other religious experiences are not veridical. We should expect, of course, that the adherents of other faiths (also seeking consistency) will characterize some of our most prized experiences as non-veridical. But that is just one more example of the general truth that some religions really do make claims that are logically incompatible with those of some other religions.

Another observation Hick makes might seem to have some bearing on this question of whether to treat all the religions alike. Hick proposes a criterion by which to judge the value of various religious traditions:

> The function of post-axial religion is to create contexts within which the transformation of human existence from self-centeredness to Reality-centeredness can take place. Accordingly the basic criterion must be soteriological. Religious traditions and their various components—beliefs, modes of experience, scriptures, rituals, disciplines, ethics and lifestyles, social rules and organisations—have greater or less value according as they promote or hinder the salvific transformation.[37]

And he goes on to say that we can recognize, in the various religions, a type of human being which he calls a "saint", and which he describes as "one in whom the transformation of human existence from self-centeredness to Reality-centeredness is so much more advanced than in the generality of us that it is readily noticed and

---

[36] Hick, *An Interpretation of Religion*, p. 234.

[37] Ibid., p. 300. He also puts forward another criterion, presumably of secondary importance, "the ethical criterion" (pp. 316–42). The upshot of this criterion seems to be pretty much the same as that of the soteriological criterion.

acknowledged."[38] In such persons the process of salvation and liberation is so far advanced as to be evident, and such people are in fact recognized across religious boundaries. One might hope, therefore, to make some religion-neutral estimate of the comparative value of various religious traditions by reference to their success in producing saints.

Well, how do the great religions stack up relative to this criterion? Hick says that "the criterion of saintliness, then, enables us to recognize the great traditions as areas of salvation/liberation, but does not enable us to go on to grade them comparatively." And that is because "we do not have sufficient information for an answer" to the comparative question. Apparently, we do not have enough detailed information to judge the comparative efficiency of the various religions in the salvific enterprise. However, Hick ventures his own "impressionistic judgment that no one tradition stands out as more productive of sainthood than another."[39] Assuming this to be true, then, so far as we can tell, the great religions are pretty much on a par.

Yes, but parity along which dimension? Assuming that Hick's "impressionistic judgment" is roughly correct, they are on a par with respect to the production of saints, and therefore (perhaps) they are on a par as vehicles of salvation and liberation. Must they also be on a par with respect to the veridicality of the experiences associated with them or on a par with respect to the ontological status of their gods and absolutes? It would not seem so. Why should not a Hindu, for example, maintain that in all the religions it is Vishnu who is active, turning men and women away from self and toward a way of life centered on Reality? And this man—the one I imagine, anyway—will add that it is Vishnu who is fully real, and so it is Vishnu who is the proper referent of the expression "the Real".

To whatever extent it is plausible to suppose that Vishnu might be identical with the gods of some other religions, this man will say that in those other religions also Vishnu is recognized and experienced *an sich*, though under some other name. And what of the religions whose fitness to be vehicles of salvation is attested by the men and women who have come to saintliness within them but whose gods or absolutes are construed so differently that it is implausible to think that they could be identical with Vishnu? Here, so

[38] Ibid., p. 301.
[39] Ibid., p. 307.

far as I can see, the enthusiast of Vishnu can avail himself of either
of Hick's alternatives. He may say that the gods of these conceptually remote religions are imaginary entities, or hallucinations,
which nevertheless encode some veridical information derived from
Vishnu, and who perhaps also mediate some causal influence origi-
nating in the power of Vishnu. Or he may say that these other gods
and absolutes are real at some level, though not at the same deep
level as Vishnu. They are something like phenomena, of which
Vishnu is the noumenal reality. The experiences in which these gods
are present to their worshippers are perhaps veridical in some sense
but not in the deep sense in which the experiences of Vishnu are
veridical. And the reason for this is that the categories that are available in those conceptually remote religions are such that they cannot
plausibly be fitted to Vishnu. Those categories do not permit a veridical experience of Vishnu. The best that can be done with them is to
construct something like a phenomenal entity which they will indeed fit. And that is what those worshippers have done.

Now, what can be said against that enthusiast of Vishnu? We can
observe, of course, that the enthusiasts of Adonai, the Trinity, Nirvana, and so on, may make similar claims about their gods and absolutes. These claims cannot all be true. But (as I have argued) this
does not show that no one of them is true, and hence it does not
count against someone who claims only that his or her particular
god is the noumenal reality, the Real.

Might someone argue that the similarity of effects—the production of saints—is evidence of a single underlying cause?[40] Well, perhaps so. But that need not bother the enthusiast of Vishnu. For he
himself posits a single underlying cause for the occurrence of sainthood. He attributes it everywhere and in all the religions to the self-
same cause, the saving power of Vishnu.

Perhaps it will be said that this partisan of Vishnu cannot be right,
because it is impossible, or at least unlikely, that such profound effects as salvation, liberation from self-centeredness, and sainthood
could be effected through the mediation of imaginary, hallucinatory,
or merely phenomenal entities. These things can occur only in religious contexts in which the Real is present *an sich*, and acknowl-

---

[40] Someone who did argue in this way, it seems to me, would have departed a long
way from the Kantian notion of phenomena and noumena. I would suppose that in
the Kantian metaphysics the causal relations and the arguments that appeal to these
relations have their place entirely within the phenomenal world. They do not provide
a bridge from the phenomenal to the noumenal.

edged in his (or its) own true character. But, in the first place, this objection would not be available to someone like Hick. For Hick holds that salvation, the production of saints, and so on normally does take place within the particular religious traditions and under the aegis of their phenomenal (or even imaginary) gods and ultimates.[41] The Hindu whom I am imagining simply acknowledges that this is indeed what sometimes happens. And anyway, why should anyone who thinks that salvation and saintliness are to be accounted for, at some level, by a divine activity be so doctrinaire as this objection requires? Why should we suppose that the divine power for this great purpose could not, or should not, or would not be mediated through phenomenal entities or something like them? It isn't as if we had an immediate insight into every aspect of the preferred mode of divine activity in the soteriological project.

It seems to me, therefore, that along these lines there is nothing strong which can be said against the sort of partisan of Vishnu whom I am imagining.

Furthermore, this man has (or may have) an argument. He has an experience of Vishnu as the ultimate reality. That is, he has an experience which comes to consciousness in him conceptualized in terms of Vishnu and ultimate reality. And he takes that experience to be veridical. If he did not take it to be veridical, he might well have no reason at all to bother himself about Vishnu. And if he were not rational in taking it to be veridical, he might well not be rational in giving his allegiance to Vishnu. But he does take it to be veridical, and (following Hick here) he is rational in doing so. So he believes, and rationally believes, that Vishnu is identical with the Real. He also recognizes that not all the other gods can be identical with Vishnu. Consequently, he denies of some of them that they are ultimately real. And therefore he also denies that experiences of them as ultimately real are veridical.

What could we say against this argument, seeing it now for a second time? The logic of it seems to be persuasive. Substantively, if this man's experience of Vishnu really is veridical, then he is right— Vishnu is the Real, and the other gods are either identical with Vishnu or else they are not ultimately real. We can reject his conclusion, in a strong way, only if we can reject the premiss that his experience of Vishnu as ultimately real is veridical. Is it possible to do that?

---

[41] "The soteriological transformation normally occurs within the context of a particular tradition." Hick, *An Interpretation of Religion*, p. 301.

Yes, or so at least it seems to me. There might be more than one way to do it. But what seems most relevant in this context is that someone—I?, we?, you?—should have an experience whose veridicality is incompatible with the veridicality of the Vishnu experience, and that it should be this other experience that is in fact veridical. If in fact, for example, the Trinity of Christian theism is so diverse from Vishnu that they could not possibly be the same God, and if someone veridically experiences the Trinity as the Real, the ultimate reality, then the Vishnu premiss is mistaken and the Vishnu experience is not veridical.[42]

I think that there will not be a lack of candidates for this role. That fact is just one more manifestation of the conflict of religions. Maybe someone thinks that no one has, or could have, any reason to prefer one of these candidates to another. It is hard to imagine, however, how such a claim could be substantiated. Each of these religionists, after all, will have what seems to her or him a good reason, for each is relying on her or his own experience. It is not easy to think of a good argument which could show that every such person is mistaken and that every such reliance is improper. Perhaps an observer who stood outside the whole religious enterprise and who had no religious experience of her or his own would be unable to decide among these competing claims. But I don't know why such a person should be thought to be in any specially favorable epistemic position with respect to this question. Nor is it clear why anyone within one or another of the religious traditions should feel obliged to defer to this outside judgment.

Hick's version of the T-move seems to me, then, to attract a rather different sort of response than Tillich's version attracts. Hick's version emphasizes the reality of the super-transcendent entity. That, I think, makes it very attractive to a person within a religous tradition. For the idea that one should concern oneself with the most fundamental of all realities, with whatever it is that "casts the last stone", as James put it, is deep in religious sensibility. Maybe that just is the religious enterprise. But the religious thinker who reflects on his or her own experience, and on the god or absolute who seems to be revealed there, is likely to think that this feature has already been incorporated into his or her own faith. "But isn't that just what the Dharmakaya is, the truly Real, the rock-bottom level?"

---

[42] As I have noted before, it would not follow that the enthusiast of Vishnu was not reasonable in his or her beliefs or that the religion oriented around Vishnu was not a vehicle of salvation.

she or he may ask. "The Real could not be more basic than the Dharmakaya; it just is the Dharmakaya." And within the other traditions similar things will be said about the Trinity, about Allah, and the others. The Real is religiously attractive because of the deep religious orientation toward what is real. The suggestion, therefore, that there is something still *more* real than the religious object will be intolerable to many believers. Their move, in response to the T-move, is likely to be that of identifying the religious object with the allegedly more basic reality. And thus the high gods, of Hick's sort, always stand in danger of being eaten and absorbed by some allegedly lower deity.

3. Conclusion

I have argued here that the high gods, postulated by the super-transcendentalizing move that has often seemed attractive to philosophers of religion, are characteristically vulnerable. They may, on the one hand, be construed in a way which makes them irrelevant to religious life and experience. Kicked upstairs, they can thenceforth largely be ignored. On the other hand, they may be construed in ways that make them religiously attractive. In that case, they are likely to be assimilated by some allegedly lower gods that belong to the particular religions. My argument here has been carried out mostly in terms of two recent attempts at identifying such a high god. There can, of course, be other such attempts, and my conclusions may not automatically carry over to them. But my conjecture is that these dangers are endemic to the project of super-transcendentalizing.

RICHARD SWINBURNE

God and Time

An occasional change of view about a very difficult philosophical topic can only be a sign of openness to argument. In this essay I defend some of the theses of one of Norman Kretzmann's two main essays on God and time against some of the theses of the other; I also offer a rebuttal of a thesis that I had previously defended in print. The essay is offered in grateful appreciation of all that Norman has done to bring into the current debate the achievements of medieval thought on the great issues of the philosophy of religion, as well as in appreciation of his own contributions to that subject.

Let us understand by "God", in line with the tradition of Western religion, the Lord of the universe who alone brings about (or permits others to bring about) as it happens what happens at all moments of time, and who is as "great" as such a being can logically be (and thus has, in such logically possible respects as to maximize that greatness, the traditional properties of omnipotence, omniscience, perfect freedom, and perfect goodness). How will such a God be related to time?

The simple, naive, initial answer is that God is everlasting. He determines what happens at all moments of time "as it happens" because he exists at all moments of time. He exists now; he has existed at each moment of past time; he will exist at each moment of future time. This is, I believe, the view explicit or implicit in Old and New Testaments and in virtually all the writings of the church fathers of the first three centuries.

Why should any theist find that view unsatisfactory? Because it seems to make God less than sovereign over the universe. It seems to imply that time stands outside God, who is caught in its stream. The cosmic clock ticks inexorably away, and God can do nothing about it. More and more of history is becoming past, accessible to God only by remote memory, and unaffectible by any action of his. The future, however, God does not yet enjoy, but more and more of it is unavoidably looming up on God; and, as it keeps on appearing, if creatures have free will, it may contain some surprises for him. God can only act at the present moment of time, and his lordship of the universe is ever confined to the narrow slice of time between past and future.

Let us call the view of God's relation to time stated in the last paragraph "the view of God as time's prisoner". That it implies these unwelcome consequences was the burden of a major Neo-platonist criticism of the view that God was everlasting—it involved too low a view of God.[1] Hence later theologians took over from Neoplatonism the view that God is outside time; he is timeless or eternal. Origen had expressed that view at the beginning of the third century,[2] but it became the orthodox view only with Augustine at the end of the fourth century. It was then universally taken for granted for the next millennium and in general also assumed by Catholic theologians for the last five hundred years.

The view of God as eternal was given its classical exposition by Boethius: "Eternity is the complete and perfect possession all at once of illimitable life".[3] Everything God knows or does is done all-at-once in a moment of time which has no beginning or end. Hence there are no limits to God's knowledge or action. He knows everything "at once" in his eternal present; but because that present is not

---

[1] These criticisms are contained in Boethius, *De consolatione philosophiae* 5.6. "Whatsoever liveth in time . . . has not yet attained tomorrow, but has already lost yesterday", he wrote. He went on to claim also that divine timelessness leaves "unrestrained the free will of mortals", and hence reward and punishment and prayer to God have a part, which, he implies, they would not if God were within time and still foreknew all our actions. I do not discuss in this essay the latter objection to the view that God is everlasting—the objection that if God is in time and his omniscience involves foreknowledge of future human actions, then those actions could not be free. I stand by what I wrote on this issue in *The Coherence of Theism* (Clarendon Press, 1977), pp. 167–78.

[2] "The phrase which we use . . . that there never was a time when [the Son] did not exist, must be accepted with a reservation. For the very words, when, or never, have a temporal significance, whereas the statements we make about the Father and the Son and the Holy Spirit must be understood as transcending all time and all ages and all eternity." Origen, *De principiis* 4.4.1 (Latin version), trans. G. W. Butterworth (New York: Harper and Row, 1966).

[3] Boethius, *De consolatione philosophiae*, 5.6.

"before" the time of any human action, he *fore*knows no human action. Hence his knowledge of that action is no more incompatible with the action's being free than our observation of someone else's present action is incompatible with its being free. Likewise God can "at once" in his eternal present choose to bring about at any moment of time any (consistently describable) state of affairs. If backward causation is impossible, that imposes no limit on God—for his "eternal present" is later than no time of any state of affairs. We are like travelers moving along a road at the bottom of a mountain. The stages on the road are the moments of time through which we pass. We cannot see or act except at the stage at which we are. But God is like an observer standing on the mountain who can see the road (all of time) in one glance and cast a rock from above onto whatever stage of the road he chooses.

I argue in this essay that the "timeless" view is incoherent. I also argue that to the extent that the "everlasting" view does have the consequence that God is time's prisoner, this only arises from God's voluntary choice.

In order to justify these claims, I need first to establish four principles about time. The first principle is that everything that happens in time happens over a period of time and never at an instant of time—everything, that is, apart from anything analyzable in terms of things happening over periods of time. Instants are the bounding points of the periods during which things happen. Among instants are 2:00.00 P.M. on Friday, 3 November 1989, and 7:30.02 A.M. Saturday, 4 November 1989. Among periods is the period between these two instants. Periods may last for varying intervals such as two hours or three days.

In general our ascription of properties to objects is ascription to them over periods of time—things are green or wet or weigh ten pounds for periods of time. And normally when we do ascribe properties to objects at instants, our doing so is to be read as ascribing them to objects for periods which include the instant. To say that the object is green at 2 P.M. is to say that it is green for some period that includes 2 P.M. It is difficult to see what would be meant by an object being green at 2 P.M. although it was not green either before or after 2 P.M. If it were green for a period of zero duration, how could that differ from its not being green at all? Certainly, things like winning a race or becoming sixty years old can happen at an instant. But one becomes sixty at an instant if and only if that instant is the boundary of a period of sixty years during which one has lived. And one wins a race if and only if one has run it for a period and there is a final segment of that period (however small) during all of which one is ahead of the field. These things apparently happening at an instant are thus analyzable in terms of things happening over periods of time.

The same applies to talk in a scientific context of instantaneous possession of a property by an object, when it does not possess that property before or after the instant in question. Such talk is introduced by a special definition in terms of limits. We say that a particle has instantaneous velocity of 10ft./sec. at 2 P.M. if

$$\lim_{t \to t_2} \frac{s_2 - s}{t_2 - t} \to 10$$

(when $t_2 = 2$ P.M. and s_2 the distance covered at t_2 since some arbitrary origin; $t < t_2$ but is taken closer and closer to it; s is the distance covered at t since the origin; s is measured in feet; t in seconds), where also

$$\lim_{t \to t_2} \frac{s - s_2}{t - t_2} \to 10$$

(t_2 and s_2, t and s as before, but this time $t > t_2$). As we take smaller and smaller intervals of time bounded above *and* below by 2 P.M., the velocity over those intervals converges on 10 ft./sec. But since "instantaneous velocity" is introduced by such careful mathematical definition, the obvious thing to say is that that is what instantaneous velocity is. It's not a velocity possessed at an instant discovered via study of limits but rather a limit of velocities possessed over series of periods bounded by that instant. That that is the right thing to say is brought out by the fact that where velocities from above converge on a different limit from velocities from below, not merely does physics not ascribe an instantaneous velocity, but it provides no grip on what would be meant by a claim about it.[4] My earlier use of "moments" was meant to cover both instants and periods; I can now make my points more precisely, using the latter notions.[5]

---

[4] The conclusion is that of George Berkeley's *The Analyst* (1734), although the argument for it is not.

[5] Any period of time during which an event occurs is infinitely divisible in thought: we can consider one half of the period, one fourth of the period, one eighth of the period, and so on ad infinitum. Hence any period of time is composed of an infinite number of smaller periods. In that sense I shall say (since nothing turns on the dense/

The second principle is that (subject to relativistic considerations which I shall ignore)[6] while time has a topology independently of whether there are laws of nature, it has a metric only if there are laws of nature, and indeed ones that attain a unique simplest form on the assumption that some periodic process measures intervals of equal time. That is, whether an event E_2 occurs after or before an event E_1 is independent of whether there are laws of nature; but whether there is a truth about how much later or earlier than E_2 E_1 occurs—e.g., one hour or two hours—depends on whether there are such laws of nature. For statements about the length of temporal intervals are statements about what would be measured by clocks. We regard some periodic mechanism as a clock because it coincides in the periods it measures with those of many other mechanisms which are or could be constructed (i.e., their periods are linearly related) and because, when natural processes are measured by those clocks, laws of nature which predict their occurrence take a unique simplest form. If there were two kinds of periodic mechanisms which could be constructed, such that clocks of one kind kept time with each other but not with clocks of the other kind (the scale of intervals measured by one might be related asymptotically to the scale of intervals measured by the other) and if clocks of one kind

---

continuous distinction) that time is a continuum. To say that time is a continuum is not to make any claim about how things behave in the natural world; for example, it is not to rule out the possibility of all change in the natural world being staccato— objects always remaining unchanging for some very small period and then changing non-continuously. It is only to say that any period consists of smaller periods, even if some of them are too small for any object to change during them more than once. The very concept of a period during which something remains changeless, or alternatively changes, involves its consisting of more than one smaller period during which things remain changeless or are different. A "period" that did not contain smaller periods would be an instant.

  [6] I ignore relativistic considerations because I do not think they make any great difference to the issues. First, because the special and general theories of relativity are perfectly compatible with the view that there are truths about which events are "abso- lutely simultaneous" with which others (i.e., that there is a unique frame of reference in which measurements of simultaneity are correct), the so-called "relativity of simul- taneity" being a limit on our knowledge of simultaneity (our ability to discover that true frame), not a limit on its existence. See my *Space and Time*, 2d ed. (London: Macmillan and Co. Ltd., 1981), pp. 181–202. And second, because even on the nor- mal interpretation of relativity theory, "the relativity of simultaneity" only applies between events that are not causally connectible (i.e., they are so far away from each other in space that no signal is fast enough to travel from one to the other). All events E_1 and E_2 which are causally connectible are such that if E_1 is earlier than E_2 in one frame of reference, it is earlier in all frames.

enabled laws of one subject matter to reach their simplest form and if clocks of the other kind enabled laws of a different subject matter to reach their simplest form, the only truth about the interval between two events E_1 and E_2 would be that it was (say) one hour by one sort of clock, and two hours by a different sort of clock.[7] If one supposed that there was a truth about temporal interval independent of what was measured by clocks, one would need an explanation of why it is in our universe that clocks measure intervals correctly; it is hard to see what such an explanation would be like. If one denies that there is any reason to suppose that they do measure intervals correctly, one loses one's grip on the notion of a temporal interval. It follows from this line of argument that if there were no laws of nature, and so no periodic mechanisms which kept time with each other, there would be no content to the notion that the interval had any definite length at all.

Periods of time are the periods they are in virtue of the actual or possible events that end or begin when they begin or that end or begin when they end; and instants are the points of time which are the boundaries of such events. By a "possible event" I mean some event of a specified kind, picked out by a uniquely identifying description, which would be brought about in virtue of the laws of nature if some earlier event of a specified kind, picked out by uniquely identifying description, had happened at some earlier period of time, as dated by an actual event. Thus one possible event is the first explosion that would have happened if I had lit a certain fuse with a certain setup at the same time that a certain man walked out the door. Or another possible event is the second coincidence of the minute hand of this clock with "12" which would have occurred if I had started the clock going when John started to run the race.

We normally pick out periods of time by their relations to actual events: the period from the end of this event to the beginning of that event, or from when the clock pointed to 2 until it pointed to 4. But some have argued—rightly, it seems to me—that there could be a universe in which nothing changed for a period of time of definite length, or there could even be a universe empty of matter for such a period of time. In Sydney Shoemaker's thought experiment there is

---

[7] E. A. Milne once suggested that dynamic and electromagnetic processes were best measured by temporal scales that were related to each other asymptotically. See his *Kinematic Relativity* (Oxford: Clarendon Press, 1948), passim and especially pp. 224–25. On this matter, see my *Space and Time*, especially chap. 11.

a universe that has three parts A, B and C, observable from each other.[8] Observers on B and C observe over a period of some fifty years that A "freezes" for a year every three years (i.e., everything on A remains totally changeless); observers on A and C observe that B freezes for a year every four years; and observers on A and B observe that C freezes for a year every five years. They therefore all extrapolate from their observations over the limited period to reach the generalization that these freezings happen outside that period and hence conclude that every sixty years the whole universe (including the observers) freezes for a year. And what content is there to the supposition that this static period when all clocks have stopped lasts for a year rather than for any other length of time? The content is that if some clock had been preserved from the freezing process (e.g., a clock on A if A had not been frozen three years before), that is the length of time it would have measured. Hence the frozen period consists of two half-years, the boundary instant separating them being the instant by which a clock exempt from freezing would have measured one-half year. We can therefore refer to such periods, picking out the beginning or end thereof by the (beginning or end of the) "possible event" of when a clock would have pointed to some figure if we had managed to exempt it from the freezing process. Since laws of nature operate during such a period, the description "instant at which a clock would have measured one half year" picks out a definite instant.

But now suppose a universe in which there are no laws of nature. There will then be no content to talk of periods of time located by their relation to possible events, for "the instant at which such and such would have begun or ceased to happen if initial conditions had been different" picks out no definite instant rather than any other. Even if it were true that if certain initial conditions had occurred, a certain event would have happened (e.g., because God would have brought it about directly), there would be no truth that the event would have begun or ceased to happen at this instant rather than at another instant of the actual temporal continuum in which there are no laws of nature and the initial conditions did not obtain. For instants are the instants they are in virtue of their temporal distance from events. There is nothing intrinsic to the instant that is 3 P.M.

---

[8] Sydney Shoemaker, "Time without Change", *Journal of Philosophy* 66 (1969): 363–81. The extension to a world temporarily lacking any physical objects was made by W. H. Newton-Smith in *The Structure of Time* (London: Routledge and Kegan Paul, 1980), chap. 2.

independent of its temporal relations to other things; nor can an instant be the instant it is in virtue of the other instants to which it is contiguous, for in a temporal continuum, between any two instants, there is always another one. Yet in the absence of laws of nature, there will be no temporal distances and so talk about the instant (of actual time) at which some possible event would have begun or ended is empty. So we could only pick out periods of time by their temporal relations of before or after to actual events—"the period between E_1 and E_2", or "the period before E_1". So if there were no God and the universe had a beginning before which there were no laws of nature, although one can talk of the time before there was a universe (and I think that we must be able to do this, for something can only have a beginning if at an earlier time it was not), one could not distinguish any one such period from any other. And by "one could not distinguish" I mean (in virtue of my earlier argument) that there would be no difference between them: every period ending with the beginning of the universe would be identical to every other. There is no content to the period of an hour before the beginning of the universe distinct from the period of half an hour before that beginning in the absence of laws of nature determining how clocks would have behaved.

The third principle is that the past is that realm of the logically contingent which it is not logically possible that any agent can now affect, and the future is that realm of the logically contingent which it is logically possible that an agent can now affect. (I understand here by "the logically contingent" actual events reported by logically contingent propositions and the periods at which such events could occur and the bounding instants of such periods.) More precisely, the past at an instant t is that realm of the logically contingent which it is not logically possible that any agent can affect by an action over a period which includes t; and conversely for the future. When the question is asked whether an effect can precede its cause, it is often supposed that we have a conception of past and future, on the one hand, and of causality, on the other, and the question asks whether they have always to be instantiated in one alignment, whether time and causation always have to have the same direction. But I do not think that we have such an independent grasp on conceptions of the past or future for the question to be raised in this way. The most primitive concepts that we acquire are the concept of the world's being this way rather than that and the concept of an ability to make it this way rather than that. We then divide events up into those that we can, or could if we were powerful enough, make this way rather than that and those that, however powerful we were, are beyond making this way or that. The former are future, the latter are past.

The present instant is the boundary between past and future. Our use of "present" (alias "happening now") with respect to events that last for a period of time is often somewhat loose and may need more careful spelling out. But roughly speaking, events that last for a period are present if the period includes or terminates with the present instant or is fairly close to it—given that the period is fairly short relative to other periods relevant to the context of discussion. The movements of the walkers I see from the window are, for most contexts of discussion, present events, loosely speaking; even if strictly speaking they are very slightly past. But in a context where we are talking of the physiological processes that produce my "present" perception of them, we would say that the movements perceived are no longer present. My present action of writing this sentence, however, includes (at this stage) both elements that (strictly speaking) are past, and elements that (strictly speaking) are future. It is in this way that the concepts of past and future are connected to the rest of our conceptual scheme.

Causation in a circle is not possible. If A causes B, then B cannot cause A (or cause anything which by a longer circle causes A). For what causes what is logically contingent—"anything can produce anything," wrote Hume.[9] Let me state the point this way: a sufficiently powerful being could—it is logically possible—alter the laws of nature in such a way that some event had, instead of its normal effect, one incompatible with it. So if A caused B and B caused A, a sufficiently powerful being at the moment of B's occurrence could have altered the laws of nature so that B caused not-A; in which case B would have (indirectly) caused B not to occur—which is absurd.

Now it might be suggested that our concepts of the past and future are connected to the rest of our conceptual scheme via the concepts of (personal) memory[10] and perception. An event is past if we

[9] David Hume, *Treatise of Human Nature* 1.3.15. There is, however, a subsequent sentence limiting the possibility of causation to objects that are "not contrary" to each other; but even that could not be deployed to rule out A causing B, and B separately causing not-A.

[10] I understand by a "personal memory" roughly a memory of what one has experienced oneself based on the previous experience of it. This definition is Norman Malcolm's. See "Three Forms of Memory", in his *Knowledge and Certainty* (Englewood Cliffs, N.J.: Prentice-Hall, 1963), p. 215. Most uses of "memory" and cognate words have such a sense. My memory of going to London when young or having toast for breakfast this morning are personal memories. My memory that $5 \times 7 = 35$ is not.

remember it or could have remembered it if we had been at the time and place in question; or if we now perceive it. But a perception of an event perceived or a personal memory of an event remembered must be caused by the event perceived or remembered. The points are logical ones; nothing would count as a "perception" or "memory" unless these causal relations held. This basic tenet of the causal theories of perception and memory are generally accepted. Hence, given the impossibility of causation in a circle, perception and memory can only give us access to what is fixed beyond our power to affect it causally. The concepts of perception and memory only link us to the concepts of past and future via the concept of causality. To label something a memory is already to have built into it the causal fixedness of what it delivers.

While admitting that, you might suppose that we derive our concept of the past from paradigm examples of past events, many of which are in fact remembered. The events of my youth which I remember, and the events in Egypt in the first millennium B.C. which I do not, are paradigm examples of events past. But the trouble with a paradigm case analysis of pastness is that the class of events past is altering all the time—events which were once paradigm cases of events not past become paradigm cases of events past. And any account that can be given of what determines when an event crosses the border from being future to being past will involve a crucial reference to causality. If it becomes past when it is perceived, it becomes past when it causally affects us, at which point we cannot causally affect it.

Finally an appeal might be made to the "present". Our "present" conscious experiences are not (by principle 1) instantaneous static experiences but extended and often changing experiences. I experience change of pattern in my visual field, of thought in my procedure of inference. My every experience is an extended experience and so contains elements that I recognize as more past than other elements. That is enough, the argument might go, to give us the concept of the past as a whole—the past is whatever is "in the same direction" as "the more past" elements of my present experience; the future is whatever is "in the other direction". The trouble with this suggested way of access to the past is that it assumes that an experience being present is something of which we can get a grasp without bringing in the concept of causation. I don't think it is. In talking of a "present" extended experience, we are talking of something logically contingent that happens over a period of time. And how am I aware of it? In what does my awareness of it consist? How is the coincidence between what is going on and my belief about what is going on sustained? Clearly what is going on causes me to be aware of what is going on. And because I think this about it, I regard my experience as now unaffectable by anything I or anyone, however powerful, might do; and so I regard the "specious present" of my experience as strictly speaking past. If I believe that some other mechanism (e.g., causation by a common cause, or some sort of non-causal awareness) was responsible for sustaining the coincidence, the question would arise why I should regard "what is going on" as happening in the specious present rather than as yet to happen; and any satisfactory answer thereto would, I suggest, involve some sort of causal story. A present experience is really one most recently past, and I can have no grasp on the notion in order to use it for other purposes unless I have already utilized the notion of causality.

So, I claim, the concepts of past and future cannot be connected to the rest of our conceptual scheme unless we understand the past as the logically contingent which is causally unaffectible, and the future as the logically contingent which is causally effectible. Unless we suppose that, any grasp we might have on the concepts would be utterly mysterious and irrelevant to anything else.

My causal account of time rules out not merely backward causation (an effect preceding its cause) but simultaneous causation (an effect being simultaneous with its cause). If simultaneous causation were possible—if A caused B simultaneously, and B caused C simultaneously—then, by Hume's principle cited earlier, it would be logically possible that B could have had, instead of its normal effect, not-A. That logically impossible conjunction of causal sequences is, given Hume's principle, only rendered impossible if we suppose simultaneous causation itself to be impossible. Hence, given that causes and effects are events that last for periods of time, an effect must begin at an instant later than its cause begins.[11]

Both memory and perception must be of things past. But there is a

---

[11] Every event that has one total cause in the sense of an event that physically necessitates its occurrence in all its detail will have infinitely many such. For if E has one such total cause C, it has also as total causes all events which are later parts of C and which begin before E does, and, given a temporal continuum (which time must be—see n. 5), there will be infinitely many such, and if there are events which include C as later parts (as normally there will be), they too will be causes of E. So if there is an effect E which depends on its cause C not merely for its coming into existence but for its continuing in existence at every period of its existence (as might perhaps be the case with the motion of my pen in my hand as I write), this will be by each segment of E beginning at a time t and ending at a time t^1 having as its total cause every segment of C beginning earlier than t and ending at t^1. It will be in this way that God acts continuously to conserve the universe in being.

contingent distinction in the kind and method of awareness we humans have of things past which leads to a natural distinction between perception and memory. We call "perceptions" those experiences of a kind which arise by an immediate causal chain from an event through sense organs to the brain, which normally give us very reliable information about the nearby state of the world so little-out-of-date as to enable us to cope with our nearby surroundings fairly effectively, experiences unavoidable if our organs are operative and we direct them aright. (Occasionally, of course, experiences of this kind are of things as they were a long time ago—as when we look at the stars. But those are exceptions.)

Memories, by contrast, are not constantly before us. They come to us erratically; it is only partly under our voluntary control whether we have them or not; they are available to us because we have in our brains stored traces of effects of immediate causal chains from the states of affairs remembered. We do not have memories of all the events of our past, and those we do have are not totally reliable. Memories often have much less sensory (as opposed to cognitive) content than perceptions have. These differences between perceptions and memories in humans clearly have their source in the different brain structures that mediate our experience of the world. Individuals of a very different kind from ourselves might not have a similar twofold scheme of awareness of the past.

The fourth principle about time is that there are truths about periods of time which can only be known at certain periods—e.g., that something is happening now can only be known now, that something is going to happen can only be known before it happens. My knowledge that it is raining today can only be had today. Many philosophers have supposed otherwise, on the grounds that my knowledge that it is raining today is—since today is 3 November 1993—the same item of knowledge as the knowledge that it is raining on 3 November 1993. But, to my mind, quite clearly that is wrong. Knowing the latter doesn't tell me whether to take an umbrella with me; to know that, I need to know whether it is raining *now*. One does, of course, need a sophisticated philosophical doctrine of what are the items of knowledge, in order to make clear what makes the two items of knowledge different; and how they are related to each other, and philosophers have had some difficulty in producing a coherent doctrine of this matter.[12] But that difficulty need cast no doubt on the fact that the two items of knowledge are

[12] I have developed my own doctrine of this matter in "Tensed Facts", *American Philosophical Quarterly* 27 (1990): 117–30.

different. That being so, the obvious conclusion would seem to be that it is raining today can only be known today.[13] Similar arguments show that there are items of knowledge which can only be possessed by certain persons; for example, the knowledge that I am cold not being the same item as the knowledge that Swinburne is cold, can be had only by me. However all non-indexical knowledge (i.e., all knowledge about individuals, times, and places not picked out by their relation to the knower) can be had by any person at any period of time.

With these four philosophical principles on board, let me return to God. I spelled out the doctrine of God's timelessness loosely in terms of his existing at a single "moment". The most natural reading of the tradition seems to me to read "moment" as "instant",[14] and in that case the doctrine is in conflict with principle 1. A state of affairs must last for a period of time; it cannot occur at an instant. God cannot be omnipotent or omniscient just at an instant. If the "moment" is a period, however, the doctrine is not open to this objection. It remains open however to a conclusive objection from principle 3: if God causes the beginning or continuing existence of the world, and perhaps interferes in its operation from time to time, his acting must be prior to the effects that his action causes. Similarly, his awareness of events in the world must be later than those events.[15]

In his 1981 essay, Norman Kretzmann with Eleonore Stump tried

---

[13] I used to endorse H.-N. Castañeda's argument against Norman Kretzmann on this point, to the effect that, since if A knows at t_1 that at t_2 B knows that p, A knows at t_1 that p; and since A could know that B knows today that it is raining today, at any time t, he could know at any time what B knows when he knows that it is raining. I am now persuaded by Richard Gale's discussion that this argument is not sound. See Norman Kretzmann, "Omniscience and Immutability", *Journal of Philosophy* 63 (1966): 409–21; H.-N. Castañeda, "Omniscience and Indexical Reference", *Journal of Philosophy* 64 (1967): 203–10; Richard M. Gale, "Omniscience-Immutability Arguments", *American Philosophical Quarterly* 23 (1986): 319–35, esp. pp. 329–31.

[14] In "Eternity" (*Journal of Philosophy* 78 [1981]: 429–56) Eleonore Stump and Norman Kretzmann claim that the "timeless" tradition is most naturally read as holding that the divine "moment" has duration and thus is a period (see pp. 432–33). Paul Fitzgerald ("Stump and Kretzmann on Time and Eternity", *Journal of Philosophy* 82 [1985]: 260–69) denies that this view can be held consistently with the rest of what Stump and Kretzmann wish to claim.

[15] Some theological accounts of God's eternity can be read as defending an even stronger view of timelessness than that of Boethius. Boethius holds that there is a moment, an eternal "all at once" moment, at which all the divine predicates are true of God. An even stronger view holds that there is no moment at which the divine predicates are true of God: he knows, acts, and so on, but there is no *moment* at which he knows, acts, and so on. This view is also ruled out by principle 3.

to spell out a notion of "ET-simultaneity"—analogous to but different from our ordinary notion of simultaneity—in which God's causal actions and awareness in an "eternity" not temporally related to our time would be ET-simultaneous with their mundane effects and objects of awareness, so that in a sense God causes them and is aware of them "as they happen" without literally being prior to, simultaneous with, or later than them. Their definition is as follows:

(ET) For every x and for every y, x and y are ET-simultaneous iff

(i) either x is eternal and y is temporal, or vice versa; and

(ii) for some observer, A, in the unique eternal reference frame, x and y are both present—i.e. either x is eternally present and y is observed as temporally present, or vice versa; and

(iii) for some observer, B, in one of the infinitely many temporal reference frames, x, and y are both present—i.e. either x is observed as eternally present and y is temporally present, or vice versa.[16]

The first clause of this definition simply lays down by fiat that every eternal event is "ET-simultaneous" with every temporal event, and vice versa. One hopes for more content from the other two clauses. What (ii) and (iii) amount to depends on what it is for an eternal observer to "observe" a mundane event as "temporally present" and for a temporal observer to "observe" an eternal event as "eternally present". Stump and Kretzmann tell us that such observations are not observations of simultaneity but of "cooccurrence" of the state observed with the observation. No further illumination is provided of what this amounts to, and hence I am unclear what (ii) and (iii) add to (i). Presumably the observers referred to, or at any rate B, need not be actual observers; potential ones will do. For there must be actual temporal events as well as eternal events (!), which are not observed by any temporal observer. Clause (iii) must be claiming that there could be such an observer; and maybe (ii) is claiming that too. But the question remains as to what it would be

---

[16] Kretzmann and Stump, "Eternity," p. 439. In a new paper, "Eternity, Awareness, and Action", *Faith and Philosophy* 9 (1992): 463–82, Stump and Kretzmann have defended their account in "Eternity", while adding a minor amendment to clauses (ii) and (iii) of their definition. This amendment requires the possibility of causal relations between A and B if x and y are to be ET-simultaneous. It thus allows the possibility of causal relations between events which in a literal sense are neither before, simultaneous with, or after each other and thus falls foul of my third principle about time.

for such observers to "observe" events of other frames as "present" when they are not "present" in the literal sense of being simultaneous with their being observed. Because such illumination is not provided, I cannot see what (ii) and (iii) add to (i), which lays down by fiat that every eternal event is "ET-simultaneous" with every temporal event. Such definitions of the supposed relation that eternal and temporal events have to each other would be harmless if some other word had been chosen to denote it—e.g., "ET-disjunction". But to call the notion "ET-simultaneity" suggests that what has been defined has some analogy to normal simultaneity, and no reason has been given for supposing that it does. Hence no reason has been given for supposing that if God has an existence outside (our) time, he can have any relation to the events of time which would be in any way analogous to "causing" or "observing" them. The objection to the coherence of the "timelessness" doctrine remains and in my view remains conclusive.

So we must revert to the doctrine that God is everlasting, which we must read as claiming that God exists throughout all periods of time. I now seek to show that that doctrine does not have the consequence that God is time's prisoner, for the reason that although God and time exist together—God is a temporal being—those aspects of time which seem so threatening to his sovereignty only occur through his own voluntary choice. To the extent to which he is time's prisoner, he has chosen to be so. It is God, not time, who calls the shots. To show this, I ask you, to start with, to think of God, the temporal being, existing by himself, not having created a universe in which there are laws of nature. There would then, by principle (2), be no "cosmic clock" which ticked unstoppably away, that is, there would be no temporal intervals of any definite length. There would just be an event or sequence of events in the divine consciousness. Think of him too as the subject of just one mental event, a conscious act without qualitatively distinguishable temporal parts (e.g., a conscious act that does not consist of one thought followed by a different thought). Now, by principle (1) any event has to take some time, but there wouldn't be a truth that this event (this act) had lasted any particular length of time rather than any other. There would be no difference between a divine act of self-awareness which lasted a millisecond and one that lasted a million years. That is hard for us to grasp, for two reasons. The first reason is that our conscious acts are distinguished by the different intervals of public clocks that tick away while they occur (and we can usually recognize roughly how long an interval is for a given act). But that difference would not be there with this divine act. The second is that any acts of ours which are qualitatively identical throughout are usually immediately followed and preceded by acts of different kinds. But that is a contingent matter, and I am supposing otherwise with respect to this divine act.

Would there be a difference between a divine conscious act that was God's only conscious act and was qualitatively identical throughout which was of finite length, and one which was of infinite length? No—so long as the former really is qualitatively identical throughout and thus contains no experience of a beginning or end; and so long as there is no time at which God is not. For consider a supposedly finite act—call it the *SF* act that has the instants *A* and *B* as its bounding instants. Compare the *SF* act with an act of supposedly infinite duration—call it the *SID* act—which will of course have no boundaries. Represent the two lines geometrically, impose upon them some arbitrary metric. Take the midpoint *Z* of the *SF* line, *AB*, under that metric. Take any point *Q* on the *SID* line. Divide *AZ* by a midpoint *Y*. Mark on the *SID* line an interval equal in length to *YZ*; call it *PQ*. Then divide *AY* by a midpoint *W*; mark on the other line an interval *KP*, of the same length as *PQ*.

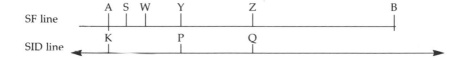

Divide the interval *AW* by a midpoint *S*. Mark on the *SID* line another interval of the length of *PQ* corresponding to *SW*. Continue this process ad infinitum, so that for each yet smaller interval of *AB*, you mark on the *SID* line an interval of the same length as each other length. Perform the corresponding process for the other half of the two lines. Then the two lines will have been divided in such a way that all intervals of the *SF* line will have been put into a one-to-one correspondence with intervals of the *SID* line. By previous arguments, there can be no difference between a segment of a divine act qualitatively identical throughout and such a segment of twice or any other finite number of times the temporal length. Hence there will be no difference between a divine act qualitatively identical throughout of "finite duration" and one of "infinite duration"—for the segments of each will be qualitatively identical to the segments of the other.

So if God does not choose to disturb his one act of self-awareness (within the Trinity), or whatever the one act qualitatively identical throughout is, any "duration" for it will be the same as any other. Although such an act does not in a literal sense have its "duration" "all at once" in the sense of "at a single instant", it does have the feature for which I believe theorists of timelessness were groping— that it is not qualitatively distinguishable from an act which lasted a millisecond or any period at all, however small.

If God had left himself like that, the aspects of time which seem to threaten his sovereignty would not hold. There would be no cosmic clock ticking away, for there would be no laws of nature. The past would not be getting lengthier by any measurable amount. God would be aware of every period of the past as directly as we are of events that we have just that millisecond experienced, for in God there is no distinction between perception and memory. God's whole experience would remain qualitatively indistinguishable from an experience that lasted only a millisecond. God cannot affect the past, but all there would ever be to the past is his having his one divine act, that is, what he is always aware of in his own experience. Anything else could be brought about and made past in the twinkling of an eye. The future however remains under God's total control; he need not make free creatures—in which case nothing will surprise him—or anything at all—in which case nothing will loom upon him.

In his 1966 essay, Norman Kretzmann[17] drew our attention to what I have called principle (4). Does not this principle suggest that even in this universe the progress of time would have the consequence that God would ever be losing items of knowledge. For surely at each period of time God knows that he is "now" in some state S, and although his experiential state remains experientially indistinguishable from any other state, the knowledge it contains is different, for its "now" refers to a different "now"; as time moves on, God no longer knows what he knew in the previous period. So would there not be more to the past than God's one present divine act, and some of it lost forever? That might be so if knowledge occurred at instants and was about instants; but, by principle (1) it occurs over periods and concerns periods. And how are these periods to be picked out and distinguished from other periods? And the answer is, of course, that they can't be. In the universe described, the only period to which reference can be made is the whole

---

[17] See Kretzmann, "Omniscience and Immutability".

of time in which God is in state *S*, and the only period at which reference can be made is the same period. The "now" refers to a period, of which there is no way of marking a beginning or an end —so long as change does not occur in God's experiential state or unless he brings about something outside himself. So time is not ever depriving God of knowledge.[18]

But God need not leave things like that, and if there is a God, he has not done so. God may choose to have a succession of qualitatively distinct mental acts, and in that case temporal order (though not a temporal metric) will have been introduced into the divine life. By bringing about some effect *A*,[19] God divides time into the realm where it is not logically possible that anyone (even God) could make any difference to whether or not *A* occurs, and the realm where that is logically possible; and by bringing about many such effects, he creates a rich assembly of the unalterable, ever present to God by perception.

God may choose to create a universe distinct from himself, governed by laws of nature. In that case there will be a temporal metric by which things in the universe are governed. And we can date God's acts by the time at which they occur on the universe's clock. And we can even say that they last as long as those events in the universe with which they coincide. To say the latter would be a little misleading, for it would suggest that they seem as long to God as they do to us—and there is no reason to suppose that. And God may choose to create creatures with indeterministic free will, and in that case the universe may indeed contain the occasional surprise for God, for no one can foreknow such free actions.[20]

The unwelcome features of time—the increase of events that cannot be changed, the cosmic clock ticking away as they happen, the uncertainty about the future—may indeed invade God's time; but they come by invitation, not by force—and they continue for such

---

[18] In "Omniscience and Immutability" Norman Kretzmann argued that if God was to be omniscient at any time, he would need to know what was happening at that time; and so, as the world changed, he would need to change with it. But Kretzmann added that "if as a matter of fact nothing else [i.e., apart from God] ever did change, an omniscient being could of course remain immutable". That is what I am arguing here.

[19] God's bringing about things "as they happen" is to be read in terms of his bringing them about by temporally contiguous causation in the sense described in note 11. His keeping a universe in being is an act of continuous creation in this sense.

[20] For the classic exposition of this point (with respect to divine foreknowledge of human free will) see Nelson Pike, "Divine Omniscience and Voluntary Action", *Philosophical Review* 74 (1965): 27–46.

periods of time as God chooses that they shall. So there is no reason for the theist to object to the view that God is everlasting on the grounds that it makes God time's prisoner; and since the rival view is incoherent, the theist should adopt the view that God is everlasting.[21]

[21] Some of the ideas of this essay were sparked off by discussions with my doctoral supervisee, Alan Padgett. I am grateful to him for stimulating and contributing to these ideas. See his "God and Time: Towards a New Doctrine of Divine Timeless Eternity", *Religious Studies* 25 (1989): 209–15. An earlier version of the essay was read to philosophy departments or societies at the University of Kent; the University of California, Los Angeles; the University of Wisconsin, Milwaukee; the University of Wisconsin, Madison; and to a graduate class at Oxford. I am grateful for all the helpful criticisms received on these occasions, of which I was able to take account in preparing the final version.

WILLIAM ROWE

❦

The Problem of Divine
Perfection and Freedom

Though God is a most perfectly free agent, he cannot but do always what is best and wisest in the whole.

Samuel Clarke

Many thinkers in the theistic tradition have held that in addition
to omnipotence and omniscience God's attributes must include perfect goodness and freedom. For the theistic God deserves unconditional gratitude, praise, and worship. But if a being were to fall short
of perfect goodness, it would not be worthy of unreserved praise
and worship. So, too, for divine freedom. If God were not free in
some of his significant actions, if he always lacked the freedom not
to do what he in fact does, we could hardly thank him or praise him
for anything that he does. He would not be deserving of our gratitude and praise for the simple reason that he would act of necessity
and not freely. So, along with omnipotence and omniscience, perfect goodness and significant freedom are fundamental attributes of
the theistic God.

Some attributes are essential to an object. That object could not
exist were it not to possess those attributes. Other attributes are
such that the object could still exist were it to lack them. If the theistic God does exist, to which class do his attributes of omnipotence,
omniscience, perfect goodness, and freedom belong? Are they essential to that being? Does that being possess those attributes in
every possible world in which he exists? Or are they not essential?
Most thinkers in the theistic tradition have held the view that these
attributes are constitutive of God's nature; they are essential attributes of the being that has them. With this view in mind, my aim in
this essay is to consider the question of whether God's perfect goodness, specifically his moral perfection, is consistent with his being
free in many significant actions. Throughout, we will suppose that if

223

God exists he is *essentially* omnipotent, omniscient, perfectly good, and free in many of his actions. What I want to determine is whether there is a serious difficulty in the endeavor to reconcile God's essential goodness and moral perfection with any significant degree of divine freedom.[1]

I begin the investigation with the question of whether God is ever free to do an evil (morally wrong) act. The answer, I believe, is no. Of course, being morally perfect, omnipotent, and omniscient, God will never in fact do an evil act. No being who knowingly and willingly performs an evil act is morally perfect. Since being free to do an evil act is consistent with never in fact doing an evil act, it may seem initially plausible to think that God could be free to perform such an act. But if God is free to perform an evil act, then he has it in his power to perform that act. And, if God has it in his power to perform an evil act, then he has it in his power to deprive himself of one of his essential attributes (moral perfection). But no being has the power to deprive itself of one of its essential attributes.[2] Therefore, God does not have it in his power to perform an evil act.

The reasoning in this argument proceeds as follows.

1. God has it in his power to bring it about that he performs an evil act. (Assumption to be refuted)
2. From God's performing an evil act it follows that God is not morally perfect.
3. If X has it in its power to bring about p, q follows from p, and q does not obtain, then X has it in its power to bring about q.
4. God has it in his power to bring it about that he is not morally perfect. (From 1 to 3.)
5. Being morally perfect is an essential attribute of God.

Therefore,

6. God has it in his power to bring it about that he lacks one of his essential attributes.

Because (6) is clearly false, we must deny the initial assumption that God has power to bring it about that he performs an evil act. But if God does not have it in his power to perform an evil act, then performing an evil act is not something God is free to do.

It may seem that my argument to show that God is not free to do

---

[1] I take God's moral perfection to be logically implied by his perfect goodness.
[2] It is understood here that a being has the power to deprive itself of a property only if it is possible for that being to lose that property and *continue to exist.*

an evil act has already produced a serious difficulty in the theistic concept of God. For if God cannot do evil, what becomes of his omnipotence? After all, even we humans, with our quite limited power, are able to perform evil deeds. If God does not have the power to do what even we can do, how can we reasonably hold that he is essentially omnipotent?

So long as we hold that omnipotence does not imply power to do what is not possible to be done, we need not conclude that God's lacking power to bring it about that he do something morally wrong renders him less than omnipotent.[3] For, as we've seen, it is strictly impossible for a being who logically cannot be other than morally perfect to do something evil.

If God is not free to do a morally wrong action, might he be free to do a morally right act? 'Morally right act' may mean either what is morally obligatory or what is morally permissible. If we are willing to countenance refraining from performing a certain action as an "action", then it is clear that God is not free with respect to performing any action that is morally obligatory for him to perform. For refraining from that action would be morally wrong, and, as we've seen, God is not free to do anything that is morally wrong for him to do. For God to be free in performing any action, it must be both in his power to perform it and in his power to refrain from performing it. But since refraining from doing what is morally obligatory is morally wrong, and being morally perfect is essential to God, he does not have the power to refrain from doing what is morally obligatory. In short, God does what is morally obligatory of necessity, not freely.

The way I've just put the point about God doing what is morally obligatory for him to do is not quite right. For it suggests that even though God does not freely do what he is morally obligated to do, he nevertheless does (of necessity) what he has a moral obligation to do. But the truth is that no action is such that God can have a moral obligation to perform it. For one cannot have a moral obligation to do what one cannot do freely. If a person freely does some act, then it was in the person's power not to do it.[4] Since it would be morally wrong for God not to do what he is obligated to do, it follows from my previous argument that God cannot do freely what he

[3] For a discussion of this point see Joshua Hoffman, "Can God Do Evil?" *Southern Journal of Philosophy* 17 (1979): 213–20.

[4] To avoid Frankfurt-type counterexamples, we should say that when an agent freely performs some action she caused her action and had the power not to cause that action. The power not to cause one's action is *not* the same as the power to prevent one's action. I ignore this complication in the text.

is morally obligated to do. But, since one cannot be morally obligated to do what one is not free to do, there are no actions God has a moral obligation to perform. At best we can say that God does of necessity those acts he would be morally obligated to do were he free to do them.

We've seen that because he is essentially a morally perfect being, God is neither free to do a morally wrong action nor free in doing a morally obligatory action. We've also seen that no action can be such that God has a moral obligation to do it (or not to do it). It looks, then, as though my initial efforts have yielded the result that God's absolute moral perfection places significant restraints on the scope of divine freedom. However, the fact that God is neither free to do what is wrong nor free in doing what is morally obligatory (what would be morally obligatory were God free with respect to doing or not doing it) may still leave considerable scope for God's freedom to be exercised.[5] For, so long as some of his important actions are morally permissible but not morally obligatory, we thus far have no reason to deny that God is free with respect to all such actions, that he has it in his power to do them and in his power not to do them. For example, it has long been held that God's action in creating the world was a free action, that God was free to create a world and free not to create a world.[6] Creating the world is certainly a very significant act, involving, as it does, a vast number of divine acts in actualizing the contingent states of affairs that constitute our world. If God enjoys freedom with respect to the world he creates, then, although his freedom is constrained in ways that ours is not, there would not appear to be any insurmountable problem to reconciling perfection and freedom.[7] To pursue the investigation of a possible conflict between God's moral perfection and his freedom, therefore, it will be helpful to turn our attention to God's action in creating the world. Specifically, we need to consider whether God's moral perfection leaves God free with respect to his creation of the world.

---

[5] If we take *significant freedom*, as Alvin Plantinga does, to be the freedom to do or refrain from doing what is morally obligatory, it can be shown that God cannot be significantly free. See Wes Morriston, "Is God 'Significantly Free'?" *Faith and Philosophy* 2 (1983): 257–63.

[6] For an excellent discussion and critical evaluation of the classical Judeo-Christian views on God's freedom with respect to creation see Norman Kretzmann, "A General Problem of Creation", and "A Particular Problem of Creation", in *Being and Goodness*, ed. Scott MacDonald (Ithaca and London: Cornell University Press, 1990).

[7] There is a problem of understanding what God's moral perfection comes to, given that he can have no moral obligations. But this problem may not be unresolvable. See Thomas Morris, *Anselmian Explorations* (Notre Dame: University of Notre Dame Press, 1987), pp. 31–41.

It is important to distinguish two questions concerning God's freedom in creating a world. There is the question of whether God is free to select among creatable worlds the one he will create.[8] There is also the question of whether God is free not to create a world at all. That these are quite different questions can be seen as follows. Suppose that among worlds creatable by an omnipotent being there is one that is morally better than all other worlds. On this supposition, one can imagine arguments for any of four positions. Someone might argue that although God is free not to create a world at all, if he chooses to create, he must create the best world he can. Hence, although he is free not to create the morally best world, he is not free to create any world other than it. Alternatively, someone might argue that God's perfect goodness absolutely necessitates that he create a good world. God is not free not to create a world. But God's perfection does not necessitate that he create the best world he can. He is free to create among the class of creatable good worlds. Third, someone might argue that God enjoys both sorts of freedom. He is free not to create at all. He is also free to create some good world other than the best that he can create. Finally, one might argue that God's being essentially perfect necessitates his creating that world which is superior to all others. God is not free to create some world other than the best, and he is not free not to create any world at all. In what follows, I focus primarily on my first question (whether God is free to select among creatable worlds).

In an important article, Robert Adams has argued that it need not be wrong for God to create a world that is *not as good as* some other world he could create.[9] Adams supposes that the world God creates contains creatures each of whom is as happy as it is in any possible world in which it exists. Moreover, no creature in this world is so miserable that it would be better had it not existed. Let's suppose there is some other possible world, with different creatures, that exceeds this world in its degree of happiness, a world that God could have created. So, God has created a world with a lesser degree of happiness than he could have. Has God wronged anyone in creating this world? Adams argues that God cannot have wronged the creatures in the other possible world, for merely possible beings don't have rights. Nor can he have wronged the creatures in the world he has created, for their lives could not be made more happy. Adams notes that God would have done something wrong in creating this

---

[8] Since there may be possible worlds that an omnipotent being cannot create, we need to restrict our discussion to the class of worlds creatable by God.

[9] Robert Adams, "Must God Create the Best?" *Philosophical Review* 81 (1972): 317–32.

world were the following principle true: "It is wrong to bring into existence, knowingly, a being less excellent than one could have brought into existence."[10] But this principle, Adams argues, is subject to counterexamples. Parents do no wrong when they refrain from taking drugs that would result in an abnormal gene structure in their children, even though taking the drugs would result in children who are superhuman both in intelligence and in prospects for happiness.

Suppose we agree with Adams on these points. Suppose, that is, that we agree that God is not morally obligated to create the best world that he can, that it would be morally permissible for God to create the best world he can, but also morally permissible for God to create any of a number of other good worlds of the sort Adams describes. If so, can't we conclude that there is no unresolvable conflict between God's being essentially morally perfect and his enjoying a significant degree of genuine freedom? For it now appears that God's moral perfection does not require him to create the best world. In short, he is free to create (or not create) any of a number of good worlds.

As forceful and persuasive as Adams's arguments are, I don't think they yield the conclusion that God's perfect goodness imposes no requirement on God to create the best world that he can create. What Adams's arguments show, at best, is that God's moral perfection imposes no *moral obligation* on God to create the best world he can. His arguments establish, at best, that God need not be doing anything *morally wrong* in creating some world other than the best world. But this isn't quite the same thing as showing that God's perfect goodness does not render it necessary that he create the best world he can. For, even conceding the points Adams tries to make, there still may be an inconsistency in a morally perfect being creating some world other than the best world he can create. My point here is this. One being may be morally better than another even though it is not better by virtue of the performance of some obligation that the other failed to perform. It may be morally better by virtue of performing some supererogatory act that the other being could have but did not perform. Analogously, a being who creates a better world than another being may be morally better, even though the being who creates the morally inferior world does not thereby do anything wrong. Following Philip Quinn, I'm inclined to think that if an omnipotent being creates some world other than the best

10 Ibid., p. 329.

world it can create, then it is possible there should exist a being morally better than it is.[11] For it would be possible for there to be an omnipotent being who creates the best world that the first being could create but did not. I conclude then that if an essentially omnipotent, perfectly good being creates any world at all, it must create the best world it can. For although a being may do no wrong in creating less than the best it can create, a being whose nature is to be *perfectly good* is not such that it is possible for there to be a being morally better than it. If, however, a being were to create a world when there is a morally better world it could create, then it would be possible for there to be a being morally better than it.

What we have seen is that a being who is morally perfect and creates a world must create the very best world it can create. But what if there is no best world among those it can create? This would be so in either of two cases. First, it might be that for any world it creates there is a morally better world it can create. Second, it might be that there is no *unique* best world. Perhaps, instead, there are many morally unsurpassable worlds among the worlds God can create. Let's consider these two cases in turn.

On the assumption that for any world God creates there is a morally better world he can create, it is clear that it is impossible for God to do the best that he can. Whatever he does, it will be the case that he could have done better. This being so, it would seem only reasonable that God's perfect goodness is fully satisfied should he create a very good world. And we may safely assume that there are a large number of such worlds that he can create. So long as he creates one of these worlds, he will have satisfied the demands of his morally perfect nature. For the idea that he should create the best world he can is an idea that logically cannot be implemented. Hence, on the assumption of there being no morally unsurpassable world among the worlds God can create, it would seem that God's absolute moral perfection is fully compatible with his freely creating any one of a number of good worlds that lie in his power to create. To complain that God cannot then be perfect because he could have created a better world is to raise a complaint that no creative action

---

[11] Philip L. Quinn, "God, Moral Perfection, and Possible Worlds", in *God: The Contemporary Discussion*, ed. Frederick Sontag and M. Darrol Bryant (New York: The Rose of Sharon Press, Inc., 1982), pp. 197–213. Quinn remarks: "An omnipotent moral agent can actualize any actualizable world. If he actualizes one than which there is a morally better, he does not do the best he can, morally speaking, and so it is possible that there is an agent morally better than he is, namely an omnipotent moral agent who actualizes one of those morally better worlds" (p. 213).

God took would have enabled him to avoid. As William Wainwright notes:

> The critic complains that God could have created a better order. But even if God had created a better order, He would be exposed to the possibility of a similar complaint. Indeed, no created order better than our own is such that God would not be exposed to the possibility of a complaint of this sort. The complaint is thus inappropriate. Even though there are an infinite number of created orders better than our own, God can't be faulted simply because He created an order inferior to other orders that He might have created in their place.[12]

There is something forceful and right about this reasoning. If, no matter what world an omnipotent being creates, there is a morally better world that being can create, then, provided that the omnipotent being creates a significantly good world, it cannot be morally at fault for not having created a morally better world. But our question is whether a being in such a situation can be an *absolutely perfect being*. And for reasons I have already uncovered, I think the answer is no. A being is necessarily an absolutely perfect moral being only if it is not possible for there to be a being morally better than it. If a being creates a world when there is some morally better world that it could have created, then it is possible that there be a being morally better than it. Since our assumption implies that for any world an omnipotent being creates there is a morally better world it can create, it follows that any such being who creates even a very good world cannot be an absolutely perfect moral being. Although the omnipotent being in question could be a very good moral agent and enjoy a significant degree of freedom in creating among a number of very good worlds, it could not be an absolutely perfect moral being. The existence of the theistic God who creates a world is inconsistent with the supposition that among the worlds he can create there is no morally unsurpassable world.

Let's now consider the second way in which it could be true that no creatable world is better than all others. Suppose that among the worlds God can create there are a number of worlds that are morally unsurpassable. For reasons we've already considered, if God creates a world, he cannot create some world that is morally inferior to some other that he can create. Therefore, if there are a number of morally unsurpassable worlds among the worlds he can create, then

¹² William Wainwright, *Philosophy of Religion* (Belmont, Calif.: Wadsworth Publishing Company, 1988), p. 90.

if he creates at all he must create one of these worlds. But unlike the case when there is exactly one morally unsurpassable world among the worlds he can create, here we do seem to have found a wedge to open up space for some degree of divine freedom to exist in harmony with God's absolute moral perfection. For God would seem to be free to create any one of the morally unsurpassable worlds. In any case, God's absolute moral perfection imposes no requirement on his creation among the set of morally unsurpassable worlds.

Among the worlds creatable by an omnipotent being, either (1) there is exactly one morally unsurpassable world or (2) there is not. If there is not, then either (2a) there is no morally unsurpassable world or (2b) there are a number of morally unsurpassable worlds. If (1) is the case, then God is not free to select among creatable worlds. If (2a) is the case, God's being essentially morally perfect is inconsistent with his act of creating a world. If (2b) is the case, God's moral perfection leaves him free to select among morally unsurpassable worlds the one he will create.

Earlier, I distinguished two questions concerning God's freedom in creating a world. We have been discussing the question of God's freedom to select among creatable worlds the one he will create. It is now time to consider the other question of whether God is free not to create a world at all. Here we may limit our inquiry to the possibility that there is exactly one morally unsurpassable world among the worlds creatable by an omnipotent being. As we've seen, in this case God is not free to select any other world to create. If God creates, he must create the one world that is morally best. Our present question is whether in this situation God is free not to create at all.

Some possible world must be actual. What possible world would be actual if God exists but does not create at all? Presumably, it would be a world in which no positive, contingent state of affairs obtains. By 'a positive, contingent state of affairs' I mean any state of affairs such that from the fact that it obtains it follows that some contingent being (other than God, if he should be contingent) exists. Apart from God and whatever necessarily existing entities there are, in a world God inhabits but does not create no other being would exist. To answer our question of whether God is free not to create a world at all, we must compare the best world God can create with a world whose inhabitants are simply God and whatever necessarily existing entities there are. Assuming such a world would not be morally incommensurate with the morally unsurpassable world among worlds God can create, it is plausible to think that God is not free with respect to whether he will not create at all. For either the world he inhabits but does not create is better than the best world he can create or it is not. If it is better, then he is not free not to create a world at all; he necessarily refrains from creating. If it is worse, then he is not free not to create a world at all; he necessarily creates a world.[13] Might the world he inhabits but does not create be on a moral par with the best world among those an omnipotent being can create? If so, then, as in the case where there are a number of morally unsurpassable worlds omnipotence can create, we again have a wedge for creating space for some degree of divine freedom. But, in this scarcely possible situation, God's freedom would be restricted to creating the morally unsurpassable world or not creating at all.

I now can draw together the results of my study of the problem of divine perfection and freedom. The conclusions may be presented as follows.

1. God is not free to perform any evil act, nor is he free in doing what is morally obligatory.

2. If there is a world creatable by God that is morally better than any world he inhabits but does not create, God is *not* free not to create a world at all. If he exists, he is a creator of necessity.

3. If for any world creatable by an omnipotent being there is another creatable world that is morally better, the theistic God cannot exist and be a creator of anything.

4. If there is a single, morally best creatable world, God enjoys neither sort of freedom: he is not free not to create and he is not free to select among creatable worlds.[14]

5. If there are a number of morally unsurpassable, creatable worlds, then, although God necessarily creates one or the other of them, he is free (so far as his moral perfection is concerned) to select among the morally unsurpassable worlds the one he will create.[15]

Traditional theists who hold that God is essentially perfect and yet possesses libertarian freedom of will and action have neglected, I believe, some of the implications that appear to follow from God's

[13] This point is a plausible extension of our earlier principle: If X creates a morally inferior world to one X can create, then it is possible that there be a being morally better than X. Extending this principle, it is plausible to hold that if X can but does not create a world that is morally better than the one X inhabits, then it is possible that there be a being morally better than X.

[14] The plausible assumption here is that if there is a single, morally best creatable world, then that world is morally better than any world God inhabits but does not create.

[15] See n. 13.

perfect goodness. For all we know about possible worlds, it may well be that God's perfect goodness is inconsistent with any degree of divine freedom in whether he creates or what world he creates. In any case, it would seem that his perfection places rather severe limitations on the scope of his freedom in creating a world.

The problem we have been considering is rooted in two basic points: God's perfect goodness is such as to preclude the *possibility* of a morally better being; God's freedom is such that he acts and wills freely only if it is in his power not to so act and will. If either point is significantly qualified or given up, the conclusions I've drawn may no longer obtain. If, for example, we give up the libertarian idea of freedom, then, following Jonathan Edwards, we might hold that God's actions are free even though necessitated by his perfect goodness.[16] On the other hand, we might endeavor to qualify God's perfect goodness so that it permits the possibility for God to have been better than he is.[17] Neither of these alternatives has been addressed in this essay.

[16] Jonathan Edwards, *Freedom of the Will*, ed. Paul Ramsey (New Haven, Yale University Press, 1957).

[17] See, for example, the suggestion by William Wainwright (drawn from Charles Hartshorne) that God's perfection might require only that he be unsurpassable by some *other* being (*Philosophy of Religion*, p. 9).

THOMAS V. MORRIS

❦

Perfection and Creation

1. Two Streams of Theology

There are many different ways of thinking about what is most ultimate. There are many different ways of thinking about God. Some philosophers attempt to articulate a conception of divinity by focusing on considerations having to do with *ultimacy in value*. This line of thinking I call "perfect being theology". It generates a conception of God as the maximally perfect or greatest possible being. Other philosophers prefer to take as their major guide for theological construction a cluster of considerations having to do with *ultimacy in causation*. This approach I call "creation theology". It centers on a conception of God as first cause, creative source of all else.

Each of these streams of philosophical theology has been seen by its adherents as a rational method for articulating an idea of God. And both methods can be thought to be revelational as well, insofar as they pick up on, and are developed in the light of, central strands of biblical thought about God. A tendency among some philosophers and theologians has been to act as if they view these methods as relatively independent and even competing ways of defining the divine. It has been my concern in some recent essays to resist this tendency and to attempt to point out what I see as a deep confluence of these two streams of thought. I believe we must conceive of God as the maximally perfect absolute creator of all, drawing on the best resources of both these ancient theological methods.[1]

---

[1] These ideas are developed in my "Defining the Divine", in *Definitions and De-*

But a problem has come to light in some recent philosophical work that makes any confluence of these two streams look like extremely troubled waters. We have been offered new reason to believe that a greatest possible being could not possibly create less than a best possible world. To the extent that our world does not seem to fit the bill, it looks like it could not be the creation of a perfect creator. And to the extent that we have reason to believe that no world could possibly fit the bill, it looks like there could not possibly be a maximally perfect creator of all. At least, this is how things appear from the perspective I want to examine. The simple reasoning I want to investigate can be seen as a direct attack on perfect being theology, or it can be viewed as an argument displaying an incompatibility between perfect being theology and creation theology. It consists in a set of considerations which together seem to imply that insofar as God is thought of as creator of this world he cannot be thought of as perfect or, on the other hand, that insofar as God is thought of as perfect then either he cannot be thought of as our world's creator or we must, in the face of any evidence and all arguments to the contrary, agree with Leibniz that this must be the best of all possible worlds.

2. The Problem

What sort of world would we expect to be created by an altogether perfect creator? The very posing of the question seems to suggest its answer. How could a perfectly wise, good, and powerful being choose to create anything less than a perfect world? Leibniz reasoned like this:

> Now this supreme wisdom, united to a goodness that is no less infinite, cannot but have chosen the best. For as a lesser evil is a kind of good, so a lesser good is a kind of evil if it stands in the way of a greater good; and there would be something to correct in the actions of God if it were possible to do better.[2]

---

finability: Philosophical Perspectives, ed. J. H. Fetzer, D. Shatz, and George Schlesinger (Dordrecht: Kluwer Academic Publishers, 1991), pp. 269–83, and in my *Our Idea of God* (Notre Dame: University of Notre Dame Press, 1991).
[2] Gottfried Wilhelm Leibniz, *Theodicy*, abridged edition, ed. Diogenes Allen (Indianapolis: Bobbs-Merrill, 1966), p. 35.

God would be doing something wrong, something subject to correction, Leibniz seems to suggest, if he were to create anything less than the best possible world. Since God is completely perfect, he cannot do anything wrong. Therefore, if God creates, he must produce the best possible world.

Leibniz's reasoning has been attacked in two basic ways. In his well-known essay "Must God Create the Best?" Robert M. Adams has argued that God could create a less than best possible world without wronging anyone and without treating anyone, all things considered, unkindly.[3] He maintains that God has no obligation *to anyone* to create only the best and concludes that, as a consequence, it is compatible with God's perfect goodness to be free graciously to create good worlds that fall far short of being the best possible.

Adams's argument is certainly intriguing, but it seems seriously incomplete. Suppose he is right that God would have no moral obligation *to anyone* to create the best. And suppose it follows from that fact that God has no such obligation *simpliciter*. Even if we allow the inference that if no one would be wronged by creating less than the best, it would not be wrong to do so, questions still remain. Do we expect manifestations of great goodness to be restricted to contexts of obligation to some particular person or other, or even to the sphere of obligations *simpliciter*? Could the mere fact that no one need necessarily be wronged by an inferior creation suffice to justify a perfect God's creating less than the best? Adams does not rule out there being principles governing perfect goodness, truths constitutive of perfection, that would still generate Leibniz's ultimate conclusion that a perfect God must create no less than the best.

But of course Leibniz's conclusion has been attacked more directly by numerous theistic philosophers who contend that the idea of a best of all possible worlds is itself an incoherence. Some point out that it is extremely difficult to suppose that there is a single scale of value on which all possible creations could be ranked, with one and only one surpassing all others with respect to degree of overall value. There are all sorts of values, or valuable properties, that different sorts of creatures might exemplify. And there is no good reason to think that all these creaturely values are commensurable, comparable on a single scale of measurement. Some world *A* might be better than rival world *B* in some respects, but with *B* surpassing *A* in others, and the relevant values not such that they could be

---

[3] Robert M. Adams, "Must God Create the Best?" *Philosophical Review* 81 (July 1972): 317–32.

summed over and compared overall. There is no reason to suppose that things are as tidy as the Leibnizian perspective requires.

But more critics have focused on a simpler consideration. For any world composed of a certain number of good creatures, or exemplifying a certain number of goods, n, there is always conceivable a greater world with $n + 1$ goods, or good creatures. So, on the simplest, barest grounds of additive value alone, it seems impossible to suppose there could be a single best possible world. And without this, of course, the Leibnizian demand collapses.

For one such reason or another, it seems that the majority of religious philosophers nowadays hold that the notion of a best possible world, or of a maximally perfect creation, is the idea of an impossibility. And they typically welcome this discovery, for it seems to eliminate the most difficult form of the problem of evil. A logical impossibility cannot be expected even of God. We thus do not face the daunting challenge of arguing that, despite all appearances to the contrary, our world is indeed the best of all possible worlds. No such argument is required of us because no such creation is required of God.

But, a number of philosophers have suggested that trouble may not be quite so easy to escape. For just as it seems initially very natural to suppose that a superlatively good, wise, and powerful being will produce only an unsurpassably perfect creation, so likewise it can seem every bit as natural to suppose that an incoherence or impossibility discovered in the latter notion indicates an incoherence or impossibility buried within the former. Summing up a way in which this sort of problem can be thought to arise, Norman Kretzmann has said:

> It might occur to someone to think that if the best of all possible beings cannot avoid choosing something less good than he could choose, then no being is or can be perfectly good. Perhaps "perfectly good" is just the expression of a confusion, like "perfectly long".[4]

Kretzmann goes on to respond to this worry by saying in the same passage that:

> Like Aquinas, I think that the logical truth that God's actions conform to the principle of noncontradiction entails no limit on his power. And

[4] Norman Kretzmann, "A Particular Problem of Creation", in *Being and Goodness: The Concept of the Good in Metaphysics and Philosophical Theology*, ed. Scott MacDonald (Ithaca: Cornell University Press, 1991), p. 238.

if it would be a violation of the principle of noncontradiction for God to create a world better than any other world he could create, then a fortiori that logical truth which does not diminish his power also leaves his *goodness* undiminished. God's being that than which nothing better can be conceived of cannot entail his producing a world than which none better can be conceived of.

Some other writers on the issue, however, have not thought it so easily settled.

God's power and God's goodness, which Kretzmann compares, are not exactly modal equals. Omnipotence is not a matter of what God *does*, it is just a matter of what he is *able to do*. Perfect goodness, which is a matter of what God is, may be thought to be quite differently related to the question of what God does, as in some way a function of that. The difference is such as to appear to break the analogy Kretzmann suggests.

In a paper called "God, Moral Perfection, and Possible Worlds", Philip L. Quinn has argued like this:

> An omnipotent moral agent can actualize any actualizable world. If he actualizes one than which there is a morally better, he does not do the best he can, morally speaking, and so it is possible that there is an agent morally better than he is, namely an omnipotent moral agent who actualizes one of those morally better worlds.[5]

Quinn takes care to make it clear that he is not suggesting it would be *wrong* for God to create a world less good than one that could be created instead. He suggests only that "a being who acted in this way would not do the best that could be done, which in turn implies that such a being would not be a superlatively good moral agent."[6]

Quinn's paper was written in response to Adams's critique of the Leibnizian connection between divine and creaturely maximality. In "The Problem of Divine Perfection and Freedom", in this volume, William L. Rowe writes: "Following Philip Quinn, I'm inclined to think that if an omnipotent being creates some world other than the best it can create, then it is possible there should exist a being morally better than it is."[7] He sums up by saying:

---

[5] Philip L. Quinn, "God, Moral Perfection, and Possible Worlds", in *God: The Contemporary Discussion*, ed. Frederick Sontag and M. Darrol Bryant (New York: The Rose of Sharon, Inc., 1982), p. 213.

[6] Ibid., p. 214.

[7] William L. Rowe, "The Problem of Divine Perfection and Freedom", in *Reasoned Faith*, ed. Eleonore Stump (Ithaca: Cornell University Press, 1993), pp. 228–29.

I conclude then that if an essentially omnipotent, perfectly good being creates any world at all, it must create the best world it can. For although a being may do no wrong in creating less than the best it can create, a being whose nature is to be *perfectly good* is not such that it is possible for there to be a being morally better than it. If, however, a being were to create a world when there is a morally better world it could create, then it would be possible for there to be a being morally better than it.

The point is basically quite simple. If it is impossible to create a best possible world, then any world God might create is such that a better could have been created. Adams may have shown how this can be compatible with a certain kind of flawlessness or sinlessness in the divine character. But absolute moral perfection is thought of as encompassing much more than merely a duty-bound or principled flawlessness, or sinlessness. It includes the idea of unsurpassable *completeness in goodness* as well. The suggestion of Quinn and Rowe is that a being who creates less than the best exhibits at best only surpassable moral goodness, a goodness which therefore is not absolute, or unsurpassably complete. If it is impossible to create a best possible world, as so many defenders of theism have recently believed, then by this reasoning it is impossible for any being to exemplify unsurpassable moral goodness. The concept of perfect goodness is thus an incoherence. This is the problem. Or it can be put a bit differently. Insofar as God is a creator, God cannot be absolutely perfect. If we want to hold on to the conception of God as perfect, we must cease to think of him as a creator, or even as any sort of creative personal agent with distinctively moral goodness at all. But all this is of course absolutely unacceptable to traditional theists, for whom both perfection and creation are important ideas.

3. Sources of the Problem

I think we can best understand and evaluate this problem of perfection and creation if we ferret out some of the assumptions required for its formulation. First, and most obviously, it is assumed that divine goodness is at least in part a matter of moral goodness, or of something very much like moral goodness. Adams argued that God was under no moral obligation to create the best possible world. Most theists, regardless of how they view the basic modality of creation, would deny that God was under any moral obligation to create at all. Insofar as the act of creation takes place and is good, it falls into another category of moral characterizability. It is an act of grace, or of moral supererogation. It is a good act that God was not duty-bound to perform.

It is further assumed in the formulation of our problem that moral goodness can be a characteristic of both agents and their actions, as well as of the results of their actions. In the case of God, a good being performs a good action in the creating of a good world. Moreover, results, acts, and agents can all be compared with other results, acts, and agents, respectively, as to their moral value. In addition, states of any one moral agent are commensurable across time and across possible worlds. I may be a better person now than I was fifteen years ago. And perhaps I could have been even better a person now if I had been subject to other influences and had made better use than I have of the resources available to me.

One of the ways in which we make comparative judgments between agents and between states of an agent across time or across possible worlds is by attending to the actions performed by those agents or by that agent at different times or in different possible circumstances. And one of the ways in which we grade actions as better or worse is in light of the relative value of their consequences. One act can be better than another in virtue of bringing about better consequences. The moral status of an agent is not altogether independent of the moral status of that agent's actions. And the moral status of an action is not altogether independent of the moral status of at least the intended consequences of the action.

But how exactly are we to understand these connections? Consider the following reasoning, which would apparently be endorsed by Quinn and Rowe, as well as by other critics who formulate our problem:

(1) It is possible for the product of divine creation to have been morally better.

Therefore,

(2) It is possible for the action of the divine creator to have been morally better.

Therefore,

(3) It is possible for the divine creator to have been morally better.

Quinn says that, as far as he can tell, the following proposition expresses "a fairly obvious truth":

(13) Necessarily, for all w, w' and x, if w is an actualizable world and
      w' is an actualizable world and w is a morally better world than
      w', then if x is an omnipotent moral agent and x actualizes w',
      then x is such that there is some possible world in which there is
      a y such that y is a better moral agent in that world than he (x) is
      in w'.[8]

Simply put, the idea seems to be that, all else equal, the better the
product, the better the act; the better the act, the better the agent.
  Rowe says:

One being may be morally better than another even though it is not
better by virtue of the performance of some obligation that the other
failed to perform. It may be morally better by virtue of performing some
supererogatory act that the other being could have but did not perform.[9]

Suppose that I give you five dollars. I could have given you ten, but
I give you five. Suppose you do not particularly need the gift, nor
do you need to be the recipient of a gift. Suppose, in other words,
that it's pure supererogation on my part. I do a good deed that did
not need to be done. If someone else instead had given you ten
dollars, would it have been the case that she did a better deed than
I? Would she therefore, all else equal, have been a better person
than I? I'm not convinced that this follows at all. And it's not just
because it's my generosity and stature we're discussing.
  Is there a simple additive relation between what is produced by
supererogatory acts and the moral status of the acts themselves? Is
there a simple additive relation between the value of the acts and
the moral status of their agents? We can think we have some reason
to suppose so, but then the implications of so supposing can turn
out to be counterintuitive. Or, at least, so it seems to me.

4. Subjunctives of Supererogation

Consider the following compound conditional statement form,
which for convenience we can refer to as a "subjunctive of supererogation":

---

[8] Quinn, "God, Moral Perfection, and Possible Worlds," p. 213. Parenthetical addition mine.
[9] Rowe, "The Problem of Divine Perfection and Freedom," p. 228.

(SS)   If an act of supererogation *A* is better than another such act *B*,
and an agent *S* does *B*, having been able to do *A* instead, without
any overriding negative consequences, then *S* would have been a
better agent if *S* had done *A* rather than *B*.

This subjunctive of supererogation seems to convey an assumption
that is central in the construction of our problem. What we need to
ask is this: Is there a relation between the moral status of an agent
and the moral status of the agent's acts such as to ground the truth
of subjunctives of this sort?

There are obviously connections of various kinds between our actions and our characters. The following theses lay out two possible
relations:

The Production Thesis: The goodness of an agent's actions is productive
of the agent's goodness.

The Expression Thesis: The goodness of an agent's actions is expressive of
the agent's goodness.

What could warrant the truth of statements of the form of (SS)?
Well, of course, the production thesis would. If an agent's goodness
is, at least in part, an additive result of the goodness of his or her
actions, then doing more good, or doing better, would result in being better. Since at least the time of Aristotle, we have realized that
we can become good, at least in part, by doing good. This thesis, if
it is an altogether general truth about agents and their actions,
would seem to warrant the inference that if God had created a better
world, God would have been better, or if a being like God in every
other way had created a world morally superior to this one, then
that being would have been better than God is. A greater action
produces greater goodness. And in that case, God wouldn't be the
greatest possible being in his current state as creator of this world.

But can the production thesis apply to God? The production relation it expresses could not possibly hold in the case of a temporally
everlasting and morally immutable yet ceaselessly active being, as
many theists hold God to be. The goodness of such a being could
not additively increase as a product of the ceaseless summation of its
ongoing actions precisely because of its moral immutability. But
what of an atemporally or timelessly eternal mode of divine existence? It might seem that the production relation could indeed hold
with respect to the action of an atemporal or timelessly eternal, morally immutable being. For as such a being does not perform actions

that are in themselves, that is to say, with respect to their performance, temporally sequential, the moral productivity with respect to the character of the agent would not involve sequentially different levels of character, or moral mutability. But if the eternal, immutable being is also thought of as maximally perfect, then there is an intuitively insurmountable modal problem with any supposition that the production relation holds between divine action and God. For if God is the greatest possible being, then it is impossible for God or any other being to have been better. If the moral value of creation is, as a matter of logic, arithmetic, or for any other purely conceptual reason, upwardly open-ended, then if the production relation held true of God, an inconsistency would arise. The resultant impossibility displays the inapplicability of the production thesis to God, and thus its lack of completely general, unrestricted truth.

The production thesis can seem to be true when we consider the relation between act and character in the case of human beings. But humans are, at least in this life, morally improvable beings. We have moral potential. And if anything like the production thesis is true of any sorts of beings at all, it is true only of beings with moral potential. A greatest possible being is by definition not a being with moral potential. Thus, to assume the unrestricted truth of the production thesis is just to beg the question against perfect being theology.

But what of the expression thesis? It could be that statements of the form of (SS) are true not because doing better makes one better but because how we do is either good evidence for, or a criterion of, what we are. A strong enough expressive connection between acts and agents could perhaps ground the truth of (SS)-type statements.

Something like the production thesis can seem to be true of human beings; the main question we raised was whether it can be true of God, although as I indicated earlier, I do not believe that even in the human domain supererogation is always productive of good in the agent in any highly specific, additive way. The expression thesis can seem to lay out a very commonsensical connection in the case of humans and God. Our actions at least most often express our character, we are inclined to say, but of course we can act out of character. Logically and precisely speaking, however, even this is a manifestation of character: it is in our characters occasionally to act out of character. That is to say, none of us is as firmly entrenched in our own principles and as fully imbued with the virtues we have in fact developed as never to act in a way unbecoming those principles and contrary to those virtues. We are weak. And any act that is "out of character" gives expression to this weakness. So it can look as if the

expressive connection holds between agent and action in the human
domain without exception, despite what we might otherwise initially be inclined to think.

But what of God? Well, first of all, surely God's goodness will be
expressed in his actions. Moral goodness is just like that. A good
God will thus make a good world. But doesn't it then follow from
this that a perfect God will make a perfect world? The question we
seem forced to is this: If the expressive connection must hold, must
it hold perfectly? In the case of God, if it must be the case that his
character is expressed in his actions, must it further be the case that
his character is perfectly expressed in his actions? An affirmative
answer to this question could certainly ground the truth of propositions about God which take the form of (SS) and could thus give rise
to our problem.

But what is the notion of a perfect expression of character, and are
there any limits to the application of such a notion? If you and I do
less well than we're capable of doing, then those around us may
conclude, and may sometimes justifiably conclude, that we are not
at the level of goodness that could be exemplified. But failing to do
the best you can is a flaw or manifests an incompleteness in moral
character in this way only if doing the best you can is at least a
logical possibility. If doing the best he can in creating a world is for
God an impossibility, given the range of omnipotence and the nature of those considerations making the notion of a best of all possible worlds an incoherence, then not doing his best in creating cannot be seen as a flaw or as manifesting an incompleteness in the
character of God. The notion of a perfect expression of an unsurpassable character would then itself be an incoherence. To assume
otherwise would, again, just be to beg the question against perfect
being theology.

So, as far as I can see, neither the production thesis nor the expression thesis can be used to ground the general, unrestricted
truth of (SS)-style propositions. In particular, neither can be used to
generate the inferences Quinn and Rowe employ to construct the
problem of perfection and creation we have examined. And without
the inference that if God could have done better, God would have
been better, the lack of any upward moral maximality with respect
to a world cannot be taken to imply the lack of any such determinate
maximality with respect to the character of God. So, despite the lack
of analogy between perfect power and perfect goodness, I believe
Norman Kretzmann was right to say that neither of these exalted

properties is threatened by any divine inability to create a best of all possible worlds.

5. Some Suggestions

To end here, though, would be a bit misleading. For although I am inclined to believe that it is in fact, and as a matter of logic, impossible for God to actualize a best of all possible worlds, I do not in the least think that this impugns the perfection of creation.

For one thing, I am unconvinced that it is helpful to attempt to elucidate the basic act of creation in terms of the actualization of any state of affairs or of any possible world. God most basically brings into existence stuff. Ex nihilo he produces very basic things. It brings no illumination here to employ locutions and concepts helpful elsewhere and say that he actualizes the state of affairs of something's existing other than God. Quinn parses creation in terms of the actualizing of a possible world. And so does Rowe, who writes, "Creating the world is certainly a very significant act, involving, as it does, a vast number of divine acts in actualizing the contingent states of affairs that constitute our world."[10] I don't see any reason to think that God's most basic productive activity in creation involves "a vast number" of distinct divine acts at all. And I suspect that to understand *creating* as *actualizing* is in some respects to obscure more than to clarify.

What is it to actualize a state of affairs, according to the analytic metaphysics both Quinn and Rowe draw on? To actualize a state of affairs is roughly something like this: An action actualizes a state of affairs just in case the performance of the action, or a causal or logical result of the action's being performed in its context, is such that *in virtue of it* a proposition expressing the obtaining of that state of affairs, and having no other semantic content, is true. In creating, God, through a metaphysical exercise of his *power*, brings about the existence of stuff ontologically distinct from himself. The *in-virtue-of* relation involved in actualization need not consist in any such exercise of causal power at all. Thus, there is a certain specificity about creation which actualization locutions do not in themselves necessarily capture.

Of course, in contemporary philosophy, there are at least two dis-

[10] Ibid., p. 226.

tinct senses of the word *world* that are sometimes intertwined, one from analytic modal metaphysics, the other of a more common origin. In the former, a world is a maximal state of affairs; in the latter it is a concrete cosmic entity or cluster of entities of a certain type, whether as small as a planet or as large as the universe. When traditional believers have said that God created the world, they have had in mind the latter. But philosophers quickly translate into terms of the former. I am suggesting that such translations into favored philosophical conceptualities may not always be useful or enlightening. And in the case of creation, such a translation has gotten our attention off one sort of matter and focused it on something else instead. God cannot create a best of all possible worlds in the sense of a best possible maximal state of affairs. But it still may be the case that there is a way in which God can do his best in creating and in some important sense bring about a perfect creation.

What is it that comes directly from the hand of God? We wait upon a more complete physical science and a more fully developed attendant metaphysics to identify with relative certainty the basic building blocks of our world. Whatever they are, whether one-dimensional strings of energy, with all their essential combinatorial properties, or something else, these can be thought of as the most direct or as the most immediate products of the divine activity of creation. In what sense can they be assessed as "good", relevant to the distinctively moral goodness of their creator? In what sense as "perfect"?

Insofar as the direct objects of creation are such that, by them, a universe would come into existence in which sentient, moral life could be produced and flourish, those objects of creation are good. And insofar as each basic unit of creation is in itself non-defective, fully what it is intended to be, it is perfect (etymologically, "thoroughly or completely made"). In fact it can be argued that the most basic units of divine creation, the simple ultimate ingredients of our world, given their status, could not fail this test for perfection.

But could the whole cluster of direct objects of creation have been, overall, better than the array composing our world? Well, presumably, there could have been more of them. We have no reason to think that the metaphysical or physical space available for their introduction into reality is limited in such a way as to constrain their number. So with respect to number there is presumably no maximization or completeness available to God. But with respect to order there very well may be.

If the basic units of creation are ordered with respect to one another, overall, in a way that is maximally productive given their number and maximally efficiently productive of all the values wholly dependent on them, their number, their ordering and their combinatorial functions, then their arrangement is perfect.[11] In that teleological sense, the realm of creation they make up would be as good as it could possibly be. Insofar as the existence of these basic units is perfect and their arrangement is perfect, and the direct product of divine creation is just such simples, with their ordering, there could then be a straightforward sense in which creation is perfect, appropriate as the production of a perfect being.

What results from the creation environment once sentient moral creatures come onto the scene may seem far from perfect. And in many respects it can fail to be a best of all possible worlds, a best possible maximal state of affairs, without its following from this that the product of creation, the act of creation, or the character of the creator must be judged inconsistent with the assurances of perfect being theology. Thus, again, I see nothing here to prevent the confluence of perfect being theology and creation theology into one powerful stream of thought, despite any appearances to the contrary. There is still much that needs explaining about our world, but I think we can draw deeply on both these traditions in our attempts to provide some of that explanation.

[11] For remarks on the perfection of divine ordering, see Norman Kretzmann, "Goodness, Knowledge, and Indeterminacy in the Philosophy of Thomas Aquinas", *Journal of Philosophy* 80 (October 1983): 631–49.

PART IV

❦

REASON AND FAITH ON THE RELATION BETWEEN GOD AND CREATURES

WILLIAM E. MANN

Hope

Paul concludes the well-known thirteenth chapter of his first letter to the Corinthians by saying that "faith, hope, love abide, these three; but the greatest of these is love." When ordinary folk and theologians turn their attention to this passage, they typically suppose that Paul was commending faith, hope, and love (or charity) as three different yet compatible things. In supposing this they have grounds in Paul's own testimony. For he tells us that had he faith enough to move mountains, he would still be nothing without love (1 Cor. 13:2), and that one has faith in Christ Jesus, love for all the saints, and hope laid up for one in heaven (Col. 1:4–5).

If faith, hope, and love are different, two general questions will occur immediately to the philosophically inclined. What sorts of things are they? How do they differ from each other? Although I address these questions, I do so only insofar as they are germane to the central issue of this essay—what is hope, that it should be in the company of faith and love? It can easily appear as if the credentials of hope are counterfeit for two reasons, one having to do with hope's autonomous identity, the other with hope's laudability.

What could hope do that is not done by faith or love? Hope appears to be in danger of being annexed, either by faith or by love. For if one's hope for one's salvation—that is what Paul takes the content of hope to be—is a *belief* that one will be saved, then hope seems to be just a part of faith. Suppose, then, that hope is a *desire* for one's salvation. In that case there seems to be a territorial dispute between hope and love, a dispute that, no matter how it is settled, reflects unfavorably on hope. Ought I to hope for your salvation as earnestly as I hope for my salvation? If the answer is Yes, then it is

natural to think that hope is simply a part of love, since in this case I
am just one among many about whom I should wish and work for
the best, which is surely included in the notion of Christian charity.
If on the other hand the answer is No, hope retains its autonomous
identity, but only by being taxed with a disagreeable burden of egoism. For now it appears that my hope for my salvation takes precedence over my hope for your salvation (assuming that the latter hope
is even possible), and in that case, hope is shot through with a kind of
self-love for which I deserve no moral credit. Faith and love are hard to
achieve: they make demands on aspiring Christians that are anything
but easy to satisfy. But hoping for one's own salvation might seem to
be as easy as falling off a log. How can hope count as a great thing if it,
like wishful thinking, is so apparently—even unavoidably—easy to
have? Perhaps true Christian love or charity is incompatible with
hope: to the extent to which one has the former, one cannot have
the latter. But then Paul's yoking together of faith, hope, and love
will have to be understood in some way different from the interpretation typically placed on it by ordinary folk and theologians.

I shall examine and defend hope's credentials in the face of these
kinds of suspicions. I shall examine and defend, that is, the case for
the autonomous identity of hope, its compatibility with faith and
love, and its claim to moral legitimacy within the framework of
Christian ethical theorizing. The examination will make heavy use of
historical texts, not because they are historical, but because they
contain some of the finest discussions available. I begin with a brief
excursion into St. Augustine's and St. Thomas Aquinas's remarks on
the extent of hope. I then turn to a series of passages from Martin
Luther's Lectures on Romans. Together these passages constitute an
elaborate and sophisticated argument, one of whose tacit implications is the indictment of hope. The shrewdness and subtlety of Luther's argument can best be appreciated by seeing how it can be
defended sympathetically against a number of philosophical objections. Even so, I ultimately offer an argument for rejecting Luther's
view, placing in its stead the picture of hope that emerges from a
reading of Aquinas's Summa theologiae.

1. Augustine and Aquinas on the Extent of Hope

Early in the Enchiridion, Augustine offers the following observations in order to contrast faith and hope:

> Faith, then, is both of things bad and good, since both good things and
> bad things are believed, and this faith is good, not bad. Faith is also of

things past and present and future. For we believe in the death of
Christ, which is now past; we believe that he sits at the right hand of
the Father, which now is; we believe that he will be coming as judge,
which is future. Again, faith is of things of one's own and of others; for
everyone believes both of himself and of other people and other things
that they began to exist at some time, and were not somehow everlasting. We believe many things that pertain to religion, not only concerning other people but even concerning the angels. Hope, however, is
held of nothing but good things, of nothing but future things, and of
those things pertaining to him who sustains the hope. On account of
these given reasons, faith is distinguished from hope, by name as well
as by rational difference.[1]

The third contrast between faith and hope pointed out by Augustine asserts what we may call the self-exclusiveness thesis about
hope. Since faith is said to be directed toward "things of one's own
and of others," hope, in contrast, pertains exclusively to oneself and
not to others. It is not clear, however, whether Augustine sees the
implications of this thesis, taken *au pied de la lettre*. Near the end of
the *Enchiridion*, Augustine says that the petitions in the Lord's
Prayer are expressions of hope.[2] On a literal, unimaginative interpretation of Augustine's claim, it would seem to follow that when
we utter the petition, "Give us this day our daily bread," we are
praying distributively, not collectively: *I* ask for *my* daily bread, *you*
for *your* daily bread, and so on. Although it is possible to place this
gloss on the petition, it is difficult to square the gloss with any plausibly rich notion of Christian fellowship.[3]

Aquinas may have seen and sought to avoid that interpretation of
Augustine's remarks. He cites Augustine's pronouncement about
the self-exclusiveness of hope in the *sed contra* to *Summa theologiae*,
IIaIIae, Q. 17, a. 3: Whether One Can Hope for Another's Eternal
Happiness.[4] Aquinas's resolution is to distinguish two ways in

---

[1] St. Augustine, *Enchiridion ad Laurentium de fide et spe et caritate*, 2.8. My translation
is based on the Latin text in *Corpus Christianorum Series Latina* (Turnholt: Typographi
Brepols Editores Pontifici, 1969), 46:51–52.

[2] St. Augustine, *Enchiridion*, 30.114–16.

[3] The version of the Lord's Prayer in Matthew 6:9–13 is preceded by Jesus' injunction not to make a show of one's praying, as the hypocrites do, but rather to pray in
private (Matthew 6:5–6). It is not clear whether this injunction is intended to apply to
the Lord's Prayer, but even if it is, Augustine's account of hope makes it hard to see
why the petitions of the prayer are in the plural, not the singular.

[4] All citations from the *Summa theologiae* refer to the Leonine text in St. Thomas
Aquinas, *Opera omnia*, 7 vols., edited by Roberto Busa (Stuttgart-Bad Cannstatt:
Friedrich Frommann Verlag Günther Holzboog, 1980), vol. 2. Subsequent references
to the *Summa* use the abbreviation *ST* and cite part, question, and article numbers.

which one can hope for something. One can hope for something absolutely or "from the presupposition of another" (*ex praesuppositione alterius*). It is Aquinas's contention that speaking absolutely, I can hope only for what pertains to me: "Hope directly regards one's own good, and not that which pertains to another." But if I am united to another person by love, I can hope for that person's eternal life as well as for my own.

Aquinas's distinction raises two critical questions. The first concerns the Augustinian thesis of the self-exclusiveness of hope. Neither Augustine nor Aquinas tarry to justify the thesis. What justification can it have? Second, if the thesis is true, how is it that love can somehow alter the situation, allowing the lover to extend the field of hope to include the beloved? It might seem that to the extent to which we take the self-exclusiveness thesis seriously, we should deny the Thomistic extension. How can Aquinas have it both ways?

The self-exclusiveness thesis need not and probably should not be construed as a thesis about human motivation. Think of it not as a substantive thesis about our psychological constitution—to the effect, say, that we might have been, but just happen not to be, the sorts of beings who are able to hope for what does not pertain to us. Think of the self-exclusiveness thesis instead as holding that the notion of one's hoping for what does not pertain to one is incoherent. On this interpretation, there is something unintelligible about the following narrative: "It is no concern of mine that event E should happen. E's happening is utterly unconnected to all my interests, desires, and projects. Nevertheless, I hope that E happens."[5] To hope that E happens is just to have, or to adopt, E's happening as one of one's concerns. In this respect, the concept of hope is like the concept of fear. One cannot fear something that one knows will have no adverse effect on one's interests, concerns, or projects. It would seem, similarly, that one cannot hope for something that one knows will have no positive effect on one's interests, concerns, or projects. The sort of unintelligibility involved in these cases is more akin to pragmatic inconsistency than to straightforward logical contradiction. "I hope that E happens, but it is no concern of mine that E happens" has a saying-and-taking-back quality more similar to "It is raining, but I do not believe it" than to "P and not-P".

There are two noteworthy features to the self-exclusiveness thesis construed in this way. The thesis is neutral with respect to psychological egoism. Although the *content* of one's hope—what one's

---

[5] Alternatively, one could replace reference to E's happening with reference to F's being true.

hope is *for*—is always something that pertains to oneself, the thesis does not in itself maintain that the *cause* or *motive* of one's hope is always real or perceived self-interest. For all that the thesis says, a person can hope that she continues to enjoy good health because she wants to be able to continue to care for her children. Moreover, this interpretation of the thesis sheds some light on Aquinas's distinction between absolute hope and hope that presupposes another. In the case of absolute hope, the *target* of hope, that person for whom the hope is held, is identical with the subject who holds the hope. We might say that in such cases, the content of the hope *manifestly* pertains to the subject. That is, the proposition that expresses the content of the hope will typically involve explicit reference to the subject. In the case of hope that presupposes another, the target of hope is a person other than the subject, a person to whom the subject is united by love. The content of the hope *latently* pertains to the subject; the proposition expressing the hope need not and typically will not make explicit reference to the subject. Nevertheless, the content of the hope pertains to the subject. Insofar as one loves another, one adopts the interests, needs, and welfare of the other as one's own.[6] It is this adoption of another's interests as one's own that allows the content still to pertain to oneself even though the target may be someone else.

If this interpretation is correct, then Aquinas extends the self-exclusiveness thesis by pointing out that some of the things that pertain to oneself may be the interests of others. Yet those who are skeptical about the credentials of hope are not likely to be mollified by the foregoing account. If hope can extend to others only by one's appropriating their interests as one's own, then a whiff of self-centeredness still remains. There is something morally laudable about hoping for the salvation of others, but it would seem that all that is morally laudable is contributed by love, not by hope. What needs to be shown is that there is something praiseworthy—or at least something morally respectable—about hope in and by itself.

2. Luther's Love and Pilgrim's Progress

There is a vivid picture in the *Lectures on Romans* of what Luther takes to be the purest sort of love that a person can and perhaps

---

[6] One does not necessarily adopt or seek to advance all of the other's desires or projects. One can love another and still believe that some of the other's desires and projects are unwise, misguided, or self-destructive.

should have toward God. In setting Luther's picture before you, I warn you that I take liberties in the way in which I frame it, the light I focus on it, and the features of it to which I draw your attention. I do not believe, however, that I have tampered with the canvas itself. Some parts of the picture are obscure; I have tried to leave them that way. It is clear—or so I argue—that there is no legitimate space for hope in Luther's picture.

A person who loves God purely loves nothing but God alone. Pure love of God is a love for a being whom the lover cannot experience or comprehend: it is a love that does not know what it loves, although it knows what it does not love. Pure love is impervious to the ebb and flow of spiritual and physical goods in the lover. It is the only thing that can eradicate the lover's sinfulness and tendency to esteem his own righteousness. A person who has achieved a state of pure love does not love God for the sake of God's gifts or for some advantage. In contrast, a person who loves God for his gifts loves God primarily for what he can do or has done for her. Luther classifies this kind of impure love under the scholastic category of *amor concupiscentiae*,[7] thereby seeking to stigmatize it. Harking back to Augustine's distinction between *uti* and *frui*,[8] Luther claims that to love God in this impure way is to use God, not to enjoy him. The *servants* of God serve him out of a kind of motivation that betrays the same impurity. That is, they serve God either out of fear of punishment, thus unwillingly and sullenly, or out of desire for reward, thus willingly but venally. In contrast, the *children* of God serve him gladly, voluntarily, and freely, their only desire being to fulfill the will of God.[9]

Luther has more to say about what is involved in the unalloyed desire to fulfill the will of God. In the third scholium to Romans 8:28, Luther distinguishes three ranks of people predestined by God as elect. The differences between the ranks are characterized in terms of the kinds of attitudes and desires they have concerning

[7] See, for example, *ST* IaIIae, Q. 26, a. 4.

[8] See St. Augustine, *De doctrina Christiana*, I, iii–v, 3–5; I, xxii, 20–21.

[9] See Martin Luther, *Lectures on Romans*, scholium on 5:5. The text is in Luther's *Der Brief an die Römer*, vol. 56 of the *Werke* (hereafter cited as *W*, followed by the volume number, i.e., *56*, and the page numbers) (Weimar: Hermann Böhlaus, 1938), pp. 305–9. On this and other passages I have consulted the translations by Wilhelm Pauck in the Library of Christian Classics edition (Philadelphia: Westminster Press, 1961); and by Jacob A. O. Preus in *Luther's Works*, vol. 25 (St. Louis: Concordia Publishing House, 1972). The distinction between servants and children may be an adaptation of the scholastic distinction between servile and filial fear. See, for example, Aquinas, *ST* IIaIIae, Q. 19, aa. 2 and 5.

God's will with respect to them. In the lowest rank are those who are content with the will of God, trusting that they are among the elect; these people have a categorical desire not to be among the damned. The occupants of the middle rank are people who have resigned themselves to God's will. Unlike the denizens of the lowest rank, the occupants of the middle rank have a certain kind of second-order desire, namely, a desire to want to be rejected should God will it so. Although Luther does not explicitly point out this feature of their situation, what seems to be distinctive about the people in the middle rank is that their having the second-order desire coexists with their still not having the first-order desire to be rejected should God will it so. For what distinguishes the people in the third and highest rank of the elect is that they *do* have the first-order desire to be rejected if God so wills it. Thus they presumably experience no dislocation between their first-order and second-order desires: they desire to go to hell if God wills it so, and they desire to have that desire (W 56:388).

Luther's tripartite division of the elect implies that the attainment of pure love of God is not necessary for salvation: the people in the lowest and middle ranks do not have it. It seems, then, that Luther puts forward pure love as a Christian ideal, a state that is supererogatory rather than obligatory.

Luther deploys his analysis of pure love in his scholium on Paul's pronouncement in Romans 9:3: "For I could wish that I myself were accursed and cut off from Christ for the sake of my brethren, my kinsmen by race." Luther interprets the passage in the following way. Paul is willing to forgo his own salvation if that would secure the salvation of the Jews. Although Paul is willing to be cut off from God, he is not thereby willing to hate God: "For this love arising from its opposite is strongest and most extreme, wherein the highest hatred [for oneself] serves as a sign of the highest love for another" (W 56:390). This allegedly Pauline attitude thus contrasts sharply with the attitude expressed by certain "babblers" (*garrientes*), who claim that "ordered love" (*charitas ordinata*) can only proceed to a desire for one's neighbor's salvation by way of an initial desire for one's own salvation (W 56:390–91).[10] But the babblers' conception of

---

[10] W 56, cites John Duns Scotus's and Gabriel Biel's commentaries on book 3, distinction 29, question 1 of Peter Lombard's *Sentences*. For the *Ordinatio* version of Duns Scotus's commentary, see *Duns Scotus on the Will and Morality*, selected and translated by Allan B. Wolter (Washington: Catholic University of America Press, 1986), pp. 454–57.

love is not merely mistaken: it is Luther's further contention that it is a threat to our salvation. Luther's argument is complex. I believe that I can best present it by describing the psychological development that Luther deems necessary for a person to achieve the condition of pure love of God. The account that follows is a reconstruction of the fabric of Luther's argument, with some additional embroidery of my own in obvious places.

Suppose that Palmer is a Christian believer who until now has not thought very seriously about what may be required for her salvation.[11] We may suppose that Palmer has a vivid enough imagination to appreciate some of the blessings of heaven and some of the horrors of hell. In her present stage of development, Palmer wants to avoid hell and achieve salvation because she wants to do what is best for herself. Palmer loves God because she realizes that God is the only being who can vouchsafe her salvation. So far, Palmer is caught in the toils of *amor concupiscentiae*. Her attitude need not be as cynical as someone's attitude might be toward a rich but unpleasant superannuated uncle. Nevertheless, Palmer is using God, not enjoying him; she is God's servant but not God's child.

Amor concupiscentiae can only be extirpated either by an infusion of God's superabundant grace or by one's resigning oneself to hell and damnation. God's grace is not Palmer's to command. Palmer must, then, bring herself to a state of self-hatred, resignation to hell and damnation, if she is to love God perfectly. It is not enough that Palmer simply come *not to love* herself: she must come *to hate* herself. Nor does Luther suppose self-hatred to play an essential but merely instrumental role, functioning only as a corrective necessary to bring about the absence of self-love. For, according to Luther, to love God perfectly is to love the will of God, and thus to conform one's will to what God wills. But God "hates, damns, and wills evil to all sinners, that is, to all of us" (W 56:392). Thus if Palmer is to will what God wills, then, because she herself is a sinner, she must hate herself and will the evil of hell for herself.[12] And Luther goes out of his way to insist that self-hatred is genuine hatred, the same mental state as hatred for another, but directed toward oneself: "We must act toward ourselves as someone acts who hates another. For he does not

---

[11] An explanation of this Bunyanesque name: a palmer was someone who wore two crossed palm fronds in commemoration of having made a pilgrimage to the Holy Land.

[12] "To love is to hate oneself, to damn [oneself], to will evil, according to this statement of Christ's: 'He who hates his soul in this world preserves it in eternal life'" (W 56:392 [John 12:25]).

pretend to hate; instead he earnestly desires to destroy and kill and damn him whom he hates" (W 56:393).[13]

Now comes the first of two apparently paradoxical results. By earnestly resigning herself to hell, Palmer will escape hell and attain salvation. "For it is impossible that one who throws himself utterly upon the will of God should remain outside of God. For he wills what God wills; thus he pleases God. If he pleases, then he is loved; if loved, then saved" (W 56:391).[14] Part of the hellishness of hell is that its denizens are unwilling to resign themselves to it, and that is because they are unwilling to resign themselves to the will of God. Were they willing to accept damnation for God's sake, then they would escape damnation. But the damned are in a position that makes it impossible for them now to fulfill the antecedent of this counterfactual conditional. They are no longer able themselves to resign themselves—or, perhaps, even to try to resign themselves—to God's will. Their condition, brought about voluntarily by their own continued self-love, can now only be alleviated by the sheer gratuitousness of God's grace. Unlike the damned, Palmer can still at least try to bring herself to a state of resignation, and she would be a fool to defer loving God perfectly until such a time when she will no longer be able to do so.[15]

Palmer may wonder how to achieve a state of self-hatred and resignation. Desiring to have this attitude is not the same as having it, any more than wishing to be socially poised is the same as being socially poised. Moreover—this is the second apparent paradox—if self-hatred minimally requires lack of self-love, then one cannot attain lack of self-love from a motive of self-love. "If one says: 'But I do not love my soul in this world, because I seek a good for it in the future,' I reply: 'Because you do this out of love for yourself, which is temporal love, you still by that very fact love your soul in this world'" (W 56:392). Since the issues raised by reflection on this pas-

---

[13] Notice that Luther has come a long way from the sentiment explicitly enunciated in Romans 9:3. Paul was willing to *sacrifice* himself for the sake of the Jews, not necessarily to *repudiate* himself.

[14] It may be important to distinguish, on Luther's behalf, one's desire to *become* damned from one's desire to *remain* damned. (One can make sense of this distinction even if all the damned are damned from eternity.) Palmer would receive credit for having the former sort of desire. But (depending on one's demonology) Satan may have the latter sort of desire, for which he deserves no credit.

[15] For all that Luther says, God's grace may be necessary to assist Palmer during her quest. In this connection, see Eleonore Stump, "Sanctification, Hardening of the Heart, and Frankfurt's Concept of Free Will", *The Journal of Philosophy* 85 (1988): 395–420.

sage are crucial to understanding Luther's position, it is worth spending some time considering it and a variation on it.

Luther's example is cast in the form of a first-person avowal. Avowals of the form "I am not pursuing x now because I want to pursue x later" do not generally elicit the rejoinder, "You are by that very fact pursuing x now." Luther's imagined interlocutor avows more than that. A closer approximation is, "I am not pursuing x now because I want to pursue x later, and I have chosen not to pursue x now as a means of pursuing x later." But Luther's portrayal of the situation as one expressed by means of a first-person avowal dramatizes the bizarre nature of the avowal itself. Luther's interlocutor would have to be uncommonly obtuse or self-deceived to utter it. There are situations in which one might not realize that one's actions belie one's words. This avowal, however, is rather a case in which the interlocutor's words belie his self-understanding. Luther's rejoinder points out what is a painfully obvious implication of what the interlocutor has just said: "Who wills the means to the end wills the end" seems at least as secure as "Who wills the end wills the means."

Perhaps because he concentrates on a case expressed from the first-person perspective, Luther does not notice that an interesting alternative arises when we examine the third-person perspective. What makes the first-person avowal bizarre is that if it is sincerely uttered, we must suppose that the interlocutor virtually believes of himself simultaneously that he is *not* pursuing x while he *is* pursuing a course of action chosen precisely as a means to pursuing x. Consider, by way of contrast, the corresponding third-person report, "He is not pursuing x now because he wants to pursue x later, and he has chosen not to pursue x now as a means of pursuing x later." Suppose that the report is supplemented with this explanation: "Of course, since he made that choice, some time ago, he has changed significantly, in large part as a result of making the choice. Although he now still wants to pursue x later, and although his present non-x-ish pursuits have the choice as their ancestor, his present non-x-ish pursuits are now motivated by desires whose content has nothing to do with his desire to pursue x later. In other words, the pursuits and projects that he originally chose as means have become ends in their own right." The report, eked out in this way, does not invoke the rejoinder, "He really is pursuing x now."

The assessment of the case expressed by the first-person avowal bids us to consider the interlocutor's beliefs and desires as held *synchronically*. A case described by the corresponding third-person report opens up the possibility of interpreting the agent's beliefs and desires *diachronically*, as features of a dynamic psychological process changing through time. I do not mean to suggest that all first-person avowals must be interpreted synchronically or that all third-person reports can be interpreted diachronically. For my purposes, the distinction between synchronic and diachronic cases of Luther's second apparent paradox is more important than the distinction between avowals and reports. It may seem to be a deficiency of Luther's picture that the second apparent paradox neglects diachronic cases. Luther's picture is thereby incomplete, but I argue below that this portion of the picture can be completed to Luther's advantage.

We have enough of Luther's picture before us to see that hope is not one of its elements.[16] If Palmer's pure love of God entails her hatred and condemnation of herself, then it is inimical to any hope she might have for her salvation. To see that this is so, it is helpful to consider two ways of construing hope, either as a belief or as a desire. Consider first the case in which hope is construed as a desire for one's eternal salvation. In this case, Palmer's pure love of God is in mental conflict with her hope for salvation: the fulfillment of one of the desires is logically incompatible with the fulfillment of the other. Consider, secondly, hope construed as a belief in one's eternal salvation. There is no conflict of desires here, since in this case there is one desire cheek to jowl with one belief. In the abstract, there is nothing logically untoward about the pair of mental states expressed by "*S* believes that *P*" and "*S* desires that not-*P*". But Luther can claim, with some plausibility, that there is a tension between Palmer's believing that she will be saved and her desiring that she be damned. He can allege that the belief contaminates the desire, in the sense that the desire is unauthentic or insincere in direct proportion to the strength of the belief.

Whether hope is a desire or a belief, it contaminates (or is contaminated by) pure love. It is not surprising, then, that hope is conspicuous by its absence in Luther's depiction of pure love.[17]

---

[16] It is not accidental that when Richard Swinburne discusses Luther's views about faith, he investigates the possible connection between faith and love without mentioning hope. See Swinburne's *Faith and Reason* (Oxford: Clarendon Press, 1981), pp. 110–15.

[17] It is natural to ask what Luther has to say about Romans 8:24: "For in this hope we are saved. Now hope that is seen is not hope. For who hopes for what he sees?" According to Luther, "Hope, which arises from a desire for a thing that is loved, always increases the love by delay. Thus it happens that the thing hoped for and the one who hopes become as one through the intensity of the hope. . . . Love transforms

3. Admiring Luther's Picture

If Luther is right, then hope has no categorical, essential value for *homo viator*. The friends of hope are thereby obliged to find fault with Luther's picture of pure love. And they had better find fault with the picture, not a caricature. In order to put the picture in the most favorable light, I shall discuss a series of issues; some are responses to anticipated objections, others extend and clarify the picture in various ways.

3.1. Self-hatred and Self-concern

Pure love of God entails hatred of oneself. In this respect Luther's conception of pure love differs from the quietistic conception put forward later and most visibly by François de Salignac de la Mothe Fénelon.[18] According to Fénelon, in the state of pure love, the soul is indifferent to itself, freed entirely from any concern for itself, loving only the will of God and what God wills. An indifferent soul could come to hate itself if God willed that it hate itself, but the antecedent of that conditional is certainly not necessary and may be impossible. Quietistic pure love does not *entail* hatred of oneself. In fact, quietistic pure love, insofar as it aims solely at God's will being done, seems to entail having no attitude or concern directed toward oneself. In this respect also it differs from Luther's pure love. For suppose that Palmer achieves the state of self-hatred required for Luther's pure love. If, as Luther insists, it is genuine hatred, whose object is Palmer herself, then it will be crucially important to her that *she* be the one whom she wants to see in hell. Palmer will be concerned that it be *Palmer* who deservedly suffers, out of love of God. But it will be equally important to Palmer that it be Palmer who

---

the one who loves into what is loved. Thus hope transforms [the one who hopes] into what is hoped for, but what is hoped for does not appear. Thus [hope] transfers [the one who hopes] into the unknown, into the hidden, into interior darkness, so that he knows not what he hopes for, and yet he knows what he does not hope for" (*W* 56:374). I am inclined to say that in making hope consequent on love, Luther thinks of hope as a desire, not a belief. The last sentence in particular echoes what Luther had said about pure love of God in the scholium on Romans 5:5.

[18] For an excellent discussion, along with citations of the relevant texts, see Robert Merrihew Adams, "Pure Love", *The Journal of Religious Ethics* 8 (1980): 83–99; reprinted in his *The Virtue of Faith and Other Essays in Philosophical Theology* (New York: Oxford University Press, 1987), pp. 174–92.

suffers out of *her* love of God. So there are two ways at least in which self-concern enters into Luther's conception of pure love.

Since self-hatred as well as self-love entails self-involvement, it is important for Luther that there be a distinction between self-concern or self-involvement on the one hand and self-interest or self-love on the other. Surely there is such a distinction.[19] A person might care not merely that her children be provided for but that *she* be one of the providers, even when her providing for her children entails great personal sacrifice. Using the terminology deployed in discussing the self-exclusiveness thesis, we can say that her desire's *content* is self-involving, its *target* comprises (some of) those to whom she is united by love, and its *cause* or *motive* is not cither real or perceived self-interest but rather love.

Now the very distinction that is important to Luther is also crucial to the Thomistic extension of the self-exclusiveness thesis about hope. My hope that *I* will be saved is both self-interested and self-involving, and for that reason it is easy not to detect the distinction if we concentrate exclusively on this case. The two components come apart, however, in the case of my hope that *you* will be saved. That hope is not self-involving: I could have it even if I believed that I would not be saved. It is nevertheless self-interested if Aquinas is right in saying that when we are united by love, your interests become (a part of) my interests. We should note in passing, then, that since the distinction between self-concern and self-interest is common to both Aquinas's and Luther's views, neither view can consistently fault the other for relying on the distinction.

3.2. Doing and Undoing

You will search the *Lectures on Romans* in vain for a recipe for attaining the state of pure love of God. Luther's depicts an end-state, not a process leading to it. Should you have expected a recipe?

Suppose your goal is to become adept at the calculus. You would be well advised to master the concept of a function's having a limit before you tackle the notion of a derivative or the operation of integration. Although the process of learning the calculus is not mechanical, there are sequential stages to it that any would-be learner should follow. Your mastery of the calculus presupposes that you have acquired certain concepts and certain abilities. Because the con-

---

[19] I am especially indebted to Adams, "Pure Love", sec. 3, for clarification of this distinction.

cepts and abilities form a structural and sequential hierarchy, it is possible to specify a way, or a limited number of ways, in which they can be acquired. The acquisition of many cognitive states and abilities is the result of arduous, sophisticated training of an initially unformed, perhaps resistant mind. The same is true, as Aristotle emphasized, for many states of the will. No one is born courageous; courage must be acquired. Although Aristotle did not say much more about the acquisition of courage than that in situations of fear one must act as the courageous person would act, we could imagine, I suppose, the rise of a class of professional courage trainers. But the problem that Palmer faces is not so much the *acquisition* of a state of will as the *eradication* of such a state, namely, her love of self.

Suppose that, after you have become a calculus aficionado, your doctor tells you that if you want to preserve your health, you must become completely nescient about the calculus. You must, that is, unlearn the fundamental concepts and become unable to perform any of the distinctive operations. How would you go about doing that? "Quit doing the stuff, and count on forgetting" is a familiar strategy, but it may be too slow and unreliable for your needs: what we are able to forget is not entirely within our control. (Remember the adage about learning how to ride a bicycle.) There is hypnosis, behavior modification, and the golden age of neurophysiology. Whatever you may think about the chances for success of these techniques, you can by now see what the problem is. As hard as it was to learn the calculus, it may be just as hard, even harder, to unlearn it. And as desperate as your plight is, you would not fault your doctor for telling you what your goal must be, if you are to preserve your health, even though your doctor cannot offer you a reliable prescription for achieving that goal.

The goal of achieving pure love of God, Luther can plausibly argue, requires undoing what we have been doing all our lives, namely, seeking our own welfare first and subordinating most if not all other projects to that quest. It is not a criticism of Luther that he does not supply a surefire regimen for attaining pure love. But, unlike your doctor, it is not simply that Luther does not think that he *knows* of any such regimen. It is rather that Luther believes that no regimen *can be* surefire. If there really were a malaise routinely brought on by the calculus, we might then expect the rise of a class of expert calculus deprogrammers. There is no natural way, however, by which we may induce pure love in ourselves. The attitudes and actions that are inimical to pure love are so much a part of us, literally constitutive of our *second*, postlapsarian nature, that they are ineradicable by us without the aid of divine grace.

3.3. Counterproducts

Recall the two apparently paradoxical elements of Luther's picture. The first was that by desiring her damnation, Palmer will attain her salvation. The second was that enlightened self-love provides Palmer with the natural motivation to try to eradicate self-love, since absence of self-love will bring Palmer closer to ensuring her salvation, yet the motive thwarts the absence of the desire. By injecting the second apparent paradox into the first, we should get the corollary that if Palmer's desire for her own damnation is motivated by a desire for her salvation, then, although she might be saved, it will not be on account of that motivated desire.

Apparent paradoxes need not be real paradoxes. The first of Luther's claims seems to be an instance of the following thesis:

(A)   One's desire for not-S for oneself will bring about S for oneself.[20]

The second claim seems to exemplify this form:

(B)   If the motive behind one's lack of desire for S for oneself is a desire for S for oneself, then one does desire S for oneself.

Thesis (A) is surely not true in general. Your desire not to learn linear algebra is almost certain to result in your not learning linear algebra. Nevertheless, some desires are counterproductive, in direct proportion to the strength of the desire. One cannot fulfill one's desire not to have *any* desires as long as one has *that* desire. If that example has a faint aroma of sophistry, consider the desires to sleep and not to behave in a self-conscious, awkward manner: for as long as, and to the degree to which, those desires are present to one's mind, they will perpetuate the very states they seek to avoid.[21]

---

[20] I assume, for the sake of simplicity, that damnation and salvation are mutually exclusive and collectively exhaustive alternatives. I also assume that the desire not to be saved is the same desire as the desire to be damned. Luther regards this to be a universally true instance of (A):

One's desire for damnation for oneself will bring about salvation for oneself.

But Luther does not regard this instance of (A) to be universally true:

One's desire for salvation for oneself will bring about damnation for oneself.

Recall that the lowest rank of the predestined elect mentioned in the third scholium to Romans 8:28 are people who want to be saved and who will be saved.

[21] See Jon Elster, *Sour Grapes: Studies in the Subversion of Rationality* (Cambridge: Cambridge University Press, 1983), chap. 2, "States That Are Essentially By-products", for a suggestive discussion of these phenomena.

To be sure, there are dissimilarities between my desire not to be awkwardly self-conscious and Palmer's desire not to be saved. My desire is easy to come by; Palmer's is hard to cultivate. Both desires are counterproductive, but mine, if allowed to operate directly, results in a negative counterproduct, while Palmer's results in a supremely positive counterproduct. Even so, there is an important similarity between our two desires, and that is that they *are* counterproductive. There is a plausible explanation for why a desire not to behave self-consciously typically results in self-conscious behavior. Insofar as my desire leads me to monitor my own behavior, the behavior comes to lack the spontaneity I want it to have. As we have seen, Luther has an explanation for why Palmer's desire would be counterproductive: she would thereby will what God wills, thus incurring God's love and her salvation. It is not clear that Luther's explanatory mechanism is correct—I discuss that issue later—but we can at least note for now that there are legitimate instances of thesis (A), even if we might not be convinced that Luther's first apparent paradox is one of them.

3.4. By-products

My wanting to behave in a natural, unaffected way is both stimulus and impediment to my behaving less self-consciously. According to Luther, Palmer's desire for her salvation is both stimulus and impediment to her attaining salvation. What are the two of us to do?

If my actions are to become less self-conscious, they should issue directly from desires other than the desire not to behave self-consciously. (While you learn to stroke the backhand properly in tennis, you need to concentrate on your grip, the position of the racket head, and the way you follow through on your stroke. But you will become adept at the backhand only when you no longer have to concentrate on the correctness of your stroke.) My desire not to behave self-consciously will be satisfied only if, so to speak, it disappears. Nevertheless, the desire can motivate me to try to achieve the desired state in some indirect way. Wishing to become less self-conscious and more spontaneous, I might try imbibing three martinis in an hour. (Seeking to avoid the pain brought about by the dentist's drill, you might try concentrating all your attention on the pain; ironically, so the story goes, the pain ceases to hurt.)[22] That regimen

---

[22] See Daniel Dennett, "Why You Can't Make a Computer that Feels Pain", in his *Brainstorms* (Montgomery, Vt.: Bradford Books, 1978), pp. 190–229.

is risky: it might purchase diminished self-consciousness at the price of augmented boorishness. But if the regimen is to work at all, it will do so only if it extinguishes, or at least submerges below the level of consciousness, the desire that motivated it. My becoming less self-conscious and more spontaneous is, then, a by-product of other activities I have engaged in, activities that, whatever else they may involve, bring about this by-product only by making my original desire invisible to me.

In what way must my desire not to behave self-consciously become "invisible"? Must it cease to exist, thus playing only an ancestral role in the development of my present desires? If so, then, recalling our earlier discussion of Luther's second apparent paradox and applying it to my desire not to behave self-consciously, we are apt to treat thesis (B) diachronically, and interpret the preposition, "behind," contained in thesis (B), as a temporal notion:

(BD) If the motive *that was ancestral to* one's lack of desire for S for oneself is a desire for S for oneself, then one does desire S for oneself.

Or can the desire's "invisibility" be a matter of its being presently in place in my psyche but buried below the conscious level, still somehow interacting with my conscious desires? In this case we will interpret thesis (B) synchronically, glossing the "behind" in more psychoanalytic terms:

(BP) If the motive *presently beneath the conscious level of* one's lack of desire for S for oneself is a desire for S for oneself, then one does desire S for oneself.

If thesis (BP) applies to my case, does the unconscious presence of the desire not to behave self-consciously contaminate my conscious desires?

From a therapeutic point of view, as long as my behavior is no longer self-conscious, these questions are candidates for the title of philosophical extravagance. Suppose that I no longer consciously desire not to behave self-consciously, and as a result, behave in an unfeigned, unself-conscious way. Then on the first alternative we will say that thesis (BD) is false in my case, since even though my desire not to behave self-consciously was historically a motive behind my present lack of that desire, the desire no longer exists. On the second alternative we can insist that thesis (BP), on its most plausible interpretation, is false in my case. For if the motive behind my present lack of *conscious* desire not to behave self-consciously is the *unconscious* desire not to behave self-consciously, then it does not follow that I *consciously* desire not to behave self-consciously.[23] If generic thesis (B) is false in my case on either alternative reading— (BD) or (BP)—who cares which alternative is correct?[24]

I should care. Even if my behavior now flows smoothly, I have reason to want to have become the kind of person described by the first alternative rather than the second. I want my behavior to be a product of the desires, intentions, and projects of which I am or can be aware, not a product of them plus an unconscious desire. I want it that way because any unconscious desire I might have, insofar as it is unconscious, is inaccessible to me. I would thus have no way of knowing, on my own, what role the unconscious desire plays in determining my behavior. For all I could know directly, the unconscious desire might be doing all the work, making my conscious states feckless epiphenomena, making me a victim of self-deception.

If I should care, then a fortiori Palmer should care. If, as a by-product of other activities she has engaged in, Palmer does attain at the conscious level the state of not wanting salvation for herself, she should care for reasons analogous to mine whether she still has a desire for salvation operating at the unconscious level. But in addition to the kinds of concern that I have about the unconscious springs of my unself-conscious behavior, Palmer has another, big, concern. Her unconscious desires are inaccessible to her but not to God, the *inspector cordis et renum*. Thesis (BP) seemed not to be true of my case, but only so long as we focused attention exclusively on my conscious desires and observable behavior. Palmer should consider the applicability of thesis (BP) to her case when it is not only behavior that is being judged by an omniscient being but also the state of her soul.

Suppose first that Palmer still has a desire for her salvation submerged and operating at the unconscious level. Then God will know this fact about her. It is plausible to say in this case that thesis (BP), interpreted in the following way, applies to Palmer:

(BPP)   If the motive presently beneath the conscious level of Palmer's
        lack of desire for salvation for herself is an unconscious desire

---

[23] It does follow that I unconsciously desire not to behave self-consciously. That makes thesis (BP) true but trivial.

[24] Notice that the argument in this paragraph helps itself to the optimistic but dubious assumption that my unconscious desire has no deleterious effect on my behavior.

for salvation for herself, then, all things considered, Palmer still
desires salvation for herself.

"All things considered," because it is the unconscious desire that is
in the driver's seat.[25] That is enough for God to conclude that Palmer
has not achieved the state of pure love. And that is enough for Palmer to conclude that her salvation is not guaranteed by the mechanism Luther claims to discern behind thesis (A). It is fair enough,
then, for Luther to conclude that thesis (BP) applies to Palmer's case
on the hypothesis that she presently has an unconscious desire for
her salvation.

Consider now the case in which these statements are true: Palmer
once had a desire for salvation; that desire led her to take steps to
eliminate the desire; she has in fact eliminated the desire, both from
her conscious and unconscious psyche; and moreover, she has come
to desire her own damnation. There is no doubt that Palmer has
become the person she wanted to become, and it is clear that thesis
(BP) does not characterize her case. But does thesis (BD)? What will
omniscient God think of Palmer now?

3.5. Hoodwinking God

We know what Luther's answer is: because Palmer's will conforms to God's will, God will love her and she will be saved. Some
may be hankering to protest Luther's confidence in that mechanism.
They might be forgiven for thinking that Luther's claim smacks of
presumption; it reveals an overweening attitude about Luther's capacity to know the mind of God. They might unflatteringly describe
the mechanism itself as depicting God as overly complaisant and
indulgent, too eager to overlook the calculating, self-serving way in
which Palmer got to be as she now is. This objection is a member of
the same family identified and endorsed by Jon Elster:

> Christianity rests on the idea that there is one spectator clever enough
> to see through any actor, viz. God. Hence Pascal's wager argument
> must take account of the need to induce a real belief, since faking will
> not do. Moreover, the fact of God's clairvoyance explains why good
> works cannot bring about salvation if performed for the sake of salva-
> tion. The state of grace is essentially (or at most) a by-product of action.

---

[25] It might be that Palmer still has an unconscious desire for her salvation, but that
it is so vestigial that it does little or no work. In that case I suppose that thesis (BPP)
would not be true of her situation.

Let me record an objection to the wager argument. What kind of God is it that would be taken in by a genuine belief with a suspect past history—i.e. belief ultimately caused, even if not proximately justified, by instrumental rationality? Pascal's own attack in *Les Provinciales* on Jesuit casuistry shows that he is open to this objection. Here he argues against the Jesuit doctrine of *directing the intention*, i.e. the idea that an action which is blameable when performed on one intention may not be so if performed on another, so that the confessor should direct his attention to the intention behind the behaviour rather than to the behaviour itself. The obvious objection is that even if . . . one were to succeed in changing the intention, the blameable intention behind the change of intention would contaminate the action that was performed on the new intention. Yet a similar argument would seem to apply to the reasoning behind the wager: how could present belief not be contaminated by the mundane causal origin?[26]

If Elster's objection is allowed to stand, then Palmer's shield of pure love has a bar sinister: the desire for her own salvation was an ancestor. Surely, however, the requirement of causal purity implied by Elster's objection is implausibly strong. Suppose that Chumley knows and regrets that Sly has deeply racist attitudes. Sly, shrewd enough to see that the expression of these attitudes will result in disfavor from his corporate employer, Boss, keeps the attitudes to himself. While on the job, Sly acts in ways calculated to impress upon Boss Sly's commitment to racial equality. Influenced by Sly's overt actions, Boss gives Sly assignments working with minority employees. With the passage of time, Chumley comes to notice that Sly no longer gives vent to his old attitudes in private situations in which he could "get away" with it. Instead, Sly speaks approvingly of the cooperation he has received from his coworkers and the success that the corporation has thereby had. One day Chumley finds Sly angrily denouncing a mutual friend's racism. Chumley finally and correctly concludes that Sly's on-the-job dissimulation has indirectly made Sly become what he at first only pretended to be.

Chumley surely would need a heart of stone not to approve of Sly's conversion, even though it had such a shady beginning. Chumley is not "taken in" by a genuine attitude "with a suspect past history". It is rather that Chumley takes the past attitude, the present person, and the contribution of the former to the latter as an occasion for forgiving and rejoicing. Despite his presumptuous tone, Luther is right to suppose that Christianity rests on the idea of a

---

[26] Elster, *Sour Grapes*, pp. 74–75.

loving and merciful clever spectator. Palmer cannot expect to hood-wink an omniscient God, nor is it any part of Luther's view that Palmer can somehow morally oblige God to grant her salvation. Luther is nevertheless within his rights to reject the imputation of fault along the lines suggested by thesis (BD). If Palmer were to bring herself to a state of perfect love from a state of imperfect love, she would have done all that any human can do.

3.6. Oughts and Cans

Or is it that Palmer would have done *more* than any human can do? One may wonder whether it is psychologically possible for persons to achieve the state of self-hatred that Luther commends. To hate oneself, in Luther's sense, entails consciously wanting the worst for oneself. It is not clear that one really can have that desire, even if one thinks that one *deserves* the worst. Let us make the case as dire as we can for Luther. Suppose that people genuinely cannot come to hate themselves. Suppose further that when Luther wrote the *Lectures on Romans* he believed that they cannot. What follows from these two suppositions?

Less than might meet the eye. If Luther's picture is to be faulted on this score, the criticism would presumably take one or the other of the following two forms: Luther is exhorting us to do something we cannot do. Luther is exhorting us to do something that he believes we cannot do.

The first criticism rests on the principle that what is obligatory (or supererogatory) for one must be something that is within one's power. Luther is no friend of that principle. In his summary of the detailed discussion of Romans 4:7 he writes that we cannot fulfill the law of God, that we are therefore *deservedly* unrighteous, and as a result, that we must always pray for the remission—or at least the nonimputation—of our sins (see W 56:268–91). Or consider the plight of Luther's damned who are no longer able to acquiesce in God's will: it need not follow that they no longer ought so to acquiesce. In *The Freedom of a Christian*, Luther says that the Decalogue commandment against covetousness makes sinners of us all.[27] Luther's doctrine of justification by faith, not works, depends on the fact that we cannot do the works bid by this and the other commandments, even though we ought to.

[27] Martin Luther, *The Freedom of a Christian*, in *Luther's Works* (Philadelphia: Muhlenberg Press, 1957), 31:333–77, esp. p. 348.

These counterexamples to the principle that what is obligatory must be within the agent's power exhibit a common structure. In each case the agent is unable to do something obligatory because the agent is in a debilitated state. There are similar plausible counterexamples that arise in nontheological contexts. The driver should have avoided hitting the pedestrian but was unable to because the driver was drunk. The lifeguard should have saved the drowning victim but could not: the task was not too difficult, but the lifeguard was out of shape. One might protest that in the latter cases the agent is responsible for the debilitating condition; that condition was voluntarily acquired, not inherited. Luther surely does think that we are accountable in spite of our inherited tendency toward sin. Does he thus set the standards absurdly high?

In his discussion of Romans 7:14–25, Luther appeals to a distinction between "to do" (*facere*) and "to accomplish" or "to fulfill" (*perficere*) (W 56:340–54, esp. pp. 342, 353–54). The feature of the distinction relevant to our discussion is this: we can *do* the good but we cannot *fulfill* the good. To do the good is not to succumb to the sinful promptings that we find within us. To fulfill the good would be not to have the sinful promptings at all and that is not within our power. Suppose that molecular geneticists were to discover that racist attitudes in human populations are the expression of an identifiable genetic heritage. Suppose further that Blowhard and Diehard are identical twins possessing these genes but raised separately. Blowhard has become a vicious, unabashed hatemonger. From time to time in his life, Diehard has found inexplicable feelings of racial prejudice welling up within him, but because he has been taught that prejudice is wrong, he has striven not to express them in action, verbal or otherwise, and he has developed a set of techniques that he uses to derail and dissipate those attitudes whenever he becomes aware of them. Diehard does the good but does not fulfill the good; Blowhard does not even do the good. Surely Blowhard deserves censure and Diehard deserves moral credit even though they both have the same, involuntarily inherited, debilitating condition. Diehard ought not to have the feelings he disavows, but in order for that to happen he would have to become (perhaps literally!) a new person.

Let us reexamine Palmer's case from Luther's standpoint. Because of the heritage conferred on her by original sin, she is the subject of all sorts of unbidden, sinful desires. Even if she can avoid acting on those desires—and that is no mean feat—she cannot avoid having the desires. She can do the good, but she cannot fulfill the good.

The fact that she is subject to sinful desires might motivate her to hate herself. But now we return to the question whether she *can* come to hate herself. If she cannot, then it is open to Luther to say that her inability is also a product of her sinful inheritance and that, nevertheless, self-hatred is either obligatory or a supererogatory ideal.

Is it not perverse or deceitful of Luther to commend to Palmer a goal that he believes she cannot achieve? Not necessarily. Suppose that Chumley is involved in the moral education of Diehard. Believing that Diehard cannot avoid having racist attitudes, Chumley might nevertheless commend to him a life in which he does not have them, let alone act on them. Chumley might think, with some justification, that this is the best way to get Diehard to disown the attitudes, to regard them as somehow alien, as not genuinely *his*.[28] In similar fashion, even if Palmer cannot achieve self-hatred, her taking Luther seriously may be the best way for her to renounce the self-interested desires she may inescapably have. Moreover, if Luther's belief is false, if Palmer really can achieve self-hatred, her achieving it may come about by her initially trying to hate herself, seeing that her efforts have failed, and then genuinely coming to hate herself as a reaction of self-disgust to the failure of her initial efforts.

4. Why I Am Not a Lutheran

In arguing earlier that Luther's picture of pure love of God leaves no room for hope, I did not mean to suggest that Luther consciously set out to abolish hope. Luther may have thought that if pure love is a Christian ideal that has no use for hope, it might still be that hope is an essential component of the ordinary, nonsupererogatory, Christian life. Here the issues quickly become vexed, for it is natural to protest that although the supererogatory goes beyond the obligatory, it cannot nullify it. I propose not to enter that debate. I wish instead to reject Luther's assumption that pure love is a commendable ideal and to reinstate hope's credentials. The two projects are not wholly independent.

Let us return to Palmer's case. Suppose that out of devotion to

---

[28] On the notion of a desire's not being one's own, see Harry Frankfurt, "Identification and Externality", in *The Identities of Persons*, ed. Amélie Oksenberg Rorty (Berkeley: University of California Press, 1976), pp. 239–51.

God, she yearns to achieve the self-hatred required for Luther's conception of pure love, but she still finds within herself a stubborn core of self-love. Suppose further that Dr. Wheedle has developed a drug that induces the requisite state of self-hatred. In supposing this, we need not suppose that Wheedle's drug would work on the village atheist. For it is plausible to assume that the right kind of self-hatred entails a suite of cognitive states, such as belief that God exists, that he rightly judges us and finds us wanting, and the like. But Palmer, unlike the village atheist, already has or is receptive to the relevant cognitive states. Perhaps then all that Wheedle's drug has to do for Palmer is create in her a mood of self-loathing that will interact with her cognitive states: the mood will strengthen some of the beliefs, and the beliefs in turn will make the mood seem appropriate. Should Palmer take Wheedle's drug, thus sidestepping all the elaborate and chancy indirect methods that she might otherwise attempt?

Before you answer that question, consider one more fanciful example. Recall Diehard, our congenital but reluctant racist. Let us imagine that Dr. Helix has perfected gene therapy to such a degree that a simple procedure could eliminate Diehard's innate racist attitudes with no undesirable side effects. (To make the case closer to the situation with Wheedle's drug, we might even suppose that Helix's procedure would not work to eliminate the entrenched racist attitudes of Blowhard, our village bigot.) Is it permissible for Diehard to undergo Helix's procedure?

I trust that the answer is Yes; what could be wrong with one's voluntarily eliminating an involuntarily contracted affliction? Although we could understand why Diehard might not choose to undergo the procedure if he has achieved mastery over his unbidden attitudes by indirect means, there surely would be nothing morally wrong in his undergoing the procedure.

If it is permissible for Diehard to undergo Helix's procedure, should it not also be permissible for Palmer to take Wheedle's drug?

I think that the answer is No. I also think that it is important that we say No for the right reason. Some might be tempted to seek a relevant lack of parallel between Diehard's situation and Palmer's in the fact that salvation from God is involved in the latter but not the former. The claim might be that omniscient God would know about and disapprove of Palmer's instant attainment of pure love. Now the claim is not obvious: an omniscient and loving God would also know all about Palmer's intentions and motives, along with the differences between Palmer and the village atheist, and judge accordingly.[29] Moreover, an admirer of Luther's picture ought to be especially wary of making the claim. For the defense of Luther's picture against Elster's condition of causal purity depended on rejecting the wholesale applicability of that kind of claim. Thus an admirer of Luther's picture who wants to maintain the permissibility of Palmer's taking indirect steps to achieve self-hatred while denying the permissibility of her taking the drug must point to some convincing difference between the two methods that does not presume to know God's judgments.

No doubt more could be said on behalf of this kind of negative answer to the question of the permissibility of Palmer's taking the drug. My negative answer, however, depends on a different reason. Palmer should not take the drug because the state it would induce, unlike the state Helix's procedure would induce in Diehard, is bad. Since the state is bad, any attempt—direct or indirect—to induce it is misguided. Helix's procedure eliminates a vicious factor from Diehard's psyche. It thus enables Diehard more easily to exercise his ability to treat others in a fair-minded way. Helix's procedure does not produce a virtue in Diehard, but it allows one of Diehard's fledgling virtues to flourish. In contrast, the self-hatred central to Luther's conception of pure love stifles the growth of other virtues; first, the virtue of hope and then, as a consequence, the virtue of charity. These claims presuppose that hope and charity are virtues and that without hope there can be no charity. In arguing for the plausibility of these claims, I shall rely heavily on the insights of Aquinas.

Aquinas takes Paul's enumeration of faith, hope, and charity to specify three theological virtues. They are *virtues* because they are operative habits, habits governing one's actions that perfect those actions toward an end. Faith, hope, and charity are *theological* virtues because the end at which they aim, namely, eternal beatitude, is beyond the capacity of humans to attain qua natural creatures: their object is God, they are infused[30] by God, and knowledge of them depends on divine revelation (*ST* IaIIae, Q. 62, a. 1). They are *three*

---

[29] If X desires your love and you take a pill that deepens your already existing love for X by removing impediments to it, it is not clear that X is entitled to complain. If, however, X desires Y's love and Y is indifferent at best to X but cynically takes the pill in order to have a better chance of inheriting X's estate, then X is entitled to complain.

[30] *Infunduntur*, a term of art. The process of infusion contrasts with the process of the acquisition of the moral virtues by habituation. The latter is typically within our unaided power; the former is not.

virtues because they perform three distinct functions. Faith perfects the operation of the intellect by supplying it with principles beyond its natural capacities, hope heartens the operation of the will by setting beatitude before it as something that can be attained with divine assistance, and charity perfects the operation of the will by conforming its ends with God's, thus uniting it with God (*ST* IaIIae, Q. 62, a. 3; see also *ST* IIaIIae, Q. 17, a. 6).

It may help to see that hope is a genuine virtue, not merely an example of wishful thinking, by contrasting it to *despair* and *presumption*. Unlike the moral virtues, the theological virtues are not means between extremes of deficiency and excess. It is impossible to believe too strongly in God, to trust too much in God's omnipotence and mercy, or to love God too much (*ST* IaIIae, Q. 64, a. 4). In particular, hope is not a mean between despair and presumption (*ST* IaIIae, Q. 64, a. 4, ad 3; *ST* IIaIIae, Q. 17, a. 5, ad 2). Despair is not a state of hoping too little, and presumption is not hoping too much. On the contrary, despair is the abandonment of hope, a kind of turning away from God that results when salvation is deemed to be beyond the reach of the sinful creature (*ST* IaIIae, Q. 40, a. 4; *ST* IIaIIae, Q. 20, a. 1).[31] And presumption is a rejection of hope as unnecessary, either because one presumes that salvation is within one's own power or because one presumes that God's mercy will save even those who are unrepentant (*ST* IIaIIae, Q. 21, a. 1). Both despair and presumption are sinful states. Because they consist in the rejection of a virtue necessary for salvation offered by the Holy Spirit, Aquinas reckons them as sins against the Holy Spirit (*ST* IIaIIae, Q. 14, a. 2). Among the consequences of this rejection is a proneness to malice, or sinning for the sheer pleasure of sinning (*ST* IIaIIae, Q. 14, a. 1). Despair, according to Aquinas, is the more serious of the two, since it is a more serious error to mistrust God by supposing that he will exact punishment even from repentant sinners than to suppose that he will mercifully spare the unrepentant (*ST* IIaIIae, Q. 21, a. 2).

I argued earlier that the self-hatred that is central to Luther's pure love is psychologically incompatible with hope. To hold both, a person would have to desire earnestly that God's justice be fully prosecuted while at the same time trusting steadfastly that God's justice will not be prosecuted. If hope is a virtue necessary for salvation,

---

[31] For some suggestive remarks on the phenomenology of despair, see Josef Pieper, *On Hope* (San Francisco: Ignatius Press, 1986), pp. 47–61.

then Luther's pure love puts its practitioner in peril, not because of the way it has been brought about, but because of what it is.

If Luther's picture of pure love entailed only the loss of hope, that would be reason enough to reject the picture. But it also entails the loss of charity. In order to see this, we need further to explore Aquinas's views. In particular, we need to see what charity is, that charity cannot exist without hope, and that Luther's pure love is not charity.

Aquinas takes the order given in the Pauline list to be an order of precedence. Citing an interlinear gloss on Matthew 1:2, Aquinas does not demur from saying that just as Abraham begot Isaac and Isaac begot Jacob, so faith begets hope and hope begets charity (*ST* IaIIae, Q. 40, a. 7; see also *ST* IIaIIae, Q. 17, aa. 7–8). I believe that the notion of precedence here provides for some tricky exposition. Whatever account we give of it must pay heed to the following claims made by Aquinas. (1) The theological virtues are infused simultaneously (*ST* IaIIae, Q. 62, a. 4). I take this claim to imply that whenever faith is infused, so are hope and charity. I do not take it to imply that faith, hope, and charity are infused only once in a person's career. (2) Despite what has just been said under claim (1), faith and hope can exist without charity (*ST* IaIIae, Q. 65, a. 4). (3) Nevertheless, charity cannot exist without faith and hope (*ST* IaIIae, Q. 65, a. 5). (4) Despite claim (3), the blessed in heaven retain charity (*ST* IaIIae, Q. 67, a. 6; *ST* IIaIIae, Q. 26, a. 13) even though their faith and hope have been "voided" (*evacuatur*) (*ST* IIaIIae, Q. 18, a. 2; *ST* IaIIae, Q. 67, aa. 3–5).

Let us first look briefly at claims (1) and (2), then at claim (4), reserving a more detailed examination for claim (3). Even if faith, hope, and charity are infused simultaneously, it does not follow that an agent realizes them simultaneously. Suppose that Martians have simultaneously instilled in me true beliefs about the correct fingering for the *Waldstein* Sonata, the hopeful desire that I might achieve the mastery to play the sonata, and the loving desire to play it as it ought to be played. The latter desire might become both less dispositional and more determinate only as I mobilize my beliefs and hope.[32] In similar fashion, one can believe in God and hope for salvation but not yet will as one ought. To will not only *what* one ought

---

[32] My beliefs and hope, in turn, may be deepened by my developing desire. In *ST* IaIIae, Q. 65, a. 4, Aquinas claims that charity transforms faith and hope from inchoate to perfected states.

but *as* one ought is to be perfected by charity. As for claim (4), the charity enjoyed by the blessed in heaven no longer depends on faith, for faith has been superseded by something epistemically superior: direct vision of God. And hope is made otiose because the blessed possess that for which they had hoped.

Claim (3), then, is a claim about the precedence of the theological virtues as they are lodged in *homo viator*. The notion of precedence is reasonably clear in the case of faith and hope. Faith precedes hope because hope in the will presupposes some act or state of faith in the intellect: those who assent to no beliefs whatsoever about some of the propositions expressing the content of faith literally cannot have any hope *for salvation* (*ST* IaIIae, Q. 62, a. 4; *ST* IIaIIae, Q. 17, a. 7). One would expect, then, if hope precedes charity, that charity in the will presupposes some act or state of hope in the will. One would expect further that those who have no hope for their salvation cannot have charity, construed as love of God for his own sake and love of others (*ST* IIaIIae, Q. 17, a. 8; Q. 25, a. 1).

Charity is *amicitia* between God and person. Since *amicitia* has implications that go beyond those associated with the term "friendship", I leave it untranslated. *Amicitia* goes beyond *amor concupiscentiae* because it entails benevolence or goodwill toward one's friend for the friend's sake. But even benevolent love is not enough. As Aquinas puts it, *amicus est amico amicus*: a friend is a friend to a friend (*ST* IIaIIae, Q. 23, a. 1). An anonymous stranger might lovingly bestow the bulk of his estate on you; for all of that, the two of you are not friends. For that matter, if Philemon secretly and benevolently loves Amanda and vice versa, Philemon and Amanda are still not friends. As Aquinas would put it, their love is not yet communicated or shared. Communication is a dynamic process involving both cognitive and volitional components. Philemon must know that Amanda loves him; Philemon must know that Amanda knows that he loves her; and so forth. Moreover, the knowledge must shape the desires and interests that each has.

Given Aquinas's characterization of charity as an ongoing, dynamic *amicitia* between a person and God, it may not be immediately clear why charity should count as a virtue of the person. Two observations may help. First, one who loves God with the love of charity takes on God's interests and projects as one's own. That is no mean feat, since it entails that one tame or extinguish those aspects of one's will that are at variance with God's desires for us. Charity thus is demanding: it requires disciplined vigilance over oneself. Second, it must be admitted that there is a way in which charity is unlike faith and hope. Faith and hope are *internally specifiable* virtues of a person. Since faith is a kind of belief and hope a species of desire, an omniscient being could tell whether a person had the two of them solely by knowing the states of the person's soul. But an omniscient being could not tell whether the person had charity on that basis alone, any more than one could tell whether another person had a sibling solely by attending to the other persons's beliefs and desires. To have charity is to *be*, not merely to be *disposed* to be, in a certain relationship with God. But other virtues appear to have this feature of external specification built into them. Consider, on analogy, the virtue of filial respect, or respect for one's parents. It is plausible to think that filial respect requires that one be actually, not just dispositionally, in a certain relationship with one's parents. If this is so, then there is no reason to think that charity is not a virtue.

We are now in a position to see why charity, understood as *amicitia* between a person and God, presupposes hope. I cannot enter into a relationship of *amicitia* with you as long as I despair of the possibility, deeming myself unworthy of obtaining the good that the relationship would bestow (*ST* IaIIae, Q. 65, a. 5). Nor can I be bound to you by the ties of *amicitia* if I presume that the good to be obtained thereby is something that I could achieve on my own, without you. In both cases something results that is a counterfeit of *amicitia*. In the latter case I regard you with condescension if not contempt, judging you as quite literally dispensable. In the former case, my despair is compatible with my loving you, but my love is surely not *amicitia*: it is more akin to a pathological idolization, which, if unrequited, is in danger of turning into resentment. I cannot enter into *amicitia* with you, then, unless I trust that you will not spurn me as hateful and unless I deem the good to be obtained as distinctive, a good for which you are essential and irreplaceable. In sum, I cannot enter into *amicitia* with you without hope.

Although charity is *amicitia* between a person and God, Aquinas claims that once one has charity, one can extend it toward other people. Charity toward others goes beyond benevolent love for them: it is love for them mediated by one's *amicitia* with God; one loves the goodness of others because it has been bestowed on them by a loving God whom one loves (*ST* IIaIIae, Q. 25, a. 1). If one has Luther's pure love, however, it is hard to see how one could have even benevolent love—let alone charity—toward others. In commenting on Paul's claim that "Love is the fulfilling of the law" (Romans 13:10), Luther distinguishes two ways of understanding the commandment "You shall love your neighbor as yourself." The commandment might mean that we should love our neighbor *and* ourselves. But on a better interpretation of the commandment, we should love *only* our neighbor, modeling that love on our unconditional but improper love of self (W 56:482). Luther apparently thinks, then, that I could have pure love of God, which entails self-hatred, while at the same time loving my neighbor. But there are two objections to this. If to love a person is to take some, at least, of that person's interests as one's own, I cannot coherently love my neighbor without seeking to advance some interests as mine, even if they all derive from my neighbor's interests. That is, I cannot consistently consign myself to damnation and think that I should advance some of my interests, namely, the furtherance of your interests. And if I am still capable of making any inferences while in the state of pure love, I should be able to see that my neighbor's case stands or falls as mine does. For if I desire my damnation because of my sinful nature, then, since my neighbor is like me in being a sinner, I ought to desire my neighbor's damnation.

If Aquinas's views on hope and charity are correct even in general outline, they show that Luther's pure love is incompatible with hope for oneself, charity toward God, and charity toward others. Aquinas's views also make a case, not only for the legitimacy of hope, but also for the indispensability of hope for the possession of charity. Luther's pure love, insofar as it is inimical to hope, is thus hopeless in two senses. I am mindful that in pitting Aquinas against Luther, I may appear to be reliving the Counter-Reformation. Since I am not a Catholic, I prefer to give another characterization of the philosophical balance sheet I have drawn here: truth is where you find it.[33]

---

[33] An earlier version of this essay received the critical scrutiny of David Christensen and Eleonore Stump, whose efforts are deeply appreciated.

PHILIP L. QUINN

❦

Abelard on Atonement:
"Nothing Unintelligible, Arbitrary,
Illogical, or Immoral about It"

It was, according to a prominent English philosopher and theologian, a moment of theological recovery. "For the first time—or rather for the first time since the days of the earliest and most philosophical Greek fathers—the doctrine of the atonement was stated," Hastings Rashdall says, "in a way which had nothing unintelligible, arbitrary, illogical, or immoral about it."[1] Rashdall, who coined the term 'ideal utilitarianism' and ably advocated the position since then so called, made this remark in his Bampton Lectures of 1915, published in 1919 under the title *The Idea of Atonement in Christian Theology*.[2] He was referring to the account of atonement set forth by Peter Abelard in his *Commentary on Paul's Epistle to the Romans*. In this essay I argue that there is a lot to be said for Rashdall's strongly positive evaluation of Abelard's account of the Atonement.

As two good recent books on atonement make clear, Rashdall's view is not the conventional wisdom of our own times. In *The Actuality of Atonement*, Colin Gunton, who is Professor of Christian Doctrine at King's College, London, does not so much as mention Abelard; Abelard is not listed in the book's index of names or in its bibliography.[3] And in his *Responsibility and Atonement*, Richard Swin-

---

[1] Hastings Rashdall, *The Idea of Atonement in Christian Theology* (London: Macmillan, 1919), p. 360.

[2] For a brief discussion of Rashdall's life and works, see A. K. Stout, "Hastings Rashdall," in *The Encyclopedia of Philosophy*, ed. Paul Edwards (New York: Macmillan, 1967), 7:68.

[3] Colin E. Gunton, *The Actuality of Atonement* (Grand Rapids, Mich.: William B. Eerdmans, 1989).

burne, who is Nolloth Professor of Philosophy of the Christian Religion at Oxford, dismisses Abelard in a single sentence; he claims that "Abelard's exemplary theory of the atonement, that Christ's life and death work to remove our sins by inspiring us to do penance and good acts, contains no objective transaction."[4] Implicit in this remark is a criticism of Abelard's account of atonement that is often thought to be devastating. The charge is that Abelard's views on atonement are exemplarist in character. But what exactly does the charge come to: What is exemplarism? Why is it a bad thing to be an exemplarist? And is Abelard guilty as charged? These are questions to which I shall offer answers in the course of the present discussion.

The difficulty is not, I think, that it is false or unorthodox to claim that Christ's life and death are an inspiring example. Thomas Aquinas, who is surely a sound guide on this point, explicitly endorses this claim. When enumerating some of the benefits that accrue to us as a result of the Incarnation, he includes on a list of five that contribute to our furtherance in good both having our charity kindled because God's love for us stimulates us to love in return and being inspired to do good because God himself sets an example for us.[5] And Gunton remarks that if "we are to establish a case for an objective, past atonement, it cannot be at the cost of denying the subjective and exemplary implications."[6] So the difficulty must rather be that exemplarists are explicitly or implicitly committed to the view that Christ's life and death are no more than an inspiring example, a paradigm of Christian existence. Such an exclusive view would, it is alleged, leave out something important about Christ's atoning work. Exemplarists are thus to be faulted because they have an incomplete doctrine of the Atonement. What they say is sound as far as it goes, but it is not the whole truth.

What objective transaction or past fact do the exemplarists neglect? For historical reasons, it would be virtually impossible to get agreement on an answer to this question among Christian theologians or philosophers. In this respect, there is a sharp contrast between the doctrine of the Atonement and other central Christian doctrines such as the Incarnation and the Trinity. Under pressure from theological controversy, the early church felt itself obliged to

---

[4] Richard Swinburne, *Responsibility and Atonement* (Oxford: Clarendon Press, 1989), p. 162. A detailed discussion of Swinburne's impressive positive account of atonement is outside the scope of this essay.

[5] Thomas Aquinas, *Summa theologiae* III, Q. 1, A. 2; hereafter *ST*.

[6] Gunton, *The Actuality of Atonement*, p. 157.

formulate the fairly precise definitions of such doctrines that we find expressed by the familiar Nicene and Chalcedonian formulas. Such definitions have operated as a traditional constraint on theological theorizing. Nothing similar happened in the case of the doctrine of the Atonement, and so the history of theological reflection on it is richly pluralistic. It is a colorful tapestry of scriptural motifs and theological elaborations.

In the present context, it turns out to be useful to impose some taxonomic order on the otherwise bewildering variety of accounts of the Atonement by thinking of them as falling at various places in a spectrum. At one end of this spectrum would be accounts that emphasize one motif to the exclusion of all others if there were any such purely monistic accounts. The theory Anselm proposes in *Cur Deus homo* falls close to this end of the spectrum. According to Anselm, God became human in order to pay a debt that human sinners owe but cannot pay and thereby to spare sinful humans the punishment that would otherwise be consequent upon their inability to pay this debt.[7] So Anselm understands the Atonement almost exclusively in terms of the legalistic category of making satisfaction for a debt of sin. At the other end of the spectrum would be accounts that incorporate several motifs and treat them all as being of more or less equal importance. The account Gunton sets forth in *The Actuality of Atonement* is an example of such egalitarian pluralism. It focuses on three ideas: Christ's work as a victory over demonic forces, Christ's work as a contribution to cosmic justice, and Christ's work as a priestly sacrifice.[8] All three motifs are taken to be metaphoric in nature; they are not to be confused with theories and must be understood in suitably nuanced and qualified ways. But when properly understood, each of these metaphors has something vital to contribute to our admittedly imperfect grasp of the complex mystery of the Atonement. In the middle of the spectrum are accounts that draw on a plurality of motifs but assign pride of place to some and relegate others to subordinate roles. The story Aquinas tells in the *Summa theologiae* furnishes an instance of this kind of hierarchical pluralism. Like Anselm, Aquinas thinks that the principal function of Christ's atoning work is to make satisfaction for human sin by paying a debt of punishment human sinners cannot pay.[9] Aquinas

---

[7] Anselm of Canterbury, *Cur Deus homo* II, 6.

[8] Gunton, *The Actuality of Atonement*. These motifs are elaborated in chaps. 3, 4 and 5.

[9] Aquinas, *ST* III, QQ. 46–49. I argue for this interpretation of Aquinas in Philip L. Quinn, "Aquinas on Atonement", in *Trinity, Incarnation, and Atonement*, ed. Ronald J.

holds that the power to do this comes from Christ's Passion, but he insists that the Passion also has other functions. It contributes to the salvation of sinners by meriting grace for them on account of its voluntary character, by redeeming them from bondage to the devil through a ransom paid to God, and by reconciling them to God because it is an acceptable sacrifice. So although satisfaction is the dominant theme in Aquinas's account of the Atonement, he eclectically mobilizes other motifs to play subsidiary parts.

We can, I believe, clarify the question that needs to be put to Abelard's account of the Atonement if we ask where on this spectrum it is to be located. As we shall see once we begin to examine the texts, there is no room for doubt that Abelard makes much of the inspiring love displayed in God becoming incarnate and suffering unto death for his human creatures. But even if the exemplary motif is the dominant theme in Abelard's account, it does not follow without further argument that it is the only theme. Absent such argument, the possibility remains open that Abelard, like Aquinas, is a hierarchical pluralist and so is not an exemplarist in the sense of excluding part of the truth about the Atonement. Indeed, it could turn out that Abelard and Aquinas differ not so much over which motifs should be included in a fairly comprehensive account of the Atonement as over the more delicate matter of which themes are most important and deserve to be highlighted. And if this were so, Abelard too would be located somewhere in the middle of the spectrum in terms of which we are for present purposes ordering accounts of the Atonement. In that case, an evaluation of Abelard's account would involve the subtle task of determining whether it does a better job than its rivals in answering questions about which motifs ought to be regarded as central to a well-rounded doctrine of the Atonement and thus deserve emphasis in its presentation.

Should we embrace Abelard with the enthusiasm Rashdall displayed near the beginning of this century? Or should we write Abelard off as an exemplarist in the way Swinburne has done near the century's end? Let us look at what Abelard says with the possibility in mind that neither response rests on an adequate appreciation of the merits of his views.

Feenstra and Cornelius Plantinga, Jr. (Notre Dame, Ind: University of Notre Dame Press, 1989), pp. 153–77. Further support for this view is to be found in Romanus Cesario, *Christian Satisfaction in Aquinas* (Washington, D.C.: University Press of America, 1982). A rather different interpretation is set forth in Eleonore Stump, "Atonement according to Aquinas", in *Philosophy and the Christian Faith*, ed. Thomas V. Morris (Notre Dame, Ind.: University of Notre Dame Press, 1988), pp. 61–91.

1. The Central Motif of Abelard's Account

Abelard interrupts his commentary on Romans 3 to raise the question of what Christ's death does to atone for our sins. It is the solution he proposes to the problems that come up in the course of this discussion that has given rise to the charge of exemplarism. So we need to look with particular care at what he actually says in this celebrated passage.

The passage begins with arguments against the view that sinners are rightfully held in bondage by the devil until Christ ransoms them by his death. On this view, the devil holds all mere humans in bondage by right because the first man, Adam, yielded himself to the devil's authority by an act of voluntary obedience. Being perfectly just, God respects the devil's rights and so will not free sinners from their bondage by force. Instead he ransoms them from captivity at the price of Christ's blood. Abelard has three objections to this view. Two hang on rather esoteric theological points. The first is that Christ redeemed only the elect, who were never in the devil's power. Alluding to Luke 16:26, Abelard contends that Abraham there declares that a great gulf has been fixed between the elect and the wicked so that the latter can never cross over to the former. From this Abelard concludes that "still less may the devil, who is more evil than all, acquire any power in that place where no wicked person has a place or even entry."[10] The second point is that the devil never acquired rights over the first humans because he seduced them by means of a lying promise. Alluding to Genesis 3:4, Abelard maintains that "the devil could not grant that immortality which he promised man as a reward of transgression in the hope that in this way he might hold him fast by some sort of right."[11] Presumably the thought here is that the first humans were willing to grant rights over them to the devil in return for immortality, but he did not actually acquire rights over them because he could not and so did not live up to his part of the bargain.

Abelard's third objection echoes a point that Anselm had made

---

[10] Peter Abelard, *Commentaria in epistolam Pauli ad Romanos*. The Latin text is to be found in *Petri Abaelardi opera theologica*, Corpus Christianorum, Continuatio Mediaevalis 11, ed. E. M. Buytaert (Turnhout: Brepols, 1969). An English translation of selected passages is to be found in *A Scholastic Miscellany: Anselm to Ockham*, The Library of Christian Classics 10, ed. Eugene R. Fairweather (Philadelphia: Westminster, 1956). For the sake of convenience, I quote this translation whenever possible, but I also refer to the Latin text by page and lines. Thus the quoted material to which this note is appended is at Buytaert, p. 114, lines 149–51, and Fairweather, p. 281.

[11] Buytaert, p. 115, lines 171–73; Fairweather, p. 281.

earlier.[12] He concedes that God may have given express permission to the devil to torture humans by way of punishment for their sins, but he denies that the devil on that account holds sinful humans in bondage as a matter of right. If one servant of a master seduces another to depart from obedience to the master, the master properly regards the seducer as much more guilty than the seduced servant. "And how unjust it would be," Abelard exclaims, "that he who seduced the other should deserve, as a result, to have any special right or authority over him!"[13] Even the express permission to punish sinners will, according to Abelard, be withdrawn if God chooses to forgive their sins and to remit the punishment for them, as Matthew 9:2 reports Christ did in the case of a paralytic. If God were mercifully to choose to forgive other sinners, Abelard argues, then "assuredly, once the sins for which they were undergoing punishment have been forgiven, there appears to remain no reason why they should be any longer punished for them."[14] So there really is no need for God to ransom human sinners from the devil. The devil has no rights over them which God must in justice respect, and God can retract the devil's permission to punish simply by forgiving them and remitting the punishment.

But this makes the following question all the more urgent for Abelard: "What need was there, I say, that the Son of God, for our redemption, should take upon him our flesh and endure such numerous fastings, insults, scourgings and spittings, and finally that most bitter and disgraceful death upon the cross, enduring even the cross of punishment with the wicked?"[15] Would it not be reasonable to suppose, Abelard asks, that the suffering and death of his Son should increase God's anger at sinful humanity because humans acted more criminally by crucifying his Son than they did by disobeying his first command in paradise in eating a single apple? Nor does it seem promising to think of Christ's atonement as a blood price paid to God rather than to the devil for the redemption of sinful humanity, for it appears to be inconsistent with God's perfect goodness that he should demand such a price. As Abelard puts the point, "How cruel and wicked it seems that anyone should demand the blood of an innocent person as the price for anything, or that it should in any way please him that an innocent man should be

---

[12] Anselm, *Cur Deus homo* I, 7.
[13] Buytaert, p. 115, lines161–63; Fairweather, p. 281.
[14] Buytaert, p. 116, lines 198–200; Fairweather, p. 282.
[15] Buytaert, p. 116, lines 205–9; Fairweather, p. 282.

slain—still less that God should consider the death of his Son so agreeable that by it he should be reconciled to the whole world!"[16] And thus passionately put, the point has considerable force.

Having done his best to impress upon his readers the difficulty of the question, Abelard audaciously propounds an answer to it. The passage deserves to be quoted at length both on account of its intrinsic interest and because of the controversy to which it has given rise among scholars:

> Now it seems to us that we have been justified by the blood of Christ and reconciled to God in this way: through this unique act of grace manifested to us—in that his Son has taken upon himself our nature and persevered therein in teaching us by word and example even unto death—he has more fully bound us to himself by love; with the result that our hearts should be enkindled by such a gift of divine grace, and true charity should not now shrink from enduring anything for him. And we do not doubt that the ancient Fathers, waiting in faith for this same gift, were aroused to very great love of God in the same way as men of this dispensation of grace, since it is written: "And they that went before and they that followed cried, saying: 'Hosanna to the Son of David,'" etc. Yet everyone becomes more righteous—by which we mean a greater lover of the Lord—after the Passion of Christ than before, since a realized gift inspires greater love than one which is only hoped for. Wherefore, our redemption through Christ's suffering is that deeper affection [*dilectio*] in us which not only frees us from slavery to sin, but also wins for us the true liberty of sons of God, so that we do all things out of love rather than fear—love to him who has shown us such grace that no greater can be found, as he himself asserts, saying, "Greater love than this no man hath, that a man lay down his life for his friends."[17]

The case for taking Abelard to be an exemplarist rests almost entirely on interpretation of this text.

Thus, for example, after setting forth his own translation of its first and last sentences, Robert S. Franks concludes that it is evident that Abelard "has reduced the whole process of redemption to one single clear principle, viz. the manifestation of God's love to us in Christ, which awakens an answering love in us."[18] Rashdall proceeds in a similar fashion. First he sets forth his own translation of the last two sentences of the quoted passage, and then he adds his

---

[16] Buytaert, p. 117, lines 234–38; Fairweather, p. 283.
[17] Buytaert, pp. 117–18, lines 242–62; Fairweather, pp. 283–84.
[18] Robert S. Franks, *The Work of Christ* (London: Thomas Nelson, 1962), p. 146.

translation of the somewhat different version of its first two sentences to be found in the charges against Abelard drawn up and
transmitted to the pope by Bernard of Clairvaux. These texts constitute the bulk of Rashdall's evidence for the following strong claims
about Abelard's views on the nature of Christ's atoning work:

> In Abelard not only the ransom theory but any kind of substitutionary
> or expiatory atonement is explicitly denied. We get rid altogether of the
> notion of a mysterious guilt which, by an abstract necessity of things,
> required to be extinguished by death or suffering, no matter whose,
> and of all pseudo-Platonic hypostatizing of the universal "Humanity."
> The efficacy of Christ's death is now quite definitely and explicitly ex-
> plained by its subjective influence upon the mind of the sinner. The
> voluntary death of the innocent Son of God on man's behalf moves the
> sinner to gratitude and answering love—and so to consciousness of sin,
> repentance, amendment.[19]

And, needless to say, Rashdall wholeheartedly approves of all these
things he attributes to Abelard.

Is this an adequate summary of Abelard's account of the Atonement? We should, I think, approach this summary with some suspicion precisely because almost all the evidence for it comes from a
single passage, albeit an eloquent one, that covers slightly less than
one page out of a total of three hundred pages of text in the Corpus
Christianorum edition of Abelard's *Commentary on Paul's Epistle to the
Romans*. And even in and around this famous passage there are
small clues indicating that Abelard's view is more complicated than
Franks or Rashdall takes it to be. First of all, in the final sentence of
the famous passage Abelard does say that our redemption through
Christ's suffering frees us from slavery to sin, though, to be sure, he
does not at this point offer an explanation of how it does so. Second,
a few lines after the close of the famous passage Abelard indicates
that the explanation of the manner of our redemption it proposes is
incomplete but reserves further elaboration for another treatise.[20]

Moreover, the translations of the famous passage provided by
Franks and Rashdall give it an exemplarist flavor that is absent from
the Latin original. In his "Was Abelard an Exemplarist?" which chal-
lenges Rashdall's interpretation of Abelard, Robert O. P. Taylor
points to several instances of this in Rashdall. To my mind, the most
striking among them is this one. The Latin that begins the final sen-

---

[19] Rashdall, *The Idea of Atonement*, p. 358.
[20] Buytaert, p. 118, lines 271–74; Fairweather, p. 284.

tence of the famous passage goes as follows: "Redemptio itaque nostra est illa summa in nobis per passionem Christi dilectio." "But this," Taylor insists, "surely, means, 'Our redemption, therefore, is that supreme love which is *in us* through the Passion of Christ'."[21] The translation I quoted does convey the idea that the *dilectio* which is our redemption is something in us. But, as Taylor observes, this is not the idea conveyed by Rashdall's translation. Rashdall renders the Latin thus: "Our redemption, therefore, is that supreme love of Christ *shown to us* by His passion" (my emphasis).[22] Franks performs a similar transformation. His rendition of the Latin is this: "And so our redemption is that supreme love *manifested in our case* by the passion of Christ" (my emphasis).[23] In short, both Rashdall and Franks take Abelard to be saying that our redemption is the love Christ shows or manifests by suffering for our sakes. From this thought it is only a small step to the conclusion that Christ's love is no more than an example displayed for our inspection. But this is not the only possible, or even the most natural, reading of the text. And if we take seriously the idea that our redemption is a love in us through Christ's Passion, then it remains to be seen how the Passion of Christ actually works to implant or produce this love in us.

So it is not clear that the famous passage actually teaches that Christ's love is merely an example, "something displayed in the hope that we may see that it is so admirable that we ought to emulate or adopt it."[24] And even if by itself it will bear an exemplarist interpretation, it does not follow that exemplarism is the only motif at work in Abelard's thinking about the Atonement. As we shall next see, it is not.

2. Penal Substitution in Abelard

A survey of medieval accounts of the Atonement, called "The Concept of Satisfaction in Medieval Redemption Theory", argues that the key elements of Scholastic thought on this topic are satisfaction for the dishonor of sin, substitution for the punishment imposed, and the restoration of humankind. Its author, J. Patout Burns, holds that "the first is a contribution of Anselm; the second derives from Abelard; the third becomes central only in the thir-

---

[21] Robert O. P. Taylor, "Was Abelard an Exemplarist?" *Theology* 31 (1935): 212.
[22] Rashdall, *The Actuality of Atonement*, p. 358.
[23] Franks, *The Work of Christ*, p. 145.
[24] Taylor, "Was Abelard an Exemplarist?" p. 213.

teenth century."[25] It would be easy to quarrel with the last of these
conclusions on the basis of the famous passage previously discussed. After all, Abelard there tells us that our redemption not only
frees us from slavery to sin but also wins for us the true liberty of
sons of God, so that we do all things out of love rather than fear,
and the latter effect of our redemption certainly seems to involve the
restoration of fallen humans to a state of liberty God meant them to
occupy. But more interesting in the present context is the claim that
Abelard is the source of the idea that Christ substitutes for the rest
of us in bearing the punishment due to us for our sins and thereby
makes it possible for us to avoid undergoing such punishment.
There is no hint of this in the famous passage on which those who
take Abelard to be nothing but an exemplarist build their case.

Nevertheless, Abelard clearly does endorse the notion of penal
substitution in the *Commentary on Paul's Epistle to the Romans*. In discussing Romans 4:25, where it is said that Christ was handed over to
death for our sins, Abelard says this:

> In two ways he is said to have died for our faults: first, because the
> faults for which he died were ours, and we committed the sins for
> which he bore the punishment; secondly, that by dying he might re-
> move our sins, that is, the punishment of our sins, introducing us into
> paradise at the price of his own death, and might, by the display of
> grace such that he himself said "Greater love no man hath," draw our
> minds away from the will to sin and enkindle in them the highest love
> of himself.[26]

So Abelard is committed to holding that Christ removes our sins in
the sense that he, who is innocent and so deserves no punishment,
takes our place and endures the punishment we deserve. It may be
that this view is illogical because it is logically impossible for one
person to pay a debt of punishment for sin another person owes.
And it may be that it is immoral in the sense that it is morally repug-
nant to imagine that the suffering of an innocent person could remove the debt of punishment of a guilty person.[27] But, if so,
Rashdall is mistaken in claiming that there is nothing illogical or
immoral about Abelard's account of the Atonement, for this view is
part of that account.

---

[25] J. Patout Burns, S.J., "The Concept of Satisfaction in Medieval Redemption Theory", *Theological Studies* 36 (1975): 304.

[26] Buytaert, p. 153, lines 992–1000. (my translation).

[27] I have pressed this objection against Anselm's account of the Atonement in Philip
L. Quinn, "Christian Atonement and Kantian Justification," *Faith and Philosophy*, 3
(1986): 440–62 and against Aquinas's account in Quinn, "Aquinas on Atonement".

Of course, as L. W. Grensted remarks in commenting on this passage, Abelard's heart is really in the thought with which it concludes, the idea that the grace displayed in Christ's dying may work an interior transformation in us by which our minds are drawn away from sin and toward Christ in love.[28] So there is some grist for the exemplarist's mill even here but not for the strong thesis that the only benefit conferred on sinful humans by Christ's Passion is an inspiring example of love. Scholars such as Rashdall and Franks are, of course, aware that Abelard says things which do not comport well with taking him to be a pure exemplarist, but they typically dismiss such embarrassing remarks. Thus, in a note, Rashdall concedes that "it must be admitted that Abelard sometimes shows a tendency to relapse into views hardly consistent with this position."[29] And when Franks encounters evidence that undermines his contention that Abelard reduces the whole process of redemption to a single principle, his reply is that "if Abelard does in other places present views along different lines, and so himself controvert his own tendency to a simplification of doctrine, this need not prevent our recognizing that this tendency exists."[30] Grensted provides a more balanced assessment. After citing the last sentence of the famous passage quoted and another passage which expresses a similar thought, he concludes that they represent "an attempt to set the ethical, manward, aspect of Atonement in a primary and not in a secondary place."[31] It does seem fair to say that the dominant motif in Abelard's account is the power of love in us through Christ's Passion to transform us both by freeing us from slavery to sin and, more important, by winning for us the positive Christian liberty to do all things out of love for God. Godward aspects of Atonement, such as paying a debt of punishment owed to divine retributive justice, are relegated to distinctly subordinate roles in Abelard's account. But they are not altogether absent, and Rashdall is simply mistaken in claiming that any kind of substitutionary or expiatory atonement is explicitly denied. On the contrary, as we have seen, substitutionary atonement is explicitly affirmed.

In terms of the taxonomy I have proposed, it thus seems best to classify Abelard as a hierarchical pluralist. Like Aquinas, he offers an account of the Atonement that has a dominant motif to which

---

[28] L. W. Grensted, *A Short History of the Doctrine of the Atonement* (Manchester: Manchester University Press, 1962), p. 109.

[29] Rashdall, *The Idea of Atonement*, p. 363.

[30] Franks, *The Work of Christ*, p. 148.

[31] Grensted, *A Short History*, p. 105.

others are subordinated. But unlike Aquinas, for whom satisfaction for sin is the principal theme, Abelard proposes to make a love that transforms motive and character in redeemed humans the heart of the matter. Abelard's views were fiercely denounced by Bernard of Clairvaux and condemned by the church of his day. So it will be worth our while to look into the question of whether they, or modifications of them that are recognizably Abelardian in spirit, are theologically and philosophically defensible. It is to this question that I now turn my attention.

3. Is It Ill-Disguised Pelagianism?

Rashdall is far from being the first to take Abelard's views on the Atonement to be exemplarist. Although he did not put it in these terms, Bernard clearly interpreted Abelard in this way. But while exemplarism pleases Rashdall, it horrified Bernard. In a passage of considerable rhetorical power in his letter to Innocent II, Bernard thunders against Abelard's account of the Atonement: "He holds and argues that it must be reduced just to this, that by His life and teaching He handed down to men a pattern of life, that by His suffering and death He set up a standard of love. Did He then teach righteousness and not bestow it; reveal love and not infuse it; and so return to his own place?"[32] And later on in the letter he remarks with what strikes me as a touch of sarcasm: "If Christ's benefit consisted only in the display of good works, it remains but to say that Adam only harmed us by the display of sin."[33] But, though Bernard was an ecclesiastical administrator and politician of genius, and a formidable mystical theologian, he was far from being a fair-minded philosophical critic. As Grensted acknowledges, Abelard's "extremest statements were taken as representative of his whole position and were even exaggerated by Bernard's rhetoric."[34] Grensted maintains, however, that Bernard had put his finger on a real weakness in Abelard's position: a Pelagian tendency, which, if pressed to its logical conclusion, must belittle both the sin of humans and the grace of God and fail to appreciate both the solidarity of humankind in sin and the solidarity of the redeemed in Christ. If it were true that the sin of our first parents is no more than a bad example their descendants can freely imitate or shun, then it would seem that we no

<hr>

[32] Bernard of Clairvaux, *Tractatus ad Innocentium II Pontificem contra quaedam capitula errorum Abaelardi*, quoted in Grensted, *A Short History*, p. 106.

[33] Ibid.

[34] Grensted, *A Short History*, p. 107.

more need redemption from a fallen state of bondage to sin than they did in their prelapsarian state. By the same token, if it were true that Christ confers on us no more than the benefit of a good example we can freely follow or reject, then it would seem that whether we are justified in the sight of God is something wholly within our power to determine. So the Pelagian danger Bernard fears is that Abelard has rendered Christ's atoning work unnecessary for our salvation. On such a view, we are in principle capable of earning worthiness of salvation on our own.

Yet according to Richard Weingart, whose book on Abelard's soteriology is the most detailed recent treatment of the topic in English, it cannot be repeated too often that Abelard is no Pelagian. "Although he denies that Christ's work is one of appeasement or substitution," Weingart contends, "he never moves to the other extreme of presenting the atonement as nothing more than an inducement for man to effect his own salvation."[35] And there are texts in the *Commentary on Paul's Epistle to the Romans* in which Abelard explicitly denies that it is within the unaided power of mere humans in the postlapsarian state to make themselves worthy of salvation. In commenting on Romans 7:25, Abelard affirms that our redemption is "thanks to God, that is, not the law, not our own powers, not any merits, but a divine benefit of grace conferred on us through Jesus, that is, the savior of the world."[36] Nor does the famous passage I have quoted at length provide unequivocal evidential support for Bernard's charge that Abelard is committed to Pelagianism. Consider, for example, its third sentence. The Latin goes as follows: "Iustior quoque, id est amplius Deum diligens, quisque fit post passionem Christi quam ante, quia amplius in amorem accendit completum beneficium quam speratum." Those words can, I suppose, be read in a way that speaks, as the translation I quoted does, of everyone becoming more righteous after the Passion than before because a realized gift inspires greater love than one merely hoped for. But Rashdall himself offers a different translation. It goes as follows: "Every man *is* also *made* juster, that is to say, *becomes* more loving to the Lord after the passion of Christ than he was before, because a benefit actually received kindles the soul into love more than one merely hoped for" (my emphasis).[37] Noticing that there is some oddity in the fact that Rashdall uses both "made" and "becomes" to

[35] Richard E. Weingart, *The Logic of Divine Love: A Critical Analysis of the Soteriology of Peter Abailard* (Oxford: Clarendon Press, 1970), p. 150.

[36] Buytaert, p. 210, lines 779–81 (my translation).

[37] Rashdall, *The Idea of Atonement*, p. 358.

translate the word *fit*, once used and not repeated, Taylor asks: "Why not translate *fit* as 'is made' in both cases?"[38] If we adopt the suggestion implicit in this rhetorical question, the result is this: 'Every man *is* also *made* juster, that is to say, *is made* more loving to the Lord after the passion of Christ than he was before, because a benefit actually received kindles the soul into love more than one merely hoped for.' And this translation, which speaks of everyone being made more loving because a received benefit kindles love more than one merely hoped for, resists being interpreted in a way that supports attributing Pelagian tendencies to Abelard. Hence, even if it is granted that the famous passage considered in isolation permits a reading that supports the charge of Pelagian tendencies, it does not follow and it is far from clear that it is best read in this way once contextual factors are brought to bear on interpreting it. And surely a factor that should be given appreciable weight is Abelard's explicit claim that we are saved, not by our own powers, but through a benefit of grace conferred on us through Christ.

As I see it, then, the import of the famous passage is to some extent indeterminate. By itself it does not answer such questions as these: By what mechanism does the love that is in us through Christ's Passion get implanted in us? How precisely are we made or do we become more just or righteous after Christ's Passion? And what exactly is the process by which the benefit of Christ's Passion operates to inspire or kindle love in us? Because Abelard's thought does not return clear answers to these questions, interpreters can reasonably disagree about whether it commits Abelard to Pelagian views or tends to do so. I doubt that further exegetical work on this passage would yield a conclusive resolution of those disagreements. But because the principle of charity requires us not to attribute inconsistency to a thinker of Abelard's stature if we can help doing so, I think it is best to read it in a way that harmonizes with Abelard's explicit denials of Pelagian views in other passages and so to interpret it in a manner that does not clinch the case for Bernard's charge that Abelard is a Pelagian. If, as Grensted says, Bernard has identified a real weakness in Abelard's position, it is the relatively harmless flaw of having an incomplete account of how the love manifested in Christ's Passion works upon the human heart and hence of not having said enough to preclude purely exemplarist or Pelagian readings. But it may well be, as Taylor claims, that Abelard considers love to be "a spiritual force exerted by the lover on the beloved, and, in a responsive heart, setting up a reflex, which tends to

---

[38] Taylor, "Was Abelard an Exemplarist?" p. 211.

become permanent."[39] Such a conception of the transformative power of love could, perhaps, partly explain the efficacy of Christ's Passion. If it is Abelard's, however, he has not succeeded in making it clear either to friends such as Rashdall or to foes such as Bernard.

We may conclude that Abelard's account of the Atonement is neither as attractive as admirers such as Rashdall contend nor as unattractive as critics such as Bernard maintain. When the famous passage is interpreted in the light of its context, it offers no firm support for the conclusion that Abelard is either an exemplarist or a Pelagian, though it does suggest tendencies in these directions. Yet it did introduce a fresh motif into medieval discussion of the effects of Christ's life, suffering, and death, and it continues to speak with considerable power to some Christians in our own times. So it seems to me worthwhile to develop that motif with an eye to seeing whether it could play an important role in an account of the Atonement that would appeal to contemporary Christians. I devote the final section of this essay to a somewhat speculative sketch of one way in which such development might proceed.

4. Toward a Constructive Abelardian Contribution

My suggestion is that what Abelard has to contribute to our thinking about the Atonement is the idea that divine love, made manifest throughout the life of Christ but especially in his suffering and dying, has the power to transform human sinners, if they cooperate, in ways that fit them for everlasting life in intimate union with God. But before I begin to elaborate on this suggestion, I need to issue two disclaimers in order to head off potential misunderstandings. First, I am not henceforth claiming that Abelard actually held the views I am going to recommend. Although they are inspired by the famous passage and, I hope, faithful to its spirit, my aim in setting them forth is to make a contribution to philosophical theology rather than to textual exegesis. Second, I do not claim that the motif of transformative divine love is the only idea that can help us appreciate the Atonement. I am attracted to the view that the Atonement is a mystery not to be fully fathomed by human understanding but best grasped in terms of a plurality of metaphors and models. So I am willing to entertain the hypothesis, shared by Anselm and Aquinas, that it functions in some manner to persuade God to remit a debt of punishment human sinners owe but cannot by themselves

[39] Ibid., p. 212.

pay.[40] But I do not think that such legalistic considerations are the heart of the matter or should be allowed to dominate our understanding of the Atonement. Abelard strikes me as being on target in emphasizing the interior transformations wrought in sinners by God's love for them, for I am of the opinion that Christian reflection on Christ's atoning work should be rooted in a lively sense of what God has graciously done in us. And this leads me to favor a conception of the Atonement like Abelard's in which other motifs are subordinated to the theme of the transformative power of divine love.

In order to make it quite clear, as Abelard in the famous passage does not succeed in doing, that this power exceeds any merely human example's power to inspire, it is important to insist that the relation between the operations of divine love and those of merely human love is not identity but analogy of some sort. To be sure, ordinary human love has some transformative power, and that is why the analogy shows promise of being useful in soteriology. Contemplation of the lives and deeds of saintly people such as Francis of Assisi and Mother Teresa can contribute causally to making us better persons. But if we assume that examples of this kind operate in influencing beliefs and desires wholly within a natural order of causes, we should then deny that this is the only way in which divine love can operate in influencing us in order to avoid the reductionistic implications of exemplarism. We should instead affirm that divine love also operates outside the natural order, within what theologians call the order of grace, to produce changes in us. On such a view, the love of God for us exhibited in the life of Christ is a good example to imitate, but it is not merely an example. Above and beyond its exemplary value, there is in it a surplus of mysterious causal efficacy that no merely human love possesses. And the operation of divine love in that supernatural mode is a causally necessary condition of there being implanted or kindled in us the kind of responsive love of God that, as Abelard supposes, enables us to do all things out of love and so to conquer the motives that would otherwise keep us enslaved to sin.

By insisting that this supernatural operation of divine love in us is causally necessary for fallen humans to act out of love in a way that grounds God's gracious bestowal of righteousness on them, an Abelardian account of the Atonement can avoid the danger of falling into Pelagianism. What is to be shunned is a view according to

---

[40] In Quinn, "Aquinas on Atonement", I try to illustrate by means of a fable how such persuasion might work (pp. 174–75).

which fallen humans have it within their power to perform works that will justify them in the eyes of God apart from a divine assistance that goes beyond God's ordinary conserving activity. So if being a person for whom it is in character to act out of love is a large part of what freedom from bondage to sin involves, we should not suppose that becoming such a person is an accomplishment within the reach of the unaided powers of postlapsarian humans. A vexed theological question is whether this operation of divine love is a causally sufficient condition for transforming the personalities of fallen humans in such a way that they habitually act from responsive love. No doubt divine love could, if God so chose, work such a transformation because it is powerful enough to overwhelm the resistance of a stubbornly recalcitrant human will. But I am inclined to think that God does not in fact act in this way; instead he refrains from making the pressure of his love irresistible in order to leave room for a free human response to it. So I would say that the causal efficacy of supernatural divine love, though not by itself sufficient to work such transformations in the fallen human character, is a non-redundant part of any condition that is sufficient for this purpose. Thus we may come close to agreeing with Bernard by saying that God makes an essential causal contribution to the presence of love in us, and we may say that God infuses love into us and bestows righteousness upon us, provided it is understood that this is not a deterministic mechanical process and that we are free to reject these gracious divine gifts.

Finally, lest the merely exemplary power of love exhibited throughout the life of Christ and particularly in his suffering unto death be decoupled from the supernatural divine love that is necessary to transform the fallen human personality, an Abelardian account of the Atonement must insist that this supernatural transformative love somehow operates through Christ's life and especially through the Passion. I take it that this is a contingent fact; God could have used some other channel to make his transforming love available to a humanity ravaged by sin. But perhaps, as Aquinas claims, it was peculiarly fitting, for reasons we humans are unlikely to be able to comprehend fully in this life at least, that such love come to us through Christ's suffering rather than in some other way.[41] If so, there is an answer to Abelard's question about why Christ endured insults, scourgings and spittings, and finally a bitter and disgraceful death in terms of the appropriateness of this mode of access to di-

---

[41] Aquinas, *ST* III, Q. 1, A. 2.

vine love for members of our species, even if we do not know precisely what that answer is. Is Christ the exclusive channel through which transformative divine love comes to fallen humanity? If so, this is another contingent fact about how divine providence works. However, there is no good reason to deny that providence has arranged things in this fashion provided no human who could benefit from such love is excluded from access to it. It would, I think, be unfair and so unworthy of a perfectly good being to limit access to the benefits of transforming love to the members of a particular empirical church in a world like ours in which some who might respond positively to that love have, through no fault of their own, no chance to be members of the church in question. For all I know, however, God has made his transformative love available to all fallen humans, Christian and non-Christian alike, through Christ, though of course non-Christians who benefit from it will not, at least in this life, have true beliefs about the channel through which this gift comes to them if this is the case.

It might be objected that it is empirically implausible to suppose that the life and death of Jesus of Nazareth have had such an influence on subsequent history. If he had never lived, the human condition would now not be much different from what it actually is because other inspiring examples of love would have had approximately the same good effects. My response to this objection is skeptical. According to another scenario, the human condition would now be very much worse than it actually is if Jesus had never lived because fallen human nature would have been progressively enfeebled by an increasing burden of sin. I doubt that empirical information about the actual course of history by itself supports the counterfactual that underlies the objection rather than the rival counterfactual that I have set forth. Such empirical information together with certain background assumptions does lend differential support to the objection's counterfactual, but that information together with traditional Christian beliefs about original sin lends differential support to my rival counterfactual. In short, empirical information about the actual course of history alone does not settle the controversy about how much of a difference the life and death of Jesus have made to human history because such information by itself is insufficient to render plausible any particular view of what the subsequent course of history would have been like in the absence of those events.

It is no accident that the Abelardian account of transformative divine love I have been sketching bears some resemblance to accounts of the operation of grace formulated by other medieval theologians.

But many contemporary Christians do not find these highly metaphysical theories of grace credible. Speaking of Aquinas, Eleonore Stump admits that, because his account of grace is complex and problematic, the part of his theory of the Atonement that depends on it "may leave us cold and uncomprehending."[42] Part of the difficulty, as she diagnoses it, is that "he explains in medieval metaphysical terms what we would be more inclined to explain in psychological terms."[43] It seems to me that one of the advantages of the Abelardian emphasis on love in giving an account of the Atonement is precisely that it provides a model of psychological transformation rooted in ordinary human experience that can be analogically extended to divine action. Many of us have actually experienced the power of human love to influence our characters for the better by provoking a responsive love, and some of us have experienced the power of meditation on the example of love displayed in the life and death of Christ to contribute to bringing about such psychological improvements in us. So it is a genuine aid to understanding to think of the way in which God acts on us to help make us better in terms of a divine love that has among its effects making a contribution to implanting a loving disposition in us. Indeed, it does not appear to me farfetched to claim that we can in certain circumstances experience the pressure of this divine love on us in a manner analogous to the way in which we experience the force of human love. And this analogy may help us grasp the point Karl Rahner is getting at in maintaining that God's grace is experiential.[44]

We would do well not to underestimate the depth of the human longing to be able to love God. As a televangelist character puts it in a novel by Sarah Shankman, "*Of course* you think I'm a shuck. But that's because you don't come from what I come from. Don't know what I know. Don't know the mingy tight pinched little lives people like me grow up with. Don't know how much we'd love to *love* the Lord."[45] An Abelardian account of the Atonement is directly responsive to this longing because it focuses our attention on the way in which divine love contributes to kindling in us love to him who has shown us such grace that no greater can be found and thereby to making us better persons. And even traditional Christians who cannot accept Rashdall's attempt to reduce the role of God in soteriol-

---

[42] Stump, "Atonement according to Aquinas", p. 77.
[43] Ibid.
[44] Karl Rahner, *Fundamentals of Christian Faith*, trans. W. V. Dych (New York: Crossroads, 1982), p. 55.
[45] Sarah Shankman, *Now Let's Talk of Graves* (New York: Pocket Books, 1990), p. 139.

ogy to providing in Christ an example of love can endorse his claim that Abelard "sees that God can only be supposed to forgive by making the sinner better."[46] Or, if that rather casual remark seems not to leave enough room for free human response to the gracious initiative of divine love, the insight he attributes to Abelard might be more precisely formulated by saying that God can only be supposed to reconcile sinners to himself by contributing in an important way to making them better persons. Whatever we may think about other motifs such as penal substitution that show up in Abelard's comments on Paul's Epistle to the Romans and arguably have some role to play in a complete account of the Atonement, it is, I believe, safe to agree with Rashdall that there is nothing unintelligible, arbitrary, illogical, or immoral about the thought that the main thing the Atonement does to benefit us is to give us access to a divine love on whose power we must rely in order to become better persons.

My conclusion is that an account along the Abelardian lines I have been laying out shows a lot of promise of enriching our understanding of the mystery of the Atonement. Part of that promise stems from the fact that such an account's emphasis on the inward transformation of sinners would be in tune with the modern inclination to explain the Atonement largely in terms of its psychological effects. Another part derives from the fact that such an account would, by virtue of highlighting the efficacy of the Atonement in improving the characters of sinners, be better balanced than satisfaction-theoretic rivals, such as those proposed by Anselm and Aquinas, which are dominated by legalistic concerns with paying debts of honor or punishment. It is not merely that, as Gunton suggests, we should not deny the subjective implications or psychological consequences of the Atonement. I would urge that we must in an Abelardian spirit acknowledge that the transformation of the sinful human subject wrought in large part by divine love channeled to us through Christ is the most important purpose the Atonement serves. Abelard's legacy is that this motif should dominate our thinking when we reflect on the benefits graciously made available to us through Christ's life, suffering, and death.[47]

---

[46] Rashdall, *The Idea of Atonement*, p. 359.

[47] An earlier version of this essay was presented at the Claremont Graduate School's Twelfth Annual Philosophy of Religion Conference. I am grateful to Richard Rice, my commentator on that occasion, and to Marcia Colish, Alfred J. Freddoso, John Hick, James Wm. McClendon, and Eleonore Stump for helpful advice and criticism.

MARILYN McCORD ADAMS

The Problem of Hell:
A Problem of Evil for Christians

Since the 1950s, syllabi in analytic philosophy of religion have given the problem of evil pride of place. So-called atheologians have advanced as an argument against the existence of God the alleged logical incompossibility of the statements

(I) God exists, and is essentially omnipotent, omniscient, and perfectly good

and

(II) Evil exists.

The decision of Christian philosophers to reply from a posture of "defensive apologetics" and to let their (our) opponents define the value terms has carried both costs and benefits. For if it has limited the store of valuables available as defeaters of evil, it has also restricted the range of ills to be accounted for, to the ones secular philosophers believe in.

In my judgment, this bargain has proved bad, because it has been a distraction from the most important dimensions of the problem of evil. If what is fundamentally at stake—for David Hume and J. L. Mackie, as for Christian philosophers—is the consistency of *our* beliefs, then *our* value theory is the one that should come into play. Moreover, the agreement to try to solve the problem by exclusive appeal to this world's (i.e., non-transcendent, created) goods has been curiously correlated with a reluctance to confront this world's worst evils (viz., horrors participation in which seems *prima facie* to suffice to ruin individual lives). The best-of-all-possible-worlds and free-will approaches try to finesse the existence of the worst evils by operating at a vague and global level. Elsewhere I have urged Christian philosophers to renounce secular value parsimony, to reach under the lid of our theological treasure chest for the only good big enough to defeat horrendous evils—viz., God Himself![1] On the other hand, our refusal to trade with our own store of valuables has allowed us to avoid dealing publicly with our own dark side.[2] For even if, as I argue, this-worldly horrors can be given positive meaning through integration into an overall beatific relation of loving intimacy with God, what about the postmortem evil of hell, in which the omnipotent creator turns effectively and finally against a creature's good?

My own view is that hell poses the principal problem of evil for Christians. Its challenge is so deep and decisive, that to spill bottles of ink defending the logical compossibility of (I) with this-worldly evils while holding a closeted belief that

(III)   Some created persons will be consigned to hell forever

is at best incongruous and at worst disingenuous. My purpose here is to engage the problem of hell at two levels: a theoretical level, concerning the logical compossibility of (I) and (III); and a pragmatic level, concerning whether or not a God who condemned some of His creatures to hell could be a logically appropriate object of standard Christian worship. My own verdict is no secret: statement (III) should be rejected in favor of a doctrine of universal salvation.

1. The Problem, Formulated

1.1. Theoretical Dimension

The argument for the logical incompossibility of (I) with (III), mimics that for (I) with (II):

(1)   If God existed and were omnipotent, He would be able to avoid (III).

---

[1] Cf. my article "Problems of Evil: More Advice to Christian Philosophers", *Faith and Philosophy* 5 (1988): 121–43; esp. pp. 135–37; and "Theodicy without Blame", *Philosophical Topics* 16 (1988): 215–45; esp. pp. 234–37.

[2] The ability thus afforded has actually been cited as a strategic advantage by some Christian philosophers.

2. If God existed and were omniscient, He would know how to avoid (III).
3. If God existed and were perfectly good, He would want to avoid (III).
4. Therefore, if (I), not (III).

Obviously, the soundness of this argument depends on the construals given to the attribute terms and to 'hell'. As just noted, there is an important disanalogy between this and the parallel argument for the general problem of evil: viz., that if 'evil' takes on varying extensions in different value theories, nevertheless, (II) gets its bite from the fact that most people agree on a wide range of actually extant evils. By contrast, (III) enjoys no straightforward empirical support but rests on and must be in the first instance interpreted by the authorities that tell us so. Tradition counts Scripture among the witnesses. For example, the Gospel according to Matthew speaks in vivid imagery of the disobedient and unfaithful being "cast into outer darkness" where there is "weeping and gnashing of teeth" (Matt. 13:42, 50; 22:13) or being thrown into the "unquenchable fire" "prepared for the devil and all his angels" (Matt. 13:42, 50; 18:8–9; 22:13; cf. 3:10). Cashing the metaphors, it says of Judas that it would have been better for him never to have been born (Matt. 26:24). Mainstream medieval theology took such pictures at face value. Duns Scotus is typical in understanding that the reprobate will be forever given over to their guilt[3] and the torment of their inordinate appetites, deprived of both natural and supernatural happiness, and made to suffer perpetual fiery torture, which distracts their intellects so much that they can think of nothing else.[4]

Likewise, we can distinguish an *abstract* from a *concrete* version of the problem, depending on whether "some created persons" in statement (III) ranges over persons created in utopian antemortem environments and circumstances or only over persons in circumstances with combinations of obstacles and opportunities such as are found in the antemortem life experiences of persons in the actual world. Since the doctrine of hell is asserted by many Christians to be not merely logically possible but true, faith that embraces both (I) and (III) and seeks understanding will not complete its task unless it faces the concrete as well as the abstract version of the problem.

Premiss (1) is true because an omnipotent creator could altogether

[3] Duns Scotus, *Opus Oxoniense* in *Opera Omnia* (Paris: Vives, 1891), IV, d. 46, q. 4, n. 6; Wadding-Vives 20, 459.
[4] Duns Scotus, *Op. Ox.* IV, d. 46, q. 4, n. 5; Wadding-Vives 20, 457.

refrain from making any persons or could annihilate created persons any time He chose; either way, He could falsify (III). Again, many traditional theologians (e.g., Augustine, Duns Scotus, Ockham, Calvin) have understood divine sovereignty over creation—both nature and soteriology—to mean that nothing (certainly not creatures' rights) binds God as to what soteriological scheme (if any) He establishes. For example, God could have had a policy of not preserving human persons in existence after death, or He could have legislated temporary reform school followed by life in a utopian environment for all sinners. In these, and many other ways, God could avoid (III), and such was within His power.[5]

Likewise, (3) would be true if "perfectly good" is construed along the lines of person-relative goodness:

> 'God is good to a created person p' iff God guarantees to p a life that is a great good to p on the whole, and one in which p's participation in deep and horrendous evils (if any) is defeated within the context of p's life',

where

> 'Evil is horrendous' iff 'Participation in e by p (either as a victim or a perpetrator) gives everyone *prima facie* reason to believe that p's life cannot—given its inclusion of e—be a great good to p on the whole'.

The traditional hell is a paradigm horror, one which offers not merely prima facie but conclusive reason to believe that the life of the damned cannot be a great good to them on the whole. Any person who suffers eternal punishment in the traditional hell will, on the contrary, be one within whose life good is engulfed and/or defeated by evils.

For all we know, however, (3) may be false if divine goodness is evaluated in relation to God's role as producer of global goods. It is at least epistemically possible that (III) be true of a world that exhibits maximum variety with maximum unity or of a very good world that displays the best balance of moral good over moral evil which God could weakly actualize.[6] And in general, it is epis-

---

[5] Cf. my *William Ockham* (Notre Dame: University of Notre Dame Press, 1987), chap. 30, 1257–97; and "The Structure of Ockham's Moral Theory", *Franciscan Studies* 46 (1986): 1–35.

[6] Alvin Plantinga takes this line in numerous discussions, in the course of answering J. L. Mackie's objection to the free-will defense, that God could have made sinless free creatures. Plantinga insists that, given incompatibilist freedom in creatures, God cannot strongly actualize any world He wants. It is logically possible that a world

temically possible that the world have a maximally good overall order and still include the horrors of damnation for some created persons. Aquinas rationalizes this conclusion when he explains that since the purpose of creation is to show forth God's goodness, some must be damned to manifest his justice and others saved to advertise His mercy.[7]

1.2. Pragmatic Implications

The pragmatic consequences of reconciling (I) with (III) by restricting divine goodness to its global dimension are severe. First of all, this assumption makes human life a bad bet. Consider (adapting John Rawls's device) persons in a preoriginal position, surveying possible worlds containing managers of varying power, wisdom, and character, and subjects with diverse fates. The subjects are to answer, from behind a veil of ignorance as to which position they would occupy, the question whether they would willingly enter a given world as a human being. Reason would, I submit, render a negative verdict already for worlds whose omniscient and omnipotent manager permits antemortem horrors that remain undefeated within the context of the human participant's life and a fortiori for worlds some or most of whose human occupants suffer eternal torment.[8]

Second, it would make pragmatically inconsistent any worship behavior that presupposes that God is good to the worshipper or to created persons generally. For given the traditional assumption that the identity of the elect is secret, so much so that there are no certain (or even very probabilifying) empirical signs by means of which humans can make an antemortem distinction between the saved and the damned, actual created persons are left to worry about whether this latter "fate-worse-than-death" is theirs. Nor would the knowledge that *we* were among the elect greatly relieve our pragmatic difficulty, given Christ's command to love our neighbors as ourselves.

If (III) were true, open-eyed worship would have to be of a God who mysteriously creates some persons for lives so horrendous on the whole and eternally, that it would have been better for them never to have been born, of a God who is at worst cruel (not that He

---

with evils in the amounts and of the kinds found in this world is the best that He could do, Plantinga argues, given His aim of getting some moral goodness in the world. See section 2.2 below.

[7] Thomas Aquinas, *Summa theologica* I, q. 23, a. 5, ad 3.

[8] Cf. my "Horrendous Evils and the Goodness of God," *Proceedings of the Aristotelian Society*, Supplementary Volume 63 (1989): 297–310; esp. 303.

had any obligation to be otherwise) and at best indifferent to our welfare. Christian Stoicism practices a species of such worship, one in which the believer (i) recognizes his or her insignificant place in the universe and (ii) by a series of spiritual exercises humbly accepts it (thereby submitting to God's inscrutable will), (iii) praises its Maker for His world-organizing activity, and (iv) finds dignity in this capacity for self-transcendence. Some even speak of divine love for them, in making them parts of His cosmic order and endowing them with the capacity for dignity, even when they are crushed by it. But the fact of such love carries no implication that God is *good to* them in the sense defined in section 1.1.[9] Notice, however, that Stoic worship that is honest (i.e., not based on denial and repression) is very difficult, indeed psychologically impossible for many, perhaps most, people. Avoiding pragmatic inconsistency requires vigilance against smuggling in the assumption to which none would be epistemically entitled, that after all God does care for me!

2. Free Will and the Problem of Hell

Many Christians find the Stoic bullet hard to bite but insist that it is unnecessary even if (III) is true. Mounting a kind of free-will defense, they claim that God has done a good thing in making incompatibilist free creatures. Like any good governor or parent, He has established a set of general conditional decrees, specifying sanctions and rewards for various sorts of free actions. His preference ("antecedent" or "perfect" will) is that everyone should be saved, but He has given us scope to work out our own destinies. Damnation would never happen but for the errant action of incompatibilist free creatures within the framework of divine regulations. It is not something God *does*, but rather allows; it is neither God's means, nor His end, but a middle-known but unintended side effect of the order He has created. Thus, (3) is true only regarding God's antecedent but not His all-things-considered preferences, and the incompossibility argument (in section 1.1) fails.

2.1. Exclusive Salvation according to William Craig

William Craig offers a remarkably bold presentation of this position in his "'No Other Name': A Middle Knowledge Perspective on

---

[9] Cf. Diogenes Allen, "Natural Evil and the God of Love," *Religious Studies* 16 (1980): 439–56.

the Exclusivity of Salvation through Christ."[10] Motivated by his beliefs that (III) is asserted by Scripture and necessary to justify the missionary imperative, Craig takes Plantinga for his inspiration, and attempts to demonstrate the logical compossibility of (I) with

(III′)   [a] Some persons do not receive Christ, and [b] are damned,

by finding another proposition that is compossible with (I) and that together with (I) entails (III′): viz.,

(IV)   God has actualized a world containing an optimal balance between saved and unsaved, and those who are unsaved suffer from trans-world damnation.[11]

By "optimal balance" Craig means the best that God could weakly actualize and still fill heaven.[12] Nor need this ratio keep the number of damned down to a few. For Craig thinks his defense also has the makings of a theodicy[13] and insists that "if we take Scripture [Matt. 7:13–14] seriously, we must admit that *the vast majority of persons in the world* are condemned and will be forever lost."[14]

Craig recognizes a need to defend his rejection of (3) for God's all-things-considered preferences and his claim that (IV) is logically compossible with (I), against the charge that

(3′)   A perfectly good being would prefer not to create any persons at all rather than see some suffer in hell.

Once again, Craig has the courage of his convictions, insisting that even if "the terrible price of filling heaven is also filling hell",[15] God's decision to create free creatures—not merely a handful but enough to fill heaven—and to accept this price does not count against His benevolence or fairness,[16] provided God has done everything He could (supplying grace to all). For their damnation is "of their own free will", "the result of their own free choice".[17] They are "self-condemned".[18] By the same token, the sufferings of the damned should

---

[10] William Craig, "'No Other Name': A Middle Knowledge Perspective on the Exclusivity of Salvation through Christ," *Faith and Philosophy* 6 (1989): 172–88.

[11] Ibid., 184.

[12] Ibid., 182–83.

[13] Ibid., 186.

[14] Ibid., 176.

[15] Ibid., 183.

[16] Ibid., 186.

[17] Ibid., 184, 185.

[18] Ibid., 176.

not tarnish the heavenly happiness of the saved, because they too will recognize that the damned brought "this tragic circumstance" on themselves as a "result of their own free choice."[19] And Craig insists that divine distribution of graces through special and general revelation does give each created person a chance to comply with God's will.

2.2. Justice and Commensuration

Craig is concerned to maintain that God is neither "unjust"[20] nor "unfair" in damning those who do not accept Christ.[21] Here it is necessary to distinguish between (a) justice taken from the side of God (whether God would be just in the sense of living up to His obligations in weakly actualizing (III) or (III')), and (b) justice considered in relation to created agents and their acts (whether weakly actualizing (III) or (III') would exemplify a policy of treating like cases alike, of rendering to each according to his or her deserts, or of setting expectations within reasonable reach). I want to argue that either way 'justice' is the wrong concept, because justice trades in commensurables, whereas both God and eternal destinies are incommensurable with human beings and their acts.

2.2.1. *Divine Justice and the Ontological Gap.* I merely join the consensus of the great medieval and reformation theologians in recognizing that God and creatures are *ontologically incommensurate*. God is a being a greater than which cannot be conceived, the infinite being, in relation to which finite creatures are "almost nothing". Drawing on social analogies, Anselm contends that God is so far above, so different in kind from us, as not to be enmeshed in merely human networks of mutual rights and obligations; God is not the kind of thing that could be obligated to creatures in any way. Duns Scotus concurs, reasoning that God has no obligation to love creatures, because although the finite *goodness* of each provides *a* reason to love it, the fact of its *finitude* means that this reason is always defeasible, indeed negligible, almost nothing in comparison with the reason divine goodness has to love itself. Their conclusion from this ontological disproportion is that God will not be *unjust to* created persons no matter what He does.

---

[19] Ibid., 185.
[20] Ibid., 176.
[21] Ibid., 186.

2.2.2. *Finite Temporal Agency versus Eternal Destiny.* My earlier arguments[22] for the disproportion between human acts and eternal destinies centered on our limited capacities to do and suffer harm. Focusing on the "an-eye-for-an-eye" principle and its variants, I insisted that even if each human being were made to experience each of the harms she or he caused other humans, whether once, twice, or any finite multiple of times, the punishment thus mandated would eventually be over. I observed, however, that the notion of proportionate return already breaks down in ordinary cases where the numbers (though finite) get large, because in such cases we are irremediably unable to suffer precisely what we cause. For example, suppose I knock one tooth out of the mouth of each of thirty-two people each of whom has a full set of teeth. Is my losing one tooth thirty-two times and hence having no teeth not much worse than their each having thirty-one teeth? Or suppose I interrupt television transmission of the Superbowl game, thereby causing twenty million fans one hour of fury and frustration each. Surely, my suffering twenty million hours of fury and frustration is much worse. Harms are not atomic, their cumulative effect not simply additive; and so for large amounts, the notion of proportionate return already loses definition.

More recently, I have concentrated on the incommensuration between horrendous evils and human life and agency. For, on the one hand, *horrors have a power to defeat positive meaning disproportionate to their extension in the space-time worm of an individual's life.* And, on the other, *horrors are incommensurate with human cognitive capacities.* For (i) the human capacity to cause horrors unavoidably exceeds our ability to experience them. Many examples make this clear as to quantity: for example, on the traditional doctrine of the fall, Adam experiences one individual's worth of ignorance and difficulty, but his sin brought it on his many descendents; Hitler organized a holocaust of millions; small numbers of government leaders, scientists, and military personnel brought about the atomic explosions over Hiroshima and Nagasaki. Likewise for quality, it is probably true that, for example, a childless male soldier cannot experience anything like enough to the suffering of a mother whose child is murdered before her eyes. But (ii) where suffering is concerned, conceivability follows capacity to experience, in such a way that we cannot adequately conceive of what we cannot experience. Just as a blind person's

---

[22] Cf. my early article "Hell and the God of Justice," *Religious Studies* 11 (1974): 433–47.

color concepts are deficient because lack of acquaintance deprives him or her of the capacity for imaginative representation of colors, despite lots of abstract descriptive knowledge about them, so lack of experience deprives an agent of the capacity emphathetically to enter in to what it would be like to suffer this or that harm, despite more or less detailed abstract descriptive knowledge about such suffering. To these observations, I add the claim (iii) that agent responsibility is diminished in proportion to his or her unavoidable inability to conceive of the relevant dimensions of the action and its consequences, and I draw the conclusion that human agents cannot be fully responsible for the horrendous consequences of their actions.[23]

Returning to the problem of hell, I maintain that damnation is a horror that exceeds our conceptual powers. For even if we could experience for a finite period of time some aspect of hell's torments (e.g., the burning of the fire, deep depression, or consuming hatred) or heaven's bliss (e.g., St. Teresa's joyful glimpse of the Godhead), we are unavoidably unable to experience their cumulative effect in advance and so unable more than superficially to appreciate what is involved in either. It follows that human agents are unavoidably unable to exercise their free choice with fully open eyes, the way Craig implies we do.

2.2.3. *Finite Agency in the Region of the Divine.* It may be objected that the ontological incommensuration between God and creatures redounds another way, however. For Anselm pointed out that the badness of sin is to be measured not simply in terms of what the creature is or does but in terms of the creature's relation to God, a being a greater/more worthy of honor, respect, and esteem than which cannot be conceived. Since God is infinitely worthy of honor, any offense against God is immeasurably indecent and hence infinitely culpable. Even if every created *harm* we caused were finite, at the very worst the ruin of finite created lives, Anselm's principle shows how we have the capacity to cause infinite *offense*. Any and every sin would turn out to be a horrendous evil. And if eternal torment for the creature is incommensurate with human agency taken in itself, it does not adequately measure the offensiveness of one small look contrary to God's will. Eternal torment is merely the closest approximation that creatures can make to experiencing the just punishment.

My reply is that it is not "fair" in Craig's sense (b) of setting rea-

---

[23] Cf. my "Theodicy without Blame."

sonable expectations to put created agency (even if we think of its starting in utopian Eden with ideal competence of its kind) into a position where the consequences of its exercise are so disproportionate to its acts. Suppose the powers that be threaten a nuclear holocaust if I do not always put my pencil down no more than one inch from the paper on which I am writing. Although it is within my power to meet such a demand, such disproportionate consequences put my pencil-placing actions under unnatural strain. Although in some sense I *can* comply, I am also in some sense *bound* to "slip up" sooner or later. Hence, the demand is unreasonable, the responsibility too hard for me to bear. Interestingly, medieval adherents of free-will approaches to the problem of evil worried about this. In some works, Augustine confesses that the corruptibility of human nature makes failure virtually inevitable, incompatibilist freedom notwithstanding.[24] And Duns Scotus worries that it might be too risky for God to give us the liberty of indifference in heaven, because sooner or later the fall would be apt to recur.[25] Craig's own reading of Matthew—according to which the vast majority of created persons in the actual world are damned—lends credence to these probability estimates.

I do not say that were God to create persons with the intention of condemning to hell any who fail to honor him appropriately, he would be unjust in the sense (a) of violating his (non-existent) obligations to them (us). I do claim that such punishment would be *unusual*, because acting in the region of the divine levels out the differences among created act types (e.g., between peeking out at prayers and torturing babies). Moreover, God would be "unfair" in sense (b) and hence *cruel* in setting created persons conditions relative to which not only were they (we) unlikely to succeed, but also their (our) lives were as a consequence more apt than not to have all positive meaning swallowed up by horrendous evil.

2.3. The Idol of Human Agency

Where soteriology is concerned, Christians have traditionally disagreed about human nature along two parameters. First, some hold that human nature was created in ideal condition and placed in a

---

[24] Cf. John Hick, *Evil and the God of Love*, rev. ed. (New York: Harper and Row, 1966, 1978), chap. 3, pp. 37–48.

[25] Duns Scotus, *God and Creatures: The Quodlibetal Questions*, translated with introduction, notes and glossary by Felix Alluntis, O.F.M., and Allan B. Wolter, O.F.M. (Washington, D.C.: The Catholic University of America Press, 1975), q.16, art. II, 377–79.

utopian environment: i.e., that *ab initio* humans had enough cognitive and emotional maturity to grasp and accurately apply relevant normative principles, while (on the occasion of their choice) their exercise of these abilities was unobstructed by unruly passions or external determinants of any kind. Others maintain, on the contrary, that humans are created immature and grow to adult competence through a messy developmental process. Second, where salvation is concerned, some take the human race collectively, while others consider humans individualistically. According to the Augustinian doctrine of the fall, Adam and Eve began as ideal agents in utopian Eden. The consequence of their sin is not only individual but collective: agency impaired by "ignorance" (clouded moral judgment) and "difficulty" (undisciplined emotions), which passes from the first parents to the whole family of their descendants. In his earlier works, Augustine insists that despite such inherited handicaps, the reprobate still bring damnation on themselves, because God has offered help sufficient to win the difficult struggle through faith in Christ.[26] In later anti-Pelagian works, Augustine abandons the idea that God confers on each fallen human grace sufficient for salvation; he concedes that damnation is the consequence of such divine omissions and Adam's original free choice to sin. Nevertheless, the damned deserve no pity, because the family collectively brought it on themselves through Adam's free choice of will.[27] Without being fully explicit, Craig seems to proceed individualistically, assuming that by the time we reach "the age of accountability", our agency is ideal enough for each to be entrusted with and held responsible for his or her own eternal destiny. Irenaeus stands on the other side as the patristic prototype of the developmental understanding of human nature.

In my judgment, the arguments from incommensuration offered in section 2.2 hold even where ideal human nature is concerned. For my own part, I reject the notion of a historical fall and read Genesis 2–3 the Irenaean way, as about the childhood of the human race. I deny not only that we human beings do have, but also that we ever had, ideal agency. Therefore, I conclude, that reasoning about it is relevant at most to the abstract and not to the concrete problem of hell.

---

[26] Augustine, *De libero arbitrio*. Corpus Scriptorum Ecclesiasticorum Latinorum, vol. 74. (Vindobonae: Hoelder-Pichler-Tempsky, 1956), passim.

[27] This position is especially clear in Augustine, *De gratia et libero arbitrio* (A.D. 426), and Augustine, *De correptione et gratia* (A.D. 426 or 427).

By contrast, a realistic picture of human agency should recognize the following: (a) We human beings start life ignorant, weak, and helpless, psychologically so lacking in a self-concept as to be incapable of choice. (b) We learn to "construct" a picture of the world, ourselves, and other people only with difficulty over a long period of time and under the extensive influence of other non-ideal choosers. (c) Human development is the interactive product of human nature and its environment, and from early on we humans are confronted with problems that we cannot adequately grasp or cope with, and in response to which we mount (without fully conscious calculation) inefficient adaptational strategies. (d) Yet, the human psyche forms habits in such a way that these reactive patterns, based as they are on a child's inaccurate view of the world and its strategic options, become entrenched in the individual's personality. (e) Typically, the habits are unconsciously "acted out" for years, causing much suffering to self and others before (if ever) they are recognized and undone through a difficult and painful process of therapy and/or spiritual formation. (f) Having thus begun *immature*, we arrive at adulthood in a state of *impaired freedom*, as our childhood adaptational strategies continue to distort our perceptions and behavior. (g) We adults with impaired freedom are responsible for our choices, actions, and even the character molded by our unconscious adaptational strategies, in the sense that we are the *agent causes* of them. (h) Our assessments of moral responsibility, praise, and blame cannot afford to take this impairment into account, because we are not as humans capable of organizing and regulating ourselves in that fine-tuned a way. And so, except for the most severe cases of impairment, we continue to hold ourselves *responsible to one another*.[28]

Taking these estimates of human nature to heart, I draw two conclusions: first, that such impaired adult human agency is no more competent to be entrusted with its (individual or collective) eternal destiny than two-year-old agency is to be allowed choices that could result in its death or serious physical impairment; and second, that the fact that the choices of such impaired agents come between the divine creator of the environment and their infernal outcome no more reduces divine responsibility for the damnation than two-year-old agency reduces the responsibility of the adult caretaker. Suppose, for example, that a parent introduces a two-year-old child into a room filled with gas that is safe to breathe but will explode if ignited. Assume further that the room contains a stove with brightly

---

[28] Cf. my "Theodicy without Blame," pp. 231–32.

colored knobs, which if turned will light the burners and ignite the gas. If the parent warns the child not to turn the knobs and leaves, whereupon the child turns the knobs and blows itself up, surely the child is at most marginally to blame, even if it knew enough to obey the parent, while the parent is both primarily responsible and highly culpable. Or suppose a terrorist announces his intention to kill one hundred citizens if anyone in a certain village wears a red shirt on Tuesday. The village takes the threat seriously, and everyone is informed. If some adult citizen slips up and wears his favorite red shirt on Tuesday, he will be responsible and culpable, but the terrorist who set up the situation will be much more culpable.

Once again, my further conclusion is not that God would (like the parent and the terrorist) be culpable if He were to insert humans into a situation in which their eternal destiny depended on their exercise of impaired agency, for I deny that God has any obligations to creatures (see section 2.2.1). Rather, God (like the parent or the terrorist) would bear primary responsibility for any tragic outcomes,[29] and God would be cruel to create human beings in a world with combinations of obstacles and opportunities such as are found in the actual world and govern us under a scheme according to which whether or not we go to the traditional hell depends on how we exercise our impaired adult agency in this life—cruel, by virtue of imposing horrendous consequences on our all-too-likely failures.

2.4. The Possibility of Transworld Damnation?

Perhaps it will be objected that my arguments in section 2.3 are unfair because they abstract from one of Craig's important claims: that God supplies all the graces needed for success and thereby strengthens us, or at least (as early Augustine thought) offers us the means to strengthen our impaired agency, only to have such aid refused. This claim is, of course, connected with Craig's hypothesis of possible transworld damnation, which I reject twice-over.

2.4.1. *True Counterfactuals of Freedom?* First, I deny that any counterfactuals of freedom are true for the metaphysical reason that there is nothing to make them true.[30] It follows from the definition of 'in-

---

[29] Contrary to what Craig maintains, "'No Other Name'", pp. 176–77.

[30] I agree with the arguments offered by Robert Merrihew Adams in "Middle Knowledge and the Problem of Evil", reprinted in his *The Virtue of Faith and Other Essays* (New York: Oxford University Press, 1987), pp. 77–93. I am indebted to him

compatibilist freedom' that neither God's will nor causal nor logical necessity could account for the truth of propositions about the incompatibilist free choices of merely possible persons (or persons considered insofar as they are merely possible). Nor could the creature's actual character or choices make them true, because these are posterior in the order of explanation to the truth value of the counterfactuals about what the merely possible creatures would do were they to be actualized in certain circumstances.

2.4.2. *Transworld Damnation and the Logical Problem of Hell.* Second, Craig's notion of transworld damnation is supposed to mimic Plantinga's conception of transworld depravity: just as it is possible that some or all or the vast majority of created persons would be such that they would go wrong with respect to at least one morally significant action no matter what circumstances God strongly actualized, so—Craig maintains—it is possible that some or all or the vast majority of created persons would be such that they would refuse Christ and be damned no matter what situations God strongly actualized. Likewise, just as it is possible that God might be powerless to weakly actualize a world of sinless incompatabilist free creatures, so—Craig alleges—it is possible that God might be unable to weakly actualize a world in which heaven would be filled without the vast majority of created persons being damned. Moreover, just as God's powerlessness to determine the truth-values of counterfactuals of (created) freedom, together with the laudable desire of creating a world with a favorable balance of moral good over moral evil, rationalizes divine permission of moral evil, so God's powerlessness with respect to such counterfactual truth values is supposed to combine with His admirable desire to fill heaven, to explain His acceptance of damnation for some or all or the vast majority of created persons.

This comparison seems fatally flawed, however. Craig's replacement for (III) is:

(III′) [a] Some persons do not receive Christ, and [b] are damned.

Note that it splits into two parts, which, given divine sovereignty over the soteriological process, are logically independent of one another. That is, it is logically possible that some or all or the vast majority of created persons might refuse to accept Christ or might

for many helpful discussions of this material, which have corrected various errors in earlier drafts of this section.

commit the sin of final impenitence, and yet God need not condemn them to hell but might maintain them in a world much like this one or annihilate them instead. Put another way, the existence of hell and the conditions for admission are among the things that fall within God's powers of strong-actualization, even if the truth values of counterfactuals of (created) freedom are not within His power. Thus, even if, relative to some possible world, the essence of each and every created person were infected with transworld final impenitence, still none would be transworld damned. Transworld damnation is not, after all, a logical possibility.

Given Plantinga's metaphysics, it is logically possible that

(IV′)   Created persons would not accept Christ in great enough numbers to fill heaven unless some or the vast majority of created persons were finally impenitent and consigned to hell forever.

By the same token the following will be taken as logically possible:

(IV″)   Created persons would not accept Christ in great enough numbers to fill heaven unless (in addition to some or a large number who die finally impenitent) some or a large number of those who responded best to Christ were consigned to hell forever.

and

(IV‴)   Created persons would not accept Christ in great enough numbers to fill heaven unless (in addition to some or a large number who die finally impenitent) some or a large number of children two years old and under, who were never even morally competent agents, were consigned to hell.

Although each of (IV′), (IV″), and (IV‴) combines with Craig's hypothesis that God weakly actualizes a world in which heaven is filled, to entail (III′), this does not suffice to establish the compossibility of (I) with (III) or (III′), for the latter conclusion requires the additional premise that each is compossible with (I). Once again, God would not violate any of His (non-existent) obligations were He to proceed with His plans to fill heaven with incompatibilist free creatures, even in the face of such counterfactual fates. Nevertheless, I submit that God would be cruel to do so, middle knowing that He was bringing some or the vast majority into being for lives it would have been better for them never to have lived. Therefore, (I) would be compossible with (III) only if "good" in (I) were taken in a sense that does not rule out cruelty. Contrary to Craig's hopes, he will not be able to rely on omnipotent powerlessness over counterfactuals of freedom to reconcile hell with divine goodness; he will have to follow the Stoic in tampering with the notion of "good" to be understood in (I).

The logical possibility (on Plantinga's scheme) of (IV'), (IV''), and (IV''') might even call into question an assumption that Plantinga locates at the heart of free-will approaches to evil: viz., that a "world containing creatures who are sometimes significantly free (and freely perform more good than evil actions) is more valuable, all else being equal, than a world containing no free creatures at all."[31] On reflection, is it not anthropocentric, another manifestation of our idolatry of human agency (cf. section 2.2), to suppose that the latter is so valuable that God would accept unredeemed horror to include it? Since our thoughts are not like God's, how can we be so sure that omniscient creativity could not find equally good or better worlds altogether devoid of incompatibilist free creatures[32]—in which case (I) might not be compossible with (III) or (III'), even where divine goodness were evaluated solely in relation to God's role as producer of global goods.

2.4.3. *Transworld Damnation as Theodicy?* Craig offers his reflections as grist for the mill, not only of defensive apologetics, but also of theodicy. Thus, he invites us to agree (a) that (IV') is not only logically possible but true, and yet (b) that for each actual created person, God has done everything He could to win that person over. I reject both claims.

2.4.3.1. *Congruent Grace versus Transworld Final Impenitence.* If I believed that counterfactuals of freedom could be true, I would replace (a) with Suarez's doctrine of congruent grace: namely, that God is able to provide each created person with such grace that she or he would freely consent to His will, and that God is able to do this for each, no matter which other created persons He additionally makes and graces. Craig considers this move but finds it impotent against his theodicy, because "we have no good grounds for believing" the Suarezian doctrine, and the burden of proof is on the Suarezian to "demonstrate" its truth.[33] By contrast, I see the onus of proof distrib-

---

[31] Alvin Plantinga, *The Nature of Necessity*, chap. 9 (Clarendon Press, 1974), p. 166.
[32] I owe this suggestion to Robert Merrihew Adams.
[33] Craig, "'No Other Name'", p. 183.

uted otherwise: it favors his position no more than mine. The issue may be approached at two levels. First, if (as Plantinga assumes) nothing explains why one counterfactual of freedom should be true of an individual essence rather than another, their truth-values would seem to fall like "fates" independently of both the divine will and created wills. And if—so far as the theory of counterfactuals of freedom is concerned—it remains a mystery to us why or how the truth values should be distributed, we are left with appeals to ignorance or epistemic contingency about their actual distribution. Second, we might suppose with Plantinga that, while nothing makes such counterfactuals of freedom true, still some are more plausible than others. Both ways, the arguments favoring transworld impenitence or transworld redeemability[34] will be driven by other considerations: for Craig, by his belief that (III) and (III') are true because endorsed by Scripture and required to fire the missionary effort; for me, by confidence in God's ability to convince us that He is the Good that satisfies, in His power and resourcefulness to defeat evil thoroughly within the context of each created person's life.

For that matter, I, too, have a synoptic proof text (Matt. 19:24–26; Mark 10:25–27; Luke 18:25–27): Jesus' claim that all things are possible with God does not respond to worries about the size of stones God is able to make and lift or the possibility of His squaring the circle or making contradictories true but to the question how anyone can be saved, about how human hearts can be changed. I understand the answer to imply that God is so powerful, so witting and resourceful, that he can let created persons do their damnedest and still save them.[35] I prefer the mystery of how God accomplishes this

[34] David P. Hunt of Whittier College opposes the notion of 'transworld salvation' to Craig's 'transworld damnation' in his interesting paper "Middle Knowledge and the Soteriological Problem of Evil," *Religious Studies* 27 (1991): 3–26.

[35] Note, I use the term 'proof text' lightly. I am not so naive as to assume that my citation of these passages and assertion of my interpretation constitutes a proof that the doctrines of congruent grace or universal salvation are biblical. My own general impression is of a variety of different biblical, indeed New Testament views, each of which deserves separate and careful consideration. Certainly, I do not think the biblical witness is so univocal as Craig alleges ("'No Other Name'", pp. 172–74). But neither am I so confident as Thomas Talbot ("The Doctrine of Everlasting Punishment," *Faith and Philosophy* 7 (1990): 19–42; esp. 23) as to advance the doctrine of universal salvation as the biblical view; apocalyptic theology, whatever is to be made of it, strikes too strong a chord in the New Testament. At any rate, this is the work of many other papers (and volumes), some of them mine. Cf. my "Separation and Reversal in Luke-Acts," *Philosophy and the Christian Faith*, ed. Thomas V. Morris (Notre Dame: University of Notre Dame Press, 1988), pp. 92–117; and "Hell according to Matthew?" presented at the Gordon College Conference on the Future of God, May 1989.

with incompatibilist free creatures to the equally impenetrable mystery of how transworld damnation falls on some individual essences rather than others.

Empirically, given that all adults have impaired freedom—where some impairments are worse than others due to factors beyond the agent's control, some increased by the agent's own choices—the belief that any of us is saved implies that God is able to change the hearts of sinners from good to bad. When I consider the way our neuroses are integrated into the cores of our personality, and the difficulty of ripping out such dysfunctions, I doubt that there is much to choose among them from God's point of view: if God can change any of them, there is insufficient reason to believe He could not change the others, too.

2.4.3.2. "Sufficient" Grace Universally Distributed? Insofar as Craig intends not merely a defense but a soteriological theodicy, he must confront the concrete problem of hell, and construe (III) and (III') to be about, not just some possible persons in some possible situations or others, but about possible persons in antemortem situations of the sort in which people find themselves in the actual world (i.e., with like traumas, impairments, disasters, and hardships to work against). I do not find it credible that all such actual antemortem situations contain grace sufficient for faith in and cooperation with God (Christ) were it not for the creature's incompatibilist free refusal. (Consider, e.g., the predicament of gangland youths in South Central Los Angeles, individuals who have been subject to physical and sexual abuse from childhood.) Rather, God seems for the most part to have a policy of distributing the graces bit by bit, so that our way out of our sinful habits and so on is itself a developmental process. Some people die before they get very far, and sometimes this seems to be through no fault of their own.

2.5. Pragmatic Implications

In my judgment, Craig's theological picture is not only theoretically mistaken, but also pragmatically pernicious. For according to it, a created person can view God as friendly—i.e., as good to him or her—only by counting himself or herself among the elect. But this breeds Pharisaism thrice-over: (1) To the extent that I do succeed in walking the straight and narrow, I will be contrasting myself with my brothers and sisters who don't, which easily leads to self-congratulation. (2) To the extent that it is difficult for me to toe the line, because of my developmental impairments, it produces the feeling of the one-talent man (Matt. 25:14–30; Luke 19:12–27), that

God is harsh and demanding. (3) Insofar as sincere obedience to the first and great commandment needs to be laid on the psychological assurance of divine goodness to oneself, it will be difficult to obey the first while obeying the second.

3. The Hermeneutics of Charity

When authorities seem to say things that are inconsistent or unreasonable, our first move is, not to cut off, but to twist the wax nose a bit, so that without crediting the troublesome pronouncements taken literally, we can "make something" of them by finding some deeper and more palatable truths which (we may claim) they were attempting to express. In this spirit, some agree that the notion of hell as an eternal torture chamber, as a punitive consequence for not accepting Christ, is not compatible with any tolerable understanding of divine goodness. That is, if 'hell' is understood the traditional way, then they construe 'perfectly good' in such a way as to render true the statement:

3. If God existed and were perfectly good, he would want to avoid (III).

Rather than abandon the doctrine of hell altogether, they modify or reinterpret it as some other fate involving permanent exclusion from heaven.

3.1. Hell as Leaving People to the Natural Consequences of Their Choices

On Craig's politico-legal model, the relation between a person's sinning to the end and his or her suffering eternal punishment is extrinsic and contingent (as is that between speeding and paying a monetary fine). Other philosophers think there is a better chance of construing (III) in such a way as to be compatible with (I) if one discovers an intrinsic connection between the created persons' choices and their postmortem punishments or deprivations. Thus, Richard Swinburne maintains that "heaven is not a reward for good behavior" but "a home for good people"[36] He insists on the high value not only of created free agency but also of the autonomy of

---

[36] In several places, including "A Theodicy of Heaven and Hell," in *The Existence and Nature of God*, ed. Alfred Freddoso (Notre Dame, Indiana: University of Notre Dame Press, 1983), 37–54; the second quotation is from page 43.

created persons to determine their own destinies. Noting psychological commonplaces about how patterns of choice build habits of thinking, wanting, valuing, and doing, and the more entrenched the habit, the harder it is to break, Swinburne reckons such habits may become so entrenched as to be unbreakable. For a person may so thoroughly blind himself or herself to what is really worth going for, that she or he can no longer see or rationally choose it. Since heaven is a society organized around the things that are really worth wanting, being, and doing, people locked into their vices could not enjoy it there.

Swinburne is less interested in (III) than in

(III') Some persons that God creates are permanently excluded from heaven.[37]

He is willing to recognize "various possible fates for those who have finally rejected the good": (i) "they might cease to exist after death"; (ii) "they might cease to exist after suffering some limited amount of physical pain as part of the punishment for their wickedness"; or (iii) "they might continue to exist forever pursuing trivial pursuits"[38] In Swinburne's estimation, "the crucial point is that it is compatible with the goodness of God that he should allow a man to put himself beyond possibility of salvation, because it is indeed compatible with the goodness of God that he should allow a man to choose the sort of person he will be,"[39] even where these decisions have eternal consequences.

Likewise, dismissing literal construals of Matthew 25:41–46 and Luke 16:19–26 as "a crude and simplistic account of the doctrine of hell,"[40] Eleonore Stump turns to Dante, who understands the fundamental awfulness of hell in terms of eternal deprivation of union with God. Stump takes Dante's "graphic images" at theological face value and suggests that the latter is fully compatible with a Limbo of beautiful physical surroundings "in which the noblest and wisest of the ancients discuss philosophy."[41] Moreover, in the more punitive regions of hell, external tortures are not suffered the way they would be in this world but serve rather as outward and visible signs

---

[37] Swinburne, "A Theodicy of Heaven and Hell," pp. 37, 52.
[38] Ibid., p. 52.
[39] Ibid.
[40] Eleonore Stump, "The Problem of Evil," *Faith and Philosophy* 4 (1985): 392–423; esp. 400.
[41] Ibid., p. 400.

of inner psychological states—afflictions which are nevertheless compatible with long and leisurely intellectual discussions. So far as the problem of hell is concerned, Stump maintains, "Everlasting life in hell is the ultimate evil which can befall a person in this world; but the torments of hell are *the natural* conditions of some persons, and God can spare such persons those pains only by depriving them of their nature or their existence. And it is arguable that, of the alternatives open to God, maintaining such persons in existence and as human is the best."[42] In other words, when 'hell' in (III) is thus reinterpreted, Stump finds the logical compossibility of (I) with (III) defensible.

Once again, my principal complaint about these approaches centers on their understanding of human nature. Swinburne and Stump/ Dante begin by taking human psychology very seriously: that entrenched habits of character, established tastes, and concomitant states of inner conflict are *naturally* consequent upon sinful patterns of choice is supposed to explain the *intrinsic* connection between the sinner's earthly behavior and his or her exclusion from heaven and/ or consignment to hell. By contrast, their estimates of the *natural* effects of vice over the very (i.e., eternally) long run leave human psychology far behind. For vice is a psychospiritual disorder. Just as running a machine contrary to its design leads, sooner rather than later, to premature breakdown, so also persistent psychological disorders caricature and produce breakdowns even in the medium run of twenty to seventy years. My own view resonates with C. S. Lewis's suggestion in *The Problem of Pain*,[43] that vice in the soul preserved beyond three score and ten brings about a total dismantling of personality, to the torment of which this-worldly schizophrenia and depression are but the faintest approximations. A fortiori excluded is the notion that persons with characters unfit for heaven might continue forever philosophizing, delivering eloquent speeches, or engaging in trivial pursuits.[44] Likewise, either union with God is the natural human telos, in which case we cannot both eternally lack it and yet continue to enjoy this-worldly pleasures forever; or it is not, because we are personal animals and unending life is not a

---

[42] Ibid., p. 401.

[43] C. S. Lewis, *The Problem of Pain* (New York: Macmillan, 1979), chap 8, pp. 124–26.

[44] Years ago, I agreed with Dante that philosophy could keep one entertained for eternity. Extensive conversations with the Reverend A. Orley Swartzentruber persuaded me of what Augustine and Anselm confirm: that philosophy can only seem infinitely fascinating because it involves insights into the Christ, the Divine Word, clearer knowledge and love of whom is the only thing that can satisfy forever.

natural but a supernatural endowment. For God to prolong life eternally while denying access to the only good that could keep us eternally interested would likewise eventually produce unbearable misery.[45] In short, I think that the Swinburne/Stump/Dante suggestion that God might keep created persons in existence forever but abandon them to the consequences of their sinful choices collapses into the more traditional doctrine of hell, when such consequences are calculated from a realistic appraisal of human psychology.

3.2. Annihilation by the Creator?

Among others, Swinburne mentions the option of replacing (III) with

(III''') Some created persons who die with characters unfit for heaven will be annihilated, either at death or after the Judgment.

Nor is this suggestion without ancient precedent: the non-canonical apocalyptic work, I Enoch, predicts that after the Judgment, the wicked will suffer for a while until they wither away. As contrasted with the positions examined in sections 2 and 3.1, this move has the advantage of avoiding the claim that God has subjected created persons to cruel and/or unusual punishment by extending their life span into an eternity of horrendous suffering.

True to my Suarezian bias, I reject it, on the ground that it involves an uncharitable estimate of divine wisdom, goodness, and power. St. Anselm reasons that omnipotent, all-wise goodness would do the hard as well as the easy. For God, it is easy to make good from the good; what is more remarkable, it is no effort for Him to make good out of nothing. For Him, the real challenge would be to make good out of evil; so He must be able to do that.[46] Moreover, St. Anselm argued that it is unfitting to omnipotent wisdom either to change its mind or to fail in what it attempts.[47] I agree both ways. To me, it is a better theological bargain to hold the mystery that God will not give up on the wicked, will eventually somehow be able to turn them to good, than to swallow the tragic idea that created persons, finite and dependent though we are, are able ultimately and

---

[45] Cf. Swinburne, "A Theodicy of Heaven and Hell", p. 41.

[46] St. Anselm, *Proslogion*, chap. ix; *Sancti Anselmi: Opera Omnia*: 6 vols., ed. F.S. Schmitt (Edinburgh: Thomas Nelson, 1946–61); Schmitt I, 108.

[47] St. Anselm, *Cur Deus homo* II, chap. IV; Schmitt II, 99; cf. *Proslogion*, chap. vii; Schmitt I, 105–6.

finally to defeat our Creator's purpose, the mystery of transworld
final impenitence ending in the Creator's destroying His own creation.

3.3. Truths Told by the Doctrine of Hell

Like Craig, I take the Bible seriously; indeed, as an Episcopal
priest, I am sworn to the claim that "the Holy Scriptures of the Old
and New Testaments" are "the Word of God" and "contain all
things necessary to salvation".[48] Like Swinburne, Stump, and Lewis,
I feel bound to weigh the tradition behind (III). I, too, pay my respects by identifying some deep truths expressed by the doctrine of
hell. (T1) The first (mentioned in section 2.2.1 above) is that created
persons have *no rights* against God, because God has *no obligations* to
creatures: in particular, God has no obligation to be good to us; no
obligation not to ruin us whether by depriving our lives of positive
meaning, by producing or allowing the deterioration or disintegra-
tion of our personalities, by destroying our bodies, or by annihilat-
ing us. (T2) Second, the horrendous ruin of a created person represented by eternal torment in hell constitutes a (negative and mirror
image) measure—perhaps the most vivid we can understand—of
how *bad* it is, how utterly indecent, not to respond to God appropriately; and for all that, because of the radical incommensuration
between God and creatures, the measure is inadequate.

Nevertheless, I have insisted in print for more than twenty years
that (T3) the doctrine is false on its traditional construal, because
neither the ontological gap between God and creatures nor the radical impropriety of our comportment toward God is a good indication
of God's intentions and policies toward us. God does not stand on
rights and obligations, nor does He treat us according to such "deserts".

As I see it, both the defenders of hell and I are confronted with a
theological balancing act. The *prima facie* logical incompossibility of
(I) and (III) and the accompanying pragmatic difficulties force us into
a position of weighing some items of tradition more than others.
Like many Christians, Craig begins with a high doctrine of the authority of Scripture, which combines with a certain hermeneutic, to
make (III) obligatory. He then appeals to an equally high doctrine of
human freedom to try to reconcile (I) with (III). For this, he pays the
price of denying that God will be *good to* every person He creates (in

---

[48] "The Ordination of a Priest", *The Book of Common Prayer* (1979), p. 526.

the sense defined in section 1.1) and further of understanding divine goodness to be compatible with the damnation of the vast majority of actual created persons. Likewise, Craig's God shares the limitations of human social planners: (i) He cannot achieve the optimal overall good without sacrificing the welfare of some individual persons; (ii) nor can He redeem all personal evil: some of the wicked He can only quarantine or destroy.

By contrast, I emphasize a high doctrine of divine resourcefulness (assigning God the power to let creatures "do their damnedest" and still win them all over to heavenly bliss) and a low doctrine of human agency (both ontologically, in terms of the gap between God and creatures, and psychologically, in terms of developmental limitations and impairments). Because I do not regard Scripture as infallible on any interpretation, I do not feel bound to translate into theological assertion some of the apocalyptic imagery and plot lines of the New Testament. Nevertheless, I do not regard my universalist theology as un-Scriptural, because I believe the theme of definitive divine triumph is central to the Bible, is exemplified in Christ Jesus, and is the very basis of our Christian hope.

3.4. The Pragmatics of Universalism

Surprisingly many religiously serious people reject the doctrine of universal salvation, on the pragmatic ground that it leads to moral and religious laxity. Withdraw the threat, and they doubt whether others—perhaps even they themselves—would sustain the motivation for moral diligence and religious observance.

My pastoral experience suggests, on the contrary, that the disproportionate threat of hell (see sections 2.2 and 2.3) produces despair that masquerades as skepticism, rebellion, and unbelief. If your father threatens to kill you if you disobey him, you may cower in terrorized submission, but you may also (reasonably) run away from home. My brand of universalism offers all the advantages of Augustine's and Calvin's *sola gratia* approaches (like them, it makes our salvation utterly gratuitous and dependent on God's surprising and loving interest in us) and then some (because it gives everyone reason to hope and to be sincerely thankful for his or her life).[49]

---

[49] To be sure, Augustine thinks the damned should praise the divine justice that damns them, but to do this sincerely seems psychologically impossible for humans. Cf. my "Theodicy without Blame", pp. 221–34.

4. The Relevance of Feelings

Craig and Swinburne do not enter at any length into how bad horrendous sufferings are. For example, Craig hurries by with two scant mentions that damnation of many is "a terrible price" and "an admittedly tragic fate".[50] Both close their essays with a quasi-apology, anticipating that some will be offended by their value judgment that the existence of free creatures autonomously deciding their destinies, enough to fill heaven, is worth the price of the eternal exclusion and misery of many. Both imply that those who are offended will be motivated by understandable feelings, which are nevertheless not relevant to a rational consideration of the subject.[51]

I want to close with a contrary methodological contention (one already implicit in my argument in section 2.2): namely, that feelings are highly relevant to the problem of evil and to the problem of hell, because they are one source of information about how bad something is for a person. To be sure, they are not an infallible source. Certainly they are not always an articulate source. But they are *a* source. Where questions of value are concerned, reason is not an infallible source either. That is why so-called value calculations in abstraction from feelings can strike us as "cold" or "callous". I do not believe we have any infallible faculties at all. But our best shot at valuations will come from the collaboration of feelings and reason, the latter articulating the former, the former giving data to the latter.

Personally, I am appalled at Craig's and Swinburne's valuations, at levels too deep for words (although I have already said many). I invite anyone who agrees with Craig—that the saved can in good conscience let their happiness be unaffected by the plight of the damned because the destruction of the latter is self-willed—to spend a week visiting patients who are dying of emphysema or of the advanced effects of alcoholism, to listen with sympathetic presence, to enter into their point of view on their lives, to face their pain and despair. Then ask whether one could in good conscience dismiss their suffering with, "Oh well, they brought it on themselves!"[52]

---

[50] Craig, " 'No Other Name' ", pp. 183, 185.

[51] Ibid., pp. 186–87; and Richard Swinburne, "Knowledge from Experience, and the Problem of Evil," in *The Rationality of Religious Belief: Essays in Honour of Basil Mitchell*, ed. William J. Abraham and Steven W. Holtzer (Oxford: Clarendon Press, 1987) 141–67; esp. p. 167.

[52] Years ago, Rogers Albritton persuaded me, at the theoretical level, that some suffering is too bad for the guilty. My introspective and pastoral experience since then tells in the same directions.

I do not think this is sentimental. Other than experiencing such sufferings in our own persons, such sympathetic entering into the position of another is the best way we have to tell what it would be like to be that person and suffer as they do, the best data we can get on how bad it would be to suffer that way. Nor is my thesis especially new. It is but an extension of the old Augustinian-Platonist point, that where values are concerned, what and how well you see depends not simply on how well you think, but on what and how well you love (a point to which Swinburne seems otherwise sympathetic).[53] I borrow a point from Charles Hartshorne[54] when I suggest that sensitivity, sympathetic interaction, is an aspect of such loving, one that rightfully affects our judgment in ways we should not ignore.[55]

[53] Swinburne, "A Theodicy of Heaven and Hell", pp. 46–49.

[54] Charles Hartshorne, *The Divine Relativity* (New Haven: Yale University Press, 1948, 1964), chap. 3, 116–58.

[55] Over the years, my ideas about the doctrine of hell have been shaped by others, some of whom ultimately disagree with my conclusions. Among the medievals, I am especially indebted to Anselm, Aquinas, Duns Scotus, Ockham, and Julian of Norwich; among my contemporaries, Robert Merrihew Adams, John Hick, Jon Hart Olson, A. Orley Swartzentruber, and the members of the Philosophy Department at Calvin College in Grand Rapids, Michigan.

ELEONORE STUMP

Aquinas on the
Sufferings of Job

Aquinas wrote commentaries on five books of the Old Testament (Psalms, Job, Isaiah, Jeremiah, Lamentations), two Gospels (Matthew and John), and the Pauline epistles. These biblical commentaries have not received the same sort of attention as some of his other works, such as the *Summa theologiae* or the *Summa contra gentiles*, but they are a treasure trove of philosophy and theology.[1] The commentary on Job in particular is one of Aquinas's more mature and polished commentaries. Unlike many of them, which are preserved in the form of a *reportatio*, a transcription of Aquinas's lectures by someone who attended them, the commentary on Job is an *expositio*, material reworked and revised by Aquinas himself.[2] The commentary sheds light on Aquinas's understanding of God's providence and especially of the relation between God's providence and human suffering. Aquinas does discuss providence in other works

---

[1] Norman Kretzmann has discussed some of the issues raised in Aquinas's commentary on Romans in a recent paper; see his "Warring against the Law of My Mind: Aquinas on Romans 7", in *Philosophy and the Christian Faith*, ed. Thomas Morris (Notre Dame, Ind.: University of Notre Dame Press, 1988), pp. 172–95.

[2] This commentary, *Expositio super Job ad litteram*, is available in the Leonine edition of Aquinas's works, vol. 26, and in an English translation: *Thomas Aquinas, The Literal Exposition on Job: A Scriptural Commentary Concerning Providence*, trans. Anthony Damico and Martin Yaffe, The American Academy of Religion. Classics in Religious Studies (Atlanta: Scholars Press, 1989). It was probably written while Aquinas was at Orvieto, in the period 1261/2–1264. See James Weisheipl, *Friar Thomas D'Aquino: His Life, Thought, and Works*, 2d ed. (Washington, D.C.: Catholic University of America Press, 1983), p. 153; see also *Albert and Thomas: Selected Writings*, ed. Simon Tugwell, Classics of Western Spirituality (Mahwah, N. J.: Paulist Press, 1988), p. 223.

as well, most notably in book 3 of the *Summa contra gentiles*, which is roughly contemporary with the commentary on Job; and he considers problems involving suffering in many of the biblical commentaries, especially those on the Pauline epistles.[3] But the book of Job is the paradigmatic presentation of the problem of evil for anyone trying to reconcile the existence of God with the presence of evil in the world, and it is therefore particularly interesting to see how Aquinas interprets this book. So, although I turn to the *Summa contra gentiles* and the commentaries on the Pauline epistles when appropriate, my focus is on Aquinas's commentary on Job.

In recent years there has been renewed interest in the problem of evil and the argument that grows out of it. Some philosophers have adopted a hard line, often attributed to Hume, that belief in the existence of God is logically incompatible with belief in the existence of evil in the world.[4] In the wake of an apparently decisive refutation of that claim by Alvin Plantinga[5] attention has focused on what has come to be called the "evidential" or the "probabilistic" argument from evil. The strategy of this approach is to maintain that although belief in the existence of God is not logically incompatible with belief in the existence of evil in the world, evil nonetheless counts as evidence against God's existence or renders the existence of God improbable. So, for example, William Rowe has argued that since we can see no morally sufficient reason for God to allow evil, the fact of evil counts as evidence against the existence of God:

> When we consider the vast amount of intense human and animal suffering occasioned by natural forces and find ourselves utterly unable to think of outweighing or defeating goods that omnipotence can obtain only by permitting such suffering, we are, I think, rationally justified in concluding that there are instances of suffering that omnipotence could have prevented with the result that the world would have been better. Surely, if [an omnipotent, omniscient, perfectly good being] were to exist, the world would likely contain much less human and animal suffering than it does. . . . [T]he incredible amounts of seemingly pointless

---

[3] The commentaries on the Pauline epistles were probably written during Aquinas's second Parisian regency, 1269–1272, and during his subsequent stay in Naples. See Tugwell, *Alberta and Thomas*, p. 248; Weisheipl, *Friar Thomas D'Aquino*, p. 373.

[4] See, for example, J. L. Mackie, "Evil and Omnipotence", *Mind* 64 (1955): 200–212; and H. J. McCloskey, "God and Evil", *The Philosophical Quarterly* 10 (1960): 97–114.

[5] See, for example, Alvin Plantinga, "The Free Will Defense", in *Philosophy in America*, ed. Max Black (London: Allen and Unwin, 1965), pp. 204–20. A revised version of this essay is included in Plantinga's *God and Other Minds* (Ithaca: Cornell University Press, 1967), pp. 131–55.

human and animal suffering that form the history of our world *might be* related to future outweighing or defeating goods in such a manner that [an omnipotent, omniscient, perfectly good being] can obtain these goods only by permitting those amounts of suffering. But when we take into account the likelihood that the goods in question would involve good experiences of those who suffered and consider how such goods would have to be connected to the sufferings in question so as to be obtainable by omnipotence only at the cost of the sufferings, our judgment must be that this possibility is very unlikely.[6]

Some philosophers have constructed theodicies to counter such evidential arguments from evil. So, for instance, Richard Swinburne has proposed that God's allowing evil in the world enables us to know how to produce evil effects ourselves and that such knowledge is necessary if we are to have a significant exercise of our free will. Our having significant exercise of free will constitutes, in his view, a morally sufficient reason for God to allow evil.[7]

Other philosophers have responded in yet other ways to the evidential problem of evil. So, for example, Plantinga[8] holds that whatever morally sufficient reasons God has for allowing evil are and will remain mysterious. Plantinga's defense against the probabilistic argument from evil consists not in an attempt to find such a morally sufficient reason but rather in an attack on the conceptions and uses of probability which undergird the probabilistic argument. But Marilyn Adams, who shares Plantinga's view that God's reasons for allowing evil are altogether hidden from us, finds the focus of his response unsatisfying. She argues instead that union with Christ, who has suffered on our behalf, will be of such value that it will recompense all the evil in anyone's life. It is not the case, on her

[6] William Rowe, "The Empirical Argument from Evil", in *Rationality, Religious Belief, and Moral Commitment: New Essays in the Philosophy of Religion*, ed. Robert Audi and William Wainwright (Ithaca: Cornell University Press, 1986), p. 245. See also his "The Problem of Evil and Some Varieties of Atheism", *American Philosophical Quarterly* 16 (1979): 335–41. For an opposing view, see Steven Wykstra, "The Humean Obstacle to Evidential Arguments from Suffering: On Avoiding the Evils of Appearance", and Rowe's response, "Evil and the Theistic Hypothesis: A Response to Wykstra", both in *International Journal for the Philosophy of Religion* 16 (1984).

[7] Richard Swinburne, *The Existence of God* (Oxford: Clarendon Press, 1979), pp. 200–224; see also his "The Problem of Evil" in *Contemporary Philosophy of Religion*, ed. Steven M. Cahn and David Shatz (Oxford: Oxford University Press, 1982), pp. 3–19. For opposing views, see Eleonore Stump, "Knowledge, Freedom, and the Problem of Evil", *International Journal for the Philosophy of Religion* 14 (1983): 49–58, and David O'Connor, "Swinburne on Natural Evil", *Religious Studies* 19 (1983): 65–74.

[8] See, for example, Alvin Plantinga, "The Probabilistic Argument from Evil", *Philosophical Studies* 35 (1979): 1–53.

view, that human suffering is a necessary means to such union, or that the human experience of union constitutes a morally sufficient reason for God to allow evil. Rather, on her view, the experience of union with Christ will make the evil that humans suffer in this life seem minor by comparison. This approach to the problem of evil doesn't try to justify God's allowing evil; instead, it argues that on Christian doctrine all human evil is compensated, so that from the perspective of that union the sufferer does not regard the suffering she has endured with any bitterness.[9] In his commentary on the book of Job, Aquinas takes an approach to the problem of evil which is different in important ways from all these accounts.

1. Aquinas's Approach to Job

Comtemporary biblical scholars concern themselves a great deal with the provenance of the book of Job, the date of its composition, its social setting, and the broader cultural milieu of the work in its period. Although Aquinas recognizes these concerns, he sets them aside in a line or two as uninteresting to him: "It is not part of our present plan to discuss in what time Job lived or from what parents he had his origin, [or] even who the author of this book was, whether it was Job himself who wrote this book, speaking about himself as about someone else, or whether someone else related these things about him. For we intend . . . to expound the literal sense of the book of blessed Job."[10] In other words, Aquinas supposes these historical questions to be irrelevant to an exposition of the book. He is, however, explicit about taking Job to be a historical,

---

[9] See, for example, Marilyn Adams, "Redemptive Suffering: A Christian Solution to the Problem of Evil", in *Rationality, Religious Belief, and Moral Commitment*, ed. Audi and Wainwright, pp. 248–67. One criticism sometimes leveled against this approach is that although the evil is compensated, it isn't integrated into the Christian story of the sufferer's life. Because suffering isn't in any way necessary to the good that compensates it, we might wonder why God doesn't simply grant human beings the experience of union with Christ without allowing them to suffer first.

[10] Thomas Aquinas, *Expositio super Job*, prologue; Damico and Yaffe, p. 69. "Quo autem tempore fuerit vel ex quibus parentibus originem duxerit, quis etiam huius libri fuerit auctor, utrum scilicet ipse iob hunc librum conscripserit de se quasi de alio loquens, an alius de eo ista retulerit, non est praesentis intentionis discutere. Intendimus enim compendiose secundum nostram possibilitatem, de divino auxilio fiduciam habentes, librum istum qui intitulatur beati iob secundum litteralem sensum exponere." Although I have preferred to give my own translations, I have found the Damico and Yaffe translation very helpful, and I will give references to this work both to the Latin and to their translation.

rather than a fictional, personage. According to Aquinas, it makes
no difference to our understanding of the book of Job whether we
suppose that Job belongs to history or to fable, and nothing about
the book of Job compels us to take Job as historical. But, he explains,
how we understand the character of Job does make a difference to
our general attitude towards the veracity and authority of Scripture.
Aquinas points out that Ezekiel includes Job in a list with Noah and
Daniel, in a context that seems plainly to indicate that all three are
being thought of as real rather than fictional people; James also
makes reference to Job in a way which, to Aquinas, suggests the
historicity of the character. Since, on Aquinas's view, nothing in
Scripture is false,[11] and since he also takes Scripture to be consistent,
his readings of the passages in Ezekiel and James require him to take
the character Job as historical.

Two other things about Aquinas's interpretation of Job are likely
to strike a contemporary audience as unusual.

In the first place, it is sometimes difficult for contemporary
readers to find any progression in the core of the book of Job, which
consists of the speeches of Job and his friends. The friends seem to
bring the same false accusation over and over for page after page,
and Job's responses appear at best to constitute prolonged and increasingly vehement variations on the theme of his innocence. But
Aquinas sees the speeches as constituting a debate, even a medieval
disputation, determined at the end by God. As he explains the
book, the thought in the speeches progresses and the arguments
answer one another and advance; Aquinas is ingenious, often persuasive, in his presentation of the development of the arguments.
Furthermore, he is also sensitive, in a way contemporary exegetes
are sometimes not, to the play of interpersonal relationships in the
course of the speeches and to the way those relationships advance
or explain the procession of the speeches. So, for example, while
Aquinas agrees with a great deal of what Elihu, the fourth and last
speaker, says to Job, Aquinas holds that it was presumptuous of
Elihu, one human being among others, to say such things to Job.
Elihu was in effect arrogating to himself the role of determining the
disputation about the causes of Job's suffering; but, given the nature
of the subject, Aquinas sees God himself to be the only appropriate
determiner of the argument. Aquinas correctly maintains that there
are some speeches the content of which is entirely right even though

---

[11] For Aquinas's views of biblical authority and truth, see Eleonore Stump, "Medieval Biblical Exegesis and the Authority of Scripture", forthcoming.

their utterance (by this or that person on such an occasion) is none-theless wrong. On the other hand, when it comes to the most im-portant personal relationship in the book, the one between Job and God, Aquinas is peculiarly insensitive. An important part of Job's suffering stems from the fact that, in the face of all the evil that has befallen him, he remains convinced not only of the existence of God but also of his power and sovereignty, and even (or perhaps espe-cially) of his intense interest in Job. But in consequence of his suffer-ings Job has become uncertain or double-minded about the good-ness of God, and so his trust in God, which had formerly been the foundation of his life, is undermined in ways that leave Job riven to his roots. Aquinas's presentation of Job is oblivious to this side of his suffering, so that Aquinas's Job lacks the conflict with God and the bitter anguish many of the rest of us think we see in Job.

In the second place, contemporary readers tend to think of the subject of the book of Job as the problem of evil. Since the book itself says that Job was innocent and since the book is equally clear about the fact that Job's suffering is (indirectly) caused by God, who grants Satan permission to afflict him, it seems to contemporary readers that the story of Job's suffering is hard to reconcile with the claim that there is an omnipotent, omniscient, perfectly good God. How could such a being allow an innocent person to suffer the loss of his property, the death of his children, a painful and disfiguring dis-ease, and the other sufferings Job endured? And so the story of in-nocent Job, horribly afflicted with undeserved suffering, seems to many people representative of the kind of evil with which any the-odicy must come to grips. But Aquinas sees the problem in the book of Job differently. He seems not to recognize that suffering in the world, of the quantity and quality of Job's, calls into question God's goodness, let alone God's existence. Instead Aquinas understands the book as an attempt to come to grips with the nature and opera-tions of divine providence. How does God direct his creatures? Does the suffering of the just require us to say that divine providence is not extended to human affairs? Of course, this question is clearly connected to the one we today generally find in the book of Job. But the difference between the contemporary approach to Job and the one Aquinas adopts is instructive for understanding Aquinas's view of the relation between God and evil.

On Aquinas's account, the problem with Job's friends is that they have a wrong view of the way providence operates. They suppose that providence assigns adversities in this life as a punishment for sins and earthly prosperity as a reward for virtue. Job, however, has a more correct view of providence, according to Aquinas, because he recognizes that a good and loving God will nonetheless allow the worst sorts of adversities to befall a virtuous person also. The disputation constituted by the speeches of Job and his friends is a disputation concerning the correct understanding of this aspect of the operations of providence. What is of more interest to us here than the details of this disputation, as Aquinas understands it, is his analysis of the reasons the friends take such a wrong view of providence. In connection with one of Eliphaz's speeches, Aquinas says, "If in this life human beings are rewarded by God for good deeds and punished for bad, as Eliphaz was endeavoring to establish, it apparently follows that the ultimate goal for human beings is in this life. But Job intends to rebut this opinion, and he wants to show that the present life of human beings doesn't contain [that] ultimate goal, but is related to it as motion is related to rest and the road to its end."[12]

2. Constraints on Theodicy

Aquinas's idea, then, is that the things that happen to a person in this life can be justified only by reference to her or his state in the afterlife. That a medieval Christian thinker should have an otherworldly view comes as no surprise, but it is at first glance perplexing to see that Aquinas thinks taking the other world into account will settle questions about how providence operates. For we might suppose that even if all that happens in a person's life is simply a prolegomenon to her state in the afterlife, nothing in this claim allays the concerns raised by seeing that in this world bad things happen to good people. Job's comforters take the line they do, that suffering is punishment for sins, just because they see no other way to maintain God's goodness and justice. It's hard to see how indicating the existence of an afterlife would change their minds. Because Aquinas has always in mind the thought that the days of our lives here are short while the afterlife is unending,[13] he naturally supposes that things

---

[12] Aquinas, *Expositio super Job*, chap. 7, secs. 1–4, Damico and Yaffe, p. 145. "Si in hac vita homo remuneratur a deo pro bene actis et punitur pro malis, ut Eliphaz astruere nitebatur, consequens videtur quod in hac vita sit ultimus hominis finis. Hanc autem sententiam intendit iob reprobare et vult ostendere quod praesens vita hominis non habet in se ultimum finem, sed comparatur ad ipsum sicut motus ad quietem et via ad terminum."

[13] See, for example, Thomas Aquinas, *Super ad Romanos*, chap. 12, lec. 2.

having to do with the afterlife are more important than the things having to do with this life. But nothing in this attitude of his is incompatible with supposing that if God is good, things in this life ought to go well, at least for the just, if not for everybody.

We might suppose that Aquinas is here presupposing a view something like the one Adams adopts: God's reasons for allowing suffering are mysterious, and we don't know what sort of justification, if any, there is for God's allowing evil; but the immeasurable good of union with God in heaven recompenses all the finite evils we suffer here. On her view, the benefits of the afterlife don't justify God's allowing evil, but they do make up for the suffering of people who experience evil, in the sense that in union with God such people find their sufferings more than compensated. But Aquinas adopts a line different from Adams's. His line makes constructing an adequate theodicy more difficult but also (to my mind) more satisfying if successful. He supposes that we *can* know, at least in general, the good that justifies God's allowing evil. And he accepts basically the same constraints as those Rowe insists theodicies must meet: if a good God allows evil, it can only be because the evil in question produces a benefit for the sufferer and one that God could not provide without the suffering.

In his commentary on Romans, Aquinas distinguishes between the way providence works with respect to persons, on the one hand, and the rest of creation, on the other hand. As part of his defense of the line that all things work together for good for those who love God, Aquinas says this:

> Whatever happens on earth, even if it is evil, turns out for the good of the whole world. Because as Augustine says in the *Enchiridion*, God is so good that he would never permit any evil if he were not also so powerful that from any evil he could draw out a good. But the evil does not always turn out for the good of the thing in connection with which the evil occurs, because although the corruption of one animal turns out for the good of the whole world—insofar as one animal is generated from the corruption of another—nonetheless it doesn't turn out for the good of the animal which is corrupted. The reason for this is that the good of the whole world is willed by God for its own sake, and all the parts of the world are ordered to this [end]. The same reasoning appears to apply with regard to the order of the noblest parts [of the world] with respect to the other parts, because the evil of the other parts is ordered to the good of the noblest parts. But whatever happens with regard to the noblest parts is ordered only to the good of those parts themselves, because care is taken of them for their own sake, and

for their sake care is taken of other things. . . . But among the best of all the parts of the world are God's saints. . . . He takes care of them in such a way that he doesn't allow any evil for them which he doesn't turn into their good.[14]

In discussing providence in the *Summa contra gentiles*, he takes the same line. In a chapter headed "Rational creatures are governed for their own sake but others are governed in subordination to them", Aquinas repeatedly argues for the conclusion that "by divine providence, for creatures with intellects provision is made for their own sake, but for other creatures provision is made for the sake of those with intellects."[15]

In fact, Aquinas not only accepts the biblical line that (by divine providence) all things work together for good for those (rational creatures) who love God, but he has a particularly strong interpretation of it. How are we to understand the expression "all things" in this line? he asks in his commentary on Romans. The general claim that for created persons God permits only those evils he can turn into goods for them is, Aquinas says, "plainly true when it comes to the painful evils that [created persons] suffer. That is why it says in the gloss that the humility [of those who love God] is stimulated by their weakness, their patience by affliction, their wisdom by opposition, and their benevolence by animosity."[16] But what about the evils that are sins? Are they also among the things which work together for good for those who love God? "Some people say that sins are not included under 'all things' [in the biblical passage]. . . . But against this is the passage in the gloss . . . if some among the saints go

[14] Aquinas, *Super ad Romanos*, chap. 8, lec. 6. "Quidquid fit in mundo, etiamsi malum sit, cedit in bonum universi: quia, ut Augustinus dicit in Enchiridion: deus est adeo bonus, quod nihil mali esse permitteret, nisi esset adeo potens quod ex quolibet malo posset elicere aliquod bonum. Non autem semper cedit malum in bonum eius in quo est, quod sicut corruptio unius animalis cedit quidem in bonum universi, inquantum per corruptionem unius generatur aliud, non tamen in bonum eius quod corrumpitur: quia bonum universi est a deo volitum secundum se, et ad ipsum ordinantur omnes partes universi, et eadem ratio esse videtur circa ordinem nobilissimarum partium ad alias partes, quia malum aliarum partium ordinatur in bonum nobilissimarum, sed quicquid fit circa nobilissimas partes, non ordinatur nisi in bonum ipsarum. Quia de eis propter se cura habetur, de aliis autem propter ipsas. . . . inter omnes autem partes universi excellunt sancti dei. . . . sic de eis curat, quod nihil mali circa eos esse permittit, quod non in eorum bonum convertat."

[15] *SCG* III, 112. "Per divinam providentiam intellectualibus creaturis providetur propter se, ceteris autem creaturis propter ipsas." See also *Expositio super Job*, chap. 7, secs. 10–18; Damico and Yaffe, pp. 151, 153.

[16] Aquinas, *Super ad Romanos*, chap. 8, lec. 6. "Et hoc quidem manifestum est quantum ad mala poenalia quae patiuntur. Unde in glossa dicitur quod ipsorum infirmitate exercetur humilitas, afflictione patientia, contradictione sapientia, odio benevolentia."

astray and turn aside, even this God makes efficacious for good for them. . . . [S]uch people rise again [from their fall] with greater charity, since the good of human beings is charity . . . They return more humble and better instructed."[17]

So Aquinas adopts a line different from the one Adams argues for. He apparently believes that we can and in some cases do know the goods which justify suffering. Like Rowe, he feels that (at least for creatures with minds) suffering is justified only in case it is a means to good for the sufferer herself. And Aquinas's examples of such good all have at least a natural, if not a necessary, connection with the evil in question: patience brought about by affliction, humility brought about by the experience of sin and repentance.

What shall we say then about Aquinas's approach to Job? Given his understanding of the constraints governing theodicy, how shall we explain Aquinas's view that the perplexities of the story and the inadequacies of the comforters can all be satisfactorily accounted for by the recognition that there is an afterlife and that rewards and punishments are distributed there rather than in this life? The first part of the explanation comes from Aquinas's attitude toward happiness; the second part stems from his account of suffering.

3. Aquinas's Attitude toward Human Happiness

That human beings naturally desire their own happiness is a commonplace of Western philosophy. And we also suppose that any good person, but especially a perfectly good divine person, will desire the happiness of other persons. What raises the problem of evil for us is watching cases in which, it seems to us, God isn't doing enough to promote the happiness of his creatures, or is permitting their unhappiness or even, as in Job's case, actively conniving at the unhappiness of one of his creatures. But then in order to investigate the problem of evil we need first to be reflective about the nature of human happiness. It is noteworthy that in his long treatment of providence in the *Summa contra gentiles* Aquinas has virtually no discussion of what we would consider the problem of evil but fifteen chapters on the nature of human happiness.

What exactly happens to Job that makes us wonder about God's

---

[17] Ibid. "Quidam dicunt quod peccata non continentur sub hoc quod dicit omnia. . . . Sed contra hoc est quod in glossa sequitur: usque adeo talibus deus omnia cooperatur in bonum, ut si qui horum deviant et exorbitant, etiam hoc ipsum eis faciat proficere in bonum. . . . Tales in maiori charitate resurgant, quia bonum hominis in charitate consistit . . . Sibi humiliores redeunt atque doctiores."

goodness? (We might also ask about what happens to Job's children or to Job's wife, because questions about God's goodness obviously arise in connection with them, too; but I will focus here just on Job.) He loses his animals, the basis of wealth in his society. Afflicted with a miserable skin disease, he loses his health. And he loses his children, all of whom are killed in one day. We might term these losses Job's first-order afflictions. These first-order afflictions are the cause of further, second-order afflictions for him, the most notable of which is his disgrace in his own society. In consequence of the way in which his society interprets his troubles, he becomes a pariah among those who once honored him. And, finally, because Job's friends react very negatively to his insistence that he is innocent, their response to the way in which Job sees his first- and second-order afflictions provides yet more suffering for him, a third-order suffering. Because his reactions to his first- and second-order sufferings differ radically from theirs, he finds himself deeply at odds with the very people who might have been a source of comfort to him— first his wife and then the men closest to him. (His conflict with God, to which Aquinas is oblivious, seems to me the most important part of this third-order affliction, but I will leave it to one side here, and not only because Aquinas is insensitive to it. Since this part of Job's misery stems from his inability to understand how the God he trusted could let such things happen to him, the enterprise of theodicy is itself an attempt to explain this part of Job's suffering.)

We naturally take Job's losses to constitute the destruction of his happiness. But if we look at the chapters on happiness in the *Summa contra gentiles*, we find Aquinas arguing the following claims: happiness does not consist in wealth;[18] happiness does not consist in the goods of the body, such as health;[19] and happiness does not consist in honors.[20] Happiness is the greatest of goods, on Aquinas's account, but any good that is not by nature completely shareable, that is, which is such that in giving it to others one has less of it, is only a small good. Most, if not all, the gifts of fortune will therefore count just as small goods, on Aquinas's view. There is enough of medieval Christianity left in twentieth-century Western culture that many of us can read such claims and vaguely affirm them without paying much attention to what they mean. But on this view of Aquinas's, if happiness does not consist in health, honor, or riches, then it doesn't follow that a person who does not have these things is with-

---

[18] *SCG* III, 30.
[19] *SCG* III, 32.
[20] *SCG* III, 28.

out happiness. It is therefore not immediately clear, contrary to what we unreflectively assume, that Job's happiness is destroyed in consequence of not having these things.

Two things are worth noticing here. First, Aquinas, even with all his otherworldly focus, is not a Stoic. Among the many chapters in *Summa contra gentiles* saying what happiness does not consist in, there is no chapter saying that happiness does not consist in loving relations with other persons. Unlike some ancient philosophers, Aquinas does not understand happiness as a matter of self-sufficiency. So Aquinas's arguments about what happiness does not consist in are apparently not relevant to one of Job's losses, the loss of his children, or to the third-order afflictions of discord with his friends. Second, even if health, honor, riches, and the other things on Aquinas's list don't constitute happiness, it might nonetheless be the case that the loss of them or the presence of their opposites— sickness, disgrace, impoverishment—produces so much pain as to make happiness impossible. On Aquinas's view, human happiness consists in the contemplation of God. Apart from worries over whether human cognitive faculties are capable of contemplating God in this life, one might wonder whether pain and suffering don't interfere with such contemplation. And, in fact, as part of the evidence for the conclusion that true happiness cannot be achieved in this life, Aquinas himself says that weaknesses and misfortunes can impede the functions which must be exercised for happiness.[21] Consequently, even if, as Aquinas thinks, happiness consists in contemplation of God, rather than in the gifts of fortune, so that the loss of health or honor or riches doesn't by itself entail the loss of happiness, Aquinas apparently recognizes that it is possible for misfortune in any of its varieties to be an obstacle to happiness. So although it is helpful to understand Aquinas's views of happiness, we also need to consider his account of suffering in order to understand his approach to the book of Job.

4. Aquinas's Attitude toward Pain and Suffering

When from the standpoint of religion we reflect on the many evils of the world—murder, rape, torture, and oppression of apartheid, the evils of nuclear warfare, the horrors of Auschwitz and Tre-

---

[21] *SCG* III, 48. "Cuilibet enim, quantumcumque felix dicatur, possibile est infirmitates et infortuna accidere, quibus impeditur ab operatione, quaecumque sit illa, in qua ponitur felicitas."

blinka—we can hardly avoid wondering how a good God could let such things occur. But another thing to wonder about is the nature of human beings, who in all cultures and all ages can be so vicious to one another. On Aquinas's view, all human beings have a terminal cancer of soul, a proneness to evil which invariably eventuates in sin and which in the right circumstances blows up into monstrosity. On his view, even "our senses and our thoughts are prone to evil".[22] The pure and innocent among human beings are no exception to this claim. When the biblical text says that Job was righteous, Aquinas takes the text to mean that Job was pure by human standards. By the objective, uncurved standards of God, even Job was infected with the radical human tendencies toward evil.[23] No human being who remains uncured of this disease can see God. On Aquinas's view, then, the primary obstacle to contemplation of God, in which human happiness consists, is the sinful character of human beings.

Aquinas thinks that pain and suffering of all sorts are God's medicine for this spiritual cancer; and he emphasizes this view repeatedly. In his commentary on the Apostles' Creed, he says, "If all the pain a human being suffers is from God, then he ought to bear it patiently, both because it is from God and because it is ordered toward good; for pains purge sins, bring evildoers to humility, and stimulate good people to love of God".[24] In his commentary on Thessalonians he says, "As water extinguishes a burning fire, so tribulations extinguish the force of concupiscent desires, so that human beings don't follow them at will. . . . Therefore, [the Church] is not destroyed [by tribulations] but lifted up by them, and in the first place by the lifting up of the mind to God, as Gregory says: the evils which bear us down here drive us to go to God."[25] He comments in

---

[22] Thomas Aquinas, *Super ad Hebraeos*, chap. 12, lec. 2. "Sensus nostri et cogitatio nostra prona sunt ad malum".

[23] Aquinas, *Expositio super Job*, chap. 9, secs. 24–30; Damico and Yaffe, p. 179.

[24] For an excellent annotated translation of the text, see Nicholas Ayo, *The Sermon-Conferences of St. Thomas Aquinas on the Apostles' Creed* (Notre Dame, Ind.: University of Notre Dame Press, 1988). Although I have preferred to use my own translation, I found Ayo's quite helpful, and for this work I give citations both to the Latin and to Ayo's translation. Thomas Aquinas, *Collationes Credo in Deum*, sec. III; Ayo, pp. 40–42. "Si omnis pena quam homo suffert est a Deo, debet patienter sustinere, et quia est a Deo et quia ordinatur ad bonum; nam pene purgant peccata, humiliant reos, prouocant bonos ad amorem Dei."

[25] There is a translation of this commentary: *Commentary on Saint Paul's First Letter to the Thessalonians and the Letter to the Philippians by St. Thomas Aquinas*, trans. F. R. Larcher and Michael Duffy (Albany: Magi Books, 1969). Although I have preferred to use my own translations, I found the Larcher and Duffy translation helpful, and I will

great detail on the line in Hebrews: "whom the Lord loves he chastens."[26] "All the saints who have pleased God have gone through many tribulations by which they were made the sons of God."[27] "Since pains are a sort of medicine, we should apparently judge correction and medicine the same way. Now medicine in the taking of it is bitter and loathsome, but its end is desirable and intensely sweet. So discipline is also. It is hard to bear, but it blossoms into the best outcome."[28]

The same general point appears recurrently in the commentary on Job. Arguing that temporal goods such as those Job lost are given and taken away according to God's will, Aquinas says "someone's suffering adversity would not be pleasing to God except for the sake of some good coming from the adversity. And so although adversity is in itself bitter and gives rise to sadness, it should nonetheless be agreeable [to us] when we consider its usefulness, on account of which it is pleasing to God. . . . For in his reason a person rejoices over the taking of bitter medicine because of the hope of health, even though in his senses he is troubled."[29] Even the dreadful suffering Job experiences at the death of his good and virtuous children becomes transformed on this account from the unbearable awfulness of total loss to the bitter but temporary pain of separation. In being united to God in love, a person is also united with others. The ultimate good of union with God, like any great good, is by nature shareable.

In commenting on a line in Job containing the complaint that God

---

give citations for this work and for the commentary on Philippians both to the Latin and to this translation. Thomas Aquinas, *Super ad Thessalonicenses* I, prologue; Larcher and Duffy, p. 3. "Ignem ardentem extinguit aqua. Sic tribulationes extinguunt impetus concupiscentiarum, ne homines ad libitum eas sequantur. . . . Non ergo deficit, sed sublevatur, et primo per elevationem mentis ad deum. Gregorius: mala quae nos hic premunt, ad deum nos ire compellunt."

[26] Thomas Aquinas, *Super ad Hebraeos*, chap. 12, lec. 1.

[27] Ibid., lec. 2, "Omnes sancti, qui deo placuerunt per multas tribulationes transierunt, per quas filii dei facti sunt."

[28] Ibid. "Cum autem poenae sint quaedam medicinae, idem iudicium videtur esse de correctione et de medicina. Sicut autem medicina in sumptione amara est quidem et abominabilis, ita et disciplina. Quia gravis est ad sustinendum sed adducit fructum optimum."

[29] Aquinas, *Expositio super Job*, chap. 1, secs. 20–21; Damico and Yaffe, p. 89. "Non enim esset placitum deo quod aliquis adversitatem pateretur nisi propter aliquod inde proveniens bonum: unde adversitas licet ipsa ex se amara sit et tristitiam generet tamen ex consideratione utilitatis propter quam deo placet debet esse iocunda. . . . nam et de sumptione medicinae amarae aliquis ratione gaudet propter spem sanitatis licet sensu turbetur."

sometimes doesn't hear a needy person's prayers, Aquinas says, "Now it sometimes happens that God hearkens not to a person's pleas but rather to his advantage. A doctor does not hearken to the pleas of the sick person who requests that the bitter medicine be taken away (supposing that the doctor doesn't take it away because he knows that it contributes to health); instead he hearkens to [the patient's] advantage, because by doing so he produces health, which the sick person wants most of all. In the same way, God does not remove tribulations from the person stuck in them, even though he prays earnestly for God to do so, because God knows these tribulations help him forward to final salvation. And so although God truly does hearken, the person stuck in afflictions believes that God hasn't hearkened to him."[30]

In fact, on Aquinas's view, the better the person, the more likely it is that he will experience suffering. In explicating two metaphors of Job's,[31] comparing human beings in this life to soldiers on a military campaign and to employees, Aquinas makes the point in this way. "It is plain that the general of an army does not spare [his] more active soldiers dangers or exertions, but as the plan of battle requires, he sometimes lays them open to greater dangers and greater exertions. But after the attainment of victory, he bestows greater honor on the more active soldiers. So also the head of a household assigns greater exertions to his better servants, but when it is time to reward them, he lavishes greater gifts on them. And so neither is it characteristic of divine providence that it should exempt good people more from the adversities and exertions of the present life, but rather that it reward them more at the end."[32]

---

[30] Aquinas, *Expositio super Job*, chap. 9, secs. 15–21; Damico and Yaffe, p. 174. "Contingit enim quandoque quod deus hominem exaudit non ad votum sed ad profectum: sicut enim medicus non exaudit ad votum infirmum postulantem amoveri medicinam amaram, si medicus eam non removeat eo quod scit eam esse salutiferam, exaudit tamen ad profectum quia per hoc sanitatem inducit quam maxime infirmus desiderat, ita deus homini in tribulationibus constituto tribulationes non subtrahit, quamvis deprecanti, quia scit eas expedire ad finalem salutem; et sic licet deus vere exaudiat, tamen homo in miseriis constitutus se exaudiri non credit."

[31] Only one of the two metaphors is in the Revised Standard Version, the King James, and the Anchor Bible.

[32] Aquinas, *Expositio super Job*, chap. 7, sec. 1; Damico and Yaffe, p. 146. "Manifestum est enim quod dux exercitus strenuis militibus non parcit a periculis aut laboribus, sed secundum quod militiae ratio exigit interdum eos et maioribus laboribus et maioribus periculis exponit, sed post victoriam adeptam magis strenuos plus honorat. Sic et paterfamilias melioribus mercenariis maiores labores committit, sed in tempore mercedis eis maiora munera largitur; unde nec divina providentia hoc habet ut bonos magis ab adversitatibus et vitae praesentis laboribus eximat, sed quod in fine eos magis remuneret."

In his commentary on Thessalonians, Aquinas makes the same sort of point: "Many who are alive [in the eschaton] will be tried in the persecution of Antichrist, and they will surpass in greatness the many who had previously died."[33] And in his commentary on Philippians, he makes the point more generally: "from sufferings borne here a person attains to glory."[34]

With this background, we should not be surprised to find Aquinas affirming Paul's line in Romans that we should be glad of suffering: "It is a sign of the ardent hope which we have on account of Christ that we glory not only because of [our] hope of the glory to come, but we glory even regarding the evils which we suffer for it. And so [Paul] says that we not only glory (that is, in our hope of glory), but we glory even in tribulations, by which we attain to glory."[35]

5. The Oddness of Aquinas's Views

In Plato's *Gorgias* Callicles accuses Socrates of turning the world upside down; if Socrates' views are corect, Callicles says, "Everything we do is the exact opposite of what we ought to do".[36] Aquinas's views here also seem upside down. If he is right, everything we typically think about what counts as evil in the world is the exact opposite of what we ought to think. The topsy-turvy nature of this view of evil in the world is made vivid by a passage in a much earlier commentary on Job by Gregory the Great, whose views on this score are similar to Aquinas's. The ways of Providence are often hard to understand, Gregory says, but they are "still more mysterious when things go well with good people here and ill with bad people. . . . When things go well with good people here, and ill with bad people, a great uncertainty arises whether good people receive good so that they might be stimulated to grow into something [even] better or whether by a just and secret judgment they see the rewards of their deeds here so that they may be void of the rewards of the life to come. . . . Therefore since the human mind is hemmed

[33] Thomas Aquinas, *Super ad Thessalonicenses* I, chap. 4, lec. 2; Larcher and Duffy, p. 39. "De vivis multi erunt probati in persecutione antichristi, qui dignitate praecellent multos prius defunctos."

[34] Thomas Aquinas, *Super ad Philippenses*, chap. 3, lec. 2; Larcher and Duffy, p. 102. "Ex passionibus enim hic toleratis homo pervenit ad gloriam."

[35] Thomas Aquinas, *Super ad Romanos*, chap. 5, lec. 1. "Signum ergo vehementis spei quam habemus propter christum est quod non solum gloriamur ex spe futurae gloriae, sed etiam de malis quae pro ipsa patimur, unde dicit non solum autem gloriamur, scilicet in spe gloriae, sed etiam gloriamur in tribulationibus, per quas ad gloriam pervenimus."

[36] Plato, *Gorgias* 481C.

in by the thick fog of its uncertainty among the divine judgments, when holy people see the prosperity of this world coming to them, they are troubled with a frightening suspicion. For they are afraid that they might receive the fruits of their labors here; they are afraid that divine justice detects a secret wound in them and, heaping external rewards on them, drives them away from internal ones. . . . Consequently, holy people are more fearful of prosperity in this world than of adversity."[37] In other words, since it is in Gregory's view so difficult to understand how a just and benevolent providence could allow *good* things to happen to good people, when good people see that there is no adversity in their lives, they can't help but wonder whether they aren't after all to be counted among the wicked. For that reason, prosperity is more frightening to them than adversity.

This upside-down view of evil is the foreseeable conclusion of Aquinas's twin accounts of happiness and suffering. True happiness consists in the contemplation of God, shared and enjoyed together by all the redeemed in heaven. But the spiritual cancer which infects all human beings, even those who count as pure and innocent by human standards, makes it impossible for them to be united with God (or with each other) in heaven. Suffering is a kind of medicine for that disease.[38] Furthermore, at least for those who assent to the

---

[37] There is a nineteenth-century translation of this work: *Morals on the Book of Job by Gregory the Great, the First Pope of that Name* (Oxford, 1844). Although I have preferred to use my own translations, I give the reference both to the Latin and to this translation: Gregory the Great, *Moralia in Job*, book 5, introduction; *Morals*, pp. 241–42. "Cum ualde occulta sint diuina iudicia, . . . tunc occultiora sunt cum et bonis hic bene est et malis male. . . . At cum bonis hic bene est et malis male, incertum ualde fit utrum boni idcirco bona accipiant, ut prouocati ad aliquid melius crescant; an iusto latentique iudicio hic suorum operum remunerationem percipiant ut a praemiis uitae sequentis inanescant. . . . Quia ergo inter diuina iudicia graui incertitudinis suae caligine humana mens premitur, sancti uiri cum sibi suppetere prospera huius mundi conspiciunt, pauida suspicione turbantur. Timent enim ne hic laborum suorum fructus recipiant; timent ne quod diuina iustitia latens in eis uulnus aspiciat et exterioribus eos muneribus cumulans, ab intimis repellat. . . . Unde fit ut sancti uiri magis in hoc mundo prospera quam aduersa formident."

[38] One shouldn't misunderstand this claim and suppose Aquinas to be claiming that human beings can earn their way to heaven by the merit badges of suffering. Aquinas is quite explicit that salvation is through Christ only. His claim here is not about what causes salvation but only about what is efficacious in the process of salvation. It would take us too far afield here to consider Aquinas's view of the relation between Christ's work of redemption and the role of human suffering in that process. What is important for my purposes is just to see that on Aquinas's account suffering is an indispensable element in the course of human salvation, initiated and merited by Christ.

process and are eventually saved from their sinfulness, there is a direct connection between the amount of suffering in this life and the degree of glory in the life to come. Given such views, the sort of topsy-turvy thought represented by the passage from Gregory the Great is less surprising. If suffering is the chemotherapy for spiritual cancer, the patients whose regimen doesn't include any are the only ones for whom the prognosis is really bad.

This attitude on Aquinas's part also helps to explain his reaction to the book of Job. Like Aquinas, we take the attitude we do toward Job because of the values and worldview we bring to the book. Because *we* assume, unreflectively, that temporal well-being is a necessary constituent of happiness (or even the whole of it), we also suppose that Job's losses undermine or destroy his happiness. Consequently, we wonder how God could count as good if he allowed these things to happen to a good person such as Job, or we take stories of undeserved suffering to constitute evidence for thinking there is no God. Aquinas, on the other hand, begins with the conviction that neither God's goodness nor his existence are in doubt, either for the characters in the story of Job or for the readers of that story. Therefore, on his view, those who go astray in considering sufferings such as Job's do so because, like Job's comforters, they mistakenly suppose that happiness and unhappiness are functions just of things in this life. And so Aquinas takes the book of Job to be trying to instill in us the conviction that there is another life after this one, that our happiness lies there rather than here, and that we attain to that happiness only through suffering.[39] On Aquinas's view, Job has more suffering than ordinary people not because he is morally worse than ordinary, as the comforters assume, but just because he is better. Because he is a better soldier in the war against his own evil and a better servant of God's, God can give him more to bear here; and when this period of earthly life is over, his glory will also be surpassing.

---

[39] See, for example, *Expositio super Job*, chap. 7, sec. 1, Damico and Yaffe, p. 145; and chap. 19:23–29, Damico and Yaffe, pp. 268–71, where Aquinas makes these at points clear and maintains that Job was already among the redeemed awaiting the resurrection and union with God. Someone might wonder whether it is possible to maintain this approach to suffering when the suffering consists in madness, mental retardation, or some form of dementia. This doubt is based on the unreflective notion that those suffering from these afflictions have lost all the mental faculties needed for moral or spiritual development. For some suggestions to the contrary, see the sensitive and insightful discussion of retarded and autistic patients in Oliver Sacks, *The Man Who Mistook His Wife for a Hat* (New York: Summit Books, 1985).

6. Concerns about Aquinas's View

For many of us, the reaction to this view of Aquinas's will be indignation. If we take it not as piously platitudinous but as a serious expression of otherworldliness, we are likely to find it so alien to our own sensitivities that we reject it as outrageous. I think that there are two primary forms such a reaction will take.

Our more articulate reaction is likely to center on the thought that this view constitutes a reprehensible callousness toward human affliction and misfortune and a disgusting willingness to accept evil.[40] Concern for others is a good part of what prompts this reaction; the asceticism and otherworldliness of Aquinas's sort of attitude seem to rule out all attempts to alleviate the suffering of other people. And, of course, an emphasis on otherworldliness *has* in the past been used in abominable ways as a basis for exploiting and oppressing the poor and defenseless. When the labor movement in this country was trying to protect workers through unionization, part of its strategy was to cast opprobrium on hope in an afterlife. Instead of offering decent conditions and fair wages, union organizers said, the exploitative bosses held out to their workers the hope of "pie in the sky when we die".

In fact, if what we take away from Aquinas's text is just the general conclusion that on his view pain and adversity are good things, then his view will yield results worthy not only of vituperation but of ridicule as well. We might suppose, for example, that his views entail the claim that anesthetics are to be eschewed[41] or, more generally, that any attempt to palliate or end anyone's pain is a bad thing.

One thing worth noticing at the outset here is that it is perhaps not quite so obvious as we might suppose where callousness lies in this discussion. If, contrary to what Aquinas supposes, human happiness requires the gifts of fortune, then people in contemporary wealthy and developed countries, or just the middle and upper classes in them, will have a vastly greater share of happiness, and

---

[40] For a vigorous response of this sort to all kinds of theodicy, see Terrence W. Tilley, *The Evils of Theodicy* (Washington, D.C.: Georgetown University Press, 1991).

[41] As late as the end of the nineteenth century, even *Scientific American* was publishing diatribes against anesthetics (see the quotation in *Scientific American*, August 1991, p. 14), and the lamentable nineteenth-century animus against anesthetics, particularly in connection with childbirth, often had a religious basis. For a detailed discussion of nineteenth-century attitudes toward anesthetics, see Martin S. Pernick, *A Calculus of Suffering: Pain, Professionalism, and Anesthesia in Nineteenth-Century America* (New York: Columbia University Press, 1985).

the bulk of the world's population will be ruled out of that state. Aquinas's alien otherworldliness at least has the implication that the highest human good of happiness is not another monopoly of the industrialized nations.

But the more detailed and appropriate response to our emotive reaction in both its altruistic and its more general forms consists in seeing that on Aquinas's view suffering is good not *simpliciter* but only *secundum quid*. That is, suffering is not good in itself but only conditionally, insofar as it is a means to an end. "The evils which are in this world," Aquinas says, "aren't to be desired for their own sake but insofar as they are ordered to some good."[42] In itself suffering is a bad thing; it acquires positive value only when it contributes to spiritual well-being. We have no trouble seeing this sort of point when it comes to chemotherapy. In chemotherapy toxic drugs are administered to the patient, and the patient's friends and family are grateful for the treatments; but no one gets confused and supposes that it is then all right to allow the patient to ingest any sort of poisonous substance or that the medical personnel who administer the drugs are a result in favor of administering poison generally.

It is sometimes easy to confuse conditional goods with non-conditional ones. The development of muscles is a conditional good, to be valued insofar as it contributes to health and strength and their accompanying attractiveness, but steroid users can mistakenly value it as a good in its own right. No doubt, even those steroid users who aren't ignorant of the dangers of steroids would claim that they took the drugs to enhance their bodies. But their behavior belies their explanation and suggests that they have lost sight of the purported purpose; bulking up of muscles appears to have become a good in itself in their eyes, even if it is harmful to health in the long run. Similarly, not eating is good only *secundum quid*, insofar as it leads to a healthier and more attractive body, but anorexics misprogram themselves to value it even when it leads to an ugly destruction of health. An anorexic might believe of herself that she was continuing to diet because dieting is a good means to a more attractive body, but it would be hard not to suppose that she had lost sight of the goal she professed to want in her obsessed valuing of the means. It is clear from the stories of ascetic excesses in the patristic and medieval periods that it is possible to become confused in the same sort

---

[42] Thomas Aquinas, *Super I ad Corinthios*, chap. 15, lec. 2. "Mala quae sunt in hoc mundo, non sunt secundum se appetenda, sed secundum quod ordinantur ad aliquod bonum."

of way about the conditional good of suffering. Simeon Stylites spent thirty-seven years living on top of pillars, the last of which was sixty feet high and only six feet wide. He is reputed to have come close to death on one occasion as a result of wearing next to his skin an abrasive material which grew into the skin and infected it.[43] It seems not unreasonable to take him as a spiritual anorexic, mistaking a conditional good for a non-conditional one. Perhaps he believed of himself that his purpose for self-denial was spiritual progress, but like the anorexic he appears to have become obsessed with the means at the expense of the goal. No doubt, part of what the Renaissance found so repulsive about the Middle Ages was a certain tendency on the part of medievals to engage in prolonged and pointless bouts of self-destructive asceticism.

But how do we know that Simeon Stylites, or one of the other overrigorous ascetics of the patristic period, is the medieval analogue to a neurotic and unstoppable dieter? It is not so hard to know the difference between healthy dieting and anorexia, but how would we know with regard to suffering when it was serving the function of spiritual health and so was good rather than destructive? The answer, I think, is that we can't know. Sometimes in dealing with conditional goods we have to rely on experts. The steroids which some misguided athletes take to their misfortune are also important therapeutic drugs for certain sorts of cancers; but we learn this fact from medical experts, and we have to rely on them to administer the drugs in such a way that they contribute to health rather than destruction. In the case of suffering and its role in redemption, it seems clear that at least in the great majority of cases we don't know enough to turn suffering into a help toward spiritual health. We have to rely, therefore, on God's expertise instead.[44]

How do we avail ourselves of that expertise? How do we know in any given case whether God intends some suffering as a cure for evil or whether a particular degree of suffering won't produce spiritual toxicosis instead? When we see someone suffer as a result of human injustice, then on Aquinas's view (other things being equal) we have a clear obligation to do what is in our power to stop the suffering. Injustice is a mortal sin which separates a person from God; in intervening we help to rescue not only the victim of the

---

[43] David Hugh Farmer, *The Oxford Dictionary of Saints* (Oxford: Oxford University Press, 1988).

[44] Clearly sometimes we do know, or at least have a pretty good idea, as when loving parents deliberately inflict some suffering on their children in response to intolerable behavior on the children's part.

injustice but also the perpetrator, whose condition on Aquinas's view is otherwise apparently terminal. Job, in arguing for his innocence, points not just to the fact that he has not exploited any of those dependent on him but that he has even been particularly attentive to the needs of the poor and downtrodden,[45] and Aquinas comments on these passages with evident approval.[46] There is nothing in Aquinas's attitude toward suffering which is incompatible with a robust program of social justice. More generally, one way to tell if any particular suffering on the part of a given individual is ordained by God to spiritual health is if we try to alleviate that suffering and it turns out not to be possible to do so. Part of what makes Simeon Stylites repulsive to us is that he not only doesn't try to avoid suffering but even deliberately seeks it out for its own sake.[47] Gregory the Great's line, on the other hand, implies that redemptive suffering can't be instigated by us but has to be received from God's hand. Otherwise, the good men who tremble at their prosperity could stop trembling and just flagellate themselves to put a stop to their worrisome lack of adversity.

For these reasons the concern that Aquinas's account prompts indifference to suffering is mistaken; and if our indignation at his views is based on this concern, it is misplaced. But perhaps our negative reaction to Aquinas's account of evil stems from attitudes more complicated and less amenable to crisp articulation. Renaissance attitudes toward the Middle Ages were something like Callicles' reaction to Socrates. The Renaissance thought the Middle Ages had turned human values upside down, and it found medieval worldviews repellent because it saw them as inhuman. As intellectual descendants of the Renaissance (more nearly than of the Middle Ages), we might feel somewhat the same way about Aquinas's view of the world: any life really lived in accordance with this worldview would be wretched, inhumanly repudiating all the loveliness and goodness of this world, unnaturally withdrawing from all that makes life worthwhile.

---

[45] Job 31.

[46] See also *ST* II-II, 32, 5 and 6, where Aquinas argues that not giving alms, or keeping more than one needs, can be punished with damnation.

[47] By saying that he sought the suffering for its own sake, I don't mean to deny that he might have believed of himself that the purpose of the ascetic suffering he engaged in was spiritual progress. It seems nonetheless true that the immediate end of some of his actions was to inflict suffering on himself rather than to do something else which unavoidably entailed that particular suffering. And it certainly appears as if he lost sight even of the professed goal of spiritual focus in his fixation on mortifying the flesh. I am grateful to Marilyn Adams for comments on this point.

Aquinas is not oblivious to this problem. For that matter, neither is the apostle Paul. "If in this life only we have hope in Christ," he says, "we are of all people most miserable."[48] In commenting on this passage, Aquinas says, "If there is no resurrection of the dead, it follows that there is no good for human beings other than in this life. And if this is the case, then those people are more miserable who suffer many evils and tribulations in this life. Therefore, since the apostles and Christians [generally] suffer more tribulations, it follows that they, who enjoy less of the goods of this world, would be more miserable than other people." The very fact that Aquinas feels he needs to explicate this point in some detail highlights the difference between our worldview and his; no one has to explain to us that those who suffer more evils in this world are more miserable than others. But what Aquinas goes on to say spells out explicitly the difference between the worldview of his culture and our own. "If there were no resurrection of the dead," he continues, "people wouldn't think it was a power and a glory to abandon all that can give pleasure and to bear the pains of death and dishonor; instead they would think it was stupid." He assumes that Christians are people who do glory in tribulations, and so he ends his commentary on this passage in Corinthians by saying, "And so it is clear that [if there were no resurrection of the dead,] [Christians] would be more miserable than other people."[49]

So Aquinas's account of evil has inherent in it a response to objections of the Renaissance variety. If you suppose that fast-food-munching couch potatoes are just as healthy or healthier than nutrition-conscious physical-fitness advocates, you will of course find all the emphasis of the exercisers on diet and physical training perplexing or neurotic or worse. Denying oneself appealing foods and forcing oneself to sweat and strain in exercise are conditional goods only. Unless you share the view that these things do lead to desirable ends, you won't find them good in any sense. Similarly, if we don't share the worldview that holds that there is an afterlife, that

---

[48] 1 Cor. 15:19.

[49] Aquinas, *Super I ad Corinthios*, chap. 15, lec. 2. "Si resurrectio mortuorum non est, sequitur quod nihil boni habeatur ab hominibus, nisi solum in vita ista; et si hoc est, tunc illi sunt miserabiliores, qui in vita ista multa mala et tribulationes patiuntur. Cum ergo plures tribulationes apostoli et christiani patiantur, sequitur quod sint miserabiliores caeteris hominibus, qui ad minus perfruuntur huius mundi bonis. . . . quia si resurrectio mortuorum non sit, non reputatur virtus et gloria velle omnia delectabilia dimitterre, et sustinere poenas mortus et contemptus, sed potius reputatur stultitia. Et sic patet quod miserabiliores essent caeteris hominibus."

true happiness consists in union with God in the afterlife, and that suffering helps us to attain that happiness, we will naturally find Aquinas's valuing suffering even as a conditional good appalling or crazy.

7. Consolation

Even those who share with Aquinas the conviction that there is an afterlife and that the truest or deepest happiness is to be found in it might nonetheless feel queasy about or alienated from his account of evil. For many people, the supposition that suffering has the therapeutic value Aquinas claims for it will not be enough; they will still feel that there is something frighteningly inhuman in a worldview that tells us not only that the whole of our life on earth will be one prolonged spiritual analogue to chemotherapy but also that we ought to rejoice in that state of affairs. And so they are likely to side with the Renaissance humanist repudiation of such a worldview. I, too, think the Renaissance humanists were right to reject this worldview, but I think it would be a mistake to take it as the correct description of Aquinas's account. There is a more humane side to the medieval view of suffering which the Renaissance humanists missed. As Aquinas explains it, this part of his account applies primarily to the suffering of fully functional adults who are Christians. I think it is possible to see in Aquinas's thought a way in which to transpose his line so that it applies also to the suffering of children and non-Christian adults. For the sake of brevity, however, I will consider it here only in the form in which it applies to Christian adults with normally functioning faculties.

The missing element has to do with the work of the Holy Spirit. On Aquinas's view, the Holy Spirit works in the hearts of those who believe in God and produces spiritual consolation. The Holy Spirit, Aquinas says, "purges us from sin", "illumines the intellect", "brings us to keep the commandments", "confirms our hope in eternal life", "counsels us in our perplexities about the will of God", and "brings us to love God".[50] The Holy Spirit guides toward truth those whom it fills[51] and helps them to conquer their weaknesses[52] so that they can become the sort of people they are glad to be. Most impor-

---

[50] Thomas Aquinas, *Collationes Credo in Deum*, sec. 11; Ayo, pp. 116–18.
[51] Thomas Aquinas, *Super ad Philippenses*, chap. 1, lec. 2; Larcher and Duffy, p. 63.
[52] Ibid., chap. 1, lec. 3; Larcher and Duffy, p. 68.

tantly, the Holy Spirit fills a person with a sense of the love of God
and his nearness, so that one of the principal effects of the Holy
Spirit is joy.[53]

The Holy Spirit perfects us, both inwardly and outwardly, Aquinas says; and "the ultimate perfection, by which a person is made
perfect inwardly, is joy, which stems from the presence of what is
loved. Whoever has the love of God, however, already has what he
loves, as is said in 1 John 4:16: 'whoever abides in the love of God
abides in God, and God abides in him.' And joy wells up from this."[54]
"When [Paul] says 'the Lord is near', he points out the cause of joy,
because a person rejoices at the nearness of his friend."[55]

Perhaps there is no greater joy than the presence of the person
you love when that person loves you to the fulfillment of your
heart's desire. Joy of that sort, Aquinas says, is not destroyed by
either pain or tribulation. In order to keep joy whole, even in the
adversities of this life, the Holy Spirit protects people against the
evils they encounter: "and first against the evil which disturbs
peace, since peace is disturbed by adversities. But with regard to
adversities the Holy Spirit perfects [us] through patience, which enables [us] to bear adversities patiently. . . . Second, against the evil
which arrests joy, namely, the wait for what is loved. To this evil,
the Spirit opposes long-suffering, which is not broken by the wait-
ing."[56] In this way and others, Aquinas says, the Holy Spirit makes
human joy whole, even in the midst of pain.[57]

---

[53] See, for example, *Super ad Romanos*, chap. 5, lec. 1.

[54] There is an English translation of this work: *Commentary on Saint Paul's Epistle to
the Galations by St. Thomas Aquinas*, trans. F. R. Larcher and Richard Murphy (Albany:
Magi Books, 1966). Although I have preferred to use my own translations, I found the
Larcher and Murphy translation helpful, and I will give citations for this work both to
the Latin and to the Larcher and Murphy translation. *Super ad Galatas*, chap. 5, lec. 6;
Larcher and Murphy, pp. 179–80. "Ultimus autem finis, quo homo perficitur interius,
est gaudium, quod procedit ex praesentia rei amatae. Qui autem habet charitatem,
iam habet quod amat. (I John 4:16) 'qui manet in charitate, in deo manet, et deus in
eo.' Et ex hoc consurgit gaudium."

[55] *Super ad Philippenses*, chap. 4, lec. 1; Larcher and Duffy, p. 113. "Deinde cum dicit
'dominus enim prope est', tangitur causa gaudii. Homo enim gaudet de propinquitate
amici."

[56] Aquinas, *Super ad Galatas*, chap. 5, lec. 6; Larcher and Murphy, p. 180: "Et primo
contra malum quod perturbat pacem, quae perturbatur per adversa. Sed ad hoc perficit spiritus sanctus per patientiam, quae facit adversa patienter tolerare. . . . secundo, contra malum impediens gaudium est dilatio rei amatae, ad quod spiritus
opponit longanimitatem, quae expectatione non frangitur."

[57] Aquinas, *Super ad Galatas*, chap. 5, lec. 6; Larcher and Murphy, p. 179. "Dicit ergo
'fructus spiritus', qui scilicet consurgit in anima ex seminatione spiritualis gratiae, est

But what about Job? we might think at this point. Wasn't he someone who faced his troubles without consolation from God? Aquinas thinks, after all, that God sometimes heeds a suffering person's advantage, rather than his prayer, and it is in connection with Job that Aquinas develops that line. If the sufferer can't see that advantage, then, as even Aquinas recognizes, the sufferer may not be consoled but rather be afflicted in spirit also.[58] But I think Aquinas would be inclined to deny our characterization of Job as someone who suffers without divine consolation. One of the longest speeches attributed to God in the Bible is the speech he makes to Job; and when God's speech is finished, what does Job say? "I had heard of you before with the hearing of the ear, but now my eye sees you."[59] Whatever else we need to say about the complicated relations between God and Job, and that is no doubt a great deal, it is clear that with his views of happiness Aquinas would certainly attribute deep, sweet consolation to anyone who could truly claim to be seeing God. Furthermore, part of the point of Christianity, on Aquinas's account, is to make it clear to people that there is a point to suffering, so as to ward off the kind of theological perplexity and anguish many of us think we see in Job. In his passion, Christ not only makes atonement for sinners but also sets them an example, so that they will understand that the path to redemption goes through suffering.[60] The lesson learned for us by Job and the example presented by Christ make it easier for others afterwards, Aquinas thinks, to endure suffering without losing spiritual consolation during the period of pain.[61]

---

charitas, etc.; qui quidem sic distinguuntur: quia fructus aut perficiunt interius, aut exterius. Primo ergo ponit illos qui perficiunt interius; secundo illos qui perficiunt exterius. . . . Interius autem homo perficitur et dirigitur et circa bona et circa mala. . . . circa mala etaim perficit spiritus sanctus et ordinat." See also Aquinas, *Super ad Hebraeos*, chap. 12, lec. 2: "Dicit ergo quod 'omnis disciplina', scilicet quae est eruditio per flagella et molestias, 'in praesenti videtur esse non gaudii, sed maeroris', quia exterius habet tristitiam in sustinendo, sed interius habet dulcedinem ex intentione finis. Et ideo dicit 'videtur', et non dicit 'est'."

[58] Aquinas, *Expositio super Job*, chap. 9, secs. 15–21, Damico and Yaffe, p. 174.

[59] Job 42:5.

[60] See, for example, Aquinas, *Collationes Credo in Deum*, sec. 6; Ayo, pp. 69, 73. "Sed que necessitas quod Filius Dei pateretur pro nobis? Magna. Et potest colligi duplex necessitas: una est ad remedium contra peccata, alia est ad exemplum quantum ad agenda. . . . sicut dicit Augustinus, passio Christi sufficit ad informandum totaliter uitam nostram. Quicumque enim uult perfecte uiuere, nichil aliud faciat nisi ut contempnat que Christus contempsit, et appetat que Christus appetit: nullum exemplum uirtutis abest a cruce."

[61] Aquinas therefore supposes that Job's later return to worldly prosperity is at least

In fact, Aquinas thinks that for Christians the inner sweetness of God's consolation increases directly with the troubles of this life. At the start of his commentary on 1 Thessalonians he quotes with approval the line in 2 Corinthians which says that "as the sufferings of Christ abound in us, so our consolation also abounds by Christ". And in explaining that line, in his commentary on 2 Corinthians, he describes spiritual consolation in this way: "People need to be supported in the evils that happen to them. And this is what consolation is, strictly speaking. Because if a person didn't have something in which his heart could rest when he is overcome with evils, he couldn't bear up under them. And so one person consoles another when he offers him some relief, in which he can rest in the midst of evils. Now there are some evils in which one human being can console and quiet and support another, but God is the only one who consoles us in all [our] evils."[62] Even in our sins, which from Aquinas's point of view are more frightening than adversity, because unlike adversity they separate us from God, even then, Aquinas holds, we are consoled by God; that is why, Aquinas says, Paul calls him the God of *all* consolation.[63]

The Renaissance saw the Middle Ages as inhuman in part because it no longer shared the medieval worldview and in part because it had missed this side of the medieval story. On Aquinas's account, Christianity does not call people to a life of self-denying wretchedness, but to a life of joy, even in the midst of pain and trouble. Without joy, Aquinas says, no progress is possible in the Christian life.[64]

---

in part a divine concession to the fact that Job is part of a pre-Christian culture. "And [Job's return to prosperity] was appropriate to the time, because of the position of the Old Testament in which temporal goods are promised, so that in this way by the prosperity which he recovered an example was given to others, to turn them to God." *Expositio super Job*, chap. 42, secs. 10–16; Damico and Yaffe, p. 472. "Et hoc quidem tempori congruum erat propter statum veteris testamenti in quo temporalia bona promittebantur, ut sic per prosperitatem quam recuperaverat aliis daretur exemplum ut converterentur ad deum."

[62] Aquinas, *Super II ad Corinthios*, chap. 1, lec. 2. "Indigent ut sustententur in malis quae adveniunt. Et illud est proprie consolari, quia nisi homo haberet aliquid in quo quiesceret cor eius, quando superveniunt mala, non subsisteret. Tunc ergo aliquis consolatur aliquem, quando affert ei aliquod refrigerium, in quo quiescat in malis. Et licet in aliquibus malis homo possit in aliquo consolari et quiescere et sustentari, tamen solus deus est, qui nos consolatur in monibus malis."

[63] Ibid. "Et ideo dicit 'deus totius consolationis', quia si peccas, consolatur te deus". See also *Super ad Romanos*, chap. 8, lec. 7.

[64] *Super ad Philippenses*, chap. 4, lec. 1; Larcher and Duffy, p. 112. "Necessarium est enim cuilibet volenti proficere, quod habeat spirituale gaudium."

8. Conclusion

Aquinas's attitude toward evil is clearly as different from our own as Socrates' attitude toward the good life is different from Callicles'. Aquinas's analysis of the reaction of Job's comforters would also, I think, be his analysis of the reaction to evil on the part of those of us concerned with the problem of evil in this culture.

> Human beings are made up of a spiritual nature and of earthly flesh. Consequently, evil for human beings consists in their abandoning spiritual goods to which they are directed in virtue of [having] rational minds and their cleaving to earthly goods which suit them in virtue of [having] earthly flesh."[65]

> Job's loquacious friends did not understand the spiritual consolation of Job, and so he adds, 'You have put their heart far from learning'— that is, from the spiritual learning [which comes from] you, by which you teach [human beings] to disdain temporal goods and to hope for spiritual ones. And because they put their hope only in things low and temporal, they could not reach a spiritual plane to be placed next to God.[66]

It certainly does seem true, at any rate, that there is a correlation between the degree to which we associate human good with things in this world and the extent to which we see the problem of evil in its contemporary form. The story of the metamorphosis from the medieval worldview to our own is, of course, in large part a matter of a shift from a religious to a secular outlook. But even among Christians we can chart the change from the otherworldly approach of the medievals to the more common contemporary attitudes. We can see this change in its beginnings in, for example, the pious Christian adherents of the *devotio moderna*, a religious movement important in the Netherlands, particularly in the fifteenth century. There was a distinctly non-medieval attitude in the *devotio moderna* in

---

[65] Aquinas, *Expositio super Job*, chap. 1, secs. 6–7; Damico and Yaffe, p. 79. "Cum enim homo compositus sit ex natura spirituali et carne terrena, malum hominis in hoc consistit quod, derelictis spiritualibus bonis ad quae secundum rationalem mentem ordinatur, terrenis bonis inhaeret quae sibi competunt secundum carnem terrenam."

[66] Aquinas, *Expositio super Job*, chap. 17, secs. 2–9: Damico and Yaffe, p. 252. "Hanc autem spiritualem consolationem ipsius iob amici eius verbosi non intelligebant, et ideo subdit cor eorum longe fecisti a disciplina, scilicet tua spirituali, per quam doces spiritualia bona contemptis temporalibus sperare; et quia in solis temporalibus et infimis rebus spem ponunt, ad spirtualem altitudinem pervenire non possunt ut iuxta deum ponantur."

its tendency to conflate temporal and spiritual goods and in its emphasis on the religious importance of temporal concerns. Commenting on the death of a recently appointed principal of a school for religious instruction, an anonymous adherent of this movement raises the problem of evil in a way which is devout but altogether different from Aquinas's approach. He says,

> Permit me to take a moment here to allude to the wondrous and secret judgments of our Lord God, not as if scrutinizing them in a reproachful way but rather as humbly venerating the inscrutable. It is quite amazing that our fathers and brothers had set out with a single will and labored at their own expense, to the honor of God and for the salvation of souls, to erect a school here in Emmerich to do exercises with boys and clerics. . . . And now after much care and trouble, everything had been brought to a good state: we had a learned and suitable man for rector, the venerable Master Arnold of Hildesheim. . . . Then, behold, . . . our Lord God, as if totally unconcerned with all that we had in hand, which had just begun to flower, suddenly and unexpectedly threw it all into confusion and decline, nearly reducing it to nothing. For just as the sheep are dispersed when the shepherd is struck down, so when our beloved brother [Master Arnold] died the whole school was thrown into confusion. The youths left in swarms . . . not it is to be feared, without some danger to their souls. . . . Nonetheless, to [him] be the honor and the glory now and through the ages, to him whose judgments, though hidden, are yet never unjust.[67]

Between the attitude of this Christian author, who finds adversity for God's people fundamentally inexplicable, and the attitude of such Christians as Aquinas or Gregory the Great there is a world of difference.

In this paper I have only expounded Aquinas's views of evil; I have not sought to argue for them, although they seem to me impressive and admirable in many ways. No doubt, a thorough philosophical defense or refutation of his views would require book-length treatment. But what Aquinas's interpretation of Job and general account of evil show us, whether we are inclined to accept or reject them, is that our approach to the problem of evil is a consequence of our attitude toward much larger issues, such as the nature of human happiness and the goal of human life. To make progress on the problem of evil, in my view, we need to face up to these

---

[67] *Devotio Moderna: Basic Writings*, trans. John van Engen (New York: Paulist Press, 1988), p. 151. I am grateful to John van Engen for calling my attention to the intriguing material in this book.

larger issues in a reflective way. One of the benefits of the history of philosophy, especially the history of philosophy from periods such as the Middle Ages whose cultures are so different from our own, is that it helps us to see the otherwise unnoticed and unexamined assumptions we bring to philosophical issues such as the problem of evil. Aquinas's worldview, characterized by a renunciation of the things of this world and a rush toward heaven, is a particularly good one to juxtapose to the worldview of our own culture, steeped in comforts and seeking pleasure. "Theodicies," says Terrence Tilley in his passionate denunciation of them, "construct consoling dreams to distract our gaze from real evils."[68] What reflection on Aquinas's account helps us to see is that in evaluating this claim and others like it, hostile to theodicy, everything depends on what you take to be dream and what you take to be reality.[69]

[68] Tilley, *The Evils of Theodicy*, p. 219.
[69] I am grateful to Norman Kretzmann for helpful comments on an earlier draft of this paper.

Contributors

Marilyn McCord Adams is Professor of Philosophy at the University of California at Los Angeles.

Robert Merrihew Adams is Professor of Philosophy at the University of California at Los Angeles.

William P. Alston is Professor of Philosophy at Syracuse University.

Robert Audi is Professor of Philosophy at the University of Nebraska.

Harry G. Frankfurt is Professor of Philosophy at Princeton University.

Scott MacDonald is Associate Professor of Philosophy at the University of Iowa.

William E. Mann is Professor of Philosophy at the University of Vermont.

George I. Mavrodes is Professor of Philosophy at the University of Michigan.

Thomas V. Morris is Professor of Philosophy at the University of Notre Dame.

Philip L. Quinn is John A. O'Brien Professor of Philosophy at the University of Notre Dame.

William Rowe is Professor of Philosophy at Purdue University.

Eleonore Stump is Robert J. Henle Professor of Philosophy at St. Louis University.

Richard Swinburne is Nolloth Professor of Philosophy of the Christian Religion at Oxford University.

Peter van Inwagen is Professor of Philosophy at Syracuse University.

Index

Library of Congress Cataloging-in-Publication Data

Reasoned faith / edited by Eleonore Stump.
    p.   cm.
    Essays in philosophical theology in honor of Norman Kretzmann.
    Includes bibliographical references and index.
    ISBN 0-8014-2571-9 (cloth)
    ISBN 0-8014-9796-5 (paper)
    1. Philosophical theology.   2. Faith and reason—Christianity.   3. Faith and
reason—Judaism.   4. Christianity—Philosophy.   5. Judaism and philosophy.
6. Judaism—Doctrines.   I. Stump, Eleonore.   II. Kretzmann, Norman.
BT40.R43   1993
231'.042–dc20   92-33439